CREATING
LOVE

John Bradshaw

CREATING LOVE

The Next Great Stage of Growth

BANTAM BOOKS

NEW YORK · TORONTO · LONDON · SYDNEY · AUCKLAND

CREATING LOVE

A Bantam Book / December 1992

Grateful acknowledgment is made for permission to reprint from the following:

The Complete Poems of Emily Dickinson, *edited by Thomas H. Johnson. Copyright 1929 by Martha Dickinson Bianchi; copyright © renewed 1957 by Mary L. Hampson. By permission of Little, Brown and Company. Reprinted by permission of the publishers and the Trustees of Amherst College from* The Poems of Emily Dickinson, *edited by Thomas H. Johnson, Cambridge, MA: The Belknap Press of Harvard University Press, copyright 1951, © 1955, 1979, 1983 by the President and Fellows of Harvard College.*

Uncommon Therapy *by Jay Haley. Copyright 1987 by W. W. Norton & Co., Inc. Reprinted by permission of the publisher.*

Phoenix: Therapeutic Patterns of Milton H. Erickson *by David Gordon and Maribeth Meyers-Anderson. Copyright 1981 by META Publications. Reprinted by permission of the publisher.*

Library of Congress Cataloging-in-Publication Data

Bradshaw, John, 1933–
    Creating love : the next great stage of growth / John Bradshaw.
       p.   cm.
    ISBN 0-553-07510-1
    1. Love.   I. Title.
BF575.L88684   1992
152.4'1—dc20   92-23230
                                                              CIP

Published simultaneously in the United States and Canada

PRINTED IN THE UNITED STATES OF AMERICA

BVG   0 9 8 7 6 5 4 3 2 1

To my mother, Norma, whose soul shines brightly through it all.
Thank you for my life.

CONTENTS

ACKNOWLEDGMENTS

I thank the late Ronald Laing for his penetrating analysis of modern patriarchal culture and for his term *mystification*.

Thomas Moore's book *Care of the Soul* was sent to me in manuscript form and moved me deeply. Moore stimulated my whole notion of soulfulness.

I'm indebted to Ron Kurtz for sending me the manuscript of Stephen Wolinsky's book *Trances People Live*. Wolinsky's work is the source for my conception of the second stage of mystification, and I thank him.

I'm especially thankful for all the courageous people who have confronted patriarchy by battling for equality and fighting for the rights of people of color, women, children, gays, and lesbians.

Many more sources are cited in the text and bibliography.

While I stand on the shoulders of giants, I take responsibility for my interpretations of all the sources I have mentioned.

I want to acknowledge the following individuals:

Sissy Davis, who is my sweetheart and with whom I am creating love.

My brother Richard, whose ongoing assistance allows me to perform the sometimes lonely task of being an author and workshop leader.

My associate, Karen Fertitta, whose managerial talent makes my life much easier.

My colleagues Kip Flock and Mike Berman, who assure the clinical quality of my work at the John Bradshaw Center at Ingleside Hospital in Rosemead, California.

Clark Todd and Mike Drobat of Concept Health, who manage The John Bradshaw Center.

Marc Baker, the marketing director at the John Bradshaw Center, who painstakingly assists me while I am on the road.

My grandparents, Joseph and Edna, who let me know that I mattered.

My Aunt Chickie and Uncle J.E., for fifty years of marriage.

My stepdaughter, Brenda, who loves me like a daughter.

My son, John, who challenges me to love soulfully.

My late Aunt Millie, who loved unconditionally.

My sister, Barbara Bradshaw, who spent uncounted hours preparing this manuscript. I frequently called on her extensive knowledge of the English language in order to achieve greater clarity and correct usage. She's been an enormous help.

My editor, Toni Burbank, who gently guided the transformation of a cumbersome manuscript into this book. I'm grateful to the whole staff at Bantam, who are the very best in the business.

PROLOGUE

In the evening of life, we will be judged on love
alone.

—SAINT JOHN OF THE CROSS

Wanting to please my lady friend was the only reason I bought two
ridiculously expensive tickets to see *Miss Saigon*. I am not fond of
serious musicals—and *Miss Saigon* was purported to be a tearjerker.
I have had enough sadness in my life. I do a lot of work helping
folks grieve their unresolved childhood pain. I hate sad shows, especially on my vacation.

But my lady wanted to go, so here I was in the theater, trying
to make the best of it. One thing for sure, I was not going to cry!

The story is an adaptation of *Madama Butterfly,* set during the
war in Vietnam. In the first act, a Vietnamese bar girl falls in love
with a GI. They get married and vow eternal love. He is forced to
leave her but he promises to return from the States when the war is
over. She is simple, innocent, and endearing. Her love is intense and
unconditional. Unknown to ,him, she bears their child, a boy. She
hides and fiercely protects the child while she endures a dehumanizing life in a brothel.

At the intermission, I started fantasizing about the sad stuff that
might be coming. I imagined Miss Saigon dying as she gives up her
child to Communist authorities. I can handle that, I thought! I fantasized the GI coming back for her and getting killed. I can handle
that too! Nothing could get to me tonight.

The second act introduces an agency devoted to finding the GIs
who fathered children by Vietnamese mothers. As the story unfolds,
our GI has married again. Although he dreams of Miss Saigon, he is
basically happy. Then the agency finds him. He must tell his wife
about Miss Saigon and the child. He and his wife go to Vietnam in

order to handle the matter honorably. In a cross up, Miss Saigon meets the GI's wife. She is crushed beyond words. (*I'm losing it!* Tears are running down my cheeks.) Miss Saigon begs the new wife to take the child and give him the life she cannot give him. (*Sobs!* I am now trying to hold back audible sobs.)

In the last scene, Miss Saigon dresses her son (the most adorable child you've ever seen), preparing him to be given to his father and stepmother. In the tenderest of moments she kisses her son and tells him that he will understand later and asks that he not forget her. (I have given way to unobstructed abdominal sobbing.) The child walks out; his father and stepmother open their arms to him. Miss Saigon disappears behind the curtain. Bang! A gunshot is fired. She has killed herself; the GI rushes in and holds her, moaning his lamentations.

The entire audience is crying profusely. I am a mess. I am thinking that I am glad she killed herself. I could not have handled her standing there in her poverty and degradation while her husband walks away with their child. Her suicide somehow eases the pain.

Suddenly, I'm moving into my own story of love and hate, my parents' broken marriage, my childhood pain. I am identifying with the innocent child caught in the fateful vagaries of his parents' love. I think of my own passionate loves—the woman I loved and left, *the one who left me. Especially the one who left me!* I remember *that* pain. It was like someone had hammered a huge iron nail in the middle of my chest. Just for a moment I feel the traumatic shortness of breath I felt during my rejection. I remember how I obsessed about her, how I cried, raged, felt incredible remorse.

I think of my mother. How at twenty-six she was raising three children all alone. She labored for a pittance to support us. She is a devout Catholic. Her faith would not allow her to remarry. From the time my dad left her, she never touched another man. What an incredible faith! What commitment to one's beliefs.

My mother is human. She had her unconscious rage over all of this. I have often written off her love as being severely codependent. But tonight I long to hold her and tell her I love her. Tonight I want her to know that I honor the tragic and heroic sense of her life. Tonight I see its terrible dailiness and seeming triviality redeemed by the courage and passionate tenacity of her commitment to her children.

The question I ask myself as I dry my eyes is, what is this mysterious power of love and why can it be so overwhelming? Is a mother's love innate? If so, why do some mothers leave their children on someone's doorstep, or beat their children to death, or sell them into prostitution? Is giving up one's life for another always an act of love? Could it be an act of selfishness—a way of being elevated to the grandiose heights of saintliness in order to *feel* lovable?

How can we know the difference? Does love always have to be self-sacrificing and painful in order to be considered love? Are there different kinds of love? Do we know how to love naturally, or is love learned? What does it mean to love God? How do we know that God loves us?

Why do relationships that begin in ecstasy often end in hatred and bitter divorce? How can an evening, a vacation, start out so wonderful and end in anger and isolation?

Why are so many of us at times completely baffled by a relationship? How can we think we know someone so well and admit in the end that we hardly knew that person at all? Why do so few seem to find the love we all say we want more than anything else? Why do many people who work diligently and strenuously to gain wholeness and balance still feel so frustrated about having a fulfilling relationship? Why have many people given up on love, saying that it's only for the lucky or that it's just not worth the struggle?

Just one month after that night at *Miss Saigon,* I was sitting miserably in a hotel room in Philadelphia. I had just finished putting on a two-day inner child workshop. I had walked out amid a standing ovation and signed autographs in the elevator going to my room. The cleaning lady had left her copy of *Homecoming* to be autographed. As I closed the door, I felt the pervasive aloneness of the room. I thought to myself how exciting this used to be in the early days of 1985. This was right after the PBS series *On the Family* was starting to attract interest. Requests for talks and workshops were coming in from all over the country. I started traveling everywhere. People recognized me in airports. I was drunk with the excitement of it all.

But now, in my hotel room in Philadelphia, I was faced with the fact that my lady friend had told me she was losing herself in our relationship. She told me she had to take care of her own life and her own needs. I admired her for that. *But she was leaving me!!*

I loved to call her at night when I was on the road. It was so wonderful to have *one special person that you matter to more than anything.* And to have a person that matters to you more than anything. I realized that I was letting a whole lot of things matter to me more than her. I was falling back into my old patterns of power and control.

I thought I had changed these ways of false loving. At forty-two

I had awakened to the fact that I was failing at love. I was married then. I had a son and a stepdaughter.

One day, after I had yelled at my stepdaughter about her failure to do her chores, she confronted me with my selfishness and my ways of manipulation. She really got my attention. Somehow her courage and honesty forced me to face up to myself. At that point I had been sober in a 12-step program for twelve years. I thought I was doing just great because I no longer addictively used chemicals. I felt entitled to everyone's love and respect because I had stopped my crazy behavior. At times I also felt deeply depressed and even wondered whether life was really worthwhile.

My stepdaughter's confrontation led me to begin what I now see as the second stage of my recovery work.

In my book *Homecoming* I called this stage "original pain work." It involved feeling the feelings I had avoided since child-hood—the feelings of pain, sorrow, shame, and rage. Doing this work helped me to love and accept *myself* more fully. I embraced myself in the image of a wounded little boy. By so doing I embraced my rejected and disowned feelings, needs, and wants. This was essential for me because I did not know what I actually felt, needed, or wanted at any given moment. This was one reason I *couldn't really have an intimate relationship* with anyone else.

My original pain work culminated in a deeper and more loving relationship with myself. But it left me with a great uncertainty about how to be intimate and loving with others. I recognized that every relationship I had was characterized by control and emotional repression. I had to admit that *even after years of recovery and working on myself I still felt a baffling despair about love and fulfillment.*

The reclaiming of my inner child was the *beginning* of learning to love, not the *end.*

I found that many others were in the same quandary. At my workshops, people flooded me with questions and statements like:

- What does it take to have a good relationship?

- After all the changes I've made, how come my marriage is still a mess?

- I've left my rigid religious upbringing and now I'm left with nothing. How do I find my Higher Power?

- I'm getting my own life together, but my kids are totally screwed up.

• My job is driving me crazy. I'm in recovery, but my boss isn't. He shames me every day.

The list could go on. The unsolved mystery in recovery was about loving relationships. This book is the fruit of my own struggle with these issues.

As I searched for an answer, I came across three books that provided key pieces of the puzzle I was trying to solve. The first, written by psychiatrist Scott Peck, had the very fitting title *The Road Less Traveled.* I learned two important things in Peck's book that confronted my family of origin teachings. I learned that love cannot happen unless I am willing to commit myself to making it happen. And I learned that love is a process that requires hard work and courage.

This may not be news to you, but it was revolutionary to me. I was brought up to believe that love is rooted in blood relationships. You naturally loved anyone in your family. Love was not a choice. The love I learned about was bound by duty and obligation. You could never *not* love your parents or relatives, and loving them meant you couldn't ever disagree with them or want something they disapproved of.

To question any of these teachings was to risk being labeled a "black sheep" or just plain crazy. To actually go against them was to feel *cellular guilt,* the price of breaking a sacred promise you never knew you made.

At the same time, love was supposed to be easy. When you grew up and the time was right, the "right person" would come along. You would recognize this person immediately. You would fall in love and naturally know what to do to develop that love.

I'm thankful to Scott Peck for challenging these notions of love, but I do not blame my family for passing them on.

My family taught me our culture's rules and beliefs about love. Over the last few years, it has become obvious to me that everyone I knew growing up was either raised by parents who followed these cultural rules or by parents who were reacting against them. In this book, I will have much more to say than I have in the past about the culture that shaped our families. I will suggest that these cultural rules created a deficient form of love, and that even *with the best intentions* our parents often confused love with what we would now call abuse.

I ultimately named this defective love *mystification.* I took this word from one of my college heroes, the existential psychiatrist Ronald Laing. Laing spent his life exposing the destructive identity confusion that results when we become acceptable to others only by denying our own truth. He called this identity confusion *mystification.*

As I was developing my notion of mystification, another important book came to me in manuscript before publication. Called *Trances People Live,* by Stephen Wolinsky, it helped me understand exactly how mystification occurs and why it is so powerful. Wolinsky's book is a fascinating synthesis of modern hypnotherapy with the insights of Eastern philosophy. It shows how we create *protective trance states* in response to painful experiences in childhood, and how we later *continue to use* these trances to protect us even when they are no longer necessary. "Trance" is a wonderful way to describe the frozen and out-of-touch state of mystified love. There is also a hopeful element in Wolinsky's thesis. If we actually created our own trances in childhood—even if we have no memory of doing so—we can learn to break through our trances as adults. In other words, we can demystify ourselves.

I still needed a way to describe the state of being that fosters healthy love. I first thought of calling healthy love relationships "realistic" in order to contrast them with mystified relationships. That didn't seem to work. Somehow being "realistic" has the connotation for me of life without magic or passion. I didn't want a love like that.

One day I received another manuscript entitled *Care of the Soul* by Thomas Moore. Moore has a background similar to mine, and he spoke deeply to me. His book outlined a new approach for bringing depth and value into ordinary life. He called this approach the restoration of *soulfulness.* Here was the word I was after!

As it developed, my notion of soulfulness became quite different from Moore's, but I'm very grateful to him for giving me a way to talk about healthy human love. My notion of soulful love flows from the inborn potential of all human children. Children are by nature wonder-ful—filled with wonder and curiosity. This wonder and curiosity move them to explore and investigate all that is in their field of perception. They do this exploring with great courage, resiliency, and imagination. These traits of wonder, joy, curiosity, exploration, exuberance, courage, imagination, and resiliency are often thought of as childish, to be given up as we become rational and mature adults. But in fact they are basic human traits and form the core of soulfulness. And soulfulness is the source of genuine and abiding human love.

*   *   *

The Book of Genesis describes the fall of humankind in terms of four broken relationships. The story tells us that Adam and Eve, who symbolize our first parents, were given all the resources they needed to live a blissful life in Eden. They were at one with God, with themselves, with each other, and with all of creation. This joyful state of bliss had one restriction: They were not to "eat of the tree of the knowledge of good and evil."

Adam and Eve violated this limit, and their fall severed their relationship with God, with self, with each other, and with the world. Conflict, blame, and punishment were born. Childbearing became torment; work became an endless daily struggle. And their children inherited their pain.

This story, like all great theological myths, must be personalized. The Fall takes place psychologically the moment we are born. Our state of wholeness does not last. The more wounded our parents, the greater the possibility we will grow up mystified. This mystification extends to all the relationships in our lives.

The Genesis story also tells me that human relations will always be imperfect, an admixture of soulfulness and mystification. But we can grow in soulfulness, we can become more whole, and we can create a more human and fulfilling love in all our relationships.

In what follows I will look at the creation of love in the four areas described by Genesis:

I. Your relationship with a higher power—beginning with parent-child relationships and extending to God as you understand God.

II. Your relationship with yourself. As you looked into your source-figures' faces, you were psychologically born. Your original oneness with yourself was either soulfully mirrored and validated or rejected and invalidated. If your source relationships were soulful, your relationship with yourself became soulful. If your primary caretakers were wounded adult children acting out of their trancelike mystification, your relationship with yourself became mystified.

III. Your relationships with lovers, friends, and, if you've been married, your spouse or ex-spouse. If your self-relationship is mystified, your loves, marriage, and friendships will be based on mystified love. If your self-relationship is soulful, you can create soulful love relationships with friends, lovers, and spouse.

IV. Your place in the world. Our life work can be mystified or soulful, and so can our relationship to the earth itself.

As you read the following pages, I hope I can stir you to your
own soulful depth. Be aware that you are free. Choose to love yourself. You may struggle with mystified love. I certainly do. But the
trance you created saved your most vulnerable self from being violated. Love yourself for creating your trance. Love yourself for being
willing to see how you created it and how you may still be creating
it. You can stop doing it now. The danger has passed. You saved a
child from dying. You saved yourself!

Love yourself now for the hope you have. You wouldn't be working on yourself if you didn't have hope.

CREATING
LOVE

PART ONE

The Bafflement of Love

When you interact with another, an illusion is part of this dynamic. This illusion allows each soul to perceive what it needs to understand in order to heal.

GARY ZUKAV

CHAPTER 1

Mystified Love

For the good that I wish, I do not do; but I practice the very evil that I do not wish.

ROMANS 7:19

The mass of mankind live lives of quiet desperation.

HENRY DAVID THOREAU

In my early teens I worked as a grocery checker at Butera's Food Market in Houston, Texas. I was, like most young teenage boys, obsessed with thoughts about sex. One of my unofficial jobs at Butera's was to be on the lookout for specimens of female pulchritude. When a good-looking girl came in the store, I'd press a buzzer to alert Leon in the produce department and Bubba and Phil in the meat market so that they could come and look her over. This was, of course, raw objectification and unhealthy male chauvinism. That's what I grew up with, but that is not the point of the story.

What inevitably happened, to our amazement, was that the shapely woman was accompanied by an unshapely, and to our mind, unattractive partner. "It's a goddamn shame," Leon would mutter. "Too bad there ain't more of *me*." (With two front teeth missing—lost in a brawl—Leon would not have won any beauty contests himself.) It was also astonishing to me how many handsome men came in with very plain partners.

This is a rather raw, physical, almost primitive example, but it was my first impression of what I am calling the bafflement of love. It all seemed so illogical to my 16½-year-old mind.

When I started dating I was often bewildered by the strange reversals that could take place in the course of an evening. I can remember starting out on a date full of excitement and vitality, and having it end in harsh words and door-slamming separation. Trying to reconstruct the sequence of events was never enlightening. I always felt confused, sad, and lonely.

Years later, I came to see that human beings live out the drama of their relational lives motivated by feeling and desire rather than by logical assessment. When it comes to love, reason is not our guiding light. In over twenty years of marriage counseling, I rarely saw a marriage where the partners could have been predicted. Love is not logical. This is one reason it baffles us.

In almost every case I dealt with as a counselor the spouses had made the seemingly illogical choice of marrying someone who had the undesirable character traits of one or both of their parents. They were repeating the destructive relationships they had in childhood.

Another baffling aspect of love is our hatefulness with loved ones. I have often been the most hateful and mean with the people I love the most.

After I married, I can remember driving home, vowing to be sweet and loving no matter what, and then walking in the house and immediately saying something critical. Afterward I would feel terrible about what I did or said. A week or so later I would do it again.

THE "IN-LOVE" BAFFLEMENT

I remember the day Jack and Jill married. What a joyous occasion! The dinner toasts the night before, the beautiful maids-in-waiting, the bridegroom, the flowers, Jill herself in her shimmering dress. I had counseled them during the year of their engagement. I had some serious reservations about their getting married, but no two people were more truly in love, I thought.

Jack's whole demeanor changed in their early days together. He started exercising, ate nutritious food, and completely came out of the depression he'd been in. Jill was radiant. She had started therapy, and she went at it with the excitement of a child exploring the world. Jack and Jill said they were happier than they had ever been. They *seemed* happy.

After two years of intensely dramatic conflict, affairs, and an unsuccessful attempt at annulment, Jack and Jill divorced. A split-screen movie showing this couple's courtship and early marriage on one screen and their bitter fighting and divorce on the other would offer an amazing, almost unbelievable contrast.

I remember how confused Jill was at the very end. I remember how baffled Jack was as he asked me, "What happened? What happened? How could this happen?"

This was the second marriage I had been through with Jack. There would be a third after I was gone.

THE LOVE-AS-ENDURANCE BAFFLEMENT

For some the sad story never ends.

I think of another woman I counseled. Let's call her Lady G. She had been married thirty-eight years. Her husband was a top-notch salesman. He had also been a great athlete, honored in the press, popular. He was Mr. Nice Guy to everyone—everyone but Lady G. At home he was petty, mean, and self-centered. Lady G told me what had become by then a familiar story. They were college sweethearts. He was the star football player, and she was a cheerleader and the most popular girl. After they married, the nightmare began for her. Within six years she had four children. She raised them mostly alone, as he traveled most of the time. His company provided him a liberal expense account. He partied and entertained his clients, wining and dining them at the most expensive places. Lady G was given an *allowance,* as she called it. Whenever she spent any money on herself, her husband railed at her for sending him to the poorhouse.

When he was not traveling, her husband demanded sex daily. Lady G had rarely had an orgasm. She said she enjoyed the sense of closeness she felt when they were making love. However, she claimed that he had not actually kissed her in twenty years.

Their kids were grown when she saw me, and she was terribly lonely. She spent most of her time playing tennis, going to luncheons with her friends, doing volunteer hospital work, and preparing her husband's meals. He was seldom home; when he wasn't working, he spent most of his time at the company country club.

One day, in an unguarded moment, she said that she really detested her husband. She said if he were a beggar dying of thirst, she wouldn't give him a drink of water. "Why do you stay with him?" I asked. *"Because I love him,"* she replied.

How could this be love? I thought to myself. I thought of some of the people I knew who had been married a long time. I remembered how members of my family used to point to these long marriages as examples of what marital love was all about. I remember thinking how unhappy and lonely such and such a couple used to look. Endurance seemed to be what it was all about. *True love means endurance.* Lady G was miserable, frustrated, and totally unfulfilled. Surprisingly, so was her husband, although he came to only two counseling sessions. "We have never had a divorce in our family," he stated, "and I do not intend to be the first. Besides," he told me, "in spite of all her annoying foibles and idiosyncrasies, *I love* her."

The delight and promises of their college days had ended with two strangers bonded together by the terrors of aloneness. Again we ask, what happened?

MYSTIFICATION

Our bafflement about love stems from behaviors rooted in what I will call *mystification.* I first heard this term used by the pioneering psychiatrist Ronald Laing. He spoke about parents mystifying their children. He also pointed out that therapy could itself reenact parental mystification. He told the story of a teenage boy who was taken to therapy because of his intense rage toward his father. According to Laing, this boy had a lot to be angry about. His father was chronically demanding, intrusive, and controlling. But the therapist worked to reduce the boy's anger, taking the position that there was something *wrong with the boy* for having so much rage. Laing pointed out that the boy's rage was *invalidated* by the therapist, just as his other feelings, needs, and wants had been invalidated by his father.

Once the boy saw that the psychiatrist thought there was something wrong with him because of his anger, he became shameful and confused. His anger was invalidated. He was made an *invalid.* This simply reinforced the source of his original rage. A child whose every feeling, thought, and desire is being controlled and measured learns I only matter to my dad *when I'm not being myself.* This is *confusing:* In this state of confusion, the child inevitably has another thought: *The only time I am lovable is when I'm not being myself.* Such a thought engenders self-defensive anger.

Anger gives us the energy and strength to protect ourselves. Yet anger at a parent is almost always threatening to a child. So in order to dispel this threat, most children will create a false identity which pleases their parent. The strongest children, however, become rebels and intensify their anger. This was the case with Laing's subject. His rage was evidence of his courage and inner integrity. When the therapist finished with him, he was once again reduced to confusion.

This confusion is the most general way to convey the concept of mystification. I will describe the mystified state in more detail later on. For now let me define mystification as an altered state of consciousness in which a person feels and believes that there is something wrong with them as they are, and creates a false self in order to be accepted by their parents or other crucial survival figures.

Once we come to believe that we *are* this false self, *we do not know that we do not know who we are*. For most of us the false self confusion occurred in our preschool years. Once the false self is created, the authentic self is frozen in past time. In my book *Homecoming: Reclaiming and Championing Your Inner Child*, I called this frozen self the *wounded inner child*. The wounded inner child is always mystified to some degree. The degree of mystification depends upon the nature of the abuse the child experienced, the chronicity of abuse, and whether or not there was anyone who did value the child for who they really were.

Believing that we are lovable only when we are not being ourself is the result of what I call toxic shame. (See my book *Healing the Shame That Binds You*.) Toxic shame says that the way you *are* is not okay, that there is something wrong with you in your very being.

When one is frozen in the past, one lacks a *sense of presence*. Most of us have had the experience of being with someone who is physically present but not really there. Most of us have also had the experience of overreacting to something someone has done or said to us. Overreactions are good examples of lacking presence. We do not see or hear what is actually being done or said. We see or hear something from the past. It may be the sound of someone's voice or the look on their face that takes us back to some incident from our past. We act the way we did then, rather than appropriately responding to what is going on now.

Lack of presence and a shame-based false self are the pillars of the altered state of being I'm calling mystification.

Let's take a deeper look at Jack and Jill. Jack was a shy and awkward child. He was teased and ridiculed from an early age. His mother deserted him to be raised by an alcoholic father who used him in the cruelest fashion. When he was 5, his father put him on a street corner to sell newspapers. Jack was later severely burned in a fire started by his drunken father's smoking in bed. He underwent many skin grafts on his face. He was in his mid-fifties and was divorcing his first wife when he met Jill. To Jack, for a beautiful young woman to want him was everything. His wounded child felt totally unloved and unwanted. He also could father Jill in a loving and nurturing way, the way he longed for his father to love him.

Jill had grown up in a southern town where her family was considered riffraff. When Jill was 3 years old, her father deserted her mother. Her mother had a series of lovers; she was a young woman with five kids and needed male support in her life. Early on, Jill felt there was something wrong with her. Her oldest brother and two of her mother's lovers sexually abused her. She was desperate for a father who loved her. Jack represented the perfect father—kind, gentle, and nurturing. Her inner child desperately wanted to be taken care of.

When Jack and Jill married, it was like two 3-year-old kids trying to negotiate a life together. Each was a needy child. Neither had gotten any of their real dependency needs met.

After they married, Jill's neediness became too much for Jack's needy little boy. He began to lash out at her with the anger that really belonged to his father. Jill punished Jack by having an affair with a younger man. She did it almost in front of his eyes. Shortly before they divorced, Jill confessed that she had been married three times before, each time to a wealthy older man. All three marriages had ended with her having an affair with a man her own age. She was humiliating her husband and getting even with her father. She had put her father's face on all her husbands. In punishing them, she was punishing him.

As I learned more about the G's, it became clear that both of them had re-created key aspects of their parents' marriage and sex life. Lady G was the spitting image of her mother, who had endured a forty-five-year marriage to a man who was antisocial and reclusive. When Lady G married, her mother told her that she had never been orgasmic. She instructed Lady G that as a good Catholic woman, sex was her obligation, not her choice.

Mr. G's father was macho and basically controlled his wife with money. Mr. G and his dad shared his athletic achievements, and they spent time together hunting and fishing. Mr. G had seen his dad party and cheat on his mom. But his dad was clear that divorce was never an option. "It's against God's law. If you don't like it, you have to gut it out. That's the manly thing to do."

The G's were like sleepwalkers reenacting what was familiar. They were both mystified.

FORMS OF MYSTIFIED LOVE

Mystified love causes so much bafflement because what the mystified child believed to be love is not love at all. Beliefs govern our lives. People learn about love from their *culture as embodied in their parents or other survival figures.* I call these our *source relationships,* because they are the model for every other relationship of our lives, even outside the family. If we are mystified, the patterns established in our source relationships may be manifested in a surprising number of ways. We may:

• Create an *idealized* or *degraded* image of what a partner in a relationship is supposed to be.

• Act out our culture's notion of romantic love.

• Slavishly act out our mother's and/or father's belief about love and relationships.

• Re-create the defensive strategies we used to survive our relationship with an abusive parent.

• Re-create our role in the original family system.

• Continually sabotage our happiness in all areas of life in order to be loyal to our unhappy source figure.

• Find people who are the *opposite* of our source figures, and create a marriage or committed relationship that is the opposite of our source relationships.

Here are a few examples of mystification at work that I encountered in my counseling experience.

Create an Idealized Image

Aphrodite was her father's favorite. He treated her like a princess. He anticipated her needs and often gave her things she did not need.

When she was 12 years old, he died suddenly of a heart attack. Aphrodite was heartbroken, and no one helped her to grieve his loss. Her mother hid her own grief by mood altering with frantic activity. She remarried within eight months of her husband's death.

Aphrodite hated her stepfather. He sensed her dislike and became very abusive to her.

She dreamed of her father and longed to marry a man just like him, but no man ever seemed to measure up. I counseled her when she was in her late fifties. She had been proposed to a dozen times but had never married.

She had become very religious and went to church services every day. She told me she now had her Heavenly Father and that someday she would be with her father in heaven.

Although she came to counseling because she said she wanted to get married, I knew that this could not happen unless she demystified her idealized image of her dead father.

Create a Degraded Image

Anita's father was a cruel patriarch. He physically beat Anita and her mother. When her mother was in her menstrual period, Anita was forced to be her father's sexual partner. She hated him.

Anita married as a teenager, swept off her feet by a romantic and forceful young man who promised her a better life. After they were married, he started to hit her and used her sexually in a very demanding and insensitive way. Shortly after they had a son, Anita's husband was killed in an automobile accident.

Anita loved her son, Tony. But he was always hard to handle, and she was terrified that without a father to discipline him, he would turn out badly. She often beat him and felt very frustrated when his behavior only got worse.

When she came to see me for counseling, she was sixty-one years old. She had just taken custody of her grandson because her son Tony had been put in jail for battering his wife and son!

Slavishly Act Out Source Relations' Beliefs About
Love As Duty and Obligation

When Hilliel came for counseling, he told me he thought he was losing his mind. He had recently dreamed on several occasions that he had choked his wife to death and smothered his children.

Hilliel grew up in a religious Muslim family. Although he went through an adolescent rebellion and an agnostic intellectual period while in the university, he had returned to his faith by the time he married. His wife was rigidly orthodox. She was passively controlling, moralistic, and anxiety ridden. She followed every aspect of the religiously prescribed marriage obligations to the letter.

One year into the marriage, Hilliel decided to give up his second career as a musician. His playing and practice took him away from his wife, who was now pregnant. Hilliel was a promising musician. He loved music and had played since he was 9 years old. Giving up his music was very painful. Yet he knew that his marriage vows brought new obligations and belonged to a higher order of values.

As his married life progressed, he gave up more and more of his personal joys and pleasures. As the years went by Hilliel's wife bore several more children. Hilliel had to work long hours to support his family. He had time off one day a week but that time was usually spent at the mosque. Hilliel's dreams had first occurred two years after the birth of his fifth child. All forms of birth control except abstention were strictly forbidden. For the prior 18 months, Hilliel and his wife had abstained from any kind of physical contact.

I suggested that he had effectively cast out every form of exuberance in his life. I told him that he was creating an inhuman situation. I pointed out how important his music was to him. He answered with an array of *shoulds* and *oughts*. He told me love of wife and family was a high duty, second only to the love of God. I pointed out that his dreams were telling him otherwise. I told him that his unconscious was a more powerful expression of the life force than was his conscious sense of duty. I reminded him of the places in the Koran where the direct message of God came through dreams. All of this was to no avail. After three sessions he left me, muttering that the obligations of love were what he had to live for and that I could not really understand because I was a Westerner.

I surely did understand. I myself had been totally involved in an obedience-oriented community. We read a long, tedious book of rules four times a year. We were told that we could love God perfectly if we followed these rules to the letter. We were often read stories of saints, whose every action could be accounted for by looking at the rules of their order. Saints, we were told, could always be found doing what the *rule* stated they should be doing. Love, we were taught, is consummated in doing your duty and meeting your obligations.

This understanding of love is very narrow and rigid. Such a love disregards life and creates stagnation. What could be desirable about a love that does that?

The Payoffs of Long-Suffering Love

Eve has been married thirty-one years. Her husband is an alcoholic
and a womanizer. She has caught him in bed with another woman
on two occasions. He tells her that he doesn't love her, that he stays
with her because he cannot afford to divorce her. I ask her why she
stays with him. She answers, "Because I love him."

Eve is delusional. She really *believes* she loves him.

To confront her delusion, I tell her that what she calls love is
not love at all. My job is to demystify her, to challenge a magical
belief that has gone a long way toward killing her psychologically. It
is a dangerous belief. She learned it in her family and church. Love
means completely giving up *your own needs, feelings, and wants.*
Love is complete self-negation and sacrifice. Eve saw this belief modeled by her grandmother, mother, and two aunts. They showed her
how a good loving Christian woman should behave. They told her
that this was especially a woman's role in life and that God gives
women a special place in heaven for doing their womanly duty.

What gradually became obvious to me was that her notion of
love had a lot of payoffs. This is why it was so hard to let it go.

To begin with, her husband was quite wealthy. Eve chose not to
have servants; by doing all the household chores herself, she could
temporarily escape her sadness, anger, and loneliness. She used
housework as a mood-altering activity. Marriage also kept her from
having to deal with the "terrors of aloneness." And since Eve really
had no authentic self, these terrors were magnified.

Eve had not dated much in high school. She met her husband
in college; he was her first lover. She was pregnant when they married. He was dashing, handsome, and desired by all the girls. He was
still very handsome. The only time I saw them together, they seemed
completely mismatched. Her Plain Jane looks and obesity were in
stark contrast to his dashing fitness and handsomeness. This was another obvious payoff in her staying with him. She would not even
allow herself to *think* of what it would be like to divorce him and
risk dating again.

Above all, Eve's notion of love had emotional payoffs. Eve was
praised and supported for her self-effacement and *long-suffering* per-
severance by her minister and fellow church members. Her minister
often told her that the more suffering came her way, the more God
loved her. He told her that her terrible marriage afforded her the
kind of raw material that *saints* were made of. Her children called
her a saint.

Being a saint is as high as you can go! So Eve's lowliness and long-suffering humiliation created a kind of *reverse grandiosity*. Her life of martyrdom brought her the admiration and narcissistic supplies she had been deprived of as a child.

Everything Eve was doing was geared toward enhancing *her own self-esteem*. She used self-aggrandizing, mood-altering behaviors to avoid facing the painful choices she would have to make if she let herself feel the pain and loneliness of her life. To my mind this was the pain, the true and legitimate suffering that would truly offer redemption. Facing the hurt, loneliness, and anger would move her to some action.

Eve also needs to own her self-hatred. This is the deepest wound she carries. All her addictive, mood-altering behaviors cover up this core malady. If Eve loved herself, she could not allow herself to endure her rotten life. She seemed paralyzed with despair. Despair is the direct antithesis of the vibrant faith Eve so humbly professes.

Re-create Defensive Strategies Used to Survive Abusive Parenting

Larmark tried harder at establishing friendships than perhaps anyone I have ever known. Despite all his efforts, he basically had no friends. When he talked about his friendships he would wind up contradicting himself. He would talk as if he had a host of friends, but when I queried him about the quality of a particular friendship, he would admit that it was not really a friendship at all. Sometimes he would start crying, telling me that he just didn't understand why he couldn't sustain a friendship. "What's the matter with me?" he would ask. "I bust my ass to develop friendships and no one seems to really like me."

The fact was that Larmark's behavior was offensive. He frequently raged and was critical and highly intrusive. He would interrupt, interrogate, and give patronizing lectures. He frequently asked questions that violated others' boundaries.

For example, during his second counseling session he began criticizing statements he had heard me make in a public talk, almost glaring at me and telling me that he didn't think I had finished my own therapy. He ended this particular monologue with a wink of his right eye, suggesting that he was "in the know." I remember feeling disconnected and defensive. I later realized that his behavior was aimed at putting me on the defensive. I suspected that if he was doing this to me, he was doing it to everyone else, and that we wouldn't have to probe far to know why his friendships never lasted.

Larmark had a desperate need to *control* other people. He exhibited a behavior called hypermnesia. I will describe this in greater detail in Chapter 3, but basically, it is a state of heightened alertness in which one has an abnormally sharp ability to remember details. It is a common defensive strategy developed by victims of parental control, inconsistency, and abuse.

Larmark's father was a raging, physically abusive man. As a child, Larmark had witnessed his father beating his mother and his two older brothers. His father had never beaten him, but anyone who witnesses violence is a victim of violence. Larmark had developed his hypermnesia as a way to protect himself from his father. By noticing and remembering every micro and minute detail of his father's behavior, he hoped to learn exactly which triggers set his father off. He lived in a constant state of alertness.

Larmark had been married three times and had basically driven his wives crazy by intrusively questioning and vigilantly watching every detail of their behavior. The same obsession was driving away potential friends.

Repeat the Family of Origin Role

Children are often set up to take care of their parents' pain. They are taught, really indoctrinated in, the belief that true love is giving up your self. Their role in the family is *Caretaker,* and they often continue to caretake throughout their life.

The more dysfunctional a family is, the more rigid the family roles become. In a family shamed by poverty, a child might take on the role of family *Star, Hero,* or *Heroine* in order to give the family a sense of dignity. When parents are irresponsible, an older child often becomes the *Little Parent* to his or her brothers and sisters.

Minerva was what is called in family systems work a *Lost Child.* A Lost Child is a child who was not planned or wanted. A Lost Child is often resented. Such a child often adapts by being nonintrusive, isolated, and quiet. Lost kids frequently become the "good child" in the family, conforming and not giving anyone any trouble.

As a young girl, Minerva was always perfectly behaved. She always did the right thing. Minerva was the result of an accidental pregnancy; her parents were still teenagers when she was born.

Minerva's childhood was devoid of fatherly protection or fatherly love. Her father was an alcoholic. Minerva recalls him cursing her and telling her he wished she'd never been born. He was rarely around and, by her early teens, had pretty much abandoned her.

Minerva's mother had always secretly blamed her for her early marriage and the burdens she had to bear because of her alcoholic husband's irresponsible behavior.

Minerva left home as soon as she graduated from high school and began a long and oppressive work career. Although she was what any company would call the perfect employee, she suffered greatly at work. In her thirty-five years as an executive secretary, she had had only three bosses, each of whom she described as self-aggrandizing, emotionally insensitive, and inconsiderate.

When she came for counseling, her work life had worsened. A company she had worked for for fifteen years had merged with a larger company. She had taken a demotion and a pay cut, and her job itself was in jeopardy. Her new boss was twenty years younger than she, arrogant, cocky, and stupid. For years she had risen at 5:00 A.M., caught an early bus to work, and returned home around 6:00 P.M. each evening. She had almost no personal life, and now her life at work was one of continual pressure. It had become clear to her that the new company wanted to get rid of the "older" employees.

I couldn't help but think of her life in terms of the myth of Sisyphus—the story of the man condemned to push a rock up a hill each day, knowing that when it neared the top, it would simply roll down again and he would have to start all over, day after day, year after year.

Minerva never knew she had other choices. She was lost in a mystified relationship with her *father substitute* bosses at work. In always trying to do the right thing and please her bosses, she was reenacting her original relationship with her insensitive, unavailable father.

Many people reenact their mystified source relationships at work. Their offices become exact replicas of their family of origin. I will have more to say about this later.

Sabotage Happiness Out of Loyalty to Source Figures

Many people sabotage their own chance at happiness or success right at the moment they are within reach. This seemingly illogical behavior is due to the wounded inner child's toxic guilt.

Healthy guilt is necessary; it is our moral conscience. But toxic guilt is a set of voices in our head telling us that we have no right to a life of our own, no right to be happier than our source figures. These voices can cause us to sabotage our happiness repeatedly.

Joe couldn't take risks. Several times he was offered new jobs that would help him advance. Right at the moment of decision, he would become nauseated with anxiety. And he always turned down the new job.

Joe's father had worked in the same steel mill for thirty-five years. He constantly badmouthed his job and said he kept it only because the family needed the benefits. At home he was rageful and childish when he didn't get what he wanted. One of his refrains was, "At least I'm not a phoney success." At other times, he took Joe aside and gave him long, boring lectures on how to be on the lookout for new opportunities and take advantage of them.

Gretel continually accused her husband of having affairs, although her accusations had no basis in fact. If she called her husband at work and he didn't get to the phone immediately, she would interpret his delay as caused by some kind of monkey business. If she heard a woman laugh in the background, she would bawl him out on the phone. After ten years of this behavior on Gretel's part, her husband filed for divorce. Brokenhearted, she owned that he *had* been a faithful husband. But her mother had told her over and over again that no man could be faithful. "It's just not in their nature," the mother would say. "They can't help it. So you had better be ready for the worst."

She had provoked her husband into *proving that her mother was right*.

Gretel wound up living with her mom, sharing her loneliness and isolation. She had insured that she would never be happier than her mother.

Find People Who Are the Opposite of a Source Figure ... And End Up Ourselves Just Like the Source Figure We Dislike

Maco came to counseling because he felt like a wimp in his marriage. In the beginning he had liked the fact that his wife Guinevere was a "sexpot." She flaunted her body and loved to have men ogle her. At first this turned Maco on. But over time, his feelings changed. He felt shamed and powerless. As I explored the couple's source relationships, I learned Maco's wife was an untreated incest victim; when she was a child, her father had fondled her on several occasions. But she refused to accept my strong conviction that this *was* a form of incest. Like any incest victim, she harbored a deep sense of shame. She was also terrified of abandonment. Her father was a flamboyant alcoholic and often acted out sexually. She had been a witness to one of her father's affairs. In addition, she was her mother's confidante and protector. Her mother was terrified that her husband would leave her. Guinevere carried that terror of abandonment.

Maco's father was a tyrant. He was a rageaholic and religious fanatic. Maco's mother was passive and meek. Maco had identified with his mother. He had grown up as an awkward and unobtrusive boy. He was severely shut down emotionally and painfully shy.

When they met in college, Maco could not believe that Guinevere was interested in him. In reality, he was exactly what she wanted. If she was the exact opposite of his meek mother, he was the exact opposite of her father. He adored her, and she could flaunt herself sexually while being assured that he would never stray. By marrying, Maco and his wife created the exact opposites of their parents' marriages.

Paradoxically, Maco's wife was an alcoholic and was having affairs *just like her father*. I observed this pattern frequently with couples who seemed to have marriages that were the exact opposites of their parents' marriages: One or both partners would act out the behavior of the parent they disliked the most. In this case, Maco's wife was acting exactly like the father she consciously despised and Maco was acting out the role of the mother whom he had bonded with but secretly pitied and disliked.

All these baffling behaviors of love are rooted in mystification.

MYSTIFICATION QUIZ

I believe that everyone is mystified to some degree. No one answers life's full invitation. Still, it seems that the fullest lives are the least mystified. How fully are you responding to life? Check out your level of mystification by marking an "X" on the appropriate line.

Love and Relationship in General

1. **Love means giving up yourself and putting your needs aside for another.**

   1. _____ Never   2. __X__ Occasionally

   3. _____ Frequently   4. _____ Almost always

2. **The "right" person will come along if you are willing to wait.**

   1. __X__ Never   2. _____ Occasionally

   3. _____ Frequently   4. _____ Almost always

3. My love can change another person's behavior.

1. __X__ Never   2. _____ Occasionally

3. _____ Frequently   4. _____ Almost always

4. I "fall in love" with potential lovers quickly.

1. _____ Never   2. _____ Occasionally

3. __X__ Frequently   4. _____ Almost always

5. I stay in relationships long after there is any real growth taking place.

1. _____ Never   2. _____ Occasionally

3. __X__ Frequently   4. _____ Almost always

6. I have been abused by someone I love (abuse includes abandonment and neglect).

1. _____ Never   2. _____ Occasionally

3. __X__ Frequently   4. _____ Almost always

7. I have abused someone I love.

1. _____ Never   2. _____ Occasionally

3. __X__ Frequently   4. _____ Almost always

Parenting

8. The commitment to one's children is more important than the commitment to spouse or friend.

1. _____ Never   2. __X__ Occasionally

3. _____ Frequently   4. _____ Almost always

9. One should love their parents more than anyone else in life.

1. __X__ Never   2. _____ Occasionally

3. _____ Frequently   4. _____ Almost always

10. I have been accused of being overcontrolling with my children.

1. _____ Never   2. ___X___ Occasionally

3. _____ Frequently   4. _____ Almost always

Self

11. I think I am a failure when my relationships don't work out.

1. _____ Never   2. _____ Occasionally

3. ___X___ Frequently   4. _____ Almost always

12. I compare myself to other people.

1. _____ Never   2. _____ Occasionally

3. ___X___ Frequently   4. _____ Almost always

Friendship

13. I have had trouble establishing good friendships.

1. _____ Never   2. _____ Occasionally

3. ___X___ Frequently   4. _____ Almost always

14. I have trouble sustaining relationships.

1. _____ Never   2. _____ Occasionally

3. ___X___ Frequently   4. _____ Almost always

15. Friendships are at the bottom of my personal relationship value scale. (In answering observe your actual behavior.)

1. _____ Never   2. ___X___ Occasionally

3. _____ Frequently   4. _____ Almost always

Spousal Love

This includes any committed relationships (gay, lesbian, live together, legal marriage).

16. My partner has accused me of being too controlling.

   1. _____ Never   2. _____ Occasionally

   3. __X__ Frequently   4. _____ Almost always

17. I have had conflict-free committed relationships.

   1. __X__ Never   2. _____ Occasionally

   3. _____ Frequently   4. _____ Almost always

18. I keep "secrets" (things I am ashamed of, e.g., sexual fantasies) from my partner.

   1. _____ Never   2. __X__ Occasionally

   3. _____ Frequently   4. _____ Almost always

19. The "honeymoon" can last forever if you work at it.

   1. __X__ Never   2. _____ Occasionally

   3. _____ Frequently   4. _____ Almost always

God

20. You can know what God's will is for you.

   1. _____ Never   2. __X__ Occasionally

   3. _____ Frequently   4. _____ Almost always

21. God punishes us for our failures in love.

   1. _____ Never   2. __X__ Occasionally

   3. _____ Frequently   4. _____ Almost always

World

22. One's job is more important than any other relationship. (If you don't work, you don't eat.)

1. _____ Never 2. ___X___ Occasionally

3. _____ Frequently 4. _____ Almost always

23. Political action is a waste of time. (Reflect on your *actual behavior* here. How much time do you really give to politics?)

1. _____ Never 2. _____ Occasionally

3. _____ Frequently 4. ___X___ Almost always

24. The earth and its riches are here for human pleasure and use.

1. _____ Never 2. ___X___ Occasionally

3. _____ Frequently 4. _____ Almost always

25. After God, patriotism is our highest value.

1. ___X___ Never 2. _____ Occasionally

3. _____ Frequently 4. _____ Almost always

To score this quiz look at the numbers next to the box you check. Add up the twenty-five numbers you checked.

If you scored: *Level of mystification*
25–35 Nonmystified
36–55 Mild
56–70 Fairly intense
71–90 Intense
91–100 Severe

This test is not scientific. It is based only on my experience and my beliefs about mystified love and relationships. If you agree with my beliefs, then you may want to take this test very seriously. High levels (intense to severe) of mystification mean you are in a *trance*, living your present life with part of you frozen in the past. Your life is a recycling of your childhood problems. If you don't do something about your mystification, you may go to your grave having never known who you are. You can live your whole life never being fully born. I know of no greater tragedy.

CHAPTER 2

The Sources of Mystified Love

No social problem is as universal as the oppression of the child. . . . No slave was ever so much the property of his master as the child is of his parent. . . . Never were the rights of man ever so disregarded as in the case of the child. . . .

MARIA MONTESSORI

Her father gave her only conditional acceptance—the condition being that she fulfill his fantasy of her. She learned, to her dismay, that she only felt loved when she wasn't being herself.

JOEL COVITZ

One day Wayne Kritzberg, a pioneer in adult child work, and I were walking into the parking lot of the Grand Hotel in Houston, Texas. We were talking intensely about inner child healing methods when a large bag of garbage dropped out of the sky onto the pavement right next to us. It probably came from the third or fourth level of the parking garage, but I experienced it as coming from nowhere. I walked by it continuing to talk without pausing a second. Wayne stopped and with some passion exclaimed, "Where did that come from?" *At that moment it dawned on me that bags of garbage don't just fall from nowhere.* Wayne's response was much more appropriate than mine. Then it occurred to me that in terms of the early experiences of my life in an alcoholic family, bags of garbage dropping mysteriously out of the heavens are pretty Mickey Mouse! Nothing to even break the cadence of speech over!

This is a good illustration of the trance-inducing power of our family of origin experience. What we grow up with is what we *come to view as normal*.

Our childhood is like the air we breathe—we take it for granted. Like fish which do not know they live in water until they are removed from it, we are unconscious about our childhood environment. The analogy limps but you can get the idea. Environments surround us to such a degree we take them for granted. We can only know them when we are out of them.

We can see the full impact of our family of origin only when we are far enough out of our family to view it objectively. There are many ways that people can leave their family of origin.

Physically leaving it is one way, although if the person is extremely emotionally attached, it may be the least significant way.

Other ways include giving up one's rigid family of origin role or breaking the family rules. We will discuss family roles and rules in this chapter.

The most powerful and dramatic way of leaving one's family of origin is to do what has been called original pain work. Original pain refers to the early childhood feelings one had to repress either because of the severity of the trauma or because expressing these feelings was dangerous. These repressed emotions keep us bonded to the family's emotional climate, which is made up mostly of our mother' and father's emotions. But if we can feel our own hurt and anger, we become *reconciled with ourselves*. Feeling our own feelings is the way we break away from the emotional climate of the family.

The most recent stage in my own growth occurred after I had done several years of original pain work. As I distanced myself from the emotional climate of my family, I began to see clearly that much of what I saw modeled as love in my family of origin was not love at all. That does not mean that my grandparents, parents, and relatives did not love. From a subjective viewpoint, many members of my family loved passionately and selflessly. I've already described the power of my mother's love. What I came to see was that objectively speaking what they called love was a defective and partial form of love. In fact, I now believe that many aspects of the *normal* rules that most responsible parents used when I was a child were abusive.

As a child I never questioned the beliefs about and behaviors of love that were modeled for me. They formed the grammar from which I built my language of love. When this language failed me (which it almost always did), I thought there was something wrong with *me*. I was already deeply mired in toxic shame. So it never occurred to me that *my whole notion of love was mystified*. My sense is that most people have a concept of love which they have never questioned. Folks whose love life is badly impoverished wax eloquent on the nature of love. Everyone seems to believe they *know* what love is. *It rarely occurs to people that the reason they are failing in love is because what they believe is love is not love at all.*

CULTURAL MYSTIFICATION

For most of its history, psychotherapy operated as if emotional problems originated inside a person's psyche. People certainly *experience* mystification and toxic shame as operating within themselves. But the mystification and toxic shame are the result of *what were originally interpersonal transactions*. Toxic shame originates outside the person's psyche, in their earliest relationships.

I first learned the rules of love from my family, but most of my family's rules about love were based on the teachings of our patriarchal culture.

The Rules of Patriarchy

The dictionary defines "patriarchy" as a "social organization marked by the supremacy of the father in the clan or family in both domestic and religious functions." The term "patriarch" goes all the way back to the fathers of Judeo-Christianity, Abraham, Isaac, and Jacob, and is often used to refer to the founder of a religion, clan, or race. A king is also a patriarch. Patriarchy is characterized by male domination and power. In patriarchal systems women and children have no legal rights. Most of recorded human history has been dominated by patriarchy.

Patriarchy worked in the past when life was tougher and basic security was everyone's concern. Bonding together on the basis of blood ties safeguarded survival. In the past families also sought the protection of powerful kings or landholders. Their survival depended on their king and therefore obedience and loyalty to the king were essential. Two hundred years ago the French and American Revolutions began to awaken us from our collective patriarchal trance. But patriarchal rules still govern most of the world's religions, school systems, and family systems.

The most damaging of these rules are:

- Blind obedience. You obey no matter what the content of the command because the act of obeying is itself virtuous. Blind obedience is the foundation upon which patriarchy stands. In the Judeo-Christian tradition, Abraham takes his son to the mountain to kill him in order to obey God. In a pure patriarchy the act of obeying, even if it means killing one's own child, is virtuous. This is the crux of blind obedience. No ruler could ask for a more perfect system of subjugation or devise a better scheme for getting his subjects to conform to his rules. In the religious and parental contexts, individuals are encouraged to blindly obey the leaders' rules and authority. And *one of the rules is never to question the rules*. The mere questioning of a rule is considered disobedience.

- The repression of all emotions, except fear. The emotion of anger is especially reprehensible. Once we lose our ability to be angry, we become doormats and people pleasers. We become so nice that we no longer have passion to fight for the things we stand for.

- The destruction of individual willpower. Patriarchy hates willful and exuberant children. They are hard to control. The destruction of a child's will leaves the child with two choices: conforming or rebelling. This polarized state is the core issue for all adult children.

- The repression of thinking whenever it departs from the authority figure's way of thinking.

Strangely and paradoxically, these rules stayed in place even though *political democracy was advancing*. No one seemed to notice that while democratic structures were being created in other areas, childhood was still an autocratic regime.

A major breakthrough in consciousness occurred at the end of World War II. I point to the Nuremberg trials as a decisive turning point in human history. Nazi war criminals were told that they could not plead innocence on the basis of being obedient to the authority of the state. It became clear that the men on trial did not consider themselves evil. In many instances they had been taught rigid Christian obedience. They had grown up conforming to the will of authority. They had grown up being physically punished. They were perfect specimens of pure patriarchy.

The Nazi phenomenon underscored the danger inherent in patriarchal parenting rules. As long as these rules are the dominant form of child-rearing, a totalitarian social system will always be possible. Erik Erikson suggests that "Hitler's ghost is counting on it."

From their own patriarchal upbringing, my parents and relatives learned that love was based on power, control, secrecy, shame, repression of emotions, and conformity of one's will to the will of another and of one's thoughts to the thoughts of another. These are not the bases for healthy human love.

I want to make it clear that patriarchy is not just about male domination. Patriarchal rules can be administered by women. Many women raised in patriarchal families are as controlling and repressive as their male models. Boys raised by such women can be seriously injured in their sense of masculinity.

Patriarchy is not always great for men, except for those on the top rungs of patriarchal power. Patriarchal fathers are especially hard on their sons' personhood.

But overall, patriarchy especially violates women.

All the male and female roles I grew up with were fashioned by patriarchal beliefs. My grandfather was a kind and gentle man, but he was quite limited in his range of knowledge. No one in my family ever openly challenged his viewpoint, even if they disagreed with him. I never once expressed a feeling if it was contrary to what he expected of me.

My mother was raised to be a homemaker. She felt diminished as a woman when she was forced to go to work. The patriarchal structure of the work world was the reason she couldn't make a decent living.

I remember a client who had been severely oppressed for being female. Her father wanted a boy. When she was 3 years old her parents had twin boys. The twins were the family favorites. They got all the attention. Her father felt education was a waste of time for women. He made it clear to my client that women were inferior. He made her work in her early teens in order to help the twins get a college education. Later my client was able to get a degree by going to night school. When she started her career, she met many obstacles due to male chauvinism. She was sexually harassed and was denied a promotion because she refused to respond to her boss sexually. The messages to this woman were:

From her father: There's something wrong with your sex. I'd love
                    you more if you weren't female.

From the culture: Men are more important than women. Men are
                    worth more than women. Women are valuable
                    only when they meet men's needs.

Even without her patriarchal controlling father, this client would
have experienced mystification by virtue of the fact that she was a
woman.

Some degree of cultural mystification is everyone's legacy. How
else could it be? We are measured from the moment we are born.
And we had better measure up. To be measured always involves
some degree of injustice. To be measured and not measure up is to
experience oneself as defective—as lacking in an essential way. This
deep sense of deficiency is a being wound. I call it toxic shame. No
one escapes entirely.

FAMILY MYSTIFICATION

Our parents passed on our culture's values, but we knew nothing of
this at first. Our mother and father were our first experience of
higher powers. They were gods. They knew everything. We had no
reason to mistrust them, at least not in the beginning.

We were born with an unconscious sense of our own integrity
and connectedness. There was no division within us or outside of
us. We were at one with ourselves and the world.

Still being one with our mothering source, we were unconscious. We needed to know ourselves consciously, and to do that we
needed our mother's *mirroring face*. We needed to be accepted and
reflected *exactly as we were,* because whatever was reflected back
from our mother's face became our primal self; whatever part of us
she rejected we also rejected. If she rejected all of us, if she didn't
want us, we rejected ourselves totally. We felt empty and valueless.

Psychological Death

As we grew up, we had many other developmental dependency
needs. We needed to be touched and held, to be fed and clothed.
We needed to be curious, to experience all our feelings, needs, and
wants. We needed to be affirmed and encouraged. We needed a safe
structure within which we could learn and grow. What *we needed
most of all was to be allowed to separate,* to be different from our

source figures. Separation allowed us to individuate and become self-actualized.

Without separation we would have no way of achieving our *second* or psychological birth. The failure to separate, to break the bond with our mothering source, would mean *psychological death*. Psychological death is commonplace. David Cooper, the existential psychiatrist, writes:

> Some people, in fact very many people, *have never been born,* or more usually, their birth has been only a shadow event and their lives represent only a marginal form of existence.

I call people who have never been fully born psychologically *mystified*. Failure to achieve second birth is the first and deepest level of mystification.

There are *degrees* of this failure to achieve second birth. Some separate but only conditionally. The message they received is you can separate if you honor and please me always. Or you can separate if you become what I want you to be. Or you can separate if you take care of my pain.

Some cannot separate at all. They have been so severely battered physically, sexually, or emotionally that they confuse their authentic self with the self of their abuser. This is most often the case with those who have offender status. Offenders abuse people exactly as they were abused. They lost their self during their abuse and identified with their abuser. They became con*fused* with their offender.

A lot of us never completely gave up our true self, but we went into hiding. We found that we were loved and valued *when we were not being ourselves.* Joel Covitz, in his powerful book *Emotional Child Abuse,* describes a woman who went through submissive and destructive relationships with one man after another. When she finally came for help, she traced her problems back to her rigid authoritarian father. He had decided what her life was to be before she was born. He rigidly demanded that she fulfill his fantasy for her. Covitz writes, "She learned, to her dismay, that *she only felt loved when she wasn't being herself.*"

I gulped the moment I read the part of this quote that I have italicized. I knew exactly what it meant. And I suspect you do, too. A lot of us know about this conditional, soul-marring false love. Our own mystified love is rooted in it. This is the second level of mystification—*to feel and believe that you are lovable only if you are not yourself.* This is not as deep a wound as not being born psychologically. But it is deep enough. It is enough to shrink our life so that we live only "a marginal form of existence."

EIGHT BLOCKS TO UNDERSTANDING MYSTIFICATION

It is impossible to grasp the sources of our wounded inner child's mystification all at once. I ask you to keep an open mind. There are at least eight blocks to recognizing the truth:

1. We are to some degree still mystified—still asleep in our original trance playing out the role our family system needed to maintain balance and control.
2. The patriarchal rules we were all raised with crushed our *will-power.* We learned that any adult was to be obeyed, simply because they were an adult, and that the act of obeying was in itself virtuous. We either slavishly believed this and gave up our wills in conformity to it or became compulsive rebels addicted to fighting rules and authority.
3. From the earliest age most of us had our feelings—of curiosity, excitement, joy, fear, sadness, and, especially, self-protective anger—shamed. In order to defend against the painful feeling of shame, we learned to numb our feelings. To the degree we have become numb, we no longer know what we feel or who we are.
4. We learned at an early age not to think for ourselves. Our own ideas and opinions were devalued and/or shamed. As a result, we no longer trust them.
5. We had our needs shamed, especially our need to be empowered. We also had our need to grieve shamed. Grief is the healing feeling. Because we could not grieve, we have many unhealed wounds.
6. Having our desires, feelings, thoughts, and needs shamed set us up for psychological confusion and psychological death. Without our natural human powers, we cannot really know what happened to us.
7. We were taught that we dishonored our parents if we thought critically about their ways of acting. We were taught the ultimate parental rule—*never question the parenting rules.*
8. We were set up to take care of our parents' unlived lives. Because we were enmeshed in their unresolved abuse, disappointments,

and emptiness, we had no way to separate from them and no time to develop our own emerging potential.

Each of these blocks will be more or less a factor for you depending on your degree of mystification.

THE FAMILY AS A RULE-BOUND SOCIAL SYSTEM

New knowledge has emerged in the last forty years which shows us how we can remain unconscious to the cultural mystification which our family passes on to us. This new knowledge can also help you understand how your family, as a rule-bound social system, created a trancelike "group mind" which blocks your understanding of mystification.

Families are systems in which every individual is impacted by every other individual. The whole, we could say, is greater (has more impact) than any combination of its parts. Any disorder in the primary marriage relationship will affect the ability of the other family members to get their needs met. The disorder could relate to poverty, addiction, illness, mental illness, suicide, death or any other tragedy. Any factor that causes distress in one family member will affect the whole family system. The more severe the distress, the more obsessed with it the members become. *The distress is trance inducing because it causes mental fixation and diminishes the possibility of choice.* The more distress, the greater the trance possibilities.

Functional Families

One way to understand what constitutes functionality in a family is by dividing the word *response-ability*. Being able to respond is an *ability*. Functional families are created by functional people. Functional people have the ability to respond to each other's feelings, needs, thoughts, and wants. In functional families, all members are allowed to express what they feel, think, need, or want. Problems are dealt with openly and effectively.

I once met a minister whose family vividly illustrated functionality for me. One of the three children in this family died in a tragic accident at the age of 6. He found a hot wire left by a remodeling crew and was electrocuted while the rest of the family stood by helplessly. The remaining children, a girl who was 3 at the time and a boy who was 4, were deeply impacted by their brother's death. The minister and his wife were heartbroken.

I met this man and his wife at a workshop for ministers and their spouses. They shared their story with me afterward on a two-hour drive to the airport. They told me that they had entered grief therapy as a family. The mother and father were in a support group for bereaved parents. The children were in age-appropriate groups of their own. They were helped through the various stages of grief. They were starting their *third year* of doing this work.

The whole family met from time to time and listened to one another. Each member's feelings were valued and mirrored. Each member's unique needs were taken into account. The younger child expressed herself best by acting out her feelings with dolls. As a three-year-old at the time of the accident, she could not understand the finality of death. She felt angry that her brother got so much attention and that he was no longer there to play with her. The older child was confused and scared. He was further along in his ability to grasp the finality of death. He needed lots of social support and parental warmth.

The minister and his wife also spent time expressing their feelings and listening to each other. They had to deal with their sense of guilt, with their fear they had somehow been negligent in supervising the child. They talked about how in the beginning they had each blamed the other, how they had blamed themselves.

I was deeply impressed. Here was a family in which each member was being supported in dealing with and responding to the tragic event that had affected their lives. Despite their great loss, they were truly *functional*.

Dysfunctional Families

I think of another family that had to confront the death of a child. My client had been eleven years old when her teenage brother—whom she idolized—committed suicide. The family belonged to high society and was very image conscious. They felt shamed by the suicide and did everything they could to hush it up. My client was not even allowed to go to the funeral. No one talked to her about her brother or his death.

Later she married a very religious man whom she idolized. However, they never talked to each other about any matter of real personal significance. He would quote Scripture and philosophize about things. They had a schizophrenic daughter who was of great concern to my client. When she tried to discuss this daughter with her husband, he got very quiet and suggested they pray over her. He refused to come to counseling. He was against his wife's coming, telling her that Jesus was the answer to their daughter's problem and that all problems could be answered by reading the Scriptures.

My client was as lonely as anyone I had ever seen. Her adult life was confusing to her, just as her childhood had been. In childhood her family avoided the tragedy of suicide, creating a secret that all had to bear. In adulthood she found a husband who used religion as a kind of mood-altering drug, who avoided anything unpleasant by quoting Scripture or going to church.

She went to church with him. They looked like a happy family. In reality they were a very dysfunctional family. They were not responding to their problems. They were not dealing with their feelings and needs. This kind of dysfunction is covert. Everything looks okay on the outside, but inside nothing is being dealt with. The problems are left unresolved.

Natural or Healthy Shame

Functional families are created by parents who are in touch with their healthy shame. Shame is an innate human emotion. Its function is to signal our human limits—our finitude. Our humanity is rooted in limits. To be human is to make mistakes, to need help, and to know that there is something greater than ourselves—some higher power.

Healthy shame is an essential component of our humanness. Awareness of limits is necessary to our psychological balance. Shame is our primary human boundary. When we lose our healthy sense of shame, we lose our boundaries and our shame becomes toxic. We then try to be more than human (shameless) or less than human (shameful).

We act in a more than human way by: acting like we are perfect; trying to control everything and everyone around us; obsessively seeking power; being patronizing; criticizing, blaming, and morally judging others; acting righteous; being driven to superachieve; acting like we are superior to everyone else.

We act in a less than human way by: taking on an identity of failure; allowing ourselves to continually get out of control, as with an addiction; acting powerless and weak as a way to have power; using stupidity as a way to get others to do for you what you can do for yourself; chronically criticizing and blaming yourself; continually

LESS THAN HUMAN	**MORE THAN HUMAN**
SHAMEFUL	*SHAMELESS*
• **Failure**	• **Perfect**
• **Out of Control**	• **Controlling**
• **Powerless and Weak**	• **Powerful**
• **Stupid**	• **Patronizing**
• **Self-critical**	• **Critical**
• **Self-blaming**	• **Judgmental, blaming**
• **Degraded**	• **Self-righteous**
• **Underachiever**	• **Driven, Superachiever**
• **Inferior**	• **Superior**

choosing behaviors that are degrading; refusing to use your known abilities; and becoming chronically inferior.

Healthy shame is crucial for functionality. And as we shall see shortly, healthy shame is the core of soulful love.

Roles and Rules

All families need the structure that roles and rules provide. In traditional marriages Dad brings home money, Mom does housework, and kids have chores and go to school. These are the family roles.

If the family is functional, the roles are *flexible*. When times change and Mom decides to go to work, Dad doesn't freak out. One child does not *always* do the same chores. No one is chosen to be the scapegoat. And the traditional roles may be reversed altogether.

In dysfunctional families, the roles are rigid and inflexible. The patriarchal system created the traditional marriage. I know many patriarchal men who are threatened by their wives having careers. One person gets the job of being the scapegoat. They may be the one who is continually sick or who gets in trouble all the time. They occupy the family's attention. They take the heat off the problems in the family, covering up the lack of intimacy and connectedness.

In functional families, the rules are also flexible and negotiable. In dysfunctional families rules are rigid or chaotic.

The more rigid and inflexible the rules, the more the system becomes closed and narrowly fixed. The more the rules are unspoken and covert, the more confusing they are to family members, and the more mystification they cause.

Covert rules usually result from an incongruity between what parents say and do. Parents who are severe disciplinarians but who are themselves unselfdisciplined cause their children much confusion.

Families make up all kinds of rules. Poor families have rules about being poor. In my family of origin the ultimate rule was "There is not enough." I call this the Scarcity Rule. Every day I heard, "We can't afford it," or "You can't go because we don't have any money."

There was a complementary rule that said: "Never be extravagant." No one would think of spending money frivolously.

I remember a traumatic episode that was triggered by my sister and me going to Coston's Drug Store. We were doing an errand for my mom, and decided to buy her a candy bar as a treat. We also bought one for ourselves. I was 6 at the time and my sister was 7.

Well, we got home, and the ——— hit the fan! I can feel the fear and shame right now. We had *squandered* money. We were bad.

The Scarcity Rule was reinforced by another rule, the Starving Children in ——— Rule. Each family has its own version of it. Whenever there was a moment of plenty—a parental voice would ring out, "Remember there are starving children in Latin America [Africa, India, etc.]." This would call us back to "scarcity"! I still hear this voice when I'm having fun.

Over the years parental voices become internalized and function like inner voices. In the beginning there was a specific context for this voice. Later the voice generalizes to all areas of experience.

My family rule about money became for me an internal voice that said, "There isn't going to be enough love, friends, food, etc., to go around." The rule extends to everything.

TYPES OF DYSFUNCTIONAL FAMILIES

I find it useful to divide shame-based families into three types—the cultic, the chaotic, and the corrupt. Each is shame-based in a different way. Cultic families cover up their toxic shame by acting more than human, hence shameless. Chaotic families handle their toxic shame by acting less than human, hence shameful. Corrupt families fail to develop any sense of shame. They are shameless, not as a cover-up, but because they have not developed a sense of limits.

Cultic, chaotic, and corrupt—each type has many subtypes, depending on cultural, economic, ethnic, religious, and idiosyncratic factors. Each type also has many degrees of dysfunction.

Regardless of type, all members are mystified to some degree. Chaotic families deny their pain and avoid their problems. Cultic and corrupt families are delusional. They sincerely believe that they have no problems and minimize their pain.

All three types of dysfunctional families foster mystified love. There is always a covert rule of love and fidelity that all members are expected to follow. In each type the covert rule takes a somewhat different form:

Cultic family: "To win my love, you must obey without question."

Chaotic family: "I need you to love me; I'll love you if you do."

Corrupt family: "Love is banding together and lying for one another."

All types of dysfunctional families are held together by a "groupthink" trancelike state of consciousness. The family spell is cast on each child in some way. The charts beginning on page 38 summarize the main elements of each type. It is important to note that in real life these types are not necessarily separate. *Many dysfunctional families have elements of all three types.*

Cultic Families

A cult has been defined as a closed system which exerts absolute control over its members' thoughts, feelings, and desires. The whole system is based on a rigid ideology which is considered sacred. The system with its ideology is more important than any of the individual cult members.

The cult demands purity of commitment and fosters distrust among its members, creating habitual rituals of confession. The leader manipulates the cult's milieu and establishes rigid boundaries. All of these elements of cults can be found in perfectionistic shame-based families.

Purity of doctrine may rest on the family's religious faith. Children are often told that their religious faith is the only true faith. They are told that they must never question the faith, that questioning would in itself be an act of unfaith. In such families, prosperity is often interpreted as a sign of God's special love.

But the family doctrine may not be a religious faith. It is whatever Mom and Dad rigidly hold to be true. Cultic parents often say things like, "Make me proud of you." The implication is, if you don't turn out the way I want, I won't love you anymore.

The purity of doctrine with its demand for blind obedience leads to a phenomenon called "snapping." Psychologists Flo Conway and Jim Siegelman describe "snapping" as "the process of shutting off the mind, of not-thinking. The process leaves people numb to their own feelings and the world around them." When you "snap," you have become a nonthinking part of the family cult.

Cultic families demand blind obedience. They try to control the environment at all times. They decide who the child can associate with. They choose the children's friends. The parents' rules are the Sacred Doctrine. Behaviors are considered right *or* wrong, good *or* bad—there is no in-between.

Once the children *snap,* they are "trance-formed" and mouth the family words as loyal members. Certain words or phrases might be repeated over and over. Everyone watchfully guards that no one violates the Sacred Doctrine. Brothers and sisters tattle to the parents whenever their sibling breaks a rule.

In functional families, siblings learn to share and cooperate with one another. they learn to give and take and to compromise. They learn loyalty and fidelity. In cultic dysfunctional families, the sibling system is severed. Siblings are often pitted against one another. There emerges an undifferentiated watchful *family eye* (like Big Brother). Each child becomes an extension of the parents. I was the patriarch to my brother. I shamed and blamed him for his mistakes.

Cultic families may be coercive, cruel, and punishing. They may be obsessed with good manners, relentlessly teaching their members to be correct and polite and make the right impression. They may be obsessed with rituals. The rituals often focus on religion, eating, and sexual behavior. In the most extreme cases they might even involve torture and Satanism.

PERFECTIONISM AND BLAME

The dominant rules in cultic families are perfectionism and blame.

The rule of perfectionism is perhaps the most damaging and mystifying. Dysfunctional family perfectionism is more about a *context* rather than a *content*. Being perfect has to do with whatever your family *believes* with rigid fervor. The rigid family beliefs create a context for blame. If things go wrong, it's always somebody's fault.

Perfectionism and blame are cover-ups for dealing with toxic shame. But like the shame, they try to mood alter, perfectionism and blame have no boundaries. You can never get it quite right. No matter what you do it is never quite good enough. Perfectionism always sets us up for more toxic shame.

CONTROL

The fear of exposure lies at the heart of toxic shame. Control is a way to handle this fear. If I control you, you cannot expose me. Control in shame-based families can be based on power or weakness. Control in cultic families is based on power. In chaotic families the

---

CULTIC - "SHAMELESS"

- **DOMINANT RULES**
  Power
  Control
  Perfectionism
  Blame

- **MYSTIFIED LOVE PATTERN**
  Duty
  Obligation
  Self-sacrifice

- **BOUNDARIES**
  Rigid within and without

- **DRIVERS**
  Work hard
  Don't feel

CHAOTIC - "SHAMEFUL"

- ## DOMINANT RULE
  Inconsistency

- ## MYSTIFIED LOVE PATTERN
  Caretaking
  Love Addiction

- ## BOUNDARIES
  Enmeshed

- ## DRIVERS
  Try hard
  Please me

members learn early on in life that weakness (even craziness) is a way to manipulate and control those around them.

BOUNDARIES

Cultic families have rigid boundaries both inside and outside the family. Members are expected to strive for perfect fulfillment of the family's sacred doctrine. This usually demands self-denial and rigid control over one's emotions. The family roles are based on a hierarchy of power and patriarchal rigidity. Those outside the family are unenlightened strangers. They are potential converts. (Growing up Catholic, I could certainly try and convert my non-Catholic friends. But I was *never* to go in a non-Catholic church, temple, or synagogue. It was considered a sin to do so.) Family members are trained in "impression management" learning to "act" the "right way." They are never to talk about the family to outsiders.

DRIVERS

The most dominant motivational push in cultic families is to work hard and do your duty. The rules are there and a loving person simply does what they are supposed to do no matter how they feel about it.

The most common form of mystified love in cultic families is love defined as duty, obligation, self-sacrifice, and self-negation. Father's love is measured by the long hours he works for the family. Mother's love resides in her self-sacrificing care for the children. Children show their love by doing chores or going to work as soon as possible. Since the family system is far more important than any individual in it, the children are taught that love means giving up your own desires.

Chaotic Families

There are many species of chaotic families. One type has no rules at all. When there are no rules, the message to the child is that you don't matter enough to me for me to teach you by setting boundaries for you. The parents may be adult children whose wounded inner child wants their own children to love them as their parents never did. When this is the case, there is no one there for the child. The parents are living in the past trying to get their own narcissistic needs met.

I now realize that I created a chaotic family by rebelling against my patriarchal upbringing. In certain areas, I went to the opposite extreme and avoided putting any structure in my children's lives. A lot of parents in the 60's and early 70's did this. (Some people also reverse the process. They grow up in a chaotic family, and then enforce very rigid, perfectionistic rules in their own household. They become cultic in their attempt to escape chaos.)

Another type of chaotic family has rigid but inconsistent rules. The parents may discipline the children a lot but be unselfdisciplined in their own life. Mystified parents are often adults one minute and needy children the next. This is very confusing to a child. One day she spills her milk and Dad is patient and kind. A week later she spills her milk and he goes crazy with rage. The child never knows what's going to set him off next. It doesn't take many incidents before she quits trusting altogether.

This inconsistency is made worse by divorce, which is frequent in chaotic families, and by a series of new spousal partners as either live-ins or stepparents.

Yet another type of chaotic family is "double binding." A rule creates a double bind if it sends contradictory messages. For example, a rule like "you kids ought to be more spontaneous" poses a double bind. If you are spontaneous because it is demanded of you, you are really not being spontaneous! You're in a damned if I do, damned if I don't situation. This is a double bind.

In every type of chaotic family, children are truly confused.

INCOMPLETION

Another covert issue in chaotic families is incompletion. Some problems go on for generations without resolution. The following scenario is commonplace in alcoholic families.

> Adult Child One: "How's Mom been doing with her drinking?" (Mom has been drinking for thirty years.)

> Adult Child Two: "Well, she was doing great. She quit for Lent, but started again on Easter Sunday." (Mom has quit for Lent but started again on Easter Sunday for thirty years.)

This conversation has been repeated for years. Neither one of these adult children really gets it: Mom is a sick alcoholic and needs an intervention which will confront her life-threatening problem and get her to AA and/or a treatment center.

This same scenario could occur with Dad's sexual addiction, workaholism, or gambling, or Mom's shopping, eating, or pill addiction, to mention only a few possibilities. Because the problem is denied or minimized, it is never resolved. The Rule of Incompletion is a major reason why family dysfunction is multigenerational.

BOUNDARIES

There are fused boundaries in chaotic families. The parent/child generational boundaries are violated in the various ways I will describe later in this chapter under the heading "Enmeshment."

Enmeshment is a state of confusion in which you do not know where you end and another begins.

Children become confused about their feelings, thoughts, and desires because they are not validated by their parental models.

Physical boundaries are violated—the kids sleep with the parents, family members go to the bathroom while you are taking a bath, your brother or sister use your things and wear your clothes.

DRIVERS

The driving motivation in chaotic families is learning to *please*. Love is based on neediness and emotional hunger. Children are "spoiled" or taught to be their parents' caretakers or both. There is a lot of failure in chaotic families. People try hard but they never quite make it. Trying is a kind of magical behavior. In chaotic families, children learn that if you try hard, you don't have to do it.

Children from chaotic families are often set up to take care of the needs of their families, take care of their parents' marriage, and/ or take care of one of their parents. Since the parents are often immature and childlike, they expect their children to make them happy. The children learn that they are most lovable when they are caring for their parents—or making another person feel good.

Sometimes the parents in chaotic families want their children's love so much that they become their children's slaves. The children have all the power and often become spoiled and demanding. They may later use love as an analgesic. Falling in love and being admired is the most familiar form of love. Love addiction can also result from deprivation; then it is an attempt to fill the hole we feel inside.

Corrupt Families

In corrupt families, the parents failed to develop a conscience, often because they failed to develop a sense of shame. They are truly shameless, unlike parents in cultic families, whose shameless perfectionism is a cover-up. Many of the criminals I have corresponded with come from corrupt families. Their mothers were prostitutes or drug dealers; their fathers had deserted them or were a law unto themselves, treating them violently and cruelly. Some had parents who were criminals themselves. Many were beaten or sexually abused almost at random.

The covert rule in corrupt families is "get away with anything you can." There are no moral boundaries. It is *us* against *them,* and anything goes. No one counts except the family. Loyalty to the family is the highest form of love. This family loyalty may require that you cheat, lie to, beat up, or even murder others.

The parents in corrupt families may be sociopathic and/or psychotic. They may teach and model corruption. I remember a client who vehemently defended his right to steal. He thought it was okay if you could get away with it. I had seen his son in an earlier session because the mother called me with anxious concerns about her son's habit of stealing. She spoke of her husband's stealing, but defended him almost in the next breath. It was obvious that their son had some very corrupt modeling.

Many of my prison correspondents describe their earliest memories as filled with the shaming of their emotions and their needs. They learned to be violent because of this early shaming. They were shamed before they had developed the verbal ability necessary to express themselves. They therefore were deprived of the normal human means of expression. To handle this preverbal powerlessness they developed irrational angers as a defense system. This anger was okay as long as it was directed outside the family. If it occurred within the family, it was punished, usually with severe physical abuse. Their irrational anger had nowhere to go except underground where it became a steaming volcano waiting to erupt in violence on the outside world.

Their violence was acted out on the helpless and innocent, the "suckers" or the "chumps" who got in their way.

With new awareness and a language to express themselves, these people can now see that their anger was misdirected. They now see that they "acted out" on the innocent exactly what was done to them as innocent children.

BOUNDARIES

In corrupt families there are rigid and absolute boundaries in relation to those outside the family and usually no boundaries within the parent/child relationship. I put all sexually abusing families under the corrupt family heading. Children's boundaries are severely violated in sexual abuse. The child takes on the shame and guilt which the psychotic parents do not *feel*. Incest families generally have rigid boundaries in relation to the outside world. Very little information is allowed to come in and the child victim is often held for years like a prisoner. I had a client whose father both incested and battered her. He kept her living with him for twenty-eight years. He would threaten her with a double-barreled shotgun when she threatened to leave.

CORRUPT - "SHAMELESS"

- **DOMINANT RULES**
  Power
  Punishment
  Control

- **MYSTIFIED LOVE PATTERN**
  Punishment and
    abuse as love
  Character disordered
    I deserve love
    I'm entitled

- **BOUNDARIES**
  Rigid outside the family

- **DRIVERS**
  Be strong (tough)
  Don't feel or need

DRIVERS

The driving motivation in corrupt families is "be strong and tough" and "don't feel." It is us against them and we can never let down our guard.

The most dominant mystified love pattern for this group is love as punishment and abuse. Children also learn a kind of offender love, which says "I'm entitled to love. I'm superior to everyone else." Corrupt families also may engender sadomasochistic types of love.

THE LESSONS OF FAMILY VIOLENCE

At the heart of mystified love is violence. This violence goes far beyond the acts we read about in the newspaper. The violence that induces mystification is often more covert, hidden, subtle, and tortuous.

I consider anything that violates a person's sense of self to be violence. Such action may not be directly physical or sexual, although it quite often is. In my definition, violence occurs when a more powerful and knowledgeable person destroys the freedom of a less powerful person for whom he or she is significant. It goes without saying that it is violent to choose to bring children into the world and incest, batter, torture, imprison, starve, or morally corrupt them. Other forms of violence are not as obvious. It is violent to choose to bring children into the world and:

- Neglect their health needs

- Desert them *emotionally*

- Spank, hit, kick, push, choke, shake, or pinch them, pull their hair, hit them with an object, or threaten to hit them

- Cause them to witness any form of physical violence

- Not protect them from older siblings or school or neighborhood bullies

- Tease them about their body

- Demand of them things that are unreasonable to expect from a child

- Refuse to set limits

- Be irresponsible about giving them sexual information they need

- Model inappropriate sexual behavior, which includes having a romanticized relationship with them, giving them seductive and voyeuristic looks, exposing them to inappropriate nudity, kissing them seductively

- Touch their genitals in any sexual way or have them touch your genitals in any sexual way

- Expose them to viewing any form of sexual behavior by adults or older siblings

- Bathe, massage, hug, kiss, dance with, or sleep with them as a form of sexual titillation for yourself

- Use them to supply your own need to be admired and respected

- Use them to take away your own disappointment and sadness by demanding that they perform, achieve, be beautiful, be athletic, be smart, etc.

- Use them to keep your marriage going

- Use them as a scapegoat for your anger and shame

- Refuse to resolve your own unresolved issues from the past

The list could go on. There is enough here to give you a sense of how encompassing the category of childhood violence really is. Whenever a child is not loved and valued for the very unique being he or she is, that child is violated. Violation says, "The way you are is not okay. Your right and need to be you is not okay. What you feel, want, need, imagine, think, is not okay."

Sexual Abuse

All abusive relationships teach a form of love. Sexual abuse violates the very core of a person's being. It sends the message that you are desirable and lovable only when you are being sexual. Many sexual abuse victims believe they must be sexually attractive to be valued and loved. Survivors of sexual abuse often excel in lovemaking. It's not surprising that people who feel the only way they can truly matter to anyone is sexually would become experts about sex. Another common outcome is the exact opposite. A survivor may feel, "I'm actually not very sexually attractive or desirable; therefore, I don't matter and I'll never matter to anyone." This person might put on large amounts of weight. In our society being fat is the antithesis to being the "perfect 10." Obesity can be used as a boundary to hide one's sexual distinctiveness. The more weight, the more one can hide.

Survivors of sexual abuse learn some very damaging things about relationships. Consider the following scenario:

Mother and Father have been having a heated argument. They have been drinking heavily. At one point Mom comes into her oldest child's bedroom and climbs in bed with the child. The child feels tearful and clings to Mom. Mom holds the child for some time.

Slowly Mom takes the child's hand and has the child touch her in a place that the child knows is private. Then Mom touches the child. The child is afraid but knows that Mother doesn't want questions. Also the child already knows not to talk about any unpleasant emotion like fear. The child has never felt these sensations. They are extremely pleasurable, but they are also frightening. This scene will be repeated many times under similar circumstances. The child is confused by it. But there is no one the child can talk to. The child also feels shame. Somehow the child knows it is wrong. Yet Mother's love and attention are wonderful. It makes the child feel special—warm and intimate. The child has a special secret with Mom.

This mother is teaching her child some serious lessons about power, feelings, love, and relationships. She knows the child will not repel her advances. She knows the child will obey her and accept her authority. She knows that the child does not know that he or she has the *right* to repel her advances. The mother is exerting her superior knowledge, power, and control.

The child wants the mother's love more than anything. Yet somehow the child knows that he or she is being used by the mother as an object, as an instrument of consolation.

The child feels, the only way I matter to my mother is by being sexual. The child's need to have its whole being acknowledged and valued will inevitably be repressed. In addition to repression, the child may develop any number of strategies to help ease the pain. The child learns to avoid what is there and to create fantasies about what is not there. The child will create a fantasy mother to bond to. She will be the wonderful, nurturing mother who loves the child in a *very special* way. The reality underlying their relationship is abuse. By creating a fantasy bond with Mother, the child effectively *confuses abuse with love*.

Physical Abuse

A major consequence of physical abuse is to live in fear. When the abuse is chronic, the fear becomes terror. The fear/terror response can be so intense as to cause permanent brain chemistry imbalance. The June 18, 1990, issue of *The New York Times* reported on a study from the National Center for the Study of Post-Traumatic Stress Disorder (PTSD). This study concluded that "one catastrophic experience when one is powerless is enough to change brain chemistry." The way the brain chemistry is changed has to do with the body's natural defense system. When a person encounters a severe threat, the brain releases certain hormones called catecholamines. These hormones increase the body's strength, preparing it to fight or run. This hormonal increase is the core of the emotions of anger and fear. These are the emotions that provide us the energy of self-preservation.

Children who face traumatic abuse from their survival figures have no place to run. (Later on they may literally run away from home.) Unable to run or fight, the children may "freeze." When they freeze, they enter a trance state, a state in which they remain hypervigilant. The rheostat button that controls the flow of catecholamines gets stuck and the brain keeps releasing the hormones even though the primary threat has passed. This state is commonly described as one of hypervigilance, panic attacks, overreactivity, or excessive worrying.

A child with unresolved trauma is frozen in time. When any new experience resembling the old trauma occurs, the old trauma is activated. They experience the old threat in all its fearful potential. They then overreact, responding as if the old threat were actually there.

People who have been traumatized continually distort the *facts* of present reality. They had to distort the *facts* of the original trauma in order to survive it. Abuse creates a kind of bewitchment. PTSD is characterized by this frozen state of ungrieved trauma. Physically abused children have many of the same traits as PTSD victims. (Actually any form of violation creates some of these traits.) They are hypervigilant, overreactive, and easily startled. These are major components of the mystified state.

Impact on Later Relationships

There are four major ways that victims respond to abuse. The first and worst consequence of physical and sexual abuse is that the victim often grows up to become an offender, doing to others—especially to their children—just what was done to them. Physical and sexual abuse survivors often become child batterers and child molesters.

The second way is to become an offender to yourself, treating yourself the same way your offender treated you.

The third and fourth responses result from the fact that abuse breaks the interpersonal bridge with the parents. The child can no longer trust the parent and either builds walls of isolation, unconsciously choosing never to get close to anyone, or continues to be a victim and act out victim roles all through life. The more that children are abused, the more ashamed they feel. The more ashamed children feel, the lower their expectations for love and nurturing. In effect the child concludes: "I'd better settle for anything I can get. I'm so unlovable, I'm lucky to get anything from anybody."

What *a victim of childhood abuse learns is that relationships are based on power, control, secrecy, fear, shame, isolation, and distance.* Since survival figures are beloved and godlike to a child, children will take on their parents' shame as their own. "The abuse must be about me," a child reasons. "My godlike parents who know every-thing must be okay." A child *must* think this way for survival. "Without these godlike parents," the child thinks, "what will happen to me? I must keep a fantasy of good parents going or else I will be aban-doned and die." Robert Firestone calls this process of thinking "fan-tasy bonding." The fantasy of "good parent, bad me" is a *defensive* self-nourishing image which allows the child to survive the abuse.

More often than not, the impact of the abuse is to teach a child "how to be abused." In the act of abuse, instead of learning to protect themselves, they learn that they *can't* protect themselves. Later in their adult life, they are oblivious to dangers that others would find obvious.

Many physical and sexual abuse victims do not know what to do except wait for the danger to be over.

Emotional Abuse

Emotional abuse is the most common form of child abuse. Sexual abuse and physical abuse are, of course, also emotionally abusing. In addition, emotional abuse includes the shaming of all emotions, name calling and labeling, judgments, and sadistic teasing. Two of the most mystifying forms of emotional abuse are *narcissistic use* and *double binding*.

People who failed to get their needs for affection and admiration met by their own parents will often use their children as their major source of narcissistic gratification. They will inculcate an exaggerated sense of duty and gratitude into their children at an early age. The children will feel like they *owe* their parents everything. They will feel a toxic and pervading sense of guilt any time they seem happier or financially better off than their parents. This sense of guilt is based on an overdependent loyalty.

With double binding, the process and content of a communica-tion are incongruent. Mom always says, "I want you to grow up and be independent." But her nonverbal body clues are saying, "Please don't ever leave me. I'm so pitiful, you must always take care of me." Or she talks in the abstract about children's duty to their parents. Or she talks about her own mother's sacrifice and how much she is indebted to her.

Enmeshment is the most damaging kind of emotional abuse. No form of abuse confuses us as much about love as the various types of enmeshment I will describe here.

In an enmeshed relationship, one person or a group of persons (the social system) *uses* another person (who is unequal in knowledge or power) to supply something that they need and are lacking. Children are more than eager to be the supply source in exchange for the *special* love and attention they seem to get for it. A child has a basic need to matter to their parents. When parental enmeshment occurs, the child feels like they are their parents' most special child. They cannot know they are being used by their parents and that *use* is *abuse*. Enmeshment is covert abuse and covert abuse is more crazy making than overt abuse.

FAMILY SYSTEM ENMESHMENT

In a family system, the whole system functions like an individual. And like an individual, a family system can have needs that aren't being met. In such cases, one or more family members become enmeshed with the system, supplying what the family is lacking. I used a mobile on my PBS series on the family to illustrate the system's need for balance. I would touch the mobile frequently to illustrate that touching one part would affect every other part. I would also make it clear that the mobile would always return to a state of rest or equilibrium.

In concrete, specific terms, if the family system has no joy, one or more members may adopt a Little Mary Sunshine façade. If the family has no breadwinner, one or more children may drop out of school to go to work. If there is no father present, the most available family member will become a surrogate husband to the wife and a surrogate father to younger siblings. These roles are prescribed by the needs of the family system. The individual members are sacrificed for the needs of the family system.

MARITAL ENMESHMENT

I often say that every family *needs* a generation gap. When Mom and Dad are in unresolved conflict and an intimacy vacuum is created, the generation gap may be lost. Mom and Dad may use their child's problems as a way to be close, thus "triangulating" the child into their marriage. The triangle serves to ease the tension.

I see this often in my family counseling work. I remember a case of a severely depressed child who bore the loneliness and sadness of his parents' marriage. The child's depression had been treated with drug therapy. This treatment was based on the belief that the depression was "endogenous" (originating within the child). I was able to change the child's outlook on life by working only on the marriage.

The parents were the "nicest" people you would ever want to meet. But they never really *dealt* with their conflicts or the anger these conflicts caused. Since they never communicated their anger, they never really made contact. Each was quite isolated and lonely. The child was a metaphor of their loneliness, sadness, and anger.

I have seen this same kind of triangulation in families where the child is a troublemaker at school or in families with anorectic and drug-addicted children. In each case, the child's problem is used to ease tensions in the parents' marriage. A child's success can be used in the same way. Sometimes the Star, Hero, or Heroine child serves to take care of the parents' marriage. Mom and Dad become so engrossed in their child's talents, achievements, and so forth, that they can avoid looking at their own pain and conflict.

In all cases of enmeshment, the child is being *used. Use is abuse.* None of us want to be used in a relationship. When we are used, we feel intense anger. Children cannot know they are being used. They feel the anger nonetheless. Their anger leaks out in other relationships and causes severe problems.

DYADIC ENMESHMENT

Unfulfilled marriage partners often turn to their children to get their needs met. Carl Jung once said: "The most damaging thing for any family is the unlived lives of the parents." The parents' lives may be unlived for a number of reasons, including unresolved abuse issues, disappointment because of unfulfilled dreams, and feelings of emptiness and loneliness.

Let's say a father was sexually violated by his stepmother. He may have lots of unresolved rage which he acts out on his daughters. They may experience his distrust and contempt for women in general. Even though he never says so explicitly, they will feel that their sex is bad or inferior. Father may model this contempt in his relationship with Mother. His sons may pick up his anger and carry it into their relationships. Or they may side with their mother and take on her victimization as their special responsibility. They may band with her in such an enmeshed way that they cannot leave her.

Parents who have unresolved physical abuse issues might use their children to get even with their own parents. Such parents might subject children to excessive and irrational punishments. They might set up a relationship where their children become their slaves, waiting on them hand and foot.

Alternatively, the unresolved physical abuse might be actualized as need for security, comfort, and physical care. The child might be set up to sleep with the parent, cuddling the parent and taking care of their need for touch and warmth. The child might be set up to care for a parent's "somatized feelings" which are expressed in the form of constant sickness. The child might be bonded to the parent in such a way as to think it is their obligation to nurse, give massages, and fix meals.

Parents who have unfulfilled expectations and dreams often make their children extensions of themselves. Through this dyadic enmeshment, they *use* their children to get their own unfulfilled dreams met. The result is great confusion and mystification in the children, who feel obligated to please the parents because of the special and excessive love the parents are giving. Yet *this really isn't love at all*. It is pure selfishness parading as love. How could a child possibly figure this out? The children are so busy fulfilling their parents' expectations that they cannot truly develop their own reality.

Several years ago I received a letter and a poem from a man named Craig Sanchez. I'd like to share his poem with you now. It exemplifies the kind of dyadic enmeshment I am discussing here.

As you read Craig's poem, imagine how many boys have been used by their dads as extensions of their dad's disappointed inner child who never quite made it in sports. Enter this little boy's heart and experience what is happening to him. He is learning to confuse abuse with love. His dad is giving him what all kids long for—time and special attention. There is no way he can know that this show of love has nothing to do with *him*. He will surely be mystified by it and will bear his father's chains of guilt and obligation for a lifetime.

THIS SOMETHING-SETTLED MATTER IN HIS HEART

There's my dad!
He's waiting for me outside,
waiting to play where the broad sidestreet
runs quietly along our flat roofed corner house,
the house where pumpkin-orange brick
peeks from beneath the crumbling white stucco.
Fireflies are beginning to volley and salvo
across the summer evening no man's land.
There is a hush.
It is as if the night has taken a deep breath
and is holding it.

He's got a baseball in one hand.
He whacks it into his glove
over and over and over again.
It makes a clear, sharp, snapping sound
like a whip.
Suddenly he rocks back
and launches the ball straight up into
the deepening gloom.
Up, up, up it goes,
up past the lamppost
streaking up between the telephone
wires and tree branches
up higher than the three story
apartment building next door.
Will it strike a bird?

"Catch it! Catch it! Catch it!" he bellows.
I look up
craning my neck as far back as it will go.
My feet are suddenly strangers to the ground;
they swear they've never met before,
these toes, this asphalt.
I can't let my dad down.
I'll catch it.
I will.

But I can't see it.
Two years from now I will finally get
some glasses,
but tonight all I can do
is squint into the darkness.
Will it ever come down, ever, throbs
my heart?

I can see nothing,
but I can smell something.
I can smell the smooth new leather
of my bright orange baseball glove
as it slides around on my hand.
It has a life of its own.
It's a grown-up glove, a professional one,
because my dad wants me to get used to the real thing

from the beginning—
no kid gloves for me.
Oh no.
He's a swell dad to get it for me.
He even says so.
I am five years old.
I have to squeeze all four fingers
into the forefinger hole
just to keep it from falling off.
My thumb is lost somewhere in a black hole,
Tom Thumb's Cave, I suppose.

I run around in circles
hoping that somehow—
perhaps by being in perpetual motion—
I will hear the ball when it comes down
and be able to catch it at the last second.
I must never let my dad down.
Not once.
I'm his big boy.
He wants me to be a baseball player
just like he would have been
if it hadn't been for that bad break.
(Did it hurt, Dad, that bad break?)
He's going to make a sacrifice
and make sure *I* make the big leagues.
What a dad!

The ball comes down and hits me
on the head.
Is there no hole for me,
small as I am,
to crawl
into?

"You should have been born a girl.
My father never played with *me*.
Why did I waste all that money buying
you the glove?
You're such a sissy, I should have
bought you a skirt instead."

I fight back the trebly shaming tears.
Why do I have to cry *now* of all times!
I can feel the pain from the bump on
my head
all the way to my heart.

"Dad, I'm sorry.
I'm really sorry.
Give me another chance, Dad.
Please.
I won't do it again, I promise.
Please, Dad.
Please."

"Alright, alright. One more chance,"
he says,
a smile creeping across his mouth.
"But concentrate this time.
Don't fail me."

Once more the ball flies up into the
void.
Run from it, birds.
Don't get hit.
Use your white wings to be safe.

I'm so lucky to get a second chance.
What a dad!
I still can't see the ball,
but I'll catch it
somehow.
I have to.

When we grow up mystified, we spend our whole life trying to
catch a ball we cannot see.

CHAPTER 3

The Stages of Mystification

What we think is less than what we know;
What we know is less than what we love;
What we love is so much less than what there is,
and to that precise extent, we are much less than
what we are.

R. D. LAING

... most people choose an emotionally deadened,
self-limiting mode of life. They have ceased to want
what they say they want because real gratification and
accomplishments threaten the process of self-
nourishment through fantasy.

RICHARD W. FIRESTONE

A child usually does not become mystified overnight. The process
takes time and involves several stages. There are, of course, exceptions. Severe sexual and physical abuse can have an immediate and
lifelong impact.

Before I outline the various stages in the mystification process,
let me say that mystification could be prevented. There are no childhood traumas that could not be resolved and integrated. We have a
unique ability to resolve our emotional pain. It is the ability to grieve.
Grief is a kind of psychic work. It involves several stages, the most
important being the stage of deep sorrow (weeping) and the stage
of passionate anger. We will examine these stages in detail in Chapter

7, where I will present some exercises to help you separate from your internalized source figures.

As children, we needed to weep and express anger. When we are forced to repress our sadness and anger, we leave our hurts imprinted in our neurological system. We have automatic responses to safeguard us. These responses are the defenses that allowed us to survive. Unfortunately, these defenses leave us frozen in past time. The state of frozen and unresolved hurt is the state of mystification.

STAGE ONE: SHAME BINDS

Mystification begins with what has been referred to as shame binds. As I showed in *Healing the Shame That Binds You*, the whole range of our human powers can be shamed. Each kind of abuse that I've described binds one or more of our powers in shame. These shame binds are Stage One of mystification.

Our human powers include our perceptual, imaginative, intellectual (thinking), emotional (feeling), and volitional (will) powers. Our body houses all of our powers. It is the ground of our being and is our way of being in the world.

In addition to our powers we have drives (sex and hunger) and needs. Our childhood needs are dependency needs, needs that cannot be met without depending on someone.

Look at the figure on page 63. I have shown the full range of shame binds. Only in the most abusive families might we find this full range. Most of us can identify with some of these shame binds, though.

A child is born self-connected and has an organismic sense of wholeness with relation to each of its powers, drives, and needs. Once a power, drive, or need is shamed, it becomes disconnected. As the shaming continues and intensifies, the process of self-splitting and alienation takes place. We feel less and less at home with ourselves.

It is clear to me that abusive behavior is unnatural. It is not the spontaneous fruit of our human nature. The abusing person either has learned to confuse abuse with love or is getting even with his or her own abuser. Abusers are themselves mystified. They are mentally fixed without a vision of alternatives. This narrowness of abuse represents a loss of awareness about oneself and one's choices. The abuser has lost freedom. And the abuse inflicted will greatly diminish the abused's freedom. Freedom comes from within. It flows from the core of our personal power. Once our body, drives, needs, and powers are shamed, we have lost all contact with our inner resources. Our freedom of choice is thereby decommissioned.

Body

Our body is our soul's way of being in the world. This doesn't mean we are two beings, body and soul. Our whole soul is in every cell of our body. Our body is not, however, our soul. As the great medieval theologian Thomas Aquinas once said, "We are the kinds of spiritual beings that in order to be spiritual need a body."

All physical abuse, as I described it, creates body shame. When we are hit, and hit often and without warning, our body boundary is violated. We feel like we have no protection. The message we get is that any adult has the right to touch us or hit us or humiliate us.

Teasing about the size, shape, or any aspect of the child's body also creates shame binds. Children who are too tall or too short, too fat or too thin, children who are awkward, who have deformities of any kind, children who are well endowed genitally or not well endowed, children who are handsome or ugly, may be subjected to dysfunctional family shame. The continual focus on them in the form of ridicule, teasing, or even just discussion is often extremely painful and shameful.

Children who are very physically beautiful are often *used* by their parents to enhance the parents' sense of worth. I remember a woman I counseled for sexual addiction. She was very beautiful. By the age of 11, she had already developed sexually and was evidently amazingly attractive. Her mom and dad used to take her places like shopping malls and make her walk ahead of them in order to watch the men ogle her. "They used me like a piece of meat in order to enhance their own sense of value. My mother loved it when the man hitting on me told her how gorgeous her daughter was!"

From about age 3 on, children need privacy for their bodies. They need a place to be alone when they bathe and dress. They need parents with respectful boundaries. Parents also need to protect younger children from older siblings. Many of my clients were sexually, physically, or emotionally abused by older siblings. They were teased and tormented, and some were even tortured.

When our body is violated, our spirit will be violated. When our body is shamed, we experience pain at the core of our being. We are *somebody* as opposed to *nobody*. To shame our body is to shame us.

Perceptions

Children are often shamed for what they see and hear. They begin to mistrust their own sensory perceptions. Mother is crying. Her child walks in on her. "What's the matter, Mom?" the child asks. "Nothing," the mom says wiping her eyes, "go out and play." The child goes away *mystified*. The child feels scared. "I could have sworn I *saw* and *heard* her crying," the child thinks. "There must be something *wrong with me*."

Feelings

Members of dysfunctional families are mystified, and part of their mystification is loyalty to the family *don't feel, don't talk* rules. The child is told over and over again, you don't really feel what you say you feel.

I remember watching a little boy waiting in the dentist's office. He was scared silly. His dad kept saying, "Are you a cowboy?" The little boy had a play gun in a holster on his belt and was wearing cowboy boots. When his dad asked if he was a cowboy, he said, "*Yes*, sir." Then his dad said, "Well, *real* cowboys are not afraid!" The little boy looked confused and then even more afraid. While it was obvious that his father was trying to help him overcome his fear, he was invalidating his son's feelings.

The impact of invalidation is mystification. The mystified child now feels doubly afraid because he is afraid. If he could express it, he might say, "Something is wrong with me. I know I'm afraid, but my godlike parent said there was nothing to be afraid of. Maybe I'm crazy. Maybe I'm not even afraid! But I feel afraid. Something is very wrong with me."

I jokingly tell people that in my family if someone had a feeling, an *alarm* went off! Then a voice came over a loudspeaker saying, "There's a feeling in the dining room." The whole family would run to the dining room and stomp that sucker out! This was considered the right thing to do. Feelings were considered weak. "Don't be so emotional" was an oft-spoken phrase. When all the emotions are shamed, one numbs out. The numbed-out state is a setup for addiction. Once a person is numbed out, the *only* way they can feel is with their addiction.

Dependency Needs

As newborn babies we are helpless and powerless. We need to depend on our source figures. We need them to hold us, touch us, and mirror us. We need them to feed, clothe, and shelter us. We need them to watch over our nutrition and health. We need to identify with them and separate from them. Most of all, we need them to empower and affirm us. These are needs we cannot get satisfied without a nurturing other. They are developmental dependency needs.

When any, some, or all of these needs are shamed, the fundamental bond with our source figure is broken. The interpersonal bridge necessary for individuation and growth breaks down, and we feel we have no one to depend on. This is the cruelest cut of toxic shame. The belief that there is no one we have the right to depend on sets us up for either isolation or enmeshment. If we choose isolation, we build a false self that serves as a wall to keep others away from us. If we choose enmeshment, we build a false self based on what our source figures seem to want from us. Many of us go back and forth between these two false selves.

Paradoxically, dependency shame binds create a kind of bondage to our source relationships. Since we have never been allowed to separate and establish our own identity, we have no authentic self. And we continue in our quest to get our source figure's love. This kind of bind is often reenacted over the course of a lifetime.

Will

The child's life energy may also be shamed. Exuberance was scary to my source people. Their mystified inner children were terrified of life. I've often said I was raised by terrorists. Like exuberance, the child's emerging curiosity and will are also expressions of the life force.

The will, which is the driving force of the personality and the deepest energy of love, is shamed early in childhood. The willful, stubborn child was and is the prime target of patriarchy. What a king wants is willing subjects. Kings want their people to conform. So the child's willpower must be crushed at an early age. I often marvel when people are perplexed by the massive amount of addiction in our culture. Addicts are accused of lacking willpower, but my belief is that we systematically train addicts. I believe that there are genetic factors in many addictions. I welcome the new studies that prove this clinically. But in most cases genetics only points to the kind of addiction one will have if one is trained to be an addict. The training for addiction comes from abandonment, abuse, and enmeshment. Each of these is toxically shaming. Abuse and enmeshment destroy a child's will. Without willpower one is set up for addiction.

Patriarchy asks us to destroy our children's willpower at an early age. It treats their first attempts at autonomy as evidence of the innate depravity of original sin. At 2 years a child will say "no," "I won't," and "it's mine" as inevitably as night follows day. The child is being born psychologically. The child is beginning to develop a self—a sense of me that's *different* from Mom and Dad. Being different is the child's way of being psychologically born. Having one's own will is equivalent to having one's own self. Willpower is self-power.

Willpower is also the beginning of boundary building. A boundary is a limit, a definition. It protects us from others, and it is also the foundation of discipline. Until we understand our own rights, we can't understand other people's rights. Without boundaries, there are no limits. This is why the child must also develop a healthy sense of shame. Healthy shame is our first real boundary. With healthy shame we know we are limited. Healthy shame puts limits on our willpower. It tempers the natural sense of omnipotence that every child has.

Once our will is bound in toxic shame, however, we are no longer able to develop ourselves. We conform or rebel or go back and forth between rebellion and conformity. We have no way to protect ourselves. If we are shamed every time we express anger, if we can't say no or stake out what is our own, then we become doormats or rebels, without any real choice. We stop knowing what we really want. We start challenging everything (counterdependence) or take others' suggestions as orders to be obeyed (codependence).

To lose willpower is to lose our *FREEDOM*. Once we've lost our freedom, *authentic loving is impossible*. Will shame binds set us up for mystification.

Drives

Hunger is a natural drive. Children know when they are hungry and when they are not hungry. Parents do not need to make the dinner table a stall in the Marquis de Sade's dungeon. Yet I've heard stories about hunger, eating, and the dinner table that would make a Stephen King novel pale.

On one of my appearances on "Oprah Winfrey," a man in the audience told about his father making him sit at the dinner table for four hours until he ate all his dinner. The boy hated the food, squash and eggplant. He finally ate them and then vomited. His father made him eat the vomit. All this in the name of discipline and training!

Certainly children are not nutritionists and they need guidance in this area. But children do know if they like something or not. Force-feeding and shaming the hunger drive are ways to create eating disorders and destroy a child's sense of self-connection.

The *sex drive* is universally shamed, often before children are even aware of it. Children are rewarded for finding and naming their bodily parts. They are, that is, until they find their genitals—then all hell breaks loose! Imagine how mystifying it is for a child who has been rewarded and praised for finding and naming her chin, arm, hand, elbow, and so forth, to find her vagina. I can imagine her little mind saying, "If the chin, elbow, etc., got them, this will knock them out." Only to find out that the discovery of her vagina creates a furor, and that her parents take her out of the room (where she was showing it to Grandma) faster than greased lightning. Dad's face lets her know something is shameful about this part of her body. She is cast out of the Garden of Eden! Her nakedness is acceptable except for this very private part. Something is very bad about this part. The little girl has to be confused! She later finds that this part is so bad that no one will even talk to her about it. In early puberty, she will be terrified to find that she is bleeding from this mysteriously bad place. The total impact of all this will be that whenever she feels sexual or is sexual, she will feel a sense of badness and shame.

Thinking

In cultic and corrupt families, parents demand that the children's will and minds be fused with theirs. The children lose contact with their own thoughts, fantasies, and opinions. As their spontaneous thoughts and ideas are shot down, they snap into the mental fixation of the family trance. Any time children have their own ideas, they are shamed with sentences like "Where do you get such an idea? You must be running around with those Protestants (Jewish, Catholic, Buddhist, etc.) children again." Or "Don't you ever let me hear you say that again." The message is: The way you think is not okay. Once

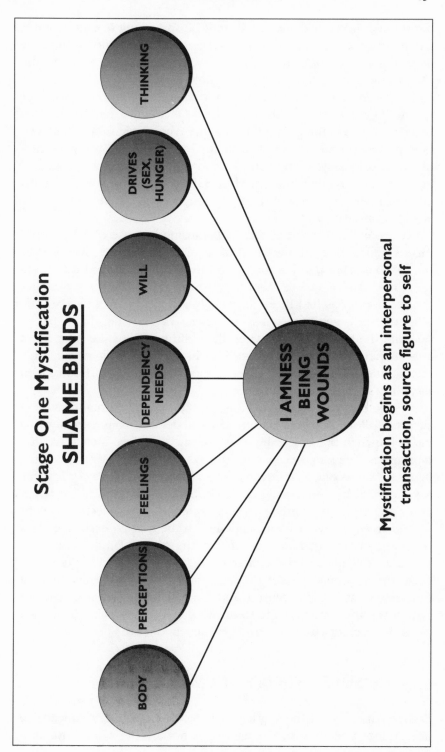

Stage One Mystification
SHAME BINDS

THINKING

DRIVES (SEX, HUNGER)

WILL

DEPENDENCY NEEDS

FEELINGS

PERCEPTIONS

BODY

I AMNESS BEING WOUNDS

Mystification begins as an interpersonal transaction, source figure to self

again the child concludes: There must be *something wrong with me.*
I don't even think correctly. I'm lovable only when I don't think my
own thoughts or have my own beliefs. A child truly comes to the
conclusion that the way he or she thinks is flawed.

A parent might say, "I know you *really* don't think badly of your
brother. I *know* you really love him." Or when a child voices an
objection to something a parent says, the parent might say, "Just who
is that talking? I know it's not really my little boy." Or, as my mother-
in-law used to say to my son, "Cranky Roy is here. John is gone."
You can't get mystification more forceful than that. She was telling my
child that when he voices a negative thought he's not even himself; he
is someone else. Wow!

Chaotic families are especially confusing because of the parents'
inconsistency. Imagine the child of an alcoholic mother who comes
home from school and is told, "Go outside and play and quit bothering me." This is before Mom has had a drink. When the girl comes
in later, Mom has had three drinks, gives her a big sloppy kiss, and
tells her she's getting a ten-speed bike. That evening, Mom passes
out, and the next morning, when the child mentions the bike, Mom
says, "Where did you get a crazy idea like that?" Children from chaotic families often spend the rest of their lives trying to find hidden
meanings and figuring things out.

Once a child's capacity to think is shut down, mental closure is
sure to follow. Mental fixation keeps a person from experiencing
the living vivid present reality they are encountering. Mental fixation
diminishes freedom, because it destroys possibility. "My way or the
highway" limits one to following the authority figure's way or leaving.
A young child views leaving as death. So the highway choice is not
really a choice. The binding of thinking with shame effectively keeps
a child from knowing what happened to them at an early age. This
is why everyone coming out of a dysfunctional family needs debriefing. They need to make their abuse real. They need to demythologize their parents. Fritz Perls often said, "Nothing changes until it
becomes what it is." Because of our narrow-minded trance state we
cannot see the forest for the trees. We cannot know what happened
to us. We cannot know the *truth* of our childhood.

STAGE TWO: DEEP TRANCE PHENOMENA

Earlier I mentioned the work of Dr. Stephen Wolinsky concerning
deep trance phenomena. Wolinsky does not use the word "mystifica-

tion," and I take full responsibility for my interpretation of his work. I refer the reader to his book *Trances People Live.* It is a pioneering and highly creative piece of work. I am indebted to Wolinsky for the discussion in this section.

Deep trance phenomena are a different way of understanding what Freud called ego defenses. We humans have the ability to defend against experiences that are too painful for us to handle. These defenses are usually formed in early childhood, when we are more powerless than later in life. We are especially powerless in the face of shame binds. It's important to underscore the feeling of *exposure* that is at the heart of a shaming experience. Shame binds always occur with someone who is important to us and more powerful. Childhood is obviously the time when there is the greatest possibility for being shamed. Shame is experienced when the child's expectations suddenly ruptured. During this rupture children feel exposed, and they feel that they have no power over their experience. It is the feelings of powerlessness and exposure that give the shaming experience its binding effect. The internal response to a shaming experience is to feel frozen or cornered. You have nowhere to run and no place to hide. You want to dig a hole and drop into it. You need relief and want it immediately.

Stage Two of mystification occurs precisely because the deep trances are *immediate* ways out of the pain. During the traumatic or painful shaming experience, the child uses the natural power of self-hypnosis as a way of coping with the overwhelming threat to his or her reality. Wolinsky writes: "All deep trance phenomena are created by a series of interpersonal interactions (parent to child) that are eventually internalized as intrapersonal communications (self to self)."

Deep trance phenomena may be created to guard against any threatening element in a child's environment. Disasters such as fire, the death of a parent, a terrible automobile accident, or a serious childhood sickness may trigger the creation of immediate and natural defensive trances. With appropriate help, these could be resolved *without* resulting in defensive deep trance phenomena. Appropriate help would consist of debriefing (talking about what happened and fully expressing the feelings). This is precisely what shame-based families prohibit the child from doing. So the trance defenses stay frozen.

The type of trance or combination of trance defenses will depend on the person's particular experience plus other factors having to do with expediency, practicality, and survival. Over a period of time a certain defensive trance may prove to be quite effective. Once it has been chosen and repeatedly used, it begins to function automatically. "One's conscious intentionality," writes Wolinsky, "is no longer necessary to initiate the trance defense." Once the person has adopted a set of effective deep trance defenses, they become the basic structure of the person's state of mystification.

The Nature of Trance

Before proceeding any further, I'd like to discuss the phenomenon of trance in general.

Perhaps the greatest authority on trance was a psychiatrist named Milton Erickson. All modern theoreticians, including Wolinsky, are indebted to him. Erickson pointed out that trance is a naturally occurring phenomenon. Trances don't just occur as defenses against threat. We go in and out of trance every day, sometimes many times. We daydream, get lost in thought, become so absorbed in something that we lose track of time. We may experience ourselves getting hungry and then be so distracted by a minor crisis that we numb out our hunger and become absorbed in figuring out how to respond to the crisis.

These natural trances are often characterized by an altered state of consciousness, by time distortion (an hour can seem like five minutes and vice versa), and by dissociation from bodily functions.

The difference between these natural trances and hypnotic trance is in the degree of conscious choice. If you come out of a daydream, you know you induced it yourself. But if you come out of a hypnotic state, you feel that it *happened to you.*

I have italicized "happened to you" because this is a crucial point. In Part 2 we will discuss ways to create soulful loving relationships. Part of the work will be demystifying the mystified love trance many of us are in. If we can grasp that we created the trance in the first place and discover how we keep creating it now, we can stop producing it and start creating the love we want.

Hypnotic Trance

According to Erickson, hypnotic trance has three core characteristics:

> (1) It is characterized by a narrowing and shrinking or
> fixing of attention. (2) It is most often experienced as hap-

pening to a person and (3) It is characterized by the emergence of various hypnotic phenomena.

To understand how it works, it is useful to look at the process of trance induction between a hypnotist and a subject. The hypnotic induction is characterized by a deepening feeling in the subject that he or she is being controlled by the hypnotist. This is not *really* the case. No one could put you in a trance unless you cooperated with them.

Yet hypnotic induction works because subjects come to believe that the hypnotist's *suggestions* are actually making things happen to them beyond their control. A good hypnotist may be using one of several methods to give subjects this feeling that they are being controlled.

ALREADY EXISTING TRANCE

The hypnotist may trigger an already existing trance state. For example, certain words may elicit some past experience associated with those words. If I, as hypnotist, know that you had a lot of trouble with your authoritarian father, I can talk about a cruel authority figure, giving sensory details, and my talk will take you back to your experiences with your father. In that way I can induce in you an age regressive state. If you have lots of unresolved traumatic experiences, they remain frozen in you and can be elicited by someone talking about experiences that are similar to your original ones.

I'm not a hypnotherapist, but, if I wanted to induce a childhood trance state, I might say the following: "As you sit relaxing in your chair, you might let your mind wander back to the many relaxing times you had in childhood. You might remember playing in the sand or sliding down a sliding board or swinging on a swing, or maybe a time you got in trouble for teasing your brother or laughing in church, or maybe even the frightening experience of waiting for your dad to come home when you knew you were going to be spanked. . . ." This is a menulike sequence aimed at letting you find whatever memory is appropriate to take you into a deep trance.

The hypnotherapist may only need to notice how the client *puts himself or herself* into the preexisting trance. Milton Erickson was fond of telling his trainees that their client was *giving* them all the data they needed. What he meant was the client was re-creating the trance they were in *as they described their problem*. The hypnotist who observes how the subject creates this self-induced trance can utilize the same process to induce the same trance later on.

CLASSIC TRANCE INDUCTION

The most familiar hypnotic trance induction involves a subject gazing at an object (a swinging pendulum or a spot on the wall). *Gazing* or *eye fixation* is an important element of classic trance induction. The reason eye fixation is used to induce trance is that, since the eye muscles are very weak, a "blinking" response necessarily occurs as the subject gazes at the object. For example, a hypnotist might say, "Gaze at the object I'm holding in my hand." When she sees the subject's eyes blink, she continues by saying, "You may feel your eyes blink." This is called *mirroring*. Whatever she sees or knows is about to come, she states as a verbal suggestion. The gazing will get tiresome very quickly. So the hypnotist usually says, "Your eyes may begin to feel heavy, you may feel an urge to close your eyes ... just let them close and you will enjoy the warm feeling of rest that comes over you as you relax."

The hypnotist may *pace* the subject by lowering the tone of speech and slowing down the words. The subject is not really giving any sensory evidence that he is enjoying a warm feeling of rest and relaxation. The hypnotist is now *leading* him to feel these states by suggesting them. The hypnotist may then say, "Now with your eyes closed, roll your eyes to the back of your head and feel them lock into place, so that the harder you try to open your eyes the tighter they close." Once again, the hypnotist knows that when you roll your eyes to the back of your head, they in fact lock and can't be opened. The subject is locking them by rolling them to the back of his head. But in the flow of the mirroring and pacing, it begins to feel like the hypnotist is doing it. After a while, the subject truly believes that the hypnotist is actually making the behaviors happen.

A hypnotic subject has to *trust* the hypnotist. The interpersonal bridge between the hypnotist and subject is crucial. The relationship of trust creates a context in which the subject believes the hypnotist. With trust established, the mirroring, pacing, and suggesting process completes the trance.

Mystified people have, in effect, been hypnotized as children. They are, therefore, quite gullible and susceptible to being hypnotized as adults. Stage hypnotists, who are total strangers, depend on this trust, naiveté, and gullibility.

Children As Hypnotic Subjects

If we look at the circumstances of childhood, it is clear that children are perfect hypnotic subjects. They are deeply trusting. Children bond with their parents and. have a *survival need* to believe that their caretakers are okay. Children are egocentric, which means they personalize everything. If a survival figure yells at them, it is about them, not about their survival figure's headache. The words that children hear impact them greatly. The words they hear continue to play in their heads and become voices that are self-nurturing or voices that blame, criticize, compare, and express contempt. Children internalize their parents at their worst. When parents are screaming, raging, hitting, or sexually violating a child, the child's security is most threatened. That is why the traumatic scenes are imprinted so much more powerfully than other scenes. We remember most vividly what has threatened our lives.

The hypnotic state is a state in which one is extremely susceptible to suggestion. Milton Erickson used the trance state to install positive voices which utilized his subjects' inner resources. He also made positive suggestions about the future which he told his subjects to forget when they awakened from the trance. He gave this instruction because he wanted the positive messages to operate directly on his subjects' unconscious mind. The future suggestions are called "posthypnotic suggestions."

Traumatic parental voices are like negative posthypnotic suggestions that play on inside our heads. We frequently think that these voices are our own thinking dialogues. They are not. They are auditory imprints, the internalized voices of our source figures. Those figures were the source of our original trances. Without resolution the voices continue to play in our adult life. Each time we hear them, the original trance is induced and maintains our mystified state of being.

DEEP TRANCE PHENOMENA

Deep trance phenomena are distinguished from ordinary trance by virtue of their depth or intensity. Deep trance phenomena occur either from threatening and traumatic events or from hypnotic induction. In the case of hypnotic induction, it usually takes many, many hours to achieve such states.

There are exceptions. Some people are more highly susceptible

Stage Two Mystification
<u>DEEP TRANCE PHENOMENA</u>

- **Posthypnotic suggestion**
- **Age regression/ Age progression**
- **Amnesia/ Hypermnesia**
- **Positive hallucinations/ Negative hallucinations**
- **Sensory distortion**
- **Dissociation**
- **Time distortion**

than others and can arrive at deep trance states rather quickly. In the case of catastrophic experiences, the trance can be induced immediately because the person is so intensely afraid.

Let me give a brief description and some examples of several deep trance phenomena.

Posthypnotic Suggestion

I have just described how our source figures' voices are internalized in the form of auditory imprints, which are activated by any experience similar to any part of our earlier experience.

As a child I used to be chided any time I acted proud of myself or my accomplishments. "Don't get a big head," someone might say. Or I might be told, "Watch out. Pride comes before a fall." I was taught that true humility consists of *never* talking about yourself, never thinking about your own strengths, and never expressing enjoyment in your own talents.

Now, as an adult, whenever I'm in touch with my own achievements or I'm feeling good about my accomplishments, I hear these voices. Two of my books have been on *The New York Times* bestseller list—*Healing the Shame That Binds You* for six weeks and *Homecoming: Reclaiming and Championing Your Inner Child* for fifty-two weeks, twenty-three of them as number one. (A voice just told me that I'm blowing my own horn and that I shouldn't name these books.) When the books hit the bestseller list, I was bombarded with voices that told me to be humble. One told me I was just lucky. Another told me that this couldn't last.

I have worked hard to recognize these voices as foreign to my true self. I try to think of them as one might think of being possessed. I answer them and replace them with new voices, which nurture me and allow me to have confidence and to enjoy my success.

Age Regression

Most people experience age regression quite frequently. A memo from the boss asking you to come to his office might trigger an earlier scene of having to go to the principal's office or to your father's room to be punished. You probably won't even be conscious that the earlier scene has been evoked, but you feel a sense of that earlier panic. The spouse who acts helpless may be age regressing to a scene where Mom always fixed things if you acted helpless. Erickson defined age regression as "the tendency on the part of the personality to revert to some method or form of expression belonging to an earlier phase of personality development." Adult children age regress frequently and seemingly automatically. An adult behaving like a child is age regressing.

It is the time-frozen quality of age regression that accounts for the fact that mystified behavior is repetitious. The compulsion to repeat can be explained by the activation of an experience in a previous time. An adult can in any present problematic situation regress to a way of thinking and behaving that he or she used at an earlier age and stage of development. As a child, I learned to pout and withdraw in order to get attention. As an adult, I have found myself using that exact behavior, in grown-up relationships and even with my children. When I pout and withdraw, I am age regressing.

Age regression undermines and impedes adult functioning. Chronic age regressions mark the places where a person's developmental process has been frozen. I think pictures make this easier to grasp. On the next page you will see my representation of two adults with a mystified wounded child.

One adult is asking another what she is angry about. The person asking the question is initiating an adult transaction. But the other adult's inner child is answering "Nothing." Frequently the person speaking from the inner child will actually *look* like a child.

Any relationship can be confusing when the adult and the age-

regressed child are operating simultaneously. Many relationships that are seemingly chosen by adults are actually chosen by their age-regressed children.

The stage is set for age regression when a child is unable to make sense of or resolve the interaction with his source figures. Wolinsky writes: "In order *not* to integrate an experience—in essence to *resist* it—the child freezes his body by tightening his muscles and holding his breath. This physiological pattern may then become the somatic basis for an automatic response—an *intra*personal self to self trance that endures for decades to come."

In my own life the most damaging effect of age regression is in relation to shamed and repressed anger. I was taught that anger was one of the seven deadly sins. Anger was a mortal sin, a sin that sends you to hell. I learned early on to hold my breath, tighten my chin, and tense my muscles when I felt anger. I cannot remember the earliest scenes of repressed anger, but I know that over time I became terrified of anger, literally scared stiff.

Carl Jung once said that any part of ourselves that we do not love unconditionally splits off and becomes more primitive. As the

years went by, my repressed anger grew in intensity. In my adult
life my age-regressed anger came out in reactions that were out of
proportion to what was triggering them. My anger often came out as
a primitive rage, a child's tantrum in a man's voice and body. Age
regression of this kind is devastating to relationships.

Age Progression

The purpose of age progression is to project oneself into a future
where things are safer and more pleasant. We often use age progression to distract from threatening interactions in the present. By creating a future picture very different from the depressing events of my
childhood, I was able to make it through many a day.

Of course age progression can be used in a positive way. The
ability to create a future time is an important part of human creativity.
Our imagination can show us the way to a better life. I can point to
many things I've done that were based on childhood visions.

The danger of age progression is in what I will call the fantastic
imagination. The fantastic imagination creates flights of fantasy in
which we distort reality. I had a friend who continually talked about
being a millionaire. He claimed it was only a matter of time before
he made it. Yet he did nothing in his life to make his fantasy a
reality. He passed over opportunities that would have allowed him to
advance his financial position. My friend had grown up with an alcoholic father. This father was a cold and punishing man, who had
greatly curtailed his son's activities. Faced with the depressing limits
his father imposed, my friend learned early on to age progress. Over
time he developed a habitual fantasy life. His self-to-self trance became a secret psychic place which functioned automatically. As with
all habituated trance defenses, this trance could be initiated without
conscious intentionality. My friend constantly used age progression
as a way to avoid reality. Instead of learning to use his conscious
energy to create a realistic future, he was stuck in the psychic space
that protected him in childhood.

I spent many of my active alcoholic years sitting in dark stinking
taverns listening to "losers" expound on great things that were going
to happen to them in the future. I can think of three men, all of
whom died before they were 45. Victims of childhood violations, they
had learned to be dreamers at an early age. They never outgrew the
fantasyland of their childhood. Like all trance defenses, age progression helps one *survive* childhood but, if left unchanged, can be the

cause of our failures in adult life. This is the paradox of early child-hood defenses—they save the person's life in childhood but cause severe problems in adulthood.

Amnesia

Milton Erickson suggests that amnesia is a natural consequence of the altered state of consciousness that constitutes hypnotic trance.

Amnesia, or forgetting, is one of the most common human expe-riences. As Stephen Wolinsky points out, we forget the time of our doctor's appointment. We forget about the business party we dread. We forget our father-in-law's birthday. It is only when we experience forgetting as a chronic part of our lives that it is problematic. And when forgetting is problematic, it is actually a trance state.

All children from dysfunctional families have learned to use the trance phenomenon of amnesia. As Wolinsky points out, a more com-mon term for amnesia is "denial." Denial is the major element in family dysfunction. Denial is the culprit that keeps the family mem-bers from dealing with their emotions and their problems. Families unconsciously agree to forget what they have seen and heard. Dad has been drunk every Christmas for twenty years. Somehow everyone *hopes* that this year will be different. This hope is part of the fantastic imagination. There is no basis in reality for this hope.

Chronic amnesiac states are intense methods to maintain the family's or the individual's balance. If a child can forget the icky things that Dad is doing to her, then the family balance can be main-tained. If the child remembers and talks about it, it will cause pain both to the child and to the family.

Denial in the form of amnesia is so common in dysfunctional families because of the family system *law* of balance. The system pressures the individuals into conformity. The more incomplete and empty each member, the more the family bands together, forming what family systems pioneer Murray Bowen called the "undifferenti-ated ego mass." Victims of sexual and physical violation feel powerful pressures to keep the secret and to forget what happened to them.

During severe abuse the self is so violated that it disappears and the victim is fused with the offender. The image of the offender is imprinted on the victim's neurological system. Amnesia is a natural consequence of losing oneself in the act of abuse.

The trauma will be remembered only when a person reenters the altered state of consciousness that first accompanied it. A person who has survived a serious accident usually has difficulty recalling the events that led up to it, because they have reentered their normal state of consciousness. If an event similar to the original accident is experienced, say in a movie, the person may reenter the traumatic state. The same holds true for incest survivors or posttraumatic stress disorder victims. A scene or other strong sense impression similar to the original can trigger the trauma.

Hypermnesia

Hypermnesia means having an abnormally sharp memory. This seems to be just the opposite of amnesia, which means having a total or partial loss of memory. But, as Wolinsky points out, the two types of trances are very similar in that they alter the normal functioning of memory. The child usually develops one or the other depending on which is more protective. But they can also overlap.

Hypermnesia is created out of the fear of not being vigilant. Typically it arises in dysfunctional families where there is inconsistency. Most often the inconsistency has to do with punishment— either raging verbal reprimands or physical abuse. But any behavioral inconsistency can trigger this trance state.

In Chapter 1, I told the story of Larmark, who saw his mother and two older brothers beaten by his alcoholic father. By watching every movement his father made, Larmark became aware of the signals that preceded his father's outbreaks of violence. There was a certain tone of voice, certain disdainful smiles and lip movements. When Larmark saw these patterns emerge, he either became very quiet and polite, or he went to his room and feigned sleep. He was never beaten. In adulthood, however, this kind of detailed vigilance caused Larmark great problems in his relationships.

Hypermnesia is an important trance defense for people who have been violated. I know many survivors of childhood violation who can tell that a stranger is a potential offender because of their abnormally sharp attention to details, especially nonverbal details.

The down side to hypermnesia is the distrustful attitude that underlies it. This trance allows people to see the thorns but not the roses, the hole but not the doughnut. Always on guard, the person is not free to consider the full range of alternatives available.

Paradoxically, hypermnesiacs miss out on a lot of the good information around them. The tunnel vision of hypermnesia seriously limits their range of perception. It sets one up for a paranoid view of the world. As in the examples here, hypermnesia often manifests itself in intimacy dysfunction and an overly critical temperament. It

may also underlie an obsessive-compulsive disorder and other disorders that involve living in watchful and fearful tension.

Positive Hallucinations

Positive hallucinations involve seeing, hearing, or feeling something
that is *not there*. At their most bizarre, these hallucinations are called
"psychotic." But there are many other sorts of positive hallucinations.
Anyone who had an imaginary playmate as a child engaged in positive
hallucinations. In the most benign case anyone who fantasizes being
in a relationship with another person or fantasizes themselves as
proficient at golf or skiing is hallucinating positively.

As a boy, I saw myself as the hero of football games and the
winner of golf tournaments. Fantasizing is a normal part of a healthy
imaginative process as long as we can will ourselves to create the
fantasy and to *stop* creating it. The moment our fantasy life begins to
function on its own, it becomes problematic.

When positive hallucinating is automatic and chronic, it is a
trance phenomenon created in childhood to survive violation. The
more severe the violation, the more powerful the positive hallucinations are likely to be.

Maxmillian had a verbally abusive mother and father. No matter
what he did, it never seemed quite right to them. "You can always
do better," his father would say. The family system was cultic in the
sense I've described. As an adult when Maxmillian goes into a group
setting, he always imagines that the people either don't like him or
are talking about him. Maxmillian hallucinates critical looks on their
faces and knows they are judging him critically.

Jealousy is another common form of positive hallucination. Jack
accused Jill of having an affair long before she actually did. When
Jack was a boy, he was left alone for long periods of time. To alleviate
his feelings of isolation, Jack created an imaginary friend. He learned
to hallucinate positively as a way to survive. Whenever Jill was talking
to another man, Jack would see things that were *not there*. I remember him saying, "I could see you were turned on by that guy; you
were smiling and breathing heavily." Jill had not even been smiling.

It is common in couple's therapy to talk about someone putting
their parent's or ex-partner's face on their new partner. We frequently
see in our new partner's face or hear in their voice negative similarities to our source figures. Any therapist doing counseling with couples has been jolted by partners' overreactive responses. Such

responses often involve positive hallucinations—pictures or voices of the past that are superimposed on the present.

Negative Hallucinations

A negative hallucination, like a positive hallucination, is a trance phenomenon that alters our perception. The word "negative" is not a value judgment. It just means that we do *not* see, hear, or feel what is there.

We have everyday experiences of negative hallucinations. I'm writing at my desk and I can't see the ruler that I've been using. We've all had the experience of looking for something that is right in front of our eyes. I'm watching a Notre Dame football game and I don't hear my son giving me the message to call my friend Johnny. During the game I completely lost touch with the ache in my shoulders that I got from working so intensely all week.

More problematically, we might completely miss the look of sadness on our partner's face. We might not hear a request that is made directly to us. We might not feel the anger in our chest.

I saw this over and over in counseling. The wife who refuses to see that her husband is an alcoholic. Or the husband who refuses to see that his wife is having an affair with his business partner when everyone else knows about it. Or the wife whose husband tells her several times during therapy sessions that he needs her to support his work. Six months later the issue comes up and she swears he never asked for support.

The trance state of negative hallucinations beings in early childhood. Many things may be too painful to see or hear or feel. A child develops the habit of not seeing, hearing, or feeling. Later the child becomes an adult child and reenacts this habit in one interpersonal relationship after another.

Negative hallucinations play a role in almost all other deep trance phenomena. For example, in age regression the person must not see the actual interpersonal context they are in. They must stop being present in the now to become present in the then. Age progression requires a similar negative hallucination. In order to see the future, the person must no longer see the present.

Many of my clients used both positive and negative hallucinations with me. This often happened when they described behavior they thought was shameful. I was most often completely neutral during these descriptions. I might say something like "That's fairly typical for a person who was abused like you were as a child." Yet my client would tell me, "I know you think I'm awful" or "I can see that you think I'm stupid for doing that." In essence, they were seeing and hearing things I wasn't saying and were not seeing and hearing what I was saying.

People who are well entrenched in the victim role make extensive use of both positive and negative hallucinations. In Chapter 1, I described Minerva, the Lost Child, who took up the victim role early in life. As an adult, she felt abused by one boss after another. When she got deeply into her therapy, however, Minerva recalled that one of those bosses had actually offered to send her to college with his own money. Another, she admitted, was a pretty good sort. Yet even in therapy, she continued to see and hear put-downs and contemptuousness that were not really there.

Frequently, sexual abuse victims create trances during the abuse, where they stop seeing and hearing what is happening. Later they become sexually dysfunctional. They no longer see or hear their *actual* partner; instead, they see and hear the person who abused them. They use both negative and positive hallucinations.

Sensory Distortion

Sensory distortion is a trance state in which the person's sensory experience is either numbed out or exaggerated. The sensory response is altered so the child can survive. The child no longer feels the pure sensory experience. Instead, the child either feels nothing or becomes hypersensitive, magnifying all stimuli.

Physical abuse is often counteracted with the trance of sensory numbing. Children who are spanked a lot or battered learn responses, like tensing their muscles and shallow breathing that allow them to stop feeling their feelings. They come to a place where they distract themselves from the physical pain and learn to numb out completely. The actual pain and physical assault are physiologically altered through the trance. Once this becomes habitual, the child can spontaneously numb out in the presence of danger.

Many times eating disorders are the result of numbing used to counteract physical or sexual abuse. The person loses contact with their bodily sensations. They literally no longer know whether they are physically hungry or not.

In hypersensory distortion, sensory stimuli are magnified. For example, some people become overly stimulated by the presence of others. I remember as a child feeling fear whenever my mother told

me that C.W. was coming over to our house. C.W. was so overstimu-
lated by the visit, he often ran up and bit me! Yes! I'm not kidding—
the kid was supercharged! C.W.'s energy was so activated, it was over-
powering to him and to those around him. This type of sensory
distortion often results from overly possessive, overly stimulating parents. They so violate their children's boundaries that the children
explode in an effort to protect themselves.

Overly intensified feeling is actually a way of avoiding feeling.
Premature ejaculation is an example. A person whose sex drive has
been shame bound may respond with premature ejaculation—they
get the dirty deed over with quickly. The quick explosion means the
person cannot experience the sensation for long.

Some people who are in emotional shame binds express their
feelings quite energetically. They have emotional outbursts. Once
again the overly intense expression of their emotions is a way not
to really feel them. The emotional blast gets the feelings over with
quickly.

Dissociation

Most incest victims use dissociation to survive as children. A sexually
victimized child learns to cope with the threatening person by "spac-
ing out," "going somewhere else," or "floating out of their body."
Wolinsky distinguishes three types of dissociation:

• Dissociation from an internal feeling or sensation

• Dissociation from a part of the body (genitalia, limbs, voice,
  muscles)

• Dissociation from the external stimuli

All of us know how to space out. We do it almost every day. We
can distract ourselves and move away from distasteful things or from
situations that threaten us.

The trance state of dissociation, in contrast, functions automatically. The range of this trance state is enormous, moving from dissociation from a feeling to the ability to have several distinct personalities
living within one's body. In the case of multiple personalities, the
dissociations can be so complete that the person's physical body actually undergoes measurable changes as the distinct personalities come
and go. For example, allergies, shoe size, and eye color may be
different in each personality.

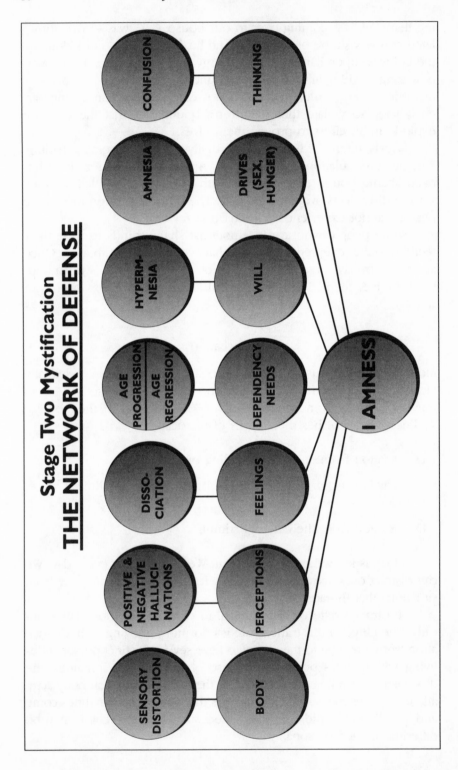

Stage Two Mystification
THE NETWORK OF DEFENSE

Some children who are physically beaten learn to dissociate from their bodies and stop experiencing the feelings of pain and sadness. In this case dissociation is the ultimate form of sensory numbing.

Dissociation allows the child to stop feeling the distress, fear, hurt, and anger that are present in the family. I learned to dissociate from my feelings by the time I was 9 years old. As a teenager I used alcohol and drugs both as a way to feel exuberance and to cover up fear and sadness. I was so numb that the only way I could feel was with the chemicals.

As I mentioned, dissociation by "leaving" the external environment is commonplace in our lives. Children stop hearing their nagging parents. Students sitting in class fantasize being somewhere else. These are normal uses of dissociation. But some children leave their environment to enter into a kind of waking sleep. They dissociate their entire psychological and emotional presence from their family life. I have had the distressing experience of working with adult children who are dissociated from their own voices. They say the family-authorized words. But the words are not their own words. They form a rote, parrotlike vocabulary. These adults sound like ventriloquists' dummies.

Time Distortion

Through time distortion, we experience time as passing more slowly or more quickly. If we listen to a boring lecture, it seems like time has slowed to a crawl. If the lecture is interesting, time seems to fly by. Time also seems to be greatly affected by our resistance to whatever we are experiencing. Obsessing on "how much longer is he going to talk" actually makes the time go slower.

A terrified child who is trying to shut out her mother's crying during a marital fight will automatically begin to shallow breathe and tense her muscles. This automatic response actually enhances the duration of the time. Wolinsky suggests that the "body in its tightened, held state actually slows down the individual's subjective experience of time, holding the breath creates a 'frozen' experience that 'holds' the feelings and impedes the outward flow of emotions." The family feud that takes twenty minutes may seem to last four hours.

In dysfunctional families, distressful events do occupy a lot of time and feel like they occupy even more. But even in families that are relatively functional a traumatic event can create time distortion. Many people's lives are ruled by a few painful events. I've seen couples who had years of good times allow one affair or other painful event to destroy their relationship.

The Network of Defense

In the figure on page 80, I have paired trance phenomena with the shame binds they help the child defend against. I have shown positive and negative hallucinations as the trance phenomena used to deal with perceptual shame binds, sensory distortion as the phenomenon used to cover up body shame binds, and so on.

Confusion, which I've put opposite the thinking shame binds, is a trance state I will describe in more detail below. Confusion ultimately becomes a generalized state that results from all shame binding, not just thinking shame binds.

In fact, the pairings in the figure are interchangeable; *any trance phenomenon could be paired with any shame bind*. For example, a person could use dissociation, rather than sensory distortion, to handle body shame binds. Each individual's unconscious choices create a distinctive pattern and combination of defenses. The figure is simply intended to show how Stage One (shame binds) and Stage Two (trance phenomena) of the process of mystification are related.

In childhood, all of these deep phenomena coalesced to form a network of defense. While the network provided protection and lessened our distress and pain, it also became the foundation of our mystification. We were no longer ourselves. We were no longer living as ourselves. Our bodies were numbed out or overly sensitive. So, too, were our thoughts, feelings, and desires. We were out of touch with our basic needs. While defending us from the shame binds, the trance phenomena kept us from resolving them, they froze us in the moment of time. We were not redeemed from injustice and the interpersonal betrayal that had caused the shame binds. Our inability to grieve, to express sadness and anger, left the original shaming scenes imprinted on our neurological systems. These imprinted scenes formed the basis for the third stage of mystification.

STAGE THREE: GOVERNING SCENES

The more severe and shaming the original scene, the more powerfully it is imprinted. Gershan Kaufman, the psychologist who pioneered the study of shame, writes:

Stage Three Mystification
<u>GOVERNING SCENES</u>

**Neurological imprints of original
shaming scenes fuse with fragments of
subsequent scenes with similar affect.**

Affect [feeling] imprints scenes, and the presence of the identical affect in two different scenes increases the likelihood of the scenes being interconnected, directly fused together. This process of psychological magnification results in the emergence of families of scenes.

Throughout our childhood, shame binding scenes coalesce and gradually emerge as whole families of scenes. They become *governing scenes*. These governing scenes form higher-order clusters of shame. Kaufman distinguishes body shame, competence shame, and relationship shame. My experience of toxic shame is that all the early experiences of shaming ultimately come together and form reservoirs of shame so deep that *all of me* feels shame. Shame has no boundaries; it pervades my whole being.

Originally, the shame binding scenes are retained in their entirety, as separate scenes. Then bits and pieces of new scenes are added until there is a collage of images that are all interconnected. These collages are the governing scenes that maintain the toxic shame.

Each collage is like a *black hole* in space, filled with powerful energy, drawing any innuendo of shame to itself. Once any piece of a governing scene is activated, the whole collage can become activated. This is called a "shame spiral" and anyone who has experienced one knows exactly how it feels. It's sort of like a string of firecrackers going off. One firecracker ignites the next, which ignites the next, and so on. One shame thought fires an image, which triggers another image, and so on, each image magnifying and intensifying the sense of shame. When you are in such a spiral, you feel overwhelmed and powerless. You feel like you have no choice. *In fact you do have a choice.* We will discuss this point later.

Consider the shame spiral of a person who was teased and ridiculed about their body as a child. They will have powerful images— both visual (faces) and auditory (voices)—of shame. Whenever they encounter someone who looks or sounds like their original shaming source, the person's deep shame scenes about their body will be activated. These scenes may be activated automatically by any external stimulus that somehow resembles the original experience of having their body shamed. The scenes can even be triggered without any external stimuli. A thought, a piece of self-talk, or a memory can activate a shame spiral. Comparing your body to someone else's can also be the trigger.

Since the image of the person who first shamed us is also recorded in the neurological memory, an offender response to the shame spiral is also always a possibility. People often shame others the way they have been shamed. This helps to explain how a person who was humiliated or beaten as a child can humiliate or beat their own children.

As the following examples show, the shame binding scenes and triggers can involve the body, the perceptions, feelings, or any other of our powers.

Wolinsky tells the story of a woman who used to stare at the gray in her father's hair when he sexually fondled her. She found the early experience pleasurable, even though she felt dirty when she thought of it. She later repressed it completely. However, as an adult, one of her favorite masturbation fantasies was to imagine being gently but forcibly taken by an older man with gray hair. She also frequently dissociated when she looked at gray hair.

Even though Joe loves to eat, he feels queasy and ashamed when he smells the turkey at Thanskgiving. His overeating problem began when he was 4 years old. He was frequently punished for bad manners at the dinner table. Joe is one hundred pounds overweight. During several age regression sessions, Joe remembered being knocked out of his chair at the dinner table. He had been eating too fast for his angry, drunken father. While he was on the floor, his father stuffed turkey and dressing into his mouth!

Sibley likes to eat quickly and on the run. He eats standing up; he eats as he drives. As a child, Sibley was forced to sit at the table for long hours until he cleaned his plate. To sit down at a table brings back the feelings of isolation and shame he once felt as a child.

The feeling shame binds are maintained in our bodies. *Whenever we feel the shamed feelings, we feel shame.* Shame has been called the master emotion. This is the reason.

Often when Bill feels fear, he sees an image of his father looking disgusted. Often he hears his father's voice saying, "You big sissy. You should have been a girl." Instead of feeling the fear, he feels shame. Bill began drinking as a way to cover up his fears. Drinking worked well, although as time went by, it took more and more booze to kill the fear. Finally, in a treatment center for alcoholism, Bill learned that fear was a normal human emotion. He learned to express his fear and came to realize that this vulnerability brought him closer to others.

The interpersonal shaming of dependency needs creates governing scenes that can be triggered by all sorts of interpersonal interactions. I'll use myself as an example.

In my patriarchal upbringing children did not say no to any adult. It was okay for adults to say no to a child, simply because they were adults. As an adult, saying no was very difficult for me.

When I said no, I had memories of a collage of faces looking at me with disdain and disapproval. My voice would tremble and I'd feel distress. Or I'd have to get angry first in order to say no.

I also felt frightened when I began to risk expressing legitimate anger. All my life I had been manipulated by other people's anger. I would do anything to stop someone from being angry at me. And I could not express anger unless I had collected so many injustices and hurts that no one could possibly object to my anger.

One day my therapist had me close my eyes and imagine myself dealing with my wife's anger. Suddenly I found a memory of a scene with my mother. She was leaving me. She said nothing, but she was rejecting me. I was about 3 years old. To a 3-year-old, rejection is death. I realized that my phobic fear of anger was rooted in this and other scenes with my mother.

The shaming of our relationship dependency needs is a mortal blow to our ability to establish a balanced dependency in later life. The shame scenes with our significant others stay riveted in our psyche. Later, as we go through the stages of a new relationship, these old scenes play like broken records.

These frozen governing scenes contaminate our relational life. The scenes are frozen because they are unresolved. Their nonresolution is due to the defenses we erected in order to avoid feeling the pain that the shaming inflicted. The defensive strategies, too, still remain. They are the various ways we got out of the living vivid present moment. When we were children, they were our salvation. When we are adults, they keep us frozen in the past.

STAGE FOUR: GENERALIZED CONFUSION

Once we are shame bound with our defenses in place and the shame is maintained by governing scenes, we arrive at a generalized state of disorientation and confusion. "Confusion," as I am using the word, is a deep trance phenomenon. It can be a defensive trance all by itself or it can be the "hub of the trance wheel," as Wolinsky says. A child will often go into a state of disorientation and confusion when faced with a threat. Confusion functions in that case as a defensive trance. As the "hub of the trance wheel," confusion accompanies all deep trance phenomena. In other words, every deep trance defensive strategy involves some disorientation and confusion.

As we get more and more entranced, we get more and more confused. Confused about what? We get more and more confused about who we really are and what is really going on around us. In the beginning of our lives we know nothing. We are totally dependent on our survival figures to teach us and guide us. As children we needed lots of security in order to learn about ourselves and our world. We needed a safe, trustworthy environment. A child's basic role is to be curious, to explore and learn. That's a very tough job when one lives in a state of constant worry and threat. When a child's environment is dangerous, they must be constantly on guard. They cannot explore and learn who they are. They can only hope to defend themselves and survive.

In dysfunctional families, children live in a chronic state of defense and confusion. This confusion forces them to find a false self that satisfies several basic needs: the need for structure, the need to belong, and the need for strokes. Strokes are any form of affirmation that tells us we are valuable. As humans, we must get these needs met. They are basic. We cannot live without them. Whatever false self identity a person chooses, the purpose of that identity will be to get those needs met.

The figure on the next page shows the kind of identity choices that result from confusion. There are two types of confusion.

Type I results from having all our powers and needs bound in

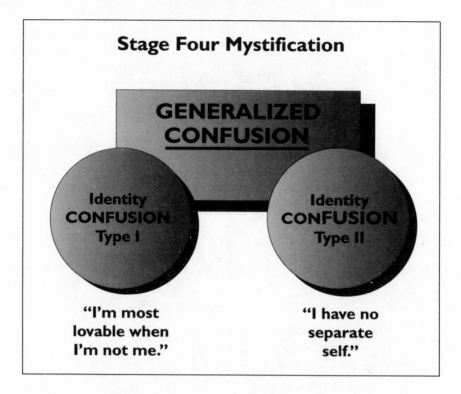

Stage Four Mystification

GENERALIZED CONFUSION

Identity CONFUSION Type I

Identity CONFUSION Type II

"I'm most lovable when I'm not me."

"I have no separate self."

shame. It is the product of family violence in the forms of perfectionism, abandonment, abuse, and neglect. These forms of violation send the terribly confusing message that "I am most lovable when I'm *not* being myself."

Type II is the result of the various enmeshment violations I discussed earlier. In this case, the child is con*fused* with the emphasis on the fusion. This type of confusion is often more covert than the other. Children in this situation may not consciously feel confused. There is so much identification and enmeshment with the primary caretaker that the children have no identity of their own. They *are* the parent they are enmeshed with. And they are fused into the fabric of the family trance.

If you live in either type of identity confusion, it is impossible to have a *real* relationship with anyone.

CHAPTER 4

Ultimate Mystification— The False Self

There is a pain—so utter—
It swallows substance up—
Then covers the Abyss with Trance—
So Memory can step
Around—across—upon it—
As one within a Swoon—
Goes safely—where an open eye—
Would drop Him—Bone by Bone.

EMILY DICKINSON

The purpose of the false self is to defend against pain—not deal with reality.

ROBERT FIRESTONE

If you want to have an interesting experience, try the following exercise. Sit across from someone and have them ask you, "Who are you?" After you give an answer, have them wait about ten seconds and then ask you, "But who are you really?" After you answer, they ask again, "But who are you really?" Continue this for at least thirty minutes. The question will become progressively harder to answer, and the more you have solidified a false self, the harder it will become. Try it and see what happens to you. I began to feel very confused after I'd answered the first five or six times.

This exercise pushes you to get past your false self masks and cultural roles and to connect with your deepest sense of self.

Ideally, in the natural sequence of human development, we form our identity as the result of experimentation, good modeling, and the healthy satisfaction of childhood dependency needs. When this identity formation process is disrupted, children experience generalized confusion which forces them to choose an identity adapted to the mystifying circumstances of their lives. The identity chosen is a false self, but it does give the child definition, structure, and some ability to control what is going on around them. They must choose the false self to keep from going crazy.

STAGE FIVE: THE FALSE SELF

The inner core of shame gives the child a sense of being flawed and defective. The flaw is felt as coming not from *doing* but from *being*. In other words, it's not just that I make mistakes or do "bad" things. The way I *am,* my very beingness, is defective.

Franz Kafka wrote about this inner sense of defectiveness brilliantly in his novel *The Trial.* Joseph K., the protagonist, wakes up one morning to find that he has been arrested. He has no idea what he has done wrong. He is simply judged and indicted.

Kafka wrote in his diary, "Healthy men dispense the phantoms of the night." But in *The Trial,* the phantoms are there in the morning, only they are not recognizable. Joseph K.'s arrest is the beginning of a series of nightmares, a lifelong sentence of mystification. He is picked up and taken to court, where he must defend himself before a judge. But he does not understand what the charges are and therefore feels powerless to defend himself.

I interpret this novel as a symbolic presentation of Kafka's awareness of the deep inner antagonism that split his life apart. All the characters in the story are aspects of his own inner life. He was plagued by an inner voice of critical accusation, which is represented in the story by a police inspector whose name is Franz.

Kafka was an unusually sensitive and highly creative child. He was dominated by a patriarchal father who had no sense of his son's uniqueness. Young Franz felt compelled to give up his own ideas and conform to the banal, standardized world of his father. Even after he left home, his father's voice continued to live on inside of him, constantly accusing him for thinking and feeling differently. In his father's world simply *being* different was a *crime*. Yet Franz could not escape the fact of his own uniqueness; he was condemned to inner secrecy, despairing of ever being able to really express his authentic self. Anyone who does not measure up to patriarchy's absolute measures is judged guilty, and Joseph K.'s crime was his wanting to be himself and therefore different.

Joseph K. is taken to court repeatedly. He stands before ghostlike judges with phantom beards and is led down long, stifling corridors leading nowhere. The court summons take place at night and on Sundays. These are the times when Joseph K. is totally alone, without the protective screen of his weekday work at a bank. He tells us, "In the bank, I am always prepared ... people keep coming to see me, clients and clerks, and above all my mind is always on my work and so kept on the alert."

At work he lives in his false self—prepared, guarded, and in control.

I understand this perfectly. I lived much of my life by staying so busy I had no time to reflect on the chronic low-grade depression that I felt. Only late at night or on days off like Sundays, when I had no way left to distract myself, did I feel the sharp pain of self-criticism and lonely shame.

As far as I know, no one has ever described the darkness of the mystified false self any better than Franz Kafka. The feeling that I've done something wrong, that I really don't know what it is, that there's something terribly wrong with my very being, leads to a sense of utter hopelessness. This hopelessness is the deepest cut of the mystified state. It means *there is no possibility for me as I am; there is no way I can matter or be worthy of anyone's love as long as I remain myself.* I must find a way to be someone else—someone who is lovable. Someone who is not me.

CREATING AN IDENTITY OUT OF CONFUSION

In order to understand the mystified false self, we have to go back to infancy. As infants, we have no real experience of self separate from our mothering source. Our self-image is based on our mother's mirroring face. The infant perceives the world through the mother's eyes. The child's self is identical with the mother's sense of the child's self. What happens when the mother fails to provide affection and approval? Dr. James Masterson, an authority on defective self-formation, writes:

> The child's intense ... need for affection and approval from his mother to build ego structure is so absolute and his rage ... at the deprivation of these very supplies on the part of his mother so great, that he fears these feelings may destroy her and himself. To deal with his fear, the infant splits the whole object of his mother into two parts, that is, a good and bad mother.

The infant does this through a primitive defense called "object splitting" (see the figure below).

The "bad" mother is not the child's mother. She is someone else. Therefore, the child can direct rage at the mother without dealing with the fear of her leaving.

A true sense of self begins to emerge during the separation-individuation stage of development, which occurs during toddlerhood. At this age, children are walking and enjoy the new sense of mastery

OBJECT SPLITTING IN INFANCY

GOOD MOTHER   **BAD MOTHER**

that locomotion brings. Just as they can now walk away from mother physically, children develop an image of themselves as an object and come to perceive themselves as separate from the mothering source. If all goes well, they also learn that mother is one and the same person in all her moods and appearances.

Children need to develop this single image of the mother—an image of the mother as both satisfying (good) and frustrating (bad). Children need at the same time to develop a whole image of themselves. In other words, children need to be able to see the mothering source as both/and and themselves as both/and—both comfortable and uncomfortable, both good and bad. The technical term for this ability is *"object constancy."*

Successful separation and individuation gives the child the capacity to relate to others and to themselves as whole persons. This ability is a crucial preparation for later satisfying interpersonal relationships, both intimate and social. To see others as whole persons, according to Masterson, means "to see them as both good and bad, gratifying and frustrating, and to have this relationship persist despite frustration at the hands of the object (the other person)." With object constancy, the person I love is the same as the person I hate. And I am the same person whether she approves or disapproves of me. *It is a both/and situation, not an either/or situation.*

If this development is interrupted—and in shame-based families it almost always is—the child cannot individuate. The child also fails to develop the capacity to relate to the mother as a whole person. If I am arrested at the infantile state of *object splitting*, I see you as all good when you meet my needs and as all bad when you fail to meet my needs. You are a good person or a bad person—not one whole person. And I view myself with the same polarization—as good *or* bad, all *or* nothing.

Object constancy is a fundamental achievement of successful separation and individuation. A child who separates well can evoke a stable and consistent memory image of their mothering source whether she is there or not. Out of sight is not out of mind. Mystified adults are often unable to connect very deeply with anyone. Out of sight *is* out of mind. I've seen clients who can leave one partner and latch onto another in the blink of an eye. They can do this because, lacking object constancy, they have no ability to evoke the image of their lost partner and hence no ability to grieve. They are cold-hearted.

If you cannot evoke an image of the person who leaves you and cannot mourn, you cannot resolve the many issues of separation life presents us with. This amounts to saying that you cannot grow up.

The figures below and on page 94 may help you get a picture of this very complex theorizing. And while it is a theory, something very like this happens to many people who exhibit mystified love. They create two images of their beloved—one is *idealized* and one is *degraded*. The beloved is idealized when they measure up to the person's image of a good lover (child, parent, partner, friend, etc.). The beloved is judged and degraded when they do not measure up to the person's image. What is missing in such love is an image that has both extremes synthesized. The synthesized image is *human* and sets up realistic expectations. The polarized image is *inhuman* and sets up unrealistic expectations.

Failure to achieve separation and individuation and, therefore, object constancy, has five disastrous consequences for both self-image and other relationships.

OBJECT CONSTANCY
IN TODDLERHOOD

**I can be both
good and bad.**

**The same mother can
be both good and bad.**

**Basis of the Ability
to Grasp Polarity**

FAILURE TO ACHIEVE OBJECT CONSTANCY

Good Mother

When I get what I want or need, Good Mother is there.

Bad Mother

When I don't get what I want or need, Bad Mother is there.

Good Child

When Mom gives me love, I am good.

Bad Child

When Mom withholds love, I am bad.

Basis of Polarization

- The mystified person relates to others as parts rather than wholes, as *objects* rather than subjects. This creates an either/or, all or nothing, type, of thinking.

- Mystified relationships cannot tolerate frustration and fluctuate widely according to feelings and needs.

- The mystified person is unable to evoke a sustaining image of another person when that other person is not present. There is a panicky sense that, when a person goes away, they will not return.

- The mystified person has a split scene of self. Either good me or bad me. Either more than human or less than human.

- The mystified person *cannot mourn*. Thus any object loss or separation is experienced as a calamity and a substitute object is quickly found.

The Split Self

The figure on page 96 shows Stage Five of the mystification process. At the bottom of the figure you can see a circle with a star. That circle is your true self; the star it contains is your wonder child. The wonder child, like all natural organisms, wants what he or she wants and has a natural urge for completion. The mystification process begins so early that the connection with, and urgings of, the true self become unconscious. Nevertheless, we all have moments when our true self breaks through. I will call these "soulful" moments. These breakthroughs may come in our dreams, in our seemingly irrational behavior, in our rage, in moments when we act uncharacteristically. When someone says, "That's not like you!"—that may be a moment when your soul is breaking through.

As you can see from the diagram, the mystified person's self-system is composed of two extremes, with the person often going from one to the other. A dominant pattern of adapting will be selected and owned—usually from the "good side" polarity of the split self, but its opposite will also be lurking in the background.

One extreme is giving in to the sense of worthlessness that's at the root of the confusion. The identity that the person has in this extreme is a negative identity. It says, "I am worthless as I am," "I am no good," "There is something wrong with me," or "There is something wrong with my body, my perceptions, my feelings, my needs, my desires, my thinking, my drives." A false self-identity trance is developed out of this extreme. The false self might be a fawning, servile people pleaser, whose core identity is "I'll do anything to please you." Alternately, the core identity might be "I'm a victim, see all the things that have happened to me, so please love me" or "I'm so dumb, stupid, crazy, inept, ugly, fat, rotten, etc., I might as well give in and be a failure, a slob, the class dunce, etc." or "I'll rebel against everyone and everything." These are strategies that give the person a definition, an identity. "I'm the class failure" is an identity.

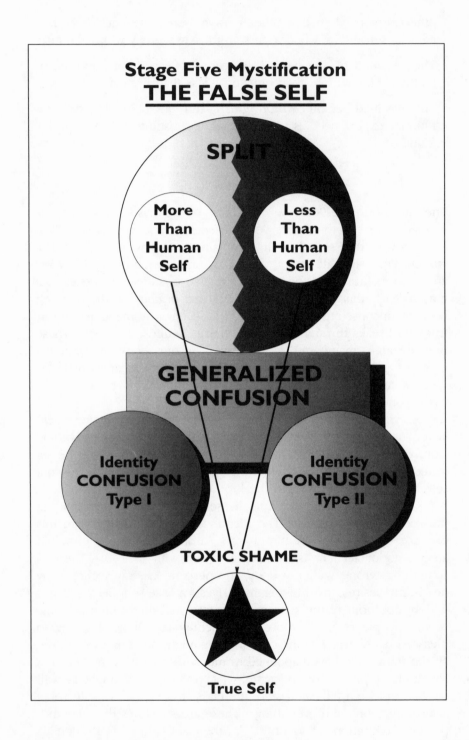

I call such strategies the less-than-human strategies. These strategies have undeniable payoffs. If I am less than human, no one can expect anything of me. If I reproach and blame myself all the time, no one else will be able to reproach or blame me. Being less than human, I can give up all discipline and responsibility. Above all, I can never fail, because I am already a failure.

At the other extreme are the more-than-human strategies. The identities that flow from this extreme involve power, control, perfectionism, judgment, righteousness, and blame. If I am in power, no one can hurt me. If I am perfect, no one can expose me. If I am in control, no one can catch me off guard. If I am righteous and saintly, no one can criticize me, and I can criticize, judge, and blame everyone. These are the "I'm OK, you're not OK" type of identities.

Only healthy shame would allow us to be human and whole. As humans we make mistakes, suffer, need help, bumble along, and know that we are not God. The false self created to deal with the confusion and disorientation of internalized shame tries to be more than human and/or less than human. Most mystified people act out both extremes. They have an all-or-nothing polarization in the center of their personality. If I can't be all, I'll be nothing. If I can't be extraordinary, I'll be a worm. Wolinsky calls these two coexisting extremes "oppositional trances."

To see how these oppositional trances develop, consider the following examples. A young child is playing with her mother's makeup. She has lipstick and powder all over her. Her father shames her for what she is doing. The little girl's natural desire is to respond by saying: "I want to keep doing this. I will do it." Her father scares her by threatening to spank her. The threat thwarts her natural response and triggers confusion. She knows what she wants and feels, but she cannot risk losing her father's love. So she may choose to do "anything to *please him.*" This is an effective choice, especially if her father chronically controls and shames her. In such a situation first one identity is tried and then another. The identity chosen is the one that most successfully resolves the confusion.

The first response the child tried was her natural self choice. "I want it my way." This is everyone's first choice. If that had worked, she would have continued to use it.

As the child was shamed, she developed a trance state that said, "I am really bad for wanting it my way." The oppositional trance is "I'll do anything to please you. I'll do it your way." The two identities, "I am bad" and "I'll do anything to please you," coexist, each sitting at one extreme. Their coexistence creates a state of tension and a power struggle within the person.

To resolve this tension, children quickly learn to *project* one identity and *own* the other. My "I'll do anything to please you, I'll be perfect" identity is the one I *own.* I project "I am bad, I want it my way" onto others—often in scathing criticism.

It's easy to spot projection in the child who innocently protests that "bad Susie" (her imaginary friend) was the one who spilled the milk. It's a lot harder to spot in ourselves. When we project our "I am bad, I want it my own way" onto others, we pick up the slightest hint of self-gratification or selfishness in them. We are often relentlessly critical of those who seem to be doing exactly what they *want* to do.

I remember an unmarried woman I counseled who passionately scorned other single women in her apartment complex for their alleged sexual promiscuity. My client belonged to a very rigid fundamentalist religion. She was moralistic and judgmental. Yet she often dreamed of being raped by dozens of men. She dressed in a way that was modest but seductive. She wore long skirts and tight long-sleeved blouses that emphasized the roundness of her breasts.

I remember this well because I was concerned about my sexual feelings about her. I thought that maybe they were coming from my own sexual issues, so I checked my perceptions with the female psychiatrist who had referred her to me for counseling. My psychiatrist colleague also found the woman seductive. This woman *projected* her erotic and desiring "I want what I want" self onto other sexy women and *owned* her "I'll do anything to please you" self in her dutiful and moralistic religious behavior.

Other people flip-flop between their oppositional false selves. My "I want it my way (I am bad)" self came out a lot in my spousal relationship, while I was most often in my "I'd do anything to please you" self in public.

Family System Enmeshment Roles

In the preschool years from ages 3 to 6, a child's developmental task is to form a first primitive identity. A new *family role* will be added to the basic sense of self. When the family is very dysfunctional, the child's choice of roles is severely narrowed.

Remember that the roles are selected to meet the needs of the system, rather than the individual. They maintain the system's balance at the expense of the individual's uniqueness and spontaneity. The rigid roles are also chosen because of the con*fusion* created by the family's enmeshment.

In the dysfunctional family system, roles are often polarized. This isn't surprising, since the dysfunctional family operates like a whole individual organism. One child may be rigidly good (behaves according to family rules) and another rigidly bad (rebels and breaks the rules). Each has the polarized opposite role. The good child *wants* to be bad some of the time and vice versa. But the systemic forces keep each one in their rigid role.

The important thing to understand, whatever role you chose, is that it gave you a sense of structure and definition. With it, you felt like you had some control. The role defined you, and you took on the boundaries or limits of that role. The role became a particular trance you lived. Over time you believed that this limited boundary was who you were. Wolinsky calls this a "thought form limitation." Your experience is narrowed by such a thought form or belief about yourself. All of your feelings, thoughts, wishes, are limited by this chosen trance identity.

I also found that over the years my trance role functioned like an *addiction*. I became so completely identified with the roles of Star and Caretaker, I had no idea how to behave if I was not being the Star or Caretaker. These identities greatly limited the possibilities of my experience and, therefore, my freedom.

The Ultimate Mystification

These false identities give us the sense of being clear of the confusion. The fact is that *they really hide the confusion.* In essence once the hypnotic identity trance is formed, we no longer know we are confused. Instead of having to face and resolve the dilemma—that "I'm most loved when I'm not being me" or "I don't know who I am"—the false self creates the ultimate level of mystification. At this level, I either *don't know that I don't know who I am* or *I think I know who I am, but I really don't.* Are you confused?

Two mystified selves trying to have a relationship and create love are asking the impossible of themselves. In a *mystified love* relationship, we have two people who are not *really present, who think they know who they are and who don't know that they don't know who they are.* It's not a pretty picture! After sitting through twenty-two years of counseling some eight hundred couples, I can guarantee you that it's mystifying.

STAGE SIX: THE INTERNALIZED FAMILY

The mystified state is maintained through the internalized family system. The false self keeps us bonded. The mystified person has never separated from the family system.

In order to grasp how this bonding works, take the following short quiz. Simply answer each question yes or no.

1. Do you get angry and/or defensive when your spouse or lover criticizes your parents? Yes _____ No_____
2. Do you get angry and/or defensive when someone outside your family makes a realistic but negative remark about one of your source figures? Yes _____ No _____
3. Do you still resent one or both of your source figures? Yes _____ No _____
4. Do you obsess on one or both of your source figures? Yes _____ No _____
5. Have you stayed in a stuck relationship long after it was healthy to be there? Yes _____ No _____
6. Have you stayed in a destructive relationship long after you understood that it was self-destructive to be in it? Yes _____ No _____
7. Whenever you take the time to reflect on it, do you feel that you are *not* afraid of death? Yes _____ No _____
8. Do you feel more comfortable talking about your faults than about your strengths? Yes _____ No _____
9. Do you complain about your parents and then quickly explain their motives in an attempt to excuse their problems or weaknesses? Yes _____ No _____
10. Have you been told that you imitate the worst qualities of your parents? Yes _____ No _____

If you answered any of these questions yes, you may still be internally bonded to your primary source figures. The more questions you answered yes, the greater the attachment.

The parental figures live on in us in the form of internalized voices and governing scenes. The family system also lives on in the internalized *rules* that we carry and in the rigid *roles* we first learned to play in the family system. As we discussed in Chapter 1, myriads of people have re-created their original family bondings in their current relationships—not only in their friendships and spousal relationships, but also in their relationships with God, self, and the world at large.

This internalized maintenance of the family system operates as a *trance*. The trance governs the person's choices like a pair of glasses with blinders on the side. Within the self-to-self interpersonal trance the person hears the family figures' voices, which operate as the beliefs governing most of what the person thinks and chooses to do.

Scared to Death

I remember listening to a guy tell his story at a 12-step meeting. He had two years of abstinence from using prescription drugs. He said that it had been hard to stop using the drugs but that it was not half as hard as dealing with an intimate relationship. "I'm scared to death of intimacy," he said. At that time I did not pay any attention to the phrase "scared to death." Since then I've given it some thought. I've come to believe that it describes what is going on in people who are mystified—and that it is an *exact* description, not a metaphorical one.

For the mystified wounded inner child, it is a *life-threatening risk* to make a true commitment to another person. Let me explain.

The false self keeps us bonded to the dysfunctional family system. The false self is maintained because of the failure to achieve object constancy. I have already described how an infant uses the primitive defense of object splitting. An infant feels helpless and utterly vulnerable. To lose the mothering source is equivalent to annihilation and death. By enabling the infant to identify with its mother (to be its own mother), this defense gives an infant an illusion of omnipotence and self-sufficiency (see the figure on the next page).

This illusion fosters the grandiose belief that the child can *meet their own needs without going outside of themselves*. The entranced child comes to prefer this defensive solution rather than venturing out and reality testing. Their world stays frozen, predictable, and static, held in place by the false self. The false self includes the source figure(s) the child is identified with. This is how and why the state of mystification is maintained. To give up the internalized parental source would mean losing the *infantile sense of self-sufficiency and immortality*.

Many people will reject any outsider's more realistic view of their source figure, often with outright anger. I remember how angry I got at the first therapist who suggested that my enmeshment with my mother was the major cause of my relationship problems. I remember how my ex-wife and I each used to lambaste our own par-

THE ILLUSION
OF SELF-SUFFICIENCY

**Enmeshed
Child**

- **Good mother internalized**
- **Child has illusion mother will never die/always protect him**
- **Mother now internal voice of self-sufficiency**

ents but then become righteously indignant when the other person started criticizing them.

The toxic shame at the root of the false self is also maintained by idealizing our source figures. Children cannot demythologize their parents. In order to feel protected and cared for, they need their parents to be godlike. I couldn't have called a meeting at age 4, with my little bags packed, in order to tell my mom and dad that their marriage was dysfunctional and that I was moving down the street to live with the neighbors where I'd get my needs better taken care of! No child could do that. If Dad and Mom are not there for me, *it must be about me*, not about them.

I remember a little boy whose mother divorced his father and moved to Houston with him. She told the boy that his father was a rotten person. The boy was acting out by getting in fights at school and misbehaving at home. He told me he was bad like his father.

The mother had worked with me for a year and a half. I had helped her to recognize some of her own intimacy problems in the marriage.

It became clear to me that the boy had overidealized his mother. I urged the mother to share some of the ways she had caused problems in her marriage and to present the boy's father in a more honest and favorable light.

The boy was quite agitated when the mother shared these things. After the discussion, he began to act out more intensely. This intensified acting out was a way of increasing his own sense of shame in order to prove that he was bad and mother was good. As long as he held on to this internal idealized fantasy bond, he did not have to deal with growing up. To see his mother with faults destroyed the identification with her and thus his illusion of omnipotence and self-sufficiency. Being bad is a small price to pay for immortality.

Look at the figure below. There you can see that it is the wounded inner child who maintains the mystified state. To the wounded inner child, the loss of the parent is equivalent to death. This is a crucial point. In Chapter 7, I will describe a process to help

Stage Six Mystification
<u>THE INTERNALIZED FAMILY</u>

Split

Disowned

- **Parent hunger**
- **My parents are all good or all bad**
- **I'll die if I separate from them**

you separate from the internalized family system. The stages in this process are difficult and frightening, because of your wounded inner child's magical beliefs.

The mystified inner child believes that:

- My "good source figure" (good mother and/or good father) is still there and will always protect me.

- All my rescue fantasies will come true. Either my "good source figure" or someone just like them will make it so I live happily ever after.

- If I find someone just like my "good source figure," or I find someone just like my "bad source figure" and act in a perfect way, I will live happily ever after.

- If I find someone exactly opposite of my "bad source figure," I will live happily ever after.

- If I were to separate from my "good or bad source figure," I would be severely punished or die. (NOTE: This is the reason the survival figure was split in the first place.)

We continue to play our family system's rigid role because the role allows us to stay connected with the omnipotent source figure. This may also be why we are so afraid to go against our family of origin's *rules*. The rules keep the mystified inner child bonded to the internal parent source.

Hopelessness and Helplessness

Another reason the wounded inner child fears separation is that toxic shame *feels hopeless*. The internal dialogue runs like this: "If I am hopeless, if I cannot count on myself, then I cannot leave my survival figures, because there is no way I can make it on my own." Some form of this internal dialogue goes on to some degree in every mystified inner child. Family violation, like all violation, strikes at the core of the self. It reduces self-worth and self-value, leading eventually to a condition called "learned helplessness." The more a person is violated, the more they feel worthless, and the more they feel worthless, the more their belief in their own competence diminishes. They have learned to feel helpless.

Hopelessness and helplessness are among the reasons many families remain dysfunctional for generations. It is very difficult to leave the internalized dysfunctional family system. It takes real commitment.

It will require your willingness to feel the hurt and anger you have about the violation you incurred.

Idealized or Degraded Image

The internalized parent described above is idealized. This parent is good and ultimately wonderful. There will be a golden age when the parent will give us everything we need. All cares will be taken away, all tears wiped from our eyes.

The internalized parent can also be maintained in a degraded image. Dad or Mom is distorted and monsterlike. Often, they are retained as totally evil or totally degraded. The mystified wounded child holds on to them in waves of recurring *resentment*. The resentment and hate keep the wounded inner child from ever having to separate. Sometimes even the degraded image is part of the idealization. The child projects such idealized and unrealistic expectations on the parent that the parent is degraded.

I carried a degraded image of my dad. Basically this image corresponded to my mother's and her family's interpretation of him. He was a no-good and irresponsible alcoholic bum. He never cared for me for one minute. The dirty rotten bastard. In my teens, I ran around with guys from broken homes who degraded their fathers. We hung out in bars calling our fathers all kinds of names. "My old man is a no-good bastard, prick, bum. He only thinks of himself." Our mothers were saints.

Neither idealized nor degraded images are accurate. And in the process of separation we will have to demythologize these images.

MYSTIFICATION IN BRIEF

I would like to summarize some key elements of mystification using the letters of the word.

Magical
Yearning for Fulfillment
Shame Based
Trancelike Existence
Incomplete, Insatiable
Fantastic Imagination
Identity Trance, Confusion
Cognitive Closure
Acting Out or Acting In the Family Violence
Time Distortion
Inability to Respond
Otheration, Codependency
Negative and Positive Hallucinations

Magical

Mystified people have never been fully born psychologically. Therefore, they still think like children. They believe that certain magical actions, behaviors, words, or rituals will bring instant happiness. Marriage is a magical act for many mystified people. They believe that just getting married will solve all their problems.

Yearning for Fulfillment

Everyone has some emptiness. But the mystified have more than average levels of emptiness. This is due to the loss of connection with their authentic self. *They are not fully present in lived experience.* There is a sense of never quite being in on anything that one does. It feels like one is always on the sidelines observing life rather than living it. This yearning is also a deep spiritual bankruptcy. There is no real inner life.

Shame Based

Being mystified is rooted in toxic shame binds. No matter what mystified people see, hear, feel, or need, they feel some degree of shame.

They have no limits or boundaries in their life. Natural or healthy shame is the permission to be human. Toxic shame tries to be more than human (shameless) or less than human (shameful). People who are shameless are compulsively perfectionistic. People who are shameful give in to impulses, stop caring about goals, and lose all concern for self-esteem. Shame-based people have been soul marred. As they have no real self, their freedom is seriously impaired.

Trancelike Existence

Mystified people wear a frozen or trancelike mask, which often confuses others. The mystified tend to overreact or underreact. More often than not, their response is inappropriate. Their vocabularies are parrotlike, and since they are not really present, they do not listen well. Depending on the nature of their final trance identity, mystified people either overly conform or overly rebel. The conformist follows others' suggestions like orders to be obeyed. The rebel is compulsively counterdependent. Mystified rebels question everything, refusing to agree no matter what.

Incomplete, Insatiable

The mystified live in the past. They have loads of unresolved developmental dependency needs. They are adult children—adults with an insatiable child inside of them. The insatiability is about their dependency needs not getting met. While they look like adults, their behavior is that of a child. It was appropriate for a needy child to act the way they are acting, but it is not appropriate for an adult. The insatiability of a mystified person is very hard to relate to. A mystified person is looking for their source figures to take care of them. This is not the basis for an adult relationship.

Fantastic Imagination

The mystified use both positive and negative hallucinations as survival mechanisms. They create fantasy bonds with their survival figures. Often, the more they have been shamed, the more their source figures have been idealized. Abandoning source figures may also be degraded in fantastic ways. The shame-based self creates more-than-human or less-than-human images. These images lead to inhuman and unrealistic expectations. Such expectations are devastating in any kind of relationship.

Identity Trance, Confusion

Because of the family violence, persons who are mystified have a deep level of confusion about their authentic self—their real identity. They either have fused with source figures or are deeply distrusting of their own perceptions, thoughts, feelings, needs, and desires. Is that person really sad or is it just my imagination? This quandary stems from continual mystification by source figures. Mother is crying. I try to console her. She says she is not crying. I must be crazy! The most damaging confusion comes from not measuring up to source figures' fantastic expectations. Early on a child realizes, I am most loved when I act like they want me to—not when I am myself. Quite often the parents' fantasies about the child are so unrealistic that the child cannot measure up and is deeply shamed. The hypnotic identity is always a cover-up and therefore a form of denial.

Cognitive Closure

Because mystified people are in a trance, they are mentally fixated. This mental fixation, known as cognitive closure, causes rigidity and great loss of flexibility and freedom. Cognitive closure is especially strong for adult children from cultic or corrupt families. They were constantly told the same things in a language characterized by thought-terminating clichés. They internalized their source people's indoctrination in the form of posthypnotic voices. Cognitive closure aids the denial process.

Acting Out or Acting In the Family Violence

The mystified will reenact the governing shame scenes, taking the part of the offender or the victim or both. They will reenact the abuse on themselves or on others. Addictions are a major way in which mystified people act out or act in their abuse. Mystification is at the root of all compulsive/addictive disorders.

Time Distortion

The time distortion of the mystified is due to earlier traumatic experience. It is accompanied by other distortions. Mystified people over-react to and distort interactions or events, especially those that are painful. The mystified are hypervigilant, catastrophic in their thinking, and easily startled. These qualities are PTSD traits. The time distortion and other distortions of the mystified make relationships very difficult.

Inability to Respond

Inability to respond leads to failure to deal with ongoing life issues. Mystified persons either lack responsibility or are overly responsible. They definitely are not balanced in this regard. The lack of responsibility is a core part of the denial and minimizing that characterize mystification. Overresponsibility and underresponsibility are evidence of the deep disorder of will that characterizes mystification.

Otheration, Codependency

The mystified are confused and have no sense of their authentic self. They either have fused with a source figure or spend all their energy manipulating others in order to get their needs met. Codependency is a dis-ease of the developing self. Happiness cannot be engendered from within. Codependent persons are spiritually bankrupt.

Negative and Positive Hallucinations

Mystified people literally see and hear things that are not there. They project unwanted parts of themselves, and they put source figures' faces on their relationship partners. Because they are stuck in the past, they *do not see the facts* that surround them. They are delusional, that is, they believe things in spite of the facts.

PART TWO

The Possibility of Love

When there is no love put love and there you will find love.

SAINT JOHN OF THE CROSS

CHAPTER 5

Soulful Love

Soul is ultimately love.

THOMAS MOORE

In the midst of winter, I found within me an invincible summer.

ALBERT CAMUS

Three years ago I stood in the middle of a run-down, empty three-story house. The front lawn and backyard were scorched by the sun, in places down to the bare ground.

Both my children were gone. Brenda had moved out years ago, and John had recently left for college. I knew they would never live in this house again.

My ex-wife and I had sealed our twenty-one years of mystified marriage with an amicable divorce. We had mutually agreed that we were stagnated and decided to give each other the opportunity to find the quality of life that we couldn't find together.

Standing in the house that had once been our family home, I wondered why I remained, why I had bought it from my ex-wife. God knows I had complained about it all during our marriage. The floors were stained, the walls needed painting, the bathrooms and kitchen were dreary and dull. On several occasions I had said I hated this house. And I had never put any effort into making it nice. I had opted for work and money-making and had put a lot of pressure on my ex-wife to do the same. It didn't seem to matter how much we accumulated, I was always scared about the future.

Now almost everyone was encouraging me to leave, to find a nice condominium or high rise, something more fitted to a single man's life-style.

But somehow I desperately wanted the house. Maybe I was afraid to leave. I thought I wanted it so that my son could come back to his boyhood home on his breaks from college, so that my children could come home for Christmas. But there seemed to be some *deeper* reason. I had kept only one piece of furniture, a fine replica of a Napoleonic desk that I had bought to celebrate my PBS series "Bradshaw On: The Family." It was the best thing I had ever given myself. But now it was sitting all alone, an elegant desk surrounded by dour emptiness.

I felt the emptiness like I had never felt it before—not the painful knife-in-the-chest stuff that comes from being rejected by a lover, but an overall sense of anomie. I felt dizzy and confused, not knowing which way to go or where to begin.

There are no rituals for this rite of passage, no ministers to lead the church service, no people to bring food to your house and say kind words. I felt very, very sad, especially at night.

I had always wanted a place for my special things, a place where I could celebrate the memories that went with them. I had a lot of Native American pieces, including an Ojibway peace pipe. I had a collection of eagles and lions, which came from all over. I called these my "power" animals.

Starting from these things, slowly, over the months, I began an incredible reformation of my house. I had no particular plan, but I kept moving on. I hired a decorator and told her things I didn't even know I wanted to do. We tore out the bathrooms and kitchen. We sanded the floors and refinished them. Before I would have begrudged every cent of expenditure. Now I loved it.

Furnishing the house became a wild, ecstatic kind of experience. At times I felt like a child just playing. I bought hand-carved chairs from India and an ancient Chinese ceremonial drum. *My soul was starting to take over!*

In New Orleans I found some Empire chairs with griffins for legs. Griffins are lions with eagle's wings, and I *had* to have them for my office. I bought a huge sleigh bed and a massive antique English armoire. In a far-out shop in a little town near Oakland, I found two old Tiffany lamps. The house was beginning to take shape.

I had never had religious pictures or crucifixes in the house. But now I bought two beautiful tramp art antique crucifixes, and in England I happened upon a handmade silver monstrance. The monstrance is the vessel that houses the host during the Catholic service of benediction and praise. I put my crucifixes together with the monstrance and created an altar at the top of the stairs on the second floor. It is there to honor God, but also to honor my ten years as a student for the priesthood. It felt good to reconnect with that part of my life.

My house was becoming my *home*. I had moved ten times during the first sixteen years of my life, living with relatives a lot of the time. I had moved five times in the seminary and four times after I left. I never really felt at home anywhere.

I filled the yards with flowers, red, blue, green, yellow, violet, orange flowers—fabulous flowers expressive of life's vibrant energy.

Then there was one ugly spot left, an enclosure on the side of the house for the air conditioners. My brother Richard suggested I do something about it. We filled it with plants—lariope, ginger, calla lilies, artesia, monkey grass, and rows of impatiens. That last ugly place became my secret garden.

I like to sit there in the warm night air and think. I think about my whole life. I think about aging and the sad/happy memories of my life. It's really happening, I am growing old! In the fires of youth, aging had never entered my mind. But here I am in the afternoon of my life, the *fourth quarter,* my buddy Mike Falls calls it, finally tending my own home and my own garden.

The emptiness and darkness of my grief and discontent provided my soul a place to make my secret garden. Out of an empty house that marked the end of one life cycle, I created a home for myself.

My secret garden is like my soul, quiet and unobtrusive, but bursting with life.

THE WONDER CHILD AND SOULFULNESS

Soulful love is rooted in the raw, unadapted depths of our human nature. It flows from our natural endowment as human beings. It develops naturally as the wonder child is nurtured. The great psychologist Carl Jung used the term "wonder child" to mean the natural state of childhood.

We are born with life-affirming emotions: curiosity, surprise, and joy. We also have life-defending and life-preserving emotions, like anger, fear, and sadness. Children are curious and are risk takers. They have lots of courage. They venture out into a world that is immense and dangerous. A child initially trusts life and the processes of life. The facts are friendly. The universe can be trusted and the child has a natural predisposition to believe this. When children are thwarted, they have the ability to bounce back. Think of the resiliency it takes in order to learn to walk.

We've discussed the way children think. I described their thinking as magical, egocentric, and nonlogical. Nonlogical *is* a way of knowing. It is our soul's most usual way of knowing. Nonlogical thinking is poetic. It involves imagination and feeling. Children love to sing and dance. They love stories and fairy tales. Stories, singing, dancing, and poetry are true modes of knowing. They are marvelous constituents of human life, of equal importance with logical ways of knowing.

Soul As Indestructible

Soulfulness is not fully definable because it is a state of being. It is the state of being fully human. Being human involves body and mind, matter and spirit. The soul bridges the gap between body and mind, matter and spirit. Thomas Moore, in his fine book *Care of the Soul*, writes: "Soul is the 'in between' factor keeping mind in touch with body and matter in touch with spirit."

We can get hints and glimmers of soul as we learn more and more about being human.

One way to get a glimpse of soul is to look at how a child responds to the forms of violence we have described. Children cannot name their abuse. They do not know that they have a *right* to stop their abuser. Enmeshed children are often terribly confused by their sense of being special to Mom or Dad. They do not know they are being *used*. Yet in all cases of violence, something *deep inside cries out in the child*. I remember hearing about a 3-year-old incest victim who could not talk about what had happened to her but who became nauseated and vomited when questioned about it. Imagine that! The child had no way of knowing that what the adult was doing was wrong. All she knew she had learned from the adults around her, including her abuser. Yet something deep inside of her could not *stomach* what had happened. Her vomiting was a metaphor for her organismic disgust, an attempt to rid herself of the shame her offender has transferred to her. Until the child's voice is heard and the abuse acknowledged, the child will cry out through addictions or in reenactment of the abuse. I see all the symptoms resulting from family violence as metaphors for the victim's soul crying out for justice.

David Mura expresses all of this when he writes: "What is the

WONDER CHILD
BEFORE ADAPTING

soul? The soul is what recognizes that we are being degraded in an act of abuse. It is the sum of what cries out in us."

Soul is what is most profoundly human in each of us, and nothing human is foreign to the soul, including mistakes, failures, and our pathology.

In the figure above, you can see my very simple drawing of the soul at the moment of birth. The star in the center of the circle will expand to the limits of the circle if we are able to let it. No one has a perfect childhood and everyone is wounded to some degree by their culture. If you add patriarchy and all the childhood violations I have described, the picture changes. A false self emerges; our feel-

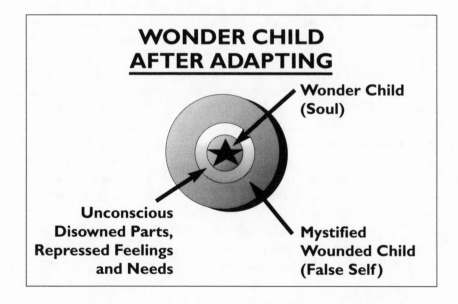

ings, needs, and wants are shamed; and our life becomes a quest for defensive security. We live in our trances defending against pain rather than vibrantly interacting with life. Our mystification binds us to the past, and we get absorbed in our wounds.

Yet no matter how bad it was, the trance you're in only feels hopeless and determined. *The trance is not really necessary.* You need to restore the interpersonal bridge. You need the mirroring face of nonshaming friends. But you *can* get demystified. Your soul may do it for you without any help.

There is nothing wrong with you; you are not ruined or defective goods. It only feels that way because of the mystification. That is the nature of trance. When you made the choice you had limited awareness and lacked experience, but you did choose the false self you're in and the deep trance defenses that support it. We all have the ability to make new choices. There are moments of grace, and there are deep reserves of determination. That star in the center circle never stops sending out life. You have an unspoiled core in you. Something refuses to die. Our most neurotic behavior is a metaphorical expression of what our soul longs for and needs.

Chronos and Kairos

Existentialist philosophers distinguish between "chronos time" and "kairos time." Chronos time is clock time, like twenty-four hours in a day. Kairos time is soul time: the time a major decision is made; a time of intensity, pattern interruption, or change of direction. We often don't realize a kairos time when it's happening, and we won't unless we look for it and believe in it. Changing a belief is a kairos time, especially a limiting belief. I saw a guy on a TV program called "That's Incredible." He was *catching arrows* shot from a powerful bow. The feat was amazing enough, but what was more amazing to me was how anyone would ever believe you could catch an arrow! But obviously this guy sat down one day and said to himself, "I wonder if I could ever catch an arrow?" And so he pursued the idea and somehow learned to catch an arrow. The *kairos* moment came when he changed his belief, when he entertained the possibility of catching an arrow. You must not think that you are doomed. I made some leaps in my own beliefs about myself in the last three years. I've totally surprised myself. You can, too. Your soul assures you that there is something there beneath the mystification.

TWO WAYS TO EXPERIENCE TIME

- **CHRONOS**
  Time as a limited measurement of duration — linear, clock time

- **KAIROS**
  Time in an intense experience, which seems to stand above time — non-linear time

The Common Expression of Soul

The idea of "soul" has fallen into disrepute in modern life. Carl Jung felt it was urgent that we restore the concept of soul to the valued and noble place it has occupied throughout human history.

It is interesting to think of ways "soul" survives in ordinary speech. This survival suggests that soul is still around.

Someone recently told me that my eyes looked "soulful." Our eyes are said to be "the mirror of the soul." People often "search their soul" to find their innocence or to find their dream. Those going through arduous trials are often told that their "soul is on trial." Those who act in a cruel and merciless way are called "soulless." We have "soul music" and "soul food." Those who seem hopelessly addicted, those who are chronic criminals, are called "lost souls." We hear talk of "troubled souls," "old souls," "innocent souls," and "inspired souls." Many religions believe in the "immortality of the soul." Some also believe that one's soul can be "possessed by the devil" or possessed by evil spirits. And some believed that one's soul can become ill or transposed into an object, animal, place, or another person.

Philosophers have said that the whole soul is in every part of the body but that the soul transcends the body. They have talked about animal, vegetable, and mineral souls.

In all cases, when the word "soul" is used the reference is to depth and value.

In his book *Re-Visioning Psychology*, the Jungian psychologist James Hillman outlines three dimensions of soul:

SOUL

Refers to:

- **What is most human**
- **Depth and value**
- **Imaginative possibilities of being**
- **What makes meaning possible**

First, soul refers to the deepening of events into experience; second, the significance soul makes possible, whether in love or in religious concern, derives from its special relation with death. And third by soul I mean the imaginative possibility in our natures, the experiencing through reflective speculation, dream, image, and fantasy—that mode which recognizes all realities ... as primarily symbolic or metaphorical.

Soul Makes Meaning Possible, Turns Events into Experience

Have you ever been surprised by the unexpected behavior of someone you thought you knew very well? It's happened to me in every close relationship I've had. And it often happened to me as a counselor. I would evaluate someone by putting them into a well-known therapeutic category. I'd work with them using the methods prescribed by the therapeutic model underlying the category I had placed them in. The majority of the time, this approach was inadequate.

I came to understand that no theoretical model can ever capture the depth of a unique human being. Soul transcends all human interpretations. People surprise us because we forget that our definitions are limited. The great therapists like Virginia Satir and Milton Erickson have soul. They baffle the rest of us because they bypass the surface and intuit the depth of possibility in the people they work with.

Good therapists are artists, not clinicians. All the *methods* in the world will not get a person in touch with their soul because soul is what allows us to grasp the inner meaning of human behavior. Soul sees the deeper meaning in all things. In a relationship, soul gives the meaning that we call love. Our earlier examples of mystified love are not mystified because they are illogical. They are mystified because they are inhuman. They do not foster mystery and spiritual depth.

The deeper meaning that soul makes possible in love and spirituality is related to death. We are, as the German existentialist Heidegger has said, "being toward death." This means that death is a boundary that gives life its meaning. Soul deals in *polarity*. There is no life without death, and death is always one of our possibilities. Death gives life an ultimate significance. Death asks us to live life while we've got it. Death is always at hand advising us to consider the uniqueness and significance of every moment. Death tempers our catastrophizing and grandiosity. It reminds us of our finitude.

Imaginative Possibilities

Soul refers to the imaginative possibilities of our nature. It reveals the depth and mystery of beings. Soul tells us that everything is inexhaustible, everything has a deeper meaning. The poet Shelley said, "There's music in all things if men had ears." Soul discovers and makes us aware of the music, the symbolic meaning, the depth of things. Soul teaches us what one of the earliest fragments of Greek philosophy taught us: "All things are full of gods." To me that means that all things have a sacred *depth* and *mystery* that we will never totally be able to fathom.

The Language of the Soul

The natural language of soul is poetry and music. It thrives on symbol, myth, and metaphor. The faculty of the soul is the imagination. That faculty is our way of reaching the larger meaning. Biblical scholars speak of the *sensus plenior,* or fuller meaning of a text in Scripture, implying that every text has a literal meaning and a fuller meaning. Life has a literal meaning, and it has a fuller meaning which is grounded in mystery. That mystery is rooted in the creative ground of being—that Higher Power that most call God.

Soulfulness would emerge spontaneously if the wonder child could develop without violence. The violence always wounds the

soul. Our partriarchal, rationalist child-rearing and educational practices have tried to lead us away from childhood. We need the foundation that childhood provides. We need to hold on to the wisdom and
talents of childhood. We need a pedagogy and education that elicits
and expands our childhood ways of knowing.

Soulfulness is not antilogical, it is nonlogical. Great minds use
logic to work out their soulful insights. Great artists use technique
to incarnate their soulful creative intuition. Great art, poetry, sanctity,
and wisdom require both soulfulness and logical thinking.

The crucial point for this book is that true human love is not
possible without soulfulness.

LEVELS OF LOVE

Soulful love takes many forms. Look at the figure on the next page. Level
1 represents eros, the life force. At its most basic, eros is the drive
in all things to complete themselves. This life force is the soul that
makes flowers blossom and acorns become oaks.

It is the energy each created reality has in seeking its own
good. In this way we can talk about nonhuman forms of love. As
minerals, vegetables, and animals become who they are—as they
achieve the ends of their maturity—they are loving themselves.
This love is not personal love. We cannot call it intimate love,
but it is an unconscious appetite that each thing has for wholeness
and completion. This is the first and most primitive level of love.
Each created reality longs for, strives for, and desires its own
completion.

As beings achieve consciouness, eros becomes appetite or libido,
the desire for physical union with another (Level 2). This sexual drive
is the force that preserves the species and insures survival. It is part
of the life force which is moving us to completion!

At a higher level of consciousness (Level 3) eros becomes
affection, the natural love for others of a species. In humans, this
is expressed in affectionate human sexuality, and becomes an arena
of soulful possibilities. Our sexuality is deeply related to our spirituality. We need our healthy human sexuality in order to create
soulful love.

At Level 4, we move beyond the natural love that we share with
other species. Eros becomes will—desire raised to the level of free
choice and executive human action. Free choice properly constitutes
human love. Soul becomes spirit in the act of freedom.

Filial love (Level 5) is created when spouses *decide* to have a child. The young child has a natural affection for his parents. But this love is a deficit love. That is, children need their parents' love. Without it they cannot really survive. Their love depends on their parents' love.

Parents have a *need* to love, but their love also involves conscious choice, will and self-discipline. Parental love involves a giving of one's time, attention, and direction. Parental love is a "gift love" rather than a need love, as parents do not need their children's love to survive.

Parents' love for their children cannot be an intimate love, because intimacy, in my definition, requires that people be equal in knowledge and power. Children are equal in dignity—but not in knowledge and power. Parents can love their children deeply and soulfully, but not intimately.

Children can experience the same kind of filial love for their parents as they become adults.

Love reaches greater soulfulness in friendship and spousal com-

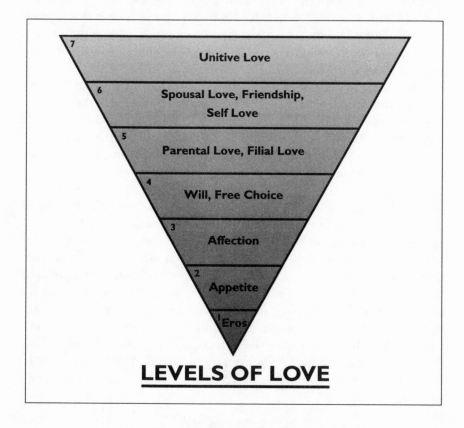

LEVELS OF LOVE

mitment (Level 6). This love, often called *agape,* is the love created by two people who commit to making each other's safety and self-actualization as important as their own.

Agape is also a love we need to extend to ourselves. One must love oneself in order to truly love another. Healthy narcissism is the true love and affection for one's self. It creates a powerful bond of self-connectedness. With healthy narcissism, one is at home with oneself. One has a sense of one's own value. One has self-esteem.

The fullest level of love, Level 7, is often called *caritas.* This is a Godlike love. We imagine that God loves with unconditional acceptance of all things. All opposites are unified in such love, and all things are valued. As we expand ourselves in *agape* love, we become more than we were. To love soulfully is to meet the other at their map of the world—to enter their very way of being. We become the other without losing ourselves. As our love extends to include more and more others, we extend ourselves more and more. We enlarge our being.

As we become progressively more connected with all other created beings, we experience a more unified consciousness. Wisdom flows from the heights of soulful love. Wisdom is seeing the larger picture. With wisdom, we experience our connectedness and relationship with everything. The great spiritual masters refer to this expanded consciousness as Unitive Vision.

No one climbs the stairs, as it were, taking these steps in the linear order the figure implies. We get glimpses of higher consciousness, we have hints of the mystery of our higher power, we have moments of grace where gifts of love come up from the depths of our soul. We work at it, we stumble, we have problems, and we see the fruits of our endurance and faithfulness.

We risk disclosure, and the rewards of our risk come to us in unexpected ways. What is soulful is often most unexpected. Our child comes to us and says "I love you" when we least expect it. Our spouse comes through when we have sort of written him or her off. Our friends appear when we really need them. And just the opposite might also happen. Our child, spouse, friend, or God, seems to let us down. We drift on the seas of concern, wander in the wilderness of withdrawal, hide in the caverns of our shame and guilt. No one seems to be there. And so we choose to change our rusty ways and our old habitual responses. The direction of our life changes. We don't know exactly how we got from there to here. But we are happy and excited again. A love that is fresh and new emerges. These are the ways of the soul!

THE PHENOMENOLOGY OF SOULFULNESS

I would like to sum up this chapter by describing various aspects of soulfulness. Remember that soul is too expansive to be defined; we can only describe aspects of soulfulness.

We must approach soul phenomenologically. Phenomenology is a method of thinking whereby we turn a topic all around and let it reveal itself to us. We look at our topic from all angles, letting each reveal something. For example, we can never see the whole earth all at once, but we can describe our experience of each part of it. In a similar way I offer my understanding of some major aspects of soulfulness:

Shame as limits
Open to the ordinary
Understanding and accepting polarity
Living in the present
Freedom
Unexpected and unusual
Love as process
Numinous
Exuberance
Symbolic
Spiritual

Shame As Limits

Healthy shame describes our essential humanness, guarding us against trying to be more than human (shameless) or less than human (shameful). Nietzsche said that shame is the source of spirituality and that it safeguards the spirit. What this means to me is that healthy shame lets us know that we are not absolute in any way—that we are not God. Healthy shame keeps us truthful and humble. Without such awareness we try to play God. We set ourselves up as the measure. We make our feelings, needs, thoughts, and fantasies the standards by which reality is judged. Once we standardize human experience, we take away its depth. We make absolutes by which we measure all other humans. Shame is our fundamental boundary. Awareness of healthy shame is the core of soulful living.

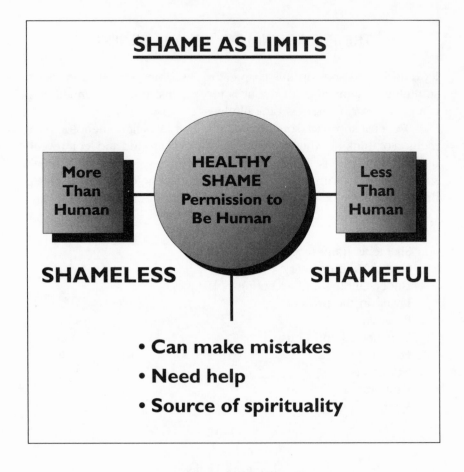

SHAME AS LIMITS

More Than Human

HEALTHY SHAME
Permission to Be Human

Less Than Human

SHAMELESS   **SHAMEFUL**

- **Can make mistakes**
- **Need help**
- **Source of spirituality**

Open to the Ordinary

When we live soulfully, we are grounded in ordinary life. Things are valuable, because they are. To be open to the ordinary is to focus on being. "Being," according to the philosopher Jacques Maritain, "is that victorious thrust by which we triumph over nothingness." Openness to the ordinary is the childlike quality of wonder. Each piece of reality is special and wondrous. For a child the world is brand new every moment of every day.

Understanding and Accepting Polarity

When we accept things as they are, we accept all of reality. Reality is polarity. Healthy shame grounds us in polarity. There is no sound without silence, no light without darkness, no life without suffering

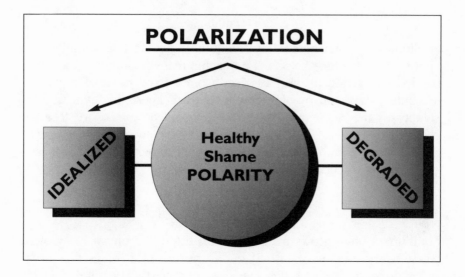

and death, no one who has no faults. All human behavior is a possibility. There is a potential Hitler and a potential Mother Teresa in us all. *Polarity keeps us from polarization.* It says that there is value in both sides of the coin. When we magnify one side of the coin, we go to one extreme and reject the other. This is polarization. Awareness of polarity keeps us from rigidity and absolutes.

We need to be conscious of polarity both in others and in ourselves. Jung called the opposite that everyone possesses their shadow side. Shadow work and shadow awareness is an important operation of soulfulness. Our own shadow is often the richest and most profound part of ourselves.

Living in the Present

It is a mark of soulfulness to be present in the here and now. When we are present, we are not fabricating inner movies. We are seeing what is before us. We are not making up stories in our head about other things or persons, we are hearing what others are saying and the way they are saying it. When we respond, we do so in a congruent way. Congruence means that the content (the words we say) is consistent with the process (the way we say the words, our tone of voice, facial expression, body posture, etc.). Conguence allows for real contact. Mystified people tend to be either confused with others or in conflict with them. Soulfulness leads to *contact* with reality.

Freedom

Soulfulness is characterized by freedom. When we live soulfully, we choose our own life projects. We imagine many possibilities, because we are not fixated in the past. Free from a fixed point of view, we are able to view many alternatives. The stuckness, frozenness, and rigidity of the deep trance defenses are released. We are free to respond to the real; we are operating in the living, vivid present. Soulful living is about acting in the present rather than reacting and overreacting to echoes of the past.

Unexpected and Unusual

Soulfulness often grows from the unexpected and unusual. My own worst happenings have turned out to be the best things that have ever happened. Persons that I've least expected to be significant in my life have been very significant (often only in retrospect). A friend of mine named Norris who drove me to the state hospital when I committed myself for alcoholism was himself a very sick alcoholic. I had committed him two years earlier. He may have even taken me to the state hospital as revenge! His motive doesn't matter. What Norris did led me to the major decision that changed my life! It was a true kairos time.

Love As Process

Love involves passion, hard work, and courage. It is a process, and it is often ambiguous and stormy.

Love is constantly developing and deepening. Expansion is its very nature. There is no "happily ever after," because soulful love is always adjusting and balancing itself. It is never arrived at and finished once and for all.

Soulful love has polarity in it. It involves not only ecstasy, but also duration. Ecstasy alone will not build a solid foundation of love.

Soulful love fosters emotive warmth, but also the capacity for conflict. Without conflict, real differences cannot be negotiated and worked out.

To love soulfully we need to be accountable. That means we need to be responsible to our partner. At the same time we need to have the possibility of negotiating our own needs.

Love seldom works out exactly as we imagined it. It has its fateful twists and turns, its unexpected moments of neglect, its betrayals and painful periods of growth.

Numinous

The numinous refers to what is mysterious in life. It refers to depth and sacredness. In his now-famous treatise *The Idea of the Holy,* Rudolph Otto looked into reported experiences of theophanies (the appearances of God). He found that every reported experience of God has two components—awe and fascination. The experience of awe involved fear and terror. The experience of fascination involved desire and obsession. One was drawn in holy terror to the experienced reality. Otto called this experience the "numinous."

In soulful living one encounters the numinous in many ways. There is an aura of fate and mystery surrounding every human being. No human life can be defined and captured by adjectival modifiers. There is a sense of sacredness in all created being. Every being has a depth to it. Life is awesome; it calls us to deeper involvement.

Exuberance

Being soulful does not always involve high-spiritedness and enthusiasm, but it often does. Children embody exuberance in its purest form. They are full of life, joy, and spirit. They are full of spontaneity and interest. They live every minute of every day. Their energy seems insatiable.

Exuberance expresses polarity. Children are the best models of this—they belly laugh and roll on the floor, they weep and sob, and they move through these emotions cleanly. A few minutes after sobbing, they may be laughing and playing. All of us need to reconnect with our original sense of exuberance. I was exuberant many times over the last three years. Many times I spontaneously did things and bought things without any plan or overall design. Spontaneity is often a part of exuberance, as is playfulness.

Exuberance is also expressed in laughter and joy. A sense of humor is a mark of healthy shame. We don't have to take life so seriously.

Symbolic

Soulfulness thrives in the sea of symbolism. A symbol is multilayered—it has many levels of meaning. Symbols are holistic. They capture the fullness of being without reducing it to closed linear concepts. Many people were outraged when protesters burned the American flag because that piece of cloth has become a symbol of revolution, courage, the willingness to die for democracy, the pioneering spirit, new frontiers, the rights of all human persons. I could go on and on. A symbol is like a pebble dropped into a pond—its ripples keep extending. A symbol is inexhaustible, because it flows from the imagination.

Imagination sees, hears, and feels new depths of possibility. Imagination is the ground of freedom. When we are unable to imagine, we lose contact with possibility. One way to look at the addicts, the criminals, the "lost souls" we encounter in modern life, is to see them as having lost their imagination. They have no more sense of meaning and, therefore, no sense of hope.

Spirituality

Soulfulness leads to spirituality. Spirituality is a state of fullness, an amplitude. With spirituality we see with a larger vision. The whole comes into view. We grasp what the philosophers call the "coincidence of opposites." We see things holistically, not as objectified parts. We have reverence for all things, and reverence pervades our life. Reverence means "to see a world in a grain of sand," as Blake wrote. Every aspect of the creation is wonderful and sacred.

Spirituality celebrates life and is in awe of higher powers. Some call the Higher Power God. Whatever we call the Higher Power, we believe that there is something or someone greater than ourselves. We are thankful for our life and feel like praising the Higher Power.

Spirituality leads us to service and solitude. We care for our fellows and take action to show it. We have a love for ourselves. We care for our own life. We love others as an expansion of our own life. We understand that by giving we receive. We grasp that by lighting others' candles, we do not lose our own light. The more candles one lights, the more enlightened the world becomes.

Soulfulness leads us to the realization that spirituality is our human destiny. To be fully human is to be fully spiritual. We are spiritual by nature. We are not material beings trying to become spiritual. We are spiritual beings on a human journey. Soul sees the depth of spirituality in everything and in everyone.

CHAPTER 6

Demystification— The Realistic Imagination

Behind all the forms of mental illness there seems to lie a generalized image of the human self as darkly unworthy and no good. It is a deep fantasy and a deep conviction that gets into everything men do.

WILLIAM LYNCH

Increase in imagination is always an increase in soul.

THOMAS MOORE

"I think I'm finally *waking* up. I'm finally getting some sense of what it takes to love someone." I heard a person make this statement at a 12-step meeting recently. It attests to what I call demystification. Demystification is a process of waking up to the facts that surround us—especially the facts about people we relate to and interact with. When our mind is no longer fixated in the past, we can fix our attention on what is really before us. Really seeing and hearing others as they *are* is crucial if we want to love them.

THE FIVE FREEDOMS

The great family therapist Virginia Satir used to say that when people are highly functional they have five freedoms available to them. They have the freedom to:

- See and hear what they see and hear rather than what they are supposed to see and hear

- Think what they think rather than what they are supposed to think

- Feel what they feel rather than what they are supposed to feel

- Want what they want rather than what they are supposed to want

- Imagine what they imagine rather than what they are supposed to imagine

Demystification is about coming out of the isolation of our self-to-self trance and owning these five freedoms. We see and hear what we see and hear rather than creating positive and negative hallucinations based on what is safe to see and hear. We think what we think rather than staying confused or thinking what we are supposed to think. We feel our own feelings rather than numbing out or taking care of someone else's feeling. We want what we want rather than what they say we should want. And we imagine our own possibilities rather than always playing out our rigid role.

These five freedoms constitute our self-connectedness. We are no longer in a defensive network of deep trance phenomena when we exercise the five freedoms. We are alive and awake, dealing with things as they are.

Earlier I described my loneliness in a Philadelphia hotel room, when the person I was in a relationship with felt that she had to break it off. She felt she was losing herself in me. She pointed to my lack of interest in the concrete issues of her life.

My first response was my old mystified response. I started defending myself, thinking immediately about all the fabulous things I had done for her. I especially focused on the money I had spent.

Many aspects of mystification come from particular facts about one's childhood—like the fact that in my family we never had any money to spend for anything except the basic survival needs. So one way my mystified wounded child feels he is acting loving is by giving expensive presents. To that part of me, giving things that cost a lot of money is a *big* act of love.

Obviously, this behavior can be a part of loving someone, but it is not love itself. And in my case, I woke up to the fact that partly what I was doing was buying time with my gifts. I have been very busy lecturing, writing, and traveling, and when I come home after a trip, I feel exhausted. But my need to please often smothers my need to just be quiet and have space. In my mystified upbringing to ask for what you needed was often met with irritability and aggravation. I learned to repress my needs. Over time I lost contact with them.

The couple of weeks we were separated woke me up to a lot. I realized that my lady friend couldn't be a mind reader about when I needed to be alone. I'd have to tell her. And I also woke up to the fact that I was paying too little attention to *her* life and needs. She has a very responsible and demanding job. My mystified inner child has been so enamored of all my celebrity goings-on that I had been neglectful in supporting her in her work. She had asked that we go to therapy together for a few clarifying sessions. I had refused, believing she was exaggerating the problem. I was using my deep trance of negative hallucination. *I was not hearing her needs* and *I was not seeing the pain on her face*. As a boy, my family system role was to caretake my mother's pain. When I couldn't take it anymore, I used negative hallucination as a way to protect myself.

Waking up helped me to see the *facts* about my relationship. I spent several days clarifying what I wanted for myself and what I was willing to give her. I proposed my new commitment to her. It included working with a therapist that she chose. This may seem like a small thing to you, but it was mammoth to me. I had to give up control and open myself to new learning—on her terms.

The shock of her deciding to end the relationship and the weeks of separation helped me demystify. In our two years of being together I had unconsciously fallen back into an old deep trance defense. The crisis forced me to *look* at the actual situation of our relationship. It forced me to view things differently and to *imagine* other real possibilities for our relationship. Crisis is one of the major ways that demystification takes place. Crisis causes pattern interruption. The habituated way we are behaving clearly isn't working anymore! A new way of behaving must be sought. The new way requires *imagination*. It demands that we look at other possibilities and other points of view. The imagining activity is a function of freedom. Imagining creates the context for new choices.

Crisis is one way demystification occurs. There are many other ways.

PATTERN INTERRUPTIONS

"It is the awareness, the full experience of how you are stuck that makes you recover," wrote Fritz Perls, the founder of Gestalt therapy.

This kind of awareness is most often the result of therapeutic intervention. A good therapist helps a person experience how they keep themselves stuck in a mystified state. Wolinsky states that he learned to observe his clients as they put themselves into a trance. I can think of a recent example of this. A woman was talking to me at a workshop. She began with a negative statement about herself. "I'm so stupid, I've done it again." She then broke eye contact with me and looked down at the floor. She said, "I know you think I'm really messed up." She held her breath and then continued, "I'm so confused, I don't even know what I wanted to ask you." At that point, she blushed and stood in frozen silence. As far as I'm concerned, she had put herself into a trance. She came to me for advice. But when she looked at me she did not see my face; she saw a parent's face (positive hallucination). She then heard an internalized parental voice, "You're so stupid," which began the trance induction. She lost all contact with me (broke eye contact) and began her self-to-self transaction. She went into her sensory numbing and confusion. She felt shame and humiliation and stood frozen.

I did not have time to work with her but I asked one of the facilitators to get her into "up time." This involves having the person look at you, breathe deeply, and answer matter-of-fact questions, such as "What color is my shirt?" "Where are you right now?" "Can you hear my voice?" These questions bring the person back into present time and restore the interpersonal bridge. Getting someone in "up time" does not completely demystify their trance state. But it does take them out of overwhelm.

Demystification takes time. But any pattern interruption is a good beginning. The goal of demystification is to operate in present reality, to see what you see and hear what you hear without distortion from the mystified wounded inner child. Demystification is best accomplished by restoring the interpersonal bridge. The mystified state began with a self-to-other transaction which turned into a self-to-self transaction. This needs to be reversed. New insight and awareness come when the interpersonal bridge is restored. The interaction with another is most powerfully done in a living, vivid present interpersonal transaction. But pattern interruption can take many forms, and I'll describe a number of them here.

Reading

Because you are reading this book, I'd like to affirm that many people have had an "Ah ha!" experience reading a book. I've had several breakthroughs into my own mystification by reading someone's presentation of how dysfunction occurs. As you read my book we enter into a personal relationship. That's why I tell you my personal stories. I've also told these stories in my PBS television series.

The great thing about a book or a TV video is that it can be read or seen before, during, and after one has started to change. And change is what it's all about.

Reading is a great supplement, but you can't become fully demystified until you take action. I can bear personal witness to gaining insights and staying stuck. I love the catharsis of intellectual insight and I love to head-trip, but it can also be a very costly form of mood alteration and denial.

Lectures and Workshops

I've also had profound experiences in lectures and workshops. And I get hundreds of testimonial letters concerning the power of my workshops to transform people's lives. The transformation comes from pattern interruptions that start the demystification process. I have put on a workshop for healing the wounded inner child for the last seven years. I have letters stating that the work has effected permanent change in their lives. I personally was puzzled by the power of this work until I began to grasp the phenomenon of mystification. By going directly to the stuck energy, imagined symbolically as one's inner child, we can create an immediate pattern interruption. Not everyone has a profound experience in the workshops, but most everyone experiences a pattern interruption.

There is a tremendous value in large groups working together. Each person is aware that all the others are there for the same reasons. The wounded inner child had no allies as a child. Violence in childhood creates isolation and loneliness. When large groups of people work together, they provide protection and support for one another. In my workshops, therapists are always available, but my therapist-facilitators constantly marvel at how well people can take care of themselves if we provide an environment of safety.

A large emphasis in current clinical work is on the power that is in the patient. Trust your own experience. Don't be discouraged if the first thing you try doesn't work for you. Talk to those who have been to workshops and who have had powerful demystification experiences.

Individual Therapy

For some people, going to a therapist may be their first real experience of a good relationship. Martin Buber, the great Jewish theologian, felt that what really brings about healing in therapy is the relationship between the therapist and the patient. True therapeutic demystification occurs because the interpersonal bridge is restored. A bond of trust is created, and some form of transference takes place. Transference means that the client usually sees in the therapist some of the positive and negative qualities of their source figures. As the therapist truly *cares* for the person, the old violent scenarios are replaced with new nurturing ones and the trance defenses are given up. The client can then feel safe enough to feel their original pain. As a person feels their own feeling, they reconnect with themselves.

There are other ways that therapy works. Steven Wolinsky works on creating pattern interruptions as he sees the person forming their trance. He maintains a strong interpersonal bridge as he does his process interruption work.

Milton Erickson had multiple approaches to entering his subject's trance. Few have been able to duplicate his imaginative genius. In fact nothing stands out more in Erickson's work than the range of his imagination. He rarely treated two people with similar symptoms the same way. He entered the unique circumstances of each person's trance in order to interrupt it.

One of his many famous case histories is of a woman in Milwaukee who had been depressed for nine months. This woman was very religious, independently wealthy, and reclusive. Erickson was asked to pay her a visit. He agreed and went to see the woman. He asked her to take him on a tour of her house. He writes:

> In looking around I saw she was a very wealthy woman
> living alone, idle, attending church but keeping to herself
> ... and I saw three African violet plants and a potting pot

with a leaf in it being sprouted as a new plant. So I knew
what I had to do for her in the way of therapy.

Erickson told the woman to buy a couple hundred gift pots for African violets. He told her that she was to grow new African violets and
that whenever there was an announcement of a child's birth in her
church she was to send an African violet. She was to do the same
for every christening, for every engagement, for every wedding, for
every sickness, for every death, for every church bazaar.

Within six months this woman was written up in a newspaper
article as the African Violet Queen of Milwaukee. She had endless
numbers of new friends, and her depression had gone away.

Erickson noted two areas in the naturally occurring events of
her life where she had lots of energy. One was going to church, and
the other was growing African violets. Erickson knew that taking care
of two hundred African violet plants would require a lot of energy
and that giving the plants as gifts would lead to friendly interactions,
which would create interpersonal bridges. He met the Milwaukee
lady at her map of the world. He entered her trance state, found the
elements that had life in them, put those elements together, and
awakened her entranced life. This is brilliant work. It required sharp
sensory observation, and it required that Erickson be totally *present*
to the depressed woman's reality.

Another very powerful model of pattern interruption is Neuro
Linguistic Programming (NLP). The NLP creators have developed various tools for interrupting the frozen states of mystification that I've
been describing.

One of NLP's most powerful tools is called "reframing." I like
the example of a reframing that Leslie Cameron Bandler used to help
a critical mother who obsessively ranted and raved at her children
about keeping the house immaculate. Bandler, who is one of the
pioneers of NLP, had the critical woman close her eyes and take a
fantasy journey through her house noting the immaculate condition
of things. When she came to the living room, Bandler said something
like "Look at your perfect rug, smooth like a sea of glass, without a
footprint, telling you that *no one else is home.* There is no one there
to mess anything up. *You are all alone.*"

At that point the woman started to sob. Leslie had reframed her
immaculate rug. Now, instead of symbolizing a neat living room, it
presented her with her loneliness. The children hated to come home.
They stayed away as much as possible. This reframe had the effect
of suddenly breaking the pattern of our critical lady's habitual way

of thinking. In a flash it revealed a new meaning and changed her consciousness.

Confrontation

Good therapists often confront their clients. This can be done in several ways. I remember a woman who was locked into a miserable and shaming job. Her trance went back to childhood. It was constituted by her mother's hypervigilant anxiety and by constant messages of terror about the threat of the outside world. A dominant family message, which operated like a posthypnotic suggestion, was "Don't take any risks, hold on to what you've got." She finally got to the point where her shame bottomed out. She desperately sought therapeutic help. As she talked to the therapist, she was stunned by the *look* on the therapist's face as the therapist said to her, "And you've stayed in this job all these years." Suddenly the woman was demystified. She saw reflected in the mirror of the therapist's face, the tragedy of what she had done to herself and how entranced she was. She made a decision to leave the job.

Intervention

The technique of intervention is very useful in treating addicts and breaking down the walls of trance denial. The trance denial is usually constituted by dissociation from one's actions, by negative hallucinations (not seeing the effect of one's irresponsible behavior), and by amnesia (forgetting the past destructive actions that the addiction caused). Addicts are in a trance. They seem to have no control over the repeated cycles of the addiction. This is *because of the trance*. When you are in a trance, it feels like you have no control over your actions.

An intervention is best done when the addict has just acted out or is experiencing the consequences of their out-of-control behavior.

The players in the intervention are the addict's significant others: spouse, children, parents, boss, best friends—as many as possible. Some professional or member of the appropriate 12-step group needs to be present also.

Each significant person gives the addict concrete specific data about an irresponsible incident which was a consequence of their addiction and in which the significant person was involved. Each begins with the concrete data describing the incident and ends by saying, "I love you and I think you're a ———— addict and in serious need of help." The last person to speak is the professional or the 12-step member, who offers to put the person in a treatment center or take them to a 12-step meeting immediately.

The impact of this kind of intervention has been profound. Many persons have stopped their addictive behavior at that very moment. Being confronted with the faces of one's loved ones and the data of one's addiction often breaks the self-to-self trance of mystification. The *group* of significant others plays a major role in the impact.

Small Group Therapy

Although I practiced one-to-one counseling for twenty-two years, I personally believe that, when done by a skillful facilitator, small group therapy has a greater potential for demystification. I have personally had very powerful experiences in groups, and I have also had some real breakthroughs in one-to-one counseling.

I do not want to give a blanket endorsement for group therapy, as I know people who have had bad experiences there. It all depends on the skill of the therapist who is facilitating the group.

The most important requirement for a group facilitator is a high level of soulfulness. Therapy is more an art than a science. Good group therapists know how to let go of ego control and let the group process unfold naturally. This requires that the therapist have good boundaries. With good boundaries, a therapist can handle silences by refusing to talk, lecture, or explain. This forces the group to take responsibility for itself. With good boundaries, a therapist can confront delusion and denial and refuse to fix others' feelings. An effective therapist creates an environment of safety. The safer the environment is, the less the group members need their defensive trances. Group therapy has more power to demystify than one-to-one therapy because groups provide more faces to give mirroring feedback. Groups provide more ways *to restore the interpersonal bridge*.

These factors make group therapy a powerful way to interrupt the isolation of the self-to-self trance state. The self-nourishing fantasies that the trance state maintains are easily interrupted by the self-to-other transactions with group members.

12-Step Groups

A very special kind of group with great power to demystify is the 12-step group. Literally millions of alcoholics and coalcoholics are living rich and fruitful lives because of Alcoholics Anonymous (AA) and

ALANON. These 12-step groups began when Bill W. and Dr. Bob, two chronic alcoholics living in isolation and self-to-self trances, turned to each other and created a supporting interpersonal relationship. Gradually, others joined and their dyad developed a full-fledged community of recovering alcoholics, which is now called AA. Through people getting together in meetings and sharing their experience in working the 12 steps, AA has become a powerful force in demystifying alcoholics around the world and rescuing them from the isolated throes of alcoholism.

Many other types of 12-step meetings have evolved from the AA and ALANON originals. Adult Children of Alcoholics (ACA) and Co-dependents Anonymous (CODA) are the most appropriate groups for working on healing the mystified wounded inner child.

The 12-step groups have great therapeutic impact on people, but the process is quite different than the process of group therapy. The 12-step groups have no official facilitator. People simply share their "experience, strength, and hope" in relation to the problem the specific group is dealing with, such as alcoholism or overeating.

In fact, you need to be wary of 12-step gurus, people who act like they are an authority on the problem. There are no authorities in 12-step groups. You can select a person who seems to be working a strong program and ask them to be your *sponsor*. A sponsor is a model and a guide. I chose my sponsor, a man named Fran, because he was a university professor. I needed someone I could identify with, as I was a university professor at the time. I was also hiding in my intellect, as Fran quickly pointed out.

Fran took me to many meetings of different groups during my first three months of sobriety. We went to groups in wealthy neighborhoods, groups of mostly businessmen, mixed groups, groups of poor folks who had hit rock bottom. The important thing in the 12-step process is identification. This meant I had to find a group where I could identify with the background and life experiences of the people there. I had a hard time with the wealthy people's group and a hard time with the skid row folks. I finally found a half dozen groups that I felt comfortable in. They spoke to my experience. Certainly not every aspect of it, as very few could share the shame and loneliness I experienced over my drinking in the seminary. But I heard enough to know I was in the right place.

Sometimes meetings are sharings about themes, such as "resentment" or "anger and rage"; sometimes they are step discussions, with members sharing how they worked the particular step in question.

In the early days, I was often lost when people shared about the steps. This is where my sponsor came in. He would explain the step to me and offer certain guidelines for taking the step. All in all, Fran was a wise and gentle teacher, modeling everything that he spoke about. I honor him as a "soul mentor" of the first degree.

There is no cross talk in 12-step meetings. Cross talk is about clarifying what others say, validating feelings, or confronting what is being shared. Cross talk is appropriate in group therapy. In 12-step groups each person's experience is acceptable as is.

The whole dynamic in 12-step groups leads to healthy shame and polarity. There is *no one right way*. Nothing is *literalized or standardized*. The only requirement for membership is an honest desire to stop the soul-marring addiction you are acting out. It is not even required that you work all the 12 steps!

Life Experiences

People also experience pattern interruptions and become demystified by virtue of life experience. The death of an old friend, the death of a parent, reaching one's 40th birthday, losing a job all challenge the narrow limits of our mystified state.

Sometimes over the years we just get sick and tired of being sick and tired. The "same old same old" becomes so boring that we seek other ways of living. Sometimes our patterns are interrupted by being with someone who thinks and feels and does things very differently. This other person shows us new choices for living.

The natural growth we experience in moving through the life cycle may also cause us to re*view* our life. Aging leads to larger vision. Just moving toward old age may force us to demystify certain beliefs. Older couples often seem to have found soulfulness. They have learned from their life experience. They have awakened from their trance and learned new and effective ways to love each other.

Any kind of trauma can be an occasion of demystification. Serious accidents may pattern interrupt in profound ways. The death of a loved one may change our life forever. Any serious illness or near death experience may cause us to look at life in a brand-new way. From the soul's point of view trauma may bring a new passion to our love. Trauma may change the habitual patterns and force us to reevaluate what is important and what is not.

Religious Conversion

William James wrote about the kind of religious belief that flows from what he called the twice born. The twice born are those that have had genuine religious conversions. They have had profound experiences that wake them up to a whole new way of seeing reality. Religious conversion comes in many forms. For some it is a personal encounter with what they interpret as the divine. For others, it is a miraculous cure or answer to a prayer. Augustine heard a voice in the next-door garden that said, "Take up and read. Take up and read." He picked up the Bible and read the exact admonition that touched upon the lascivious life he was leading. The experience changed his life. James also spoke of the once born who choose to love God profoundly right away. I'll discuss the once-born in Chapter 9.

I'm speaking here about experiences that break people out of rigidity and stagnant life-styles. Not all religious conversions do this. Some conversions are themselves mystified. I see cultic-type religions as a form of mystified faith. The devotees of a cult often claim to have powerful spiritual experiences. I believe their experience is more like *going into* a trance than coming out of one. In fact, my belief is that a lot of religious conversions are "snapping" experiences, like the ones I described in Chapter 2.

For me, true religious conversion demystifies. Our life becomes more spiritual. We become more open and loving. We expand our life-style and are more free and more creative.

Natural Mystical Experience

Sometimes just the profound experience of beauty can effect a change in consciousness. I once saw an exhibition of Vincent van Gogh's paintings in Toronto. I was awestruck. I stayed in the museum for five hours. I couldn't believe a man could create such beauty with oil and canvas. I saw another depth to life in the beauty of his paintings, and I had an encounter with van Gogh's soulfulness. He showed me images and intensities of color I had never seen before. When I left, the colors remained in my soul. My horizons were stretched. My vision was expanded.

People report soulful experiences with the world of natural beauty. Gazing at an ocean, a starry sky, or a mountain view, walking through a garden and seeing flowers in bloom, observing wildlife and the multiplicity of created species. Natural beauty can shake us

from our mystified slumber and awaken us to the expanse and trea-
sures of being.

Pain and Suffering in Relationships

Relational crises can be the vehicles that help people out of their
trance. Living with someone who is inflicting physical, sexual, and
emotional pain will eventually lead to a last straw. The last straw may
be the day you are beaten or humiliated in public, the day he beats
the children, the night she brings the neighbor in for sex. Any event
can be the last straw, and people have their own unique tolerance
levels.

It's sad that seriously abusive relationships have to go on until
they reach the nadir of humiliation and sometimes great tragedy.
Victimization and offender behavior are complementary trance states.
Victims and offenders come out of the same stockpile of shame;
people can go either way depending on their make-up and the intensity of the abuse. Often it takes extreme crisis to break the trance.

Separation

Earlier, I mentioned that my recent brief separation helped me out
of my slip into demystification. Separation can be a useful tool in
demystifying partners. As a counselor, I've been involved in several
marriages where a therapeutic separation helped both partners see
the facts of their situation.

Sometimes one of the partners was taking the other for granted
and could not see how this partner's needs had changed over the
years. The shock of separation can break down the trance defenses
of positive and negative hallucinations. One person I worked with
truly *heard* his wife's cry of loneliness during the separation. He saw
how thin and emaciated she looked. Another client gave up her fantasy of her husband as a wimp when he initiated the separation. She
heard his words as he set a firm boundary about her affair. In both
cases reconciliation was achieved.

Demystification does not always bring a couple back together.
Sometimes demystification leads to a divorce. Both partners see the
hidden contract their mystified inner kids have made. They realize
(come out of the trance) how their marriage reenacted their family
of origin relationships. They see how they made an unconscious pact

of nonintimacy, and they decide to divorce. The divorce may even
be amicable and growth producing. Mine certainly has been.

Divorce

Divorce can also be catastrophic. Couples get caught in the very
mystification that got them together. They rage at each other like they
wish they could have raged at their source figures. Since neither has
finished their grief work, the couple gets stuck at one of the stages of
grief. Often the stuck level is anger. The divorce never gets resolved.

The shock of divorce is frequently a powerful demystification.
We are forced to confront our unrealized dreams and expectations.
All the unrealistic fantasies come tumbling down. The disappointment is terrible. Often people go for therapy at this point, realizing
that something is very wrong with their beliefs about love and
relationship.

Divorce is often more life enhancing than the long-suffering,
self-negating endurance marriages we looked at in Chapter 1. The
soul emerges from pain and disruption. Once the grief work is done,
a new kind of life can emerge. A life that is more realistic, more
human, and, hence, more soulful.

Personal Encounters

An encounter with certain persons can awaken us. A certain love can
be a life-transforming experience. People say things like, "I'm sorry
it had to end, but my life will never be the same," or "So-and-so
taught me a lot. We had some very tough times but I learned from
her. I'm grateful for that relationship."

Perhaps you can remember a teacher who touched your life in
a special way. I am a teacher, and I love it when students I taught
in high school write me about their experiences in my classroom.
Sometimes I've gotten letters from those I least expected. I had no
idea I had impacted that person's life. I didn't think I had influenced
them at all. These are the ways of soulfulness. We are often the
condition of salvific change in another and we often don't know it.
Teachers especially have the possibility of awakening people from
their trance. One of the first great teachers was Socrates. He was
described as a gadfly who stung the youth of Athens into new
awareness.

Most folks can think of some person who was a source of grace
in their life. I think of Father David Belyea, a great priest in the

Basilian order. He challenged me theologically. He expanded my horizons. He also was my confessor. At a time when I felt like a rotten bag of shame, he called me to my lovableness. He refused to let me go on with my less-than-human self-contempt and self-denigration. He gently and continually called me to love myself.

I think of an Episcopalian priest, Reverend Charles Wyatt Brown. He heard me speak at a 12-step meeting. He has a soulful ability to see a person's depth and worth, and he is a man of great love and compassion. He asked me to come to Palmer Episcopal Church in Houston, and he took me into his church amid criticism and skepticism. What he saw in me I did not see. But it was there, and, with his support, my power began to unfold. I lectured at Palmer for twenty years in adult theology. It was at a Palmer Sunday lecture that Liz Kaderli, a participant in the class, saw the possibility of my doing a TV series for PBS. That was the beginning of my TV work.

Those persons saw the depths of my soul in a way I never did. Their faith and love called me to my deeper resources.

IMAGINATION AS THE FACULTY OF TRANSFORMATION

In every example I have given, mystification is reduced by some pattern interruption that creates a context for new possibilities. Finding new possibilities is primarily the work of the imagination. To create soulfulness we need lots of imagination. Soulfulness demands that we have reverence for the value and *depth* of all things. *To see the depth we need imagination.*

To be soulful we also need to be free. Mystification is rigid and unfree. When we are awakened, we have new flexibility and creativity. Imagination makes creative choices possible. Love will demand that we negotiate and choose new ways of behaving. To truly love we must be conscious and free. Freedom uses imagination as its eyes. Seeing alternatives allows us to choose. Without the ability to imagine new ways of being and behaving, we would have no choice.

Other animals seem to lack imagination; they act out their predetermined, instinctual behaviors. This is why newborn animals seem to be stronger than newborn humans. Their genetic code governs their survival. This is not true for us humans. At birth we are the most powerless of all animal species. But because we are the least determined by instinct, we have the potential to be the highest of all life forms. As evolution progressed, each new life form was less determined by instinct. Human life is the least determined of all and, therefore, the most free. Imagination is the faculty that allows us this privilege.

Mystified love is unimaginative. There is one way to love and it is the norm by which all loving behavior is viewed. Soulful love is limited only by the restraints of human nature.

Think of a painting by one of the great masters. It is limited by the nature of oil, paintbrushes, and canvas. But when we compare a Monet and a van Gogh, we are amazed at the differences.

Our ability to imagine well is not a given. Some may have a greater natural endowment for imagining well. Some of us learn this from the modeling and teaching of our source figures. But all of us can learn to use our imagination better.

Fantastic vs. Realistic Imagination

Thomas Moore tells us that "any increase in imagination is always an increase in soul." But it must be true human imagining—what I will call the realistic imagination—in order to foster soulfulness. Inadequate or fantastic imagining is the essence of mystification. The realistic imagination is rooted in the limits of human nature. The fantastic imagination is rooted in the inhuman. The realistic imagination is grounded in healthy shame. The fantastic imagination is grounded in shamelessness and shamefulness. The fantastic imagination asks us to be either "more than human" (to feel ourselves perfect, blameless, flawless) or "less than human" (to bask in imperfection and failure). The more-than-human imagination plays God. The less-than-human imagination makes failure a virtue.

The more-than-human imagination creates narrow systems like Puritanism. This kind of morality is based on the *image* of a goodness devoid of pleasure and joy. Another form of more-than-human fantasy is the mystified love of martyrdom and self-negation. Mystified martyrdom is a kind of grandiosity. It is, as Shaw observed, "the only way in which a man can become famous without ability." These more-than-human fantasies can elevate a person to inhuman heights, giving them a sense of righteousness and goodness which is addictive and mood elevating.

True martyrs, in contrast, require a realistic imagination to fuel their courage. To be a martyr one must be able to passionately envision the object of love one is dying for.

The less-than-human kind of fantasy is also a cop-out. It allows one to have self-definition and esteem by despising oneself. Nietzsche wrote, "He who despises himself esteems himself as a self despiser."

There is a paradoxical kind of reverse grandiosity in being a self-despiser. *One becomes the best of the worst!* There is also an immense payoff in choosing to imagine oneself "less than human." Once we define ourselves as bums, no one expects anything of us. We can avoid taking any responsibility.

Both extremes are fantastic. They are out of proportion to a balanced human life. To be human is to be the focal point of ambiguity and paradox. Our motives are almost always mixed, our behaviors never pure. Righteousness is an extreme, a polarization. When righteousness comes, evil won't be far behind.

Fantasy Bonding

Fantastic imagining can ruin a person's life. I'm thinking of a woman whose father died when she was 2 years old. Throughout her childhood she was told that her father had loved her more than he had loved anyone else. She was told that her father was brilliant, a brooding genius. She was told that her father wrote beautiful poetry.

When the girl was 5 years old, her mother remarried. Her stepfather was cold and critical, often demeaning her physical appearance. She hated her stepfather and longed for a warm, nurturing father who would rescue her from him. She *fantasized* a reunion with her father. Her life became dominated by her image of a brilliant man, who held her and read her the love songs he had written about her. As a child, she consciously fantasized this. As she grew up and her reasoning developed, the fantasy continued to function unconsciously.

In real life, she continually tried to please her despised stepfather, looking for any sign of affection and stooping to humiliating levels to gain any morsel of his love.

When she reached her teenage years, she went through a series of fantasy attachments with guys who were basically unavailable. They were either not interested in her or already committed to someone else. The guys she actually dated were cold and emotionally abusive. The abuse made her fantasize more about a saviorlike man, who would shower her with love and take care of her for the rest of her life. This fantasy man, of course, never came to get her.

When she came to me for counseling, she was 52 years old. Her presenting problem was that she was trying to recapture a man who had jilted her. Her lover was highly intellectual and poetic. But he had, in her words, treated her like a dog. She wanted me to help her win him over!

It seemed clear to me that her major problem stemmed from the *core fantasy* I have described. This fantasy was unrealistic; it was based on an impossible situation. She really did not know her father. She had never heard, touched, or seen a man like the man she fantasized. She was bonded to a fantasy.

Such fantasy bonding is a true *bondage*. It causes a kind of imaginative closure. By that I mean the imagination loses contact with the real images of lived experience and turns in on itself. Rather than finding images related to real things that offer new possibilities of action, the fantastic imagination just imagines in a vacuum and creates inhuman images, which crush human possibility, creating a sense of hopelessness. It was Martin Buber who termed this kind of imagination the "fantastic imagination."

In my model fantastic imagining is the source of the grandiosity that dominates the life of the mystified. It creates the daydreams and the pipe dreams that continually set the person up for failure, shame, and disappointment. The "fantastic" imagination ultimately destroys wishing and leads to apathy. Since what the person wants cannot be obtained, the person loses all sense of hope. The fantastic imagination constantly imposes its unrealistic expectations upon the person's life. Fantastic images become the norms of fulfillment and happiness. Because the fantastic vision is not rooted in reality, the expectation is *never* fulfilled.

In Part Three, we will see this type of dysfunctional imagining at work in all areas of mystified relationships. We will look at examples of parents who are totally unrealistic in their expectations about their children's behavior. We will look at a mystified kind of faith in God, one that actually destroys our humanity. I will describe the split within ourselves that occurs when our life is governed by unrealistic fantasies of how we should be, rather than by a realistic acceptance of the way we actually are. And we will look at how our unrealistic expectations of ourselves are projected onto our friends, lovers, spouses, children, and work relationships.

Realistic Imagination

In Part Three, we will also look at realistic and loving alternatives to all of these mystified, unrealistic types of relationships.

What we need in order to live and relate soulfully is what Buber called a *realistic* imagination. A realistic imagination puts pieces of *actual human* experience together in new ways. It accepts the bare facts of our existence. I will keep reminding you that soulfulness is ultimately bound up with the *human*. The more human we are, the more we are in touch with our soul. Thus Thomas Moore writes, "Soul appears most easily in those places where we feel most inferior." Our healthy shame tells us that we are limited and that we will make mistakes. "Life is trouble, Boss," as Zorba tells his professor friend, and soul appears when our rigid rules break down. And as I hope I can show you, soul is most pregnant and ready to be born in relationships, since we can't be human without them. We cannot save our soul, much less find it, alone.

This distinction between the fantastic and realistic imagination is crucial if we are to understand how to transform mystification into soulfulness. Many forms of neurotic illness are created by the fantastic imagination. Some emotionally ill people cannot imagine realistically.

Let me give another example of the distinction. At 55, single and divorced, with my children grown and gone, I felt a deep sense of depression and failure about marriage and my family. I spent a lot of time thinking of how the dinner table was never the scene of deep and attentive sharing, as I had dreamed of it being. I thought of the fact that my son never tugged at my pants and looked up at me with adoring eyes. I thought of how I often envisioned the family gathering around me on Christmas night to listen to my words of wisdom! And how I actually couldn't get anyone to pay attention to me for five minutes.

One day, feeling depressed and lonely, I shared this with a support group of male friends. Several others reported having the same disappointment. One guy finally asked, "Did any of you actually experience any of this in your own families growing up?" Not one person could answer yes. "Where did you get those fantasies?" he continued. I probed my memory. I really didn't know where they came from. I suppose I picked them up from movies or TV shows like "Ozzie and Harriet" and "Leave It to Beaver." In the light of my alcoholic family of origin's pain and sorrow, I fantasized a family life that was the exact opposite of what I had. As I spoke about it, it dawned on me that maybe such a life has *never existed in any family*. Maybe my family life, both as a child and as a father, was a lot like most people's family life.

Sure my dad's alcoholism, my parents' divorce, and our poverty made things more dramatic and more difficult than in a lot of other families. But, if each human being is unique, as different as a thumbprint, then there is no normative way for families to be and act. They are the way they are. Some have deeper scars, but all have some scars. I can certainly imagine a father who is at home a lot more than my father was. I can imagine a man who drinks in moderation. I can imagine a family sharing their feelings more spontaneously. But a family without problems! A family where everyone always thinks of everyone else! A family where Father's every word is cherished! That's unrealistic. As such, it is *inhuman* and it is the inhuman demands of such unrealistic expectations that make them so depressing and shaming.

I felt much better as I grasped this. I decided to plan something new for Christmas. I gave up all expectations about my children seeing me as the wise Buddha. I invited my best friends over Christmas night. They form my family of affiliation. I had a great Christmas dinner with my children and later that evening played games and sang carols with my support group. My kids actually wanted to join in. It may have been my best Christmas ever.

Hope, Possibility, and Freedom

In Part Three, imagination will be the tool I will use to suggest ways of transforming mystified behaviors into soulfulness. In each relationship category we will look at new possibilities for love. A realistic imagination will be my hammer and chisel.

CHAPTER 7

Reimagining Your Internalized Parents

It is not possible to live too long ... in the bosom of the family, without endangering one's psychic health. Life calls us forth to independence.

CARL JUNG

I thought I could describe a state; make a map of sorrow. Sorrow however turns out to be not a state but a process.

C. S. LEWIS

In order to create soulful relationships we need to finish our primary or source relationships. Source relationships include biological parents, stepparents, adopted parents, and surrogate parents, such as guardians, relatives, or anyone else who was significant in teaching you about loving relationships. Finishing our source relationships is the major step in transforming the wounded inner child's mystification. The process involves reimagining these relationships.

As I explained in detail in Part One, our source relationships are internalized. What that means is that they live on in us as complexes of kinesthetic, visual, and auditory images which are imprinted on our central nervous systems. We continue to be influenced by our earliest interactions with our parents. We hear their voices as our own internal self-talk. Those voices function like posthypnotic suggestions. They often govern our lives.

We carry governing scenes which represent the memories of all the painful, shaming interactions we had with our source figures. We also carry the memories of the most dramatically powerful nurturing interactions we had with them. The painful scenes are joined together by the hurt and sadness we felt when they were originally enacted. We developed deep trance phenomena as defenses against that unresolved hurt and pain. Whenever we experience an event that contains elements similar in *any* way to the original experience, the imprinted scene is triggered. It is triggered along with all the visual and auditory fragments that were connected with it. For example, a person's voice may sound similar to the voice of a source figure. When we hear it, we go back into the original trance state. So many troublesome transactions between persons are actually reenactments of scenes that took place long ago with our survival figures. Until we complete our source relationships, we will never be fully present in a current relationship. The unfinished business from the past becomes the baggage we carry into our current relationships. The anger, fear, and sadness that went unexpressed can bubble up unexpectedly in our present relationships. We must finish the past.

To finish the past, we must grieve. We have to give up the defenses that have protected us all these years. These defenses are our old familiar friends. They are the deep trance phenomena we described in Chapter 3. When we give them up, we must feel the pain we never fully felt as children. In doing this work we often feel as helpless as we did as children. We feel the old confusion. This is why this grief work is so frightening to us. But we must be willing to do it if we want to create love in our lives.

In my book *Homecoming: Reclaiming and Championing Your Inner Child*, I outlined a way to grieve our neglected developmental dependency needs. I want to make it clear that grieving is the beginning of the process, not an end in itself. I've been somewhat frustrated by the misconceptions around this point. It seems like some have gotten *stuck* in the grief work. They have focused on Part 2 of *Homecoming* and have overlooked Part 3 and Part 4. Part 3 presents a whole set of very practical corrective exercises that require time and hard work. These exercises help one unlearn dysfunctional rules and learn new skills of expressing anger safely and negotiating needs. Part 4 outlines the spiritual awakening and inner work that seems essential if one is to fully create soulful love. I recommend that book as one way to heal your wounded inner child.

In this chapter I will take you through a briefer process of grieving your internalized source relationships. This grief work amounts

THE SEPARATION–GRIEF PROCESS

STEP ONE: GRIEVING YOUR OWN GRIEF

STAGE ONE: **MOTHER/FATHER HUNGER**
Hurt and Sadness

STAGE TWO: **INRAGE TO OUTRAGE**
Embracing Your Mystified Inner Child
Making a Resource Anchor
Expressing Anger

STEP TWO: GRIEVING YOUR PARENTS' GRIEF

STAGE ONE: **DEMYTHOLOGIZING YOUR PARENTS**

STAGE TWO: **CHILD-TO-CHILD DIALOGUE**
Your Survival Figure as a Child

STAGE THREE: **FORGIVENESS**
Death and Burial

STEP THREE: BECOMING YOUR OWN PARENT

STAGE ONE: **HEADING YOUR OWN HOUSEHOLD**

STAGE TWO: **REMAPPING YOUR CHILDHOOD**
Pleasant Childhood Memories

to a process of separating your wounded child from his or her internalized source figures. What follows is an abbreviated version of my workshops on healing our mother and father wounds.

Look at the figure above. You can see that my model for doing the separation-grief process involves three steps. *You need to do the whole process with each significant source figure.* These steps are best worked through with *at least one other person present.* We need social support in doing this grief work. When we incurred our wounds in childhood, we had to bear them alone. The hard-and-fast condition of childhood abandonment and abuse is loneliness. To reexperience the feelings of that lonely, hurt child is very scary.

The social support you need for this work means that you must have at least _one_ person with whom you can share your feelings unguardedly—a person whom you trust and who will not shame you. The ideal situation is to be part of a group of people working on this with an experienced facilitator. The work _can_ be done with self-help group support only, but there are some qualifications. If you are currently working with a therapist, please get your therapist's permission to do this process. If you are in an active addiction, do not try doing this work until you've had ninety days without engaging in your primary addiction. If you've been diagnosed as mentally ill, do not do this process without your psychiatrist's permission. If you start doing this process and have feelings that frighten you, stop and consult with a professional therapist about your feelings. If you cannot afford a therapist, just stop doing the process.

These warnings are my way of telling you that the wounded little child in you is very vulnerable. The wounded child believes that if he or she separates from Mom and Dad, something terrible is going to happen. The wounded child believes that he or she _may even die._ The belief in the protection of our godlike parents is quite powerful, and that is why it's so hard to separate from them.

Yet the separation process is crucial if we truly want to create loving relationships in our life. Without separating from our internalized source figures, we contaminate all of our subsequent relationships with our unfinished issues. Let us look at the stages of the process.

STEP ONE: GRIEVING YOUR OWN GRIEF

Stage One: Mother/Father Hunger

Stage One focuses on our hurts. Although often unconsciously and unintentionally, our source figures hurt us. Whether _they intended to or not does not matter._ It doesn't matter whether what they did was just by some objective standard. What matters is that we experienced what they did as hurtful. The hurt caused us pain. The pain remains and will leak out into current relationships. It will come out as overreactions, in anger or rage, in negative behavior patterns, in age regressions. We need to make the hurt real. It needs to be validated and felt.

EXERCISE: HURT AND SADNESS

The general format that follows can be used for any of the emotional, physical, and sexual violations I outlined in Part One. Use this format for writing out the concrete details of specific episodes of abuse. Do the exercise with your support person.

The writing helps us connect with the feelings. Before actually doing the writing, find a place to relax. Insure that you won't be interrupted for at least one hour. Unplug the phone, close the door to the room you are in. Have your support person read this to you:

> Close your eyes.... Breathe deeply for three minutes.... Allow your memory to find a scene of violation. Remember you survived the actual event. *I'm asking you to deal with the memories*.... Once you've connected with a scene, open your eyes and write it out in as much detail as possible.

While you are writing, your support person should be with you, but not interrupt you. It's okay if they want to read or do something quiet, as long as they're available if you need them.

MOTHER:

(NOTE: Mother can stand for whoever was your primary maternal survival figure. It could be your biological mother, an adopted mother, a stepmother, a nanny, a grandmother, an older sister, an orphanage worker, etc.) You hurt me when:

1. _____

2. _____

3. _____

4. _____

Now go on to complete Step One and Step Two of the separation-grief process with your mother. Then come back to this exercise and begin the process with your father or primary paternal survival figure. If you had no father write about the hurt of abandonment and desertion of not having a father.

FATHER:
You hurt me when:

1. _____

2. _____

3. _____

4. _____

After you have again completed Steps One through Three with your father, come back and do the process with each of your other primary survival figures.

———— (another primary survival figure):
You hurt me when:

1. _____

2. _____

3. _____

4. _____

Here is an example taken from a male client who gave me permission to use it:

MOTHER (actually adopted mother):
You hurt me when:

1. You continually reminded me that I was adopted. You favored your natural child and suggested that I should understand why he got the new clothes and bigger shares of food and dessert.
2. You told me how fortunate I was to be adopted. You made me kneel and pray aloud, thanking God for you as my mom.
3. You called me names, like the time you called me selfish when I was playing with my blocks and my half-brother, Joe, knocked them down.

4. You were nervous all the time, so I had to walk on eggs around the house. You were sad about your life, and I had to make all A's in school so you could feel good about yourself.
5. You used me as the breadwinner after your divorce. You constantly pressured me to work after school and on weekends, telling me I owed it to you. I never had time to play and just be a kid.

Parenthetically, I'd like to share with you what so many adopted children have shared with me. Regardless of why parents gave up their children, adoption is a primal wound that *needs to be grieved.* No matter what the natural parents' intentions, the child's egocentricism interprets being given up for adoption as abandonment. No matter how nurturing the adoptive parents were, the wound needs to be grieved.

After each episode you write, take time to share it and to receive validation from your support person. The validation is essential to this process. You are attempting to feel the sadness and hurt and the longing for your source figures. In order to feel these feelings, you need validation. Validation helps legitimize your pain. It restores the interpersonal (self-to-other) bridge and thereby relieves your isolation. With validation, you have a mirroring face to be reflected in.

Take deep breaths and look at your support person frequently as you share your episodes. The deep breathing helps break the shallow-breathing pattern that is part of the defensive trance. All deep trance phenomena are related to breath patterns. By holding your breath or shallow-breathing you stopped yourself from feeling your painful emotions.

SUPPORT PERSON

As a support person your job is to validate the sharer's hurt. You need to *enter* your partner's map of the world and mirror it back so that they can see themselves more clearly.

As a supporting friend, you'll naturally want to help the person you are supporting, especially when they are in pain. You may have been taught that when a person is in painful feelings, the way to help them is to remind them of their strengths or to point out the good things they have going in their life.

There *are* times when it is valuable to help a person focus on their strengths rather than their wounds. But not in this instance. The work of these exercises is feeling work. As I explained in Part One, children who had a patriarchal upbringing almost never got their feelings validated.

The best support you can give is to mirror your partner's feelings. Examples of mirroring feelings are: "I see your mouth quivering, and I see that you are sad." "I hear your sadness as your voice breaks its rhythm." "I see your tears." "I hear the anger in your voice." "I see that your jaw is tense and that your teeth are clenched, and I can see that you are angry." As a support person you become like a VCR videorecorder. And by mirroring your partner's feelings, you validate these feelings.

Be especially careful if you have had a childhood experience similar to the one your partner is sharing. Their pain may be a catalyst for your pain, and *you* may go into your own defensive trance or a state of confusion.

If you can't observe a feeling, you might ask, "How was that for you then or how are you feeling now?" Or you might just check out what you imagine is going on with the person. An example would be a statement like "My fantasy is that you are sad (angry, afraid). Is that right?" If they answer yes, you can ask, "Do you want to talk about it?" You might solicit their feelings by asking, "*How* was that for you?"

Questions to avoid are questions that force the person to *think*. Examples of this are "*Why* do you think your mother did this to you?" and "*What* do you think your father was so angry about?"

A good support person nurtures their partner in ways that allow the partner to have their own feeling reality.

You need to agree on guidelines for touching and holding when your partner is experiencing feelings. Ask your partner's permission before touching them in *any* way. Tell them how you want to touch them. For example, you might say, "I'd like to pat your back or shoulder while you share. Would that be okay?" Be careful about hugging your partner. Hugging can take a person out of their feelings. So, before hugging them, be sure to ask them if they want a hug.

If the person you are supporting gets in a place that feels too scary to you or them, use the "up time" process: Have your partner *open their eyes and look at you, have them breathe deeply,* and ask them simple factual questions about the observable surroundings. You can also ask questions that elicit facts about your partner, such as "How old are you?" "Where do you live?" "Do you have a car? What color is it?"

OVERWHELM

It is possible to get into a state of overwhelm when doing the feeling work in this process. Overwhelm results from the fact that we develop our defensive trances because we were violated. The violation triggered hurt, anger, and sometimes rage. But since we were defenseless, the expression of that hurt and rage was too risky. The defenses kept us from feeling our feelings. We held our breath, tensed our muscles, and went into fantasy. This allowed us to numb out. The numbing out froze the feelings. They have been frozen since that time.

As you work these exercises, you will begin to feel your feelings again. You may feel them so deeply that you feel like a 3-year-old being abandoned by their mother. That feeling feels *overwhelming*. Most people do not get that deep. The more severe the violation (incest, battering), the greater is the danger of overwhelm. This is why I suggest that you get your therapist's advice before doing the work.

If you were incested, molested, or battered as a child, I strongly recommend that you get some therapeutic help before trying these exercises.

SPECIAL CAUTION ON SEXUAL ABUSE

If you have been working on your sexual abuse issues and **have your therapist's permission,** use the same format for your sexual abuse scenes.

If you have not worked on your sexual abuse issues, I recommend that you find a competent therapist to help you. If you cannot afford a therapist, find a group for survivors of sexual abuse. Survivors groups are quite common. Inquire around. Call a community service agency.

Generally, sexual abuse victims need therapeutic help. Sexual abuse is the most shaming kind of abuse. It has the greatest element of *betrayal* in it. The person abusing you says loudly and clearly, you are only an object to be used for my need. You are not valuable as a person in your own right.

A person who has been sexually abused is also bound to their offender in a very powerful way. It takes a lot of time to work out the separation, and the survivor needs to be carefully protected. The work cannot be pushed—each person must do it in *his or her own time*.

Once our emotional hurts and pain are validated, we can grieve them. This is what we could not do in the original childhood situation. We could not grieve our hurts because our source figures would not let us. They could not bear to hear our anguish. They could not tolerate our anger, because their own anger was not acceptable to their parents. They could not let us grieve our wounds, because they had not grieved their own.

Real grief activates the energy of the deep longing and sorrow that have been repressed. As the energy is expressed, it is released. The various neurological imprints that formed a governing scene coalesced because each particular unit of experience was amplified by sadness. The sadness (deep hurt and sorrow) keeps the shaming imprints grouped together in the governing scene. Once the sadness is expressed, once the tears are shed, the complex scene begins to disintegrate. The deeper the expression of sadness, the more powerful the impact on the governing scene.

THE QUESTION OF CONFRONTATION

Remember it is not your living (or deceased) parent figures that we are dealing with in this exercise. It is the images that you carry within you, the images that constitute the internalized parent. These images make up your "parent hunger." It is these images we are separating from.

Whether or not to confront your living parents is another, separate issue.

Many therapists recommend that, at a certain point in their recovery, survivors of sexual, physical, and severe emotional abuse confront their source figure offender. In the actual process of psychotherapy, there are good reasons to support this view.

But *confrontation of source figures is not part of the process I am using here.* I positively discourage it. In my workshops I tell people not to confront their flesh and blood parents and that if they do, they have missed the point of my process.

Stage Two: Inrage to Outrage

The second stage of grieving our own grief involves anger. Anger is the emotion that is most forbidden to a child. Patriarchal parents cannot tolerate anger in their children. Anger is labeled a deadly sin by religious patriarchs. Children are terrorized by being told that they will burn in the fires of hell if they express anger to their parents. Even if you escaped these threats, you probably were punished for expressing anger. Many of you were abandoned when you expressed anger.

On the other hand, some of you may have had free rein with your anger. This is usually the case in chaotic families when you had an adult child parent whose wounded child would do anything in order for you to love them. They became your people-pleasing puppet parent. You expressed your anger in an undisciplined and undifferentiated way. This lack of structure and control was also terrifying.

In both scenarios you learn to fear your own anger.

Stage Two involves your expressing the anger that lies beneath your hurts. Anger work can be dangerous because it is part of your original pain. It is the primitive anger and rage of the hurt child. Be careful of this work. If you don't feel safe doing it, commit to a couple of sessions with a therapist and get help.

COVERT EXPRESSION OF ANGER

Like the sadness, the anger is part of your *energy* that has been repressed for years. It has been held in check by your various deep trance defenses. Your anger has been unconscious. You may have expressed it in several covert ways over the years.

- Some people express anger covertly by being very nice to others in public and continually criticizing them in private.

- Anger is sometimes somatized, that is, converted into bodily ailments like headaches, backaches, stomachaches, asthma, arthritis, and ulcers. Research indicates unexpressed anger may be a component in some heart attacks and cancer.

- Some people express anger covertly through a seemingly "unemotional," rationalistic attack upon things in a never-ending thinking assault.

- Repressed anger toward source figures is reenacted in relationships with other people, usually coming at the end of a cycle of conflict or at the termination of the relationship.

- Parental rage toward children is often a reenactment of the rage the child in the parent felt toward their own parents.

• Much violent criminality is an acting out on society of the unresolved rage in one's family relationships. I have received thousands
of letters from incarcerated men and women who have seen my
TV programs and read my books and connected their criminal behavior with their families of origin.

• Lots of sexual impotency and frigidity is about repressed anger.

• Lots of sexual violence is about preverbal powerlessness and the
irrational anger that results from it.

It is essential to get to your anger and express it if you are going
to separate from your internalized source figures.

EXPRESSING ANGER

My choice for Step One anger work involves "internal remapping,"
a process based on modern cybernetics. A principle of cybernetics is
that the brain and central nervous system cannot distinguish *imagined* experience from *real* experience if the imagined experience is
sufficiently vivid and detailed. I'm sure you have had the experience
of being physically aroused by a sexual fantasy. You have also probably scared yourself with images about some threatening task you have
to do in the future. Sexual fantasies and catastrophizing about the
future are examples of imagined experiences that cause actual physiological responses. In the same way, we can use our imagination to
change the destructive experiences of the past and create new experiences that are positive. This is the power of remapping.

Before we can remap our childhood anger, however, we have
to embrace our wounded inner child. The inner child is not about to
express anger to his or her survival figures without your protection.

EXERCISE: EMBRACING YOUR MYSTIFIED INNER CHILD

(Have your partner guide you.)
The easiest way to get to the child is to spend about five minutes
doing some deep breathing. It's helpful to play soft lullaby music
while you deep breathe. (Try Steven Halpern's "Lullabies and Sweet
Dreams.")

**Close your eyes and breathe in to the count of eight,
hold your breath to the count of four, and breathe out to
the count of eight. Do this for about five minutes.**

After five minutes go to your normal breathing and help yourself to remember several long-forgotten pleasant memories from childhood. To help yourself trigger these memories, try starting with birthday parties, holidays, family vacations, playgrounds, early school days, toys, and old photographs. When you find a nice memory, let yourself go into it and imagine yourself meeting the child of long ago. Tell the child hello. Tell the child you are from their future and that you have survived. Thank them for being who they are. Thank them for their courage and goodness! *Tell your child you know better than anyone what they've gone through.* And tell your child that you are here to help them express their anger about being violated. Tell them that you will *protect* them while they express their anger to their survival figures. Ask them if they are willing to express anger now.

Be sure the internal child is ready. Sometimes you need some interaction with this child before they will trust you as their protector. This may mean fifteen minutes a day in dialogue with your child for a few weeks. Just having a simple conversation with your child is enough. Most often the child feels ready to do the work. But before going on, use your imagination to increase your power to protect the child.

EXERCISE: MAKING A RESOURCE ANCHOR

Think of a time when you were expressing anger in a nonshaming way. You were staying within your boundaries and expressing what *you* saw, heard, interpreted, and wanted from the person you were angry at. You had all your *energy available to you* and felt in control of yourself. Imagine yourself in that scene now. Pay attention to as many details as possible. When you feel the strength of that anger, make a fist with your left hand. Hold it for a minute and feel the strength it gives you. Then take a deep breath and let your fist relax. You have made a *resource anchor* which you can use while your inner child is confronting your source figure.

If you had a violent parent, you may want to make a resource anchor of someone who is more powerful than your parent. You could imagine God in whatever form you symbolize God and make a fist when you imagine God's presence. Or you could imagine someone with more physical strength than your parent, maybe Arnold

Schwarzenegger. Once you've made an anchor with your fist, it is like a switch that brings forth the powerful resource figure who will protect your inner child.

EXERCISE: EXPRESSING ANGER

Start the exercise on the expression of anger by making your fist and visualizing your adult self taking the child by the hand. Go and find the specific source figure you wish to express anger to.

> Imagine a house you lived in with that person. Or imagine where they are living now. If they are deceased, imagine them at any time of your life you can remember being with them. If you cannot find a memory, just imagine a situation in which you see the source figure.
>
> Using the list of hurts you wrote down earlier, let the child tell them, "I'm angry at you for hurting me." Be very specific. *You cannot fail with detail.* The more you give the details, the better. Let the child really get the anger out. I've sometimes referred to this process as "original justice." It is a form of justice because the child's rights were violated. The child was helpless and had no means of defense. Now the child has you for a champion.

Once anger has been completely expressed to that source figure, I advise waiting a few days before working on another source figure. Be sure all the anger is expressed. Express it as passionately as possible. We need passion if we want to affect our internal images. We want to interrupt the governing scenes. I often suggest that the person say to the source figure, "I'm angry at you and I'm giving you back your pain, loneliness, anger, unresolved sexual issues, disappointments, your marriage, and all your shame." I encourage the person's inner child to say: "I'm angry at you for dumping your pain and shame on me. I will not carry *your pain* and *shame* for you any longer. I'm not responsible for your disappointing life. I have my own life to lead."

When you are finished expressing anger to all your significant survival figures you are ready for Step Two of the separation-grief process. Remember I am abbreviating the process. It may take months for you to work out Stage One. These matters take time. Also remember we are not talking about our real flesh-and-blood parents here. Our real parents may still be around, and they may still be

shaming us. What bonds us to them is the inner child's fear of abandonment and death. This is why they can keep upsetting us and why
we keep going back for more abuse. While you are doing this work,
you may have to establish a strong boundary between yourself and
your parents. If you choose, you can tell them you are doing some
very sensitive emotional work and that you will not be in contact for
a while. Or you can choose to talk to them periodically while keeping
your distance. You have an absolute right to your own life, and you
need not let anyone shame or violate you in any way. Once you've
done this work, your boundaries will be stronger. Generally people
have a much better relationship with their parents after doing this
work.

The work I'm suggesting here and in my workshops is always
geared toward internal remapping. The parent or source figure in
question is always the *internalized image* of the parent. It is this
image that lives within us and contaminates our life.

In order to neutralize the destructive power of this image we
must internally remap it. This is the way we separate from it. Internal
remapping involves imagining vividly and in detail. We must create
images that are powerful enough to allow us to separate. Experiencing our deep sadness and anger is the first step. We must also experience deep empathy and forgiveness if we want to create new and
powerful images. Stage Two involves demythologizing our parental
images, humanizing the more-than-human (idealized) and the less-
than-human (degraded) images we created of them.

STEP TWO: GRIEVING YOUR PARENTS' GRIEF

Stage One: Demythologizing Your Parents

The images we have of our source figures are almost always unrealistic and dehumanized. All young children deify their source figures.
They need to do this for their survival. If the child was able to grasp
that Mom, for example, is severely addicted to crack, it would be
overwhelming. If a child could grasp that Mom is severely dysfunctional, the next line of thinking would be "Since mom cannot take
care of me, I will die." Children cannot let themselves think that.
So the child develops a deep trance composed of both a positive
hallucination and a negative hallucination. The child sees Mom as a
good, loving mom and stops seeing Mom as an addicted zombie.
"Mom is always good," the child fantasizes. "I am the one who is

bad." This image of the mother might change as the child grows older and is able to grasp the neglect, abuse, and abandonment. The new image might be Mom, the wicked no-good witch. The child now hates and resents the mother. The internal image is still polarized.

Resentment is a chronic state in which the person refeels the negative feelings. Resentment is also a way for the person to stay attached to their mother. For no matter how much conscious hatred is engendered, the wounded and mystified inner child *magically* believes that leaving the mother would mean death. To chronically cycle waves of hatred is a negative way to stay attached. As Fritz Perls said, so long as we hold on to the resentment for our parents, we never *grow up*. Resentment is the classic example of unfinished business. Resentment keeps us as bonded to our survival figures as idealization does. Both resentment and idealization keep us from finishing the past. Either extreme keeps the wounded inner child frozen in mystification.

You cannot see your source figures as the real human beings they were if you keep viewing them through the eyes of your wounded inner child. If you hold on to the relationship you had when you were a child, you will always remain a wounded child and they will always be your godlike or monster parent. We must demythologize our source figures. The table on the next page represents some work I did on my grandfather. As a child I followed my family's lead and canonized him (column 1). One of the family myths about his saintliness was that he prayed the rosary for Stalin's soul when he died. As I grew older and, especially as I began my own recovery work, I degraded him (column 3). Still later, after more work, I was able to humanize him (column 2).

The humanization process can be greatly enhanced by facts. Gather all the actual *facts* you know about your source figures. Be careful of family mythology. Family myths are stories told to distract you from what is really going on. They are part of a family's denial system. They are most often begun as defensive denials and passed on unconsciously for generations. Family saints are almost always exaggerated and mythologized. The more actual biographical data you can find, the better.

It is not always easy to find out about our source figures' childhoods. Consulting with aunts and uncles or other relatives can be useful. Asking our parents questions about their childhood often results in surprising new information. As children we wouldn't think to ask for the kind of information you need here. I have gotten loads of information from my mother.

IDEALIZED	REAL	DEGRADED
A saint	Loved his family	Enmeshed
Always kind and generous	A hard-working guy, who went from office boy to auditor of the SP Railroad with little education	A workaholic; so terrified he worked for ten hours a day, bringing work home on the weekend
	Took care of our family when my father left	
A very religious man, "prayed the rosary when Stalin died"	Very faithful husband Simple faith	Narrow-minded
	Somewhat mystified Achieved a lot for someone so scared	A wimp
	Saved and provided for his retirement	
	Self-centered because of shame and fear; shame functioned like a chronic toothache	No friends

If you cannot get any data from parents or relatives, try friends of your parents. Also look at old photographs. Try out the images you get from those pictures. See what comes up for you.

You see that the truth about my grandfather is somewhere in the middle. He was one of nine children in a very devout Catholic family. His childhood was constrained by narrow boundaries. He had a high school education and read very little. This limited his range of interests. He was a very faithful husband and committed to the things he believed in. He never really showed any vulnerability. He was brought up to believe that suffering should be done in silence and that real men never complain. He was fearful of taking any risks. This is the atmosphere he breathed as a child. He was taught at an early age that life is risky. He learned to play it safe.

Today I think of my grandfather as both a saint and a sinner. Like all human beings, he was the product of his family culture, the larger culture, and his individual choices. I am no longer so concerned with judging him.

I recommend that you do a three-column comparison for each of the survival figures who was significant to you. In the middle column, put as much factual data as you can find. Focus especially on your parents' childhoods, noting issues relating to family violence.

Stage Two: Child-to-Child Dialogue

Remember my drawing of a person as an adult child? I drew a big figure with a smaller figure inside. In order to demythologize your source figures, you must see them as the wounded children they were. Even if your parents had exceptional childhoods they were inevitably somewhat wounded. They were wounded by the patriarchal culture and by the inevitable human limitations of their parents. It is imperative that you see your source figure as human, that is, as carrying some woundedness.

EXERCISE: YOUR SURVIVAL FIGURE AS A CHILD

(Have your partner read this exercise to you.)
Choose the survival figure you want to work on. I'll use mother for this sample. Play Daniel Kobialka's "Going Home." Find a quiet place where you won't be interrupted.

> Breathe in to the count of eight, hold to the count of four, and breathe out to the count of eight. Do this deep breathing for four minutes. . . . Now focus on the number 8, see a black 8 on a white curtain, or a white 8 on a black curtain. . . . If you have trouble seeing the number, imagine yourself finger painting it. . . . Now focus on the number 7 and let yourself relax more and more. Find the perfect place that is a balance between holding on and letting go. You know just where the place is—you learned it long ago when you learned to ride a bicycle, . . . when you learned to climb up and slide down a sliding board, . . . when you learned to eat, . . . to walk. . . . Now see the number 7 and relax more. . . . Now the number 6. . . . Now the number 5. . . . Now the number 4. . . . When you get to number 1, you will be totally relaxed. . . . Now the number 3. . . . Now the number 2, and now. . . . The number 1. . . . Now see the number 1 become a door. . . . Open the door and walk down a hallway to a room on your left. . . . Open the door to the room and see a movie screen with scenes from your

teenage years.... Your best friend.... Your first love.... A dwelling you lived in.... Close the door and walk farther down the hallway to another door.... Open the door and see a moving picture of scenes from your early school years.... Your teacher.... Hear the bell ring for recess.... Start walking home from school....

Imagine that you are back home again. Go to your earliest memory of a dwelling you lived in as a child.... Go from room to room until your mother comes into focus. See her in as much detail as you can.... Then begin to see your mom getting younger and younger.... Finally see her as a small child.... Imagine you are the child you were when you lived in this dwelling.... Sit down with your mother and go through your list of hurts and angers. Ask her why she did those things to you.... Ask her why she abandoned you or had no time for you.... Ask about all the things she did that hurt you....

Take plenty of time for this exercise. Pay special attention to the answers that your mother gives you. Do not try to answer for her. Do not project what you *think* she would answer. Let the image of your mother as a child answer you. Ask her for the details of what happened to her as a child. Ask her to describe her own shame-bound scenarios.

After you've talked to her, walk out of the house. Take a deep breath. See the number 1, take another deep breath, see the number 2, number 3, number 4, number 5, number 6, number 7, number 8, open your eyes....

When I did this exercise with my dad's little boy, I heard him sob as he told me his father abandoned him when he was 7 and that he only saw his father two times after that. As I asked my why questions, the shameful pain and loneliness of my father's wounded and mystified inner child began to emerge. I experienced him as an abandoned child, who was used by his mother in a surrogate spouse enmeshment. I saw that what he set me up for as a child was exactly what happened to him. Having done Step One work eased my anger at him for doing to me what was done to him. We could share the pain together.

The experiences with my other survival figures were similar. The dialogue with my grandmother's wounded inner child was especially revealing. She told me of her torturous sexual abuse at the hands of her own father. She described it to me. I'm still not sure if this is factually true. But before that dialogue, it had *never entered my mind*. I want you to be careful with such an experience. It certainly could have come from my *own* imagination. But I believe we carry our source figures' unresolved issues in the undifferentiated family trance. We also carry their unexpressed wishes and ambitions. Very powerful insights can result from this meditation. Take what you get from this experience and try it on. Live with it. Look at other facts about your family history. Many other facts of my family history made me believe that this sexual abuse was factually true. *Even if it was not factually true, something quite powerful happened to me in that conversation between my inner child and my grandmother's inner child.* I experienced a sense of compassion for her that I had never felt before. I had an empathetic insight into her life. I understood why she was the way she was. I glimpsed something of her soul's true story.

Empathy and understanding are the goals of this inner-child-to-inner-child dialogue. We must somehow come to appreciate the wounds and true humanness of our survival figures if we want to separate from them.

Please be clear that empathy and understanding are not *an acceptance of their violations*. We can be empathetic without approving what they did to us. What they did really hurt, and we have anger and sadness about it. Hopefully, we have already discharged that anger and sadness in our earlier exercises.

What we want to experience in this stage is that our survival figures were originally vulnerable little children just as we were. We are separating from them, so that we can have our own lives and be available for new relationships. We are not just hurt, sad, and angry persons. We are also tender, loving, understanding, and compassionate persons. We need our anger for our strength and protection, but anger was never intended to be a chronic state. If we stay angry, we will have to hold on to the hurt and sadness in order to justify our anger. And we will be in danger of transferring the anger to ourselves or to our friends, lovers, spouses, children, and everything in our environment.

As long as we hold on to our idealizations or our resentments, we remain mystified. We remain in that caved-in mine of long ago. Our mystified self can feel a sense of strength only by being hurt and angry. Our mystified self feels alive in blaming, in seeking revenge, or in being a helpless victim.

Stage Three: Forgiveness

Now we must be willing to forgive if we want to wake up and give as before. I once read the word "forgive" written as "foregive." When we *give as before,* we live as we were before we were violated. Forgiveness allows us to reconnect with our wonder child. With this connection, we can feel our authentic strength again. Strength comes from self-connectedness. When we embrace our wonder child, we are reconciled with our feelings, our needs, our wants, and our imagination.

Empathy and understanding lead us to compassion and the recognition of our survival figures' pain. I need to see that the same kind of violation happened to my source figures as happened to me. They were reenacting their imprinted scenarios. They had not worked out their parental bondage, so they acted it out on me.

Forgiveness flows out of understanding. I now understand what made my survival figures act the way they did. I see the cycles of multigenerational pain. *I want out of that cycle!* This is why I'm willing to forgive. My forgiveness is not about sympathy for them; it's not about pitying them. It's about freedom from the bondage of the past. It's about growing up. It's about a true evolution of consciousness.

My mystified wounded inner child believes in magic and fairy tales. He believes that if he *waits* long enough a fairy godfather and godmother will come and he will live happily ever after. He believes that if he really separates from Mommy and Daddy, he will die.

The exercise with our source figures' wounded inner children showed our wounded inner child that our source figures are not *gods.* They are fellow human beings living in the "terrible dailyness" just like us. They are carrying their wound just like we are. As long as you let your mystified wounded inner child run the show, you will cling to the fairy-tale magic of waiting to find Mommy and Daddy. It is only when you *really experience* that your survival figures also had lonely and hurt inner children that you can see that they are not gods. You may still lose them; they may still hurt you. But they no longer have life-or-death power over you.

EXERCISE: DEATH AND BURIAL

The more intense and emotional Step Two is, the more you will impact your internalized, neurologically imprinted images. Your mystified inner child needs to feel the dramatic impact of separating

from your survival figures. A way to achieve this is to *imagine* their
death and burial. This is necessary whether your source figures are
alive or deceased. It is the fantasy parents, the product of the mystified wounded inner child, that we are dealing with here.

These fantasy survival figures are magical and all-powerful. The
child-to-child dialogue is usually not enough to sever the fantasy
bond. An imaginary death and burial are necessary to achieve final
separation. In my workshops this meditation is the most dramatic
and powerful of all.

For those of you who lost one or more source figures in childhood, the chances are that you never fully grieved the loss. You likely
idealized these source figures. This exercise gives you an opportunity
to demythologize them and separate from them. We must say good-
bye to them. We must experience their death, tell them whatever we
need to tell them in order to say good-bye and bury them.

Choose the survival figure you want to work on. In this example
I'll continue to use mother. Have your partner read the exercise to
you using whichever figure you choose.

> Imagine that you hear the phone ringing. You answer, and
> it's a call saying your mother is dying. Imagine yourself
> rushing to the hospital, hoping that there will be time for
> you to say your last farewell. Let your images flow sponta-
> neously as you enter the room where your mother is lying.
> You can hear her struggling to breathe as she begins the
> march of death. You go over to her bed and you see that
> she recognizes you. Look deep into her eyes and see the
> eyes of the small child you encountered earlier. Hear her
> saying, "I'm so sorry for the hurt and pain I caused you.
> Please forgive me. I never wanted our relationship to be
> this way. I really wanted to love you. Please forgive me!"
>
> Now it's your turn to say whatever you want to say
> to her. If you can, tell her you forgive her. If you can't say
> this, then you have more work to do. If you can, tell this
> survival figure, "I'm not angry anymore. I wish you could
> have been my mother in the way I wanted. I wish you
> could have held me and told me you loved me. I know
> you did the best you could." Thank her for the things you
> are grateful for. Express gratitude for what she did give
> you. Tell her you know about her pain. Tell her you know
> how hard it was for her. Tell her, "I forgive you! I love
> you and I forgive you!" Now hold her hands or hug her

or stroke her forehead. See a peaceful look come over her face. See a little smile break through on her face as she dies. Walk out of the room. . . . Let your imagination take you to the funeral service. Go through the details of the service. . . . Let yourself feel all the sadness you feel. Let it come from deep in your abdomen. Now see and hear the service ending. Go on the journey to the cemetery and hear the final words as the body is lowered into the ground, or stand in the crematorium as the body is reduced to ashes. Say your final good-bye.

It is over. You have symbolically separated from your internalized mother.

In your own time, repeat the process with your father or other survival figures. You must separate from them if you want to become demystified. The more emotion you can feel, the better. The more passionate the emotion, the more the imprinted images are impacted.

Forgiveness is for you. It allows you to finish the past. You can then take some time and decide what kind of relationship you are willing to create in the present with your flesh-and-blood survival figures. If your parents are still shaming you, you will have to set some firm boundaries. If your parent is an offender, you may decide not to stay in such a relationship. That is tragic and sad. But in some abusive circumstances, it is necessary to leave that parent to his or her fate.

Forgiveness is a way to *reform* the past. Our pain needs to have meaning. Forgiveness allows us to redeem our pain. It allows us to release the energy we were using to hold the anger and resentment and to use it creatively to shape our future. Giving up our defensive anger permits us to access the goodness within ourselves.

Carrying the unresolved anger and hurt is crippling. To resolve it is energizing. I can now use the old energy for my present interactions. I can be present to the facts of my life. I am no longer frozen in time.

STEP THREE: BECOMING YOUR OWN PARENT

Separation from your internalized survival figures leaves you with a sense of emptiness. Lots of energy was being used in the internal struggles between your mystified wounded child and your internalized parent. You experience this as a self-to-self inner dialogue. The internalized survival figures' voices are experienced as if they were our own voice. A fantasy bond is maintained with the internalized parental image. When we separate from these images, a vacuum is created and the original feeling of confusion emerges. Confusion is not to be feared, although this is easier said than done. Our culture has suppressed confusion. Actually confusion is not a bad state at all. Confusion precedes creation. In the mythology of the ancient Greeks, Chaos was the ground from which Cosmos, the universe, emerged.

The confusion we feel after separating from our internalized parents can be the source of our own self-parenting. Each of us is called to be our own person. "What I do is me, for that I came," the poet Hopkins says.

Stage One: Heading Your Own Household

The agenda for this stage is self-parenting. How do I create a mothering and fathering relationship with myself? How will I nurture my own body, my emotions, my intellect, my imagination, and my spirituality? Where will I find the practical wisdom to manage my own household? Where will I find the wisdom to reformulate my own values? How will I envision the begetting of my own life?

Maturity is marked by answering these questions and living with the choices that result. No one can answer these questions for you. The emptiness you feel after doing the separation work can be the wellspring from which you create your own life. You need all the adult information you can get and you need lots of imagination.

This time of emptiness and confusion can be the most fertile and creative time in your life. With separation you have the possibility of creating love. As long as you stayed enmeshed, your illusion of omnipotence kept you from finding your own Higher Power and your own meaning system. The feeling of emptiness tells you that there is no human security; no Mom or Dad who will protect you from harm; no one who can save you from death.

What is the meaning of your life in the face of death? To experience that question fully stirs something soulful in you. You are being called to your authentic self. Separation brings the gift of psychological birth. You must leave home in order to find your bliss.

At this stage it is valuable to find the support of a new kind of family. Your inner child feels like any child would feel who separated from the fairy-tale security of "living happily ever after." Your new family can function like an adolescent's peer group.

So the first choice I recommend is that of a support group—a group that can serve as a family of affiliation. I recommend that you try a Co-dependents Anonymous group or maybe an Adult Children of Alcoholics group. Even if you're not a child of an alcoholic, you may be a child of another kind of addict. The issues are similar. If you're an incest survivor, there are a number of survivor groups in every city. You might want to try joining a therapy group for a limited period of time.

We are reborn as we see ourselves mirrored in the eyes of others. Friends, lovers, and finally spouses will be crucial in the journey to selfhood. I will need the support of others in reclaiming my willpower and my desires. I will need support in becoming the head of my own household.

Stage Two: Remapping Your Childhood

As you begin your journey, you may also want to reconnect with your past in a new and fresh way. For most of us the pain of our mystification has distorted time. The wounds we received were painful. When we are in pain, time seems to pass slowly. The greater the pain, the more the distortion of time and the more we seem to remember only the bad times. We dwell on our wounds; we obsess on what is wrong with our life. We accentuate the negative. When we've completed our forgiveness work, we have the opportunity to look at the good things from our past. We can renew our connection with everything that was good in our childhood. I had wonderful times as a child, playing for hours—sometimes alone, sometimes with my sister, sometimes with a friend. Childhood time was a wondrous time. It had dramatic intensity and duration. I remember the Christmas when I was 6 years old. I got a tricycle and red record player and so many other toys. I remember laughing in church, holding my breath so that I didn't let go with an uproarious outburst and then exploding, not being able to keep silent. I remember wonderful times with my mother and grandparents. There were some soulful moments with my dad.

I could go on and on, but you get the picture. The past can be recaptured in its joy and its childhood wonder. Try this exercise.

EXERCISE: PLEASANT CHILDHOOD MEMORIES

(Have your partner read this exercise to you.)
For this exercise you might play Steven Halpern's "Lullabies and Sweet Dreams." Have your partner pause for ten seconds wherever indicated.

Deep breathe for five minutes.... Get in touch with the place you are sitting.... Feel your back and/or bottom touching the floor or chair or whatever.... Feel your clothes on your body.... Feel the air in the room.... Hear whatever sounds interest you.... Hear the lullaby music and let it take you to a long-forgotten childhood memory of a pleasant kind.... [one minute pause] ... Remember other pleasant times.... holidays with the family ... parties ... playing with friends ... new toys.... Remember who took you to the playground ... swings, sliding boards ... swimming ... beaches, lakes ... carnivals ... the circus ... treats like ice cream and cake and candy ... summer vacation.... Let yourself enjoy the feeling of those childhood times ... the laughter ... the excitement.... Remember your mom.... Remember something you loved about her.... Remember your dad, stepdad, granddad, ... whoever was important to you.... These memories also shaped your life. They were part of your fate. Now take a deep breath. Feel the place where you are sitting. Feel the air in the room.... Take another deep breath, wiggle your toes, and open your eyes.

The good times are the source of our hope and resilience, but the painful times can be seen as times of strengthening and times of preparation. I cannot think of any event in my past that has not prepared me for the present in some way. Each moment had its potency and its value. "Our genius comes out of our wound," Robert Bly writes. Yes, that has been true for me!

PARABLE

THE STORY OF JOE

Milton Erickson was one of the extraordinary men of our time. In 1919, at the age of 17, he suffered an attack of poliomyelitis. He was completely paralyzed, unable to do anything but move his eyes. He was not expected to survive.

Because of his tenacious will to live, Milton developed a system of concentrating mentally on the tiny details that make up each sequence of movement. He mentally practiced these movements over and over again. Slowly he began to regain his strength. He utilized every opportunity to exercise his muscles, and within a short period of time he was walking on crutches and learning to balance himself and ride his bicycle.

Before going to college and medical school he made a canoe trip, all alone, beginning on a lake near the University of Wisconsin, following the waterway to the Mississippi River, proceeding south on the Mississippi beyond St. Louis, and then returning upriver by the same route.

Throughout his life, he had recurrent attacks of pain in his muscles and joints, usually triggered by some physical stress. In the spring of 1948 he became so ill that he was hospitalized and was told he must move to a dry warm climate. He moved to Phoenix, Arizona, where he worked with every category of the mentally ill, including the "criminally insane."

After each episode of his own physical illness, Milton resumed his work, traveled extensively, did research, and wrote papers. His special expertise was the use of hypnosis in psychotherapy.

Between 1970 and 1980, the year he died, Erickson slowly lost muscular strength including tongue and cheek muscle control. He could no longer speak clearly, and he had to phase out his private practice.

But by then his fame as a therapist had spread far and wide. Many considered him the greatest artist of therapeutic change who had ever lived. Until his death, clinicians came from all over the world to participate in the teaching seminars he conducted in his home. One of my greatest regrets is that I never attended one of Erickson's seminars.

Erickson broke with all known models of psychotherapy. He had no theory of human nature or of psychotherapy. He believed that every human being is utterly unique in the way they construct their meaningful interaction with the world. He thought that the job of everyone who wanted to help others was to learn about their map of the world, enter it, and help them expand it. No therapist has ever evidenced a wider range of realistic imagination.

I personally believe that Milton Erickson was a man of profound and soulful love, and one of his great therapeutic teaching stories is also a tale of love. I first read the story of Joe in a book called *Phoenix* by David Jordan and Maribeth Meyers-Anderson. Here it is:

There once was a boy named Joe, who at the age of 12 was expelled from school because of vandalism, incorrigible behavior, and brutality to other children. Joe had also tried to set his father's house and barn on fire and had stabbed all the animals on his father's farm with a pitchfork.

His parents took Joe to court and had him committed to an industrial school for boys. At age 15, Joe was paroled, and on the way home, he committed some burglaries and was promptly returned to the industrial school, where he stayed until he was 21. The official records state that he was extremely violent and was kept in solitary confinement most of the time.

At age 21, he was discharged with a suit and $10, and he headed for Milwaukee. He was soon arrested for burglary and was sent to the young men's reformatory in Green Bay. Again, the records show that he was aggressive and violent and that he was kept in solitary. The guards were so afraid of him that whenever he was allowed to go to the exercise yard, two guards accompanied him. When he was released, he went into the town of Green Bay and committed some more burglaries. The police picked him up, and he was sentenced to the state prison.

The records at the state prison show that Joe beat up fellow convicts and spent most of his time in the dungeon. The dungeon was eight feet by eight feet, soundproof and lightproof. The thick, heavy wooden door had a small slot at its base, through which once a day, usually at 1:00 or 2:00 A.M., a tray of food was slipped. He completed every day of this sentence, was released, and went into the town and committed some more burglaries. He was arrested and sentenced to a second term in the state prison. He spent every day of this sentence either in solitary or in the darkness and silence of the dungeon.

Upon his release he returned to a village in Wisconsin. Milton Erickson lived nearby and was about 10 years old at the time. Joe had been around for about four days, Milton was sent to town on an errand. He met some of his classmates, who told him "Joe is back!" Erickson picks up the story from here. He states that there was suspicion that Joe had already stolen some goods. He goes on:

> Now it happened that there was a farmer about three miles from the village. A farmer who had three hundred acres of company land. He was a very rich man, had beautiful buildings, and to work three hundred acres it requires a hired man. And his daughter Susie ... was about five feet ten, and she could work alongside any man in the community. She could pitch hay, plow fields, help with the butchering ... any task she could handle. The entire community felt bad about Susie. She was a good-looking girl, she was famous for her housekeeping, her dressmaking and for her cooking, and she was an old maid at twenty-three years. And that should not be. Everybody thought Susie was too choosy. On that particular day when I went to the village on the errand, Susie's father's hired hand quit because of a death in the family and said he would not be back. And Susie's father sent her into the village on an errand. Susie arrived, tied up the horse and buggy, came walking down the street. And Joe stood up and blocked her pathway. And Joe looked her up and down very thoroughly, quietly ... and Susie with equal poise looked him up and down very thoroughly. Finally Joe said, "Can I take you to the dance next Friday?" Now the village always had a weekly dance on Friday nights for all the young people. And Susie was very much in demand at those dances and she regularly drove in and attended the dance. And when Joe said, "Can I take you to the dance next Friday?" Susie said coolly, "You can if you're a gentleman." Joe stepped out of her way. She performed

her errand, went back. And the next morning the merchants were very glad to find boxes full of stolen goods at their front doors. . . . And Joe was seen walking down the highway toward Susie's father's farm. Word soon got around that he had asked Susie's father for the job of hired hand, and he was hired. And made a magnificent wage of $15 per month. He was allowed to have his meals in the kitchen with the family. And Susie's father said, "We'll fix a room for you in the barn." In Wisconsin when the temperatures are down to 35° below zero you really need a well-insulated room in the barn. Joe turned out to be the best hired hand that community had ever seen. Joe worked from sunup to long past sundown, seven days a week. Joe was six feet three, a very able bodied man and, of course, Joe always walked to the village on Friday night to attend the dance. Susie drove in to attend the dance. And much to the ire of the other young men Susie usually danced with Joe every dance. And Joe's size made them wary of pointing out to Joe the error of his way by appropriating Susie. In just about a year the community was buzzing with gossip because Susie and Joe were seen going out Saturday evening for a drive, or "sparking," as the term was used. And there was even more gossip the next day—on Sunday—Susie and Joe went to church together. And thereafter for some months Joe and Susie went for a drive every Saturday evening and to church on Sunday. And after some months of this Susie and Joe were married. And Joe moved from the barn into the house. He was still the best hired man imaginable and Joe and his father-in-law, with some aid of Susie, ran the farm. And Joe was such a good worker that when a neighbor got sick, Joe was the first one to show up to help with the chores. And they soon forgot all about Joe's history of being an ex-convict. . . .

Eventually Susie's parents died and Susie inherited the farm. Joe and Susie had no children but Joe had no trouble getting hired men. He went to the state reformatory for young men and asked for any young, promising ex-convict from the reformatory. The reformatory was for first-time offenders. Some of those men lasted a day, a week, a month, and some for months. As long as they worked Joe kept them around and treated them well. And he served to rehabilitate quite a number of ex-convicts. When I got my job as state psychologist for Wisconsin to examine all inmates in penal and correctional institutions, Joe was very happy for me.

Joe told Dr. Erickson to check out his records. He wanted him to see the incredible transformation that had taken place in his life. Erickson did check out Joe's records. He found an account of a seemingly incorrigible chronic and habitual criminal. So what happened to change Joe?

Erickson comments:

All the psychotherapy Joe received was "You can if you're a gentleman." He didn't need psychoanalysis for several years. He didn't need Carl Rogers' indirect psychotherapy, he didn't need five years of Gestalt therapy, all he needed was a simple statement . . . "You can if you're a gentleman." Psychotherapy has to occur within the patient, everything has to be done by the patient, and the patient has to have a motivation. And so when I became interested in psychiatry Joe's history had a very strong influence on me.

The story of Joe speaks to my sense of the mystery of love. Our love for another can heal our broken lives. Joe's did. And no one knows exactly how or why. Pascal told us that "the heart has its reasons that reason cannot fathom." When we truly love, we are willing to change and we do often change. We lose weight, start exercising, forgive our enemies, accept others, love ourselves, feel alive, believe that life is worthwhile. Eric Berne, the founder of a mode of therapy called Transactional Analysis, termed love "nature's psychotherapy." I believe that love can dramatically heal our wounds and radically change our lives.

I want you to remember this as you look at the various models and images of love that I will present to you in Part Three. If you get bogged down by my mental gyrations, or if I succumb to my propensity for moralizing, just remember the story of Joe. Something similar and very simple may be about to happen to you. If you expect something too complicated, you may miss out on it.

Creating Love

It has often been noted that most, if not all, problems brought to therapists are issues of love. It makes sense that the cure is also love.

THOMAS MOORE

INTRODUCTION

In Part Three I will do my very best to evoke the symbols and powers of love. I will give you examples of creating love. You may like them and use them yourself. What I cannot tell you is "how to love." No one can.

Believe me, I *want* to tell you how to love. By telling you how to love I can get the feeling that I grasp what love is. To grasp love frees me from its polarity and depth. I can lull myself and you into a false sense of security. Telling you how to love would be like drinking a glass of wine. It momentarily eases my anxiety about love, my anxious need for control and predictability. But it does not help me find love. I have engaged in how-to advice a lot in my life, and some how-tos will surely slip through the cracks. But I know that whenever I slip into advice, I'm opening the door to mystification. I want you to know that, too.

Every time I watch a late-night infomercial—you know, the ones with guys rolling out wheelbarrows of hundred-dollar bills, or with Fran Tarkington and Tony Robbins in their open-collared shirts and identical sports coats offering us the *technology* of happiness and success (as if Fran Tarkington had ever been a loser!), or with Dave Del Gado and all the people holding the checks for all the money they have made using Dave's method, or with the marriage counselor who knows all the secrets about love and relationships. This guy is too much! He offers the secret to every man or woman's everything! All the issues of life are reduced to simple formulas. We are offered the *cures* of the problems of life. I want to buy it all! I take down the 800-number *every time*. Thank God I never buy the stuff!

The late-night infomercials touch a part of me. They touch my mystified false self that believes that love could be real only if I do it someone else's way. I couldn't be lovable if I did it my way. They tap into my shame and fear. They concretize the symbolic and materialize our consciousness. They continue our mystification.

Having someone else tell us how to love robs us of the very thing we need the most, *our imagination*. And imagination is the way we can truly help others. A good helper *imagines with* the one he or she is helping. This is the mutuality that grounds our hope. Sometimes we do feel stuck. We do not see any way out. At such times we need help. When we are really helped, we can see something, an alternative, that we hadn't seen before. Someone—a parent, teacher, therapist, friend, fellow worker—has *imagined* with us and helped us find new images, which give us choices. We will need lots of imagination to find our way through our relationships.

"Life is not a problem to be solved," says the great theologian Kierkegaard, "it is a mystery to be lived." I believe in teaching. I believe in motivating others to own the mystery and depth of themselves. Some of that involves packaging. Packaging is a way to present material, and all teaching comes to us in some kind of package. The picture I drew of consciousness in Chapter 5, with the star in the middle, is a way to package some very deep and mysterious matters. In my *Homecoming* book I use the image of the wounded inner child as a way to package the deep wounds that result from family violence. Packaging is a way to make things that cannot be fully understood through words and concepts more concrete and understandable. Since we cannot exhaust the meaning of anything, some packaging is necessary. But the packaging needs to at least hint at the depth and mystery it cannot contain. Offering secret formulas is a form of robbery. It robs us of our imagination. I own that I've been guilty of that.

I think we want formulas and cures because we've been mystified into believing that our desires can be attained without the fear and anxiety that goes with the hard work of love. The wounded child in all of us does not want to give up its fantastic imagination with its fantasies of cure, self-improvement, and life without problems.

Soul making requires that we experience the mysterious depths of the reality that surrounds us. To do this we have to be willing to transcend polarization and embrace polarity and paradox.

Love is especially paradoxical. No one can tell you how to love. If you listened to them and followed their advice, you would cut yourself off from your own depth and possibility. Every choice we make defines and limits us, but you need to make your own choice, not someone else's.

My goal in this part is to describe some of the wanderings and some of the possibilities of soulful loving. Soulful love takes us into the heart of the human. Soulful love rejoices in the meanderings of every day. Soulful love looks to this day as the life of life. It looks for the richness of living, taking its time to hear children laugh and to see a friend's face light up when we are reunited after an absence. Soulful love feels the worry and pain of a loved one's operation; it fears aging; it feels the unique sorrow of endings—of our children leaving home, of our parents dying. Soulful love often contradicts our expectations and reveals a depth we hadn't seen before.

I have a mailman who models love in an extraordinary way. Rain or shine, day in day out, he walks his route. He has a limp, and on cold days, he seems to experience some pain when he walks. He always smiles when I see him. He always has kind words to say. He makes it possible for me to relate to many people. Today I got a Saint Patrick's Day card from my son. It was a sweet card and brought back special memories that only he and I share. I'm thankful for my mailman. He's a model of love and devotion.

For years I've missed seeing some of the best examples of love. They are all around me, the simple expressions of everyday human devotion. I've always looked to Albert Schweitzer or Mother Teresa as the ultimate exemplars of love, and they certainly are powerful examples. But my mailman isn't any less devoted or committed to what he does. I'm sure he does not receive anything extraordinary in the way of recompense. Baseball players are getting millions to play baseball. They have their faces enshrined in baseball cards. Maybe someday when the world has soul again, we'll pay mail carriers a lot of money and have mail carrier cards and a Mail Carrier Hall of Fame. We don't need to stop there. One day we may have secretary cards, bricklayer cards, carpenter cards, housewife cards, single mother cards ... you get the idea.

We need to stop looking for love in the idealized images we ourselves have created. We need to stop looking for examples of love in the extraordinary few who truly reach transcendent heights.

In what follows we will look at the mundane human. Human parenting, human struggles with loving God, with loving ourselves, with loving each other, and loving the world. I don't think we can love well if our models are beyond our reach.

While no person is ever fully present to *the grace of every moment,* there are many highly functioning people who are making major contributions, quietly, gently, and mostly unnoticed. These people are the great lovers. The mystified go for high drama and squat on the two ends of grandiosity, trying to be either the best best or the best worst.

Since the activities of love cannot be defined, we can only catch glimpses of love in moments of ecstasy, of affection, of intuition, of insight. We know about love in parables, in poetry and song. The natural language of love is metaphoric and symbolic. "My love is like a red red rose that's newly sprung in June," says Robert Burns. "Love is like"—that's the important phrase, with emphasis on *like*.

T. S. Eliot's J. Alfred Prufrock asks, "Do I dare disturb the universe?" Each new poem, song, work of art disturbs the universe. Each is a being that has never existed before. Love also disturbs the universe. It creates something new, a reality that never existed before.

Many of you reading this book may not feel that you've found the love you really want. You may be looking at the mystified and inhuman models that are often presented as the pearls of great love. When you compare yourself to them, you feel empty and lonely— you feel like you don't measure up.

What I hope you will grasp from the third part of this book is that you *already have what you want and what you need*. You could not even think about seeking something if you had no awareness of it or familiarity with it. It would be too foreign. You seek because *something in you* has been touched. You are attracted to someone *because you already have within you what you are attracted to*.

You have a heart filled with the desire for the Good. You have a soul that will find your way. You have an imagination with which you can create a love that reveres all things, especially the depth and sacredness of every day. You can transform your ordinary life into something full of wonder.

CHAPTER 8

The Love Between Parents and Children

Almost everything we do is insignificant. But it is very important that we do it.

MAHATMA GANDHI

When I was fourteen my class had to write a home essay on ourselves. Mine began, "Time lies heavily on my hands." My parents were upset by this because they said it reflected on them ... "You always have plenty to do ... and it shows how ungrateful you are for all we have done for you." ... So I changed the opening to "I find life full of interest." They were happy, and I got a "Very Good."

R. D. LAING

As a teenager, I swore I would never have a child. This is a common feeling for people who have suffered a lot in childhood. In effect, their wounded child says, "Don't bring another child into the world. They may have to suffer like I did." The feeling of not wanting a child can also stem from the fact that the parent you were most bonded to either didn't want you or doesn't want you to have a child. In the latter case the parent does not want you to separate from them and grow up or sees your becoming a parent as competition. In my case, my early feelings were about not wanting a child to go through what I had to go through.

Some time after I was in my recovery from alcoholism, I had a strong desire for a child. Wanting to have a child is a soulful urge. Our soul desires life, and the procreative desire is a desire to extend and expand life.

The desire for a child can also be about *one's own wounded child wanting another shot at childhood*. I have had people in counseling who were in the midst of chaotic relationship crises tell me that they had an obsessive desire to have another child. This was most often about their unresolved childhood issues. I think my strong desire for a child was a mixture of soulfulness and an unconscious desire to relive my childhood.

When my son was born, I was overjoyed. I couldn't wait to be a father. I was 35 years old, and I knew a lot about developmental psychology. I had studied the then-current masters on proper discipline and good parenting techniques. I was also counseling a lot of people and giving public lectures on marriage, intimacy, and parenting. I felt highly qualified to be a father.

Unfortunately, for the first twelve years of my son's life I lacked a lot as a soulfully loving father. I was the best father I knew how to be. And most of you reading this made the best parenting decisions you could make at the time you made them. Your parents probably did the same. But I was mystified and so are many of you and so were many of your parents.

I was committed and sincere as a parent. The problem was that as a mystified person I was confused about my identity. No matter how much you *know* about parenting, you need to have some sense of your real self in order to have a healthy parental relationship with your children.

We can become more and more present to our children as we begin some kind of demystification process. In the recovery field we often refer to the demystification process in relationship to our family of origin as "passing it back."

At my treatment center at Ingleside Hospital in Rosemead, California, we often say: *"You either pass it back or you pass it on."* I don't know who first used this phrase, but it is very accurate. I actually had the experience of being a parent both before and after I passed it back.

BEFORE I "PASSED IT BACK"

Before I did this work my parental situation looked much like what I've shown on the next page. There you can see a funny-looking

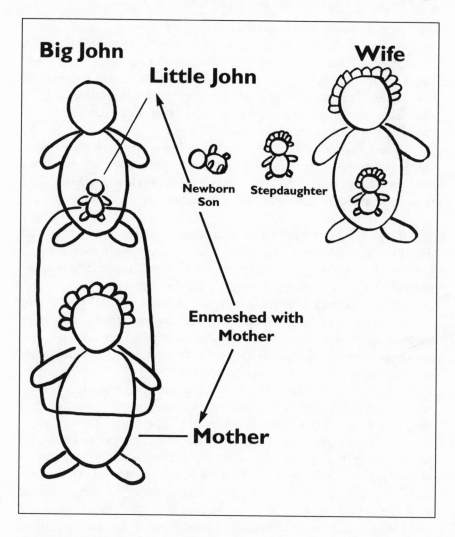

Big John

Little John

Wife

Newborn Son

Stepdaughter

Enmeshed with Mother

Mother

drawing of me with my wife, 8-year-old stepdaughter, and newborn son. In addition to my stepdaughter, I have a stepson who lives with his father. Mine is a blended family. Relationships become more complex in a blended family. Each and every relationship has to be negotiated and worked out.

In the picture, I am still an unconscious adult child who has not separated from my internalized parents. I think my now ex-wife would probably agree that neither of us had "passed it back." We still had unfinished business. What that means very simply is that our children were often being parented by our wounded inner kids. I'll assure you that was *my* situation. In the drawing I have put a rope around Little John (my inner child) and his mother. He is a wonderful little boy. He is fun loving, mischievous, curious, and interested in everything, but he is bonded to his mother, who is the tall figure at the bottom of the page. Little John lost his father at an early age and *longs* for male fathering. He has reservoirs of ungrieved sadness. He cries whenever he sees any warm father and son relationship. (I remember bawling once during an Alpo dog food commercial. A father and son were feeding the boy's dog.)

Little John's whole sense of maleness has come from his mother. He therefore feels very frightened about being a male. He has been afraid as far back as I can remember. He also feels frightened of the responsibilities of being a father, although he is overjoyed at having a newborn son.

If you keep in mind that I'm not separated from my mother, you can see that I don't have an updated relationship with myself, much less anyone else. I have not finished my own childhood. While we probably never completely finish it, I had a long way to go.

Prior to doing the internal separation work I was still looking for fairy godparents to magically take away all my pain. In my marriage I tried to set my wife up as my magical mother. With my newborn son and stepchildren, *I got to be the father I never had.* I did not know or understand this on any conscious level.

My mystification kept me in my past wounds. Instead of interacting with my son and stepchildren in the *present,* I was often a little boy in an adult's body giving them all the things I never got. I went to great lengths to protect my children from the kind of pain and suffering that I went through because of my father's abandonment. And I was so busy protecting them (as an extension of myself), that I was seldom there for them in the sense of meeting them at their map of the world. I'll come back to this point in a moment.

My children had a 185-pound 5-year-old as a parent. I was often as childish as my children. I either would play, goof off, and indulge them, or, when I couldn't take being the *nice* dad anymore, would vent years of repressed rage at them. The rage was usually accompanied by yelling, and when it was over I felt terrible. My wounded inner boy would feel terrified. I knew what I had done was inappropriate. The rage really needed to be expressed to my own *internalized father and mother.* My children got the rage that I felt as a child but was too terrified to express.

My yelling rages especially hurt my relationships with my children. Several episodes were all they needed to stop trusting me. I've already described how children internalize their parents at their worst. The image of the screaming parent becomes a *governing scene* in the child's psyche. Dad becomes a truly threatening and dangerous figure. The interpersonal bridge is shattered by a raging parent. The child selects whatever deep trance phenomena they need and stops trusting the parent.

A 185-pound mystified Little John wanted to create wonderful, nurturing, and warm father-child relationships and instead he was driving his children away. My parenting was chaotic, veering from "Mr. Santa Claus" to "Ivan the Terrible." *I feel so sad as I write these words.* The whole multigenerational cycle is tragic. It is painful to realize that I was creating just the opposite of the very thing I wanted most.

First Order Change

I mentioned that I knew a lot about parenting when I got married. I had taught courses in it. What I came to realize is that one *can use the most up-to-date techniques in a mystified way.*

I remember the night I went to the lecture on Rudolf Dreikurs' notion of the democratic family council. Dreikurs was a well-known authority on child-rearing. His idea of the democratic council is that once a week the family has a meeting covering issues like division of household chores and family outings. The leadership rotates each week. Although children under 7 are not allowed to be the leaders of the meetings, each family member has an equal vote on the issues.

The family council is a great idea and, when it is organized and run by soulful parents, it can create a wonderful context for fostering family communication and participation.

But in my own case, on my third attempt at getting the family together, I wound up screaming at the top of the stairs that I was the *president* of the family and we were going to have a democratic family council or face the consequences! Hardly what Dreikurs had in mind!

I also tried to use Thomas Gordon's *Parent Effectiveness Training,* a fine book with flexible guidelines for soulful parental modeling and nonshaming communication. For my mystified inner child *any suggestion by an authority became an order to be obeyed.* This is the major danger for a severely mystified person using how-to manuals. The mystified rigidly do what the manual says without internalizing the methods. The result is first order change: The behavior looks different on the surface but is still basically the same underneath.

One of Gordon's major tenets is that parents should use "I messages." I messages are self-responsible statements that express what one sees and hears, how one interprets what one sees and hears, how one feels on the basis of that interpretation, and what one wants. An example would be: "I saw you take your brother's candy. I think that is unfair, I feel angry that you did that, and I want you to give it back to him." The goal in this model of communication is to avoid shaming and judgment.

On a couple of occasions of rage, I heard myself saying things like "*I* think you're very selfish, and *I* think you never think of anyone but yourself." These are *not* self-responsible I messages. They are *judgments* preceded by the word "I."

As a mystified person, I was frozen in the past. Whenever there was crisis, or I was tired or hungry, my mystified child would take over. The crisis usually triggered old scenarios from my childhood. This isn't surprising, as our children inevitably pass through the *same stages in which our own developmental arrests occurred*. Their normal and age appropriate behavior often triggers issues related to our own developmental blocks.

If you are from one of the dysfunctional family types I wrote about in Chapter 2 and you remain mystified, your most spontaneous reactions to your children will often be echoes of messages you heard from your own source figures. Their voices function like post-hypnotic trance messages. We tend to shame our children the way we were shamed. And you can shame them using the most up-to-date psychological techniques.

First Order Versus Second Order Change

In my own case every technique I used was filtered through the structures of my childhood trance. I changed, but the change was a change in *content* not in *process*. I used Dreikurs and Gordon (and many others) in an absolutist manner. My thinking was still *polarized*. I used the new models in an all-or-nothing way. I shamed myself when I forgot to use I messages. I beat up on myself for failing to get the family council running in a democratic manner. I went from *RIGID patriarchy to RIGID democratic parenting methods*. I went from *RIGID overdiscipline to RIGID underdiscipline*. The content of my behavior changed, but the underlying structure remained the same. It was like I quit eating grapefruits and started eating oranges. Even though I changed my behavior, I was still eating citrus fruit.

With second order change, we have a real possibility of soulful parenting. With second order change, we let go of rigidity and polar-

ization. Second order change results from demystification. When we
separate from our internalized family system, we can see our family
of origin parenting rules in an objective light and we can use new
information to change those rules. After I had begun this work, I used
the parenting techniques I had learned from Dreikurs and Gordon in
a much more flexible manner. After finishing my business with Mom
and Dad and making peace with the past, I saw Dreikurs and Gordon
as resources who offered new alternatives for living more honestly
and humanly with my children. Their models were not *new rules* for
perfect parenting. They were ways to be more *present* to my children
and to meet them at their map of the world.

I don't mean to imply that by doing your grief work on your
childhood wounds, you will magically be able to master new ways
of child-rearing. Mastering the new ways will require your commitment and practice. But as you become demystified, you can learn to
use them effectively as part of *your own parenting style.*

As I did my grief work, I became more conscious of what was
happening. I found that I could differentiate *between my own
wounded inner child and my own flesh-and-blood child.* I learned
to check my first reaction to my children. I literally counted to ten,
questioned my response, and asked myself to *imagine* another response. This worked well for me a lot of the time. I used it often
during my children's teenage years. My first urge was to accuse them
and tell them how bad I had it when I was their age! I came to realize
how ineffective that kind of response was. If you were bleeding, it
would not help you for me to tell you how badly I bled in the past.

I know a woman who kept a rubber band around her wrist.
Every time one of her children upset her, she snapped the rubber
band. This was an adaptation of a method called "thought stopping."
The snap against her wrist was the signal for her to consider *imagining* another response.

In the beginning you might not be aware of a mystified response
until it is over. It is never too late. You can apologize to your child.
I did this often in the period after I began my work of separation
from my internalized parents. It can be very healing to say to a child,
"The response I just gave you, my loud voice, was *about me* and *not
about you.* I'm sorry for talking that way to you." Saying this allows
you to own your own shame. When I'm feeling upset and I yell at
my children or anyone else, I'm transferring my upset to them. In
effect the child who was not upset is now carrying my upset. This is
the way that much shame is interpersonally transferred from shame-

less or shameful parents to their children. Owning your shame or
any other unresolved feelings is a way to free your child from having
to carry these feelings.

I cannot own my feelings as long as I am in my trance defenses.
These defenses are there to prevent me from feeling the pain. I needed
them as a child because I did not have the knowledge or maturity
to deal with the adults (or older children) who were hurting me.
What was once my protection has now become my problem. To
respond to my children I need to be present to them. The more I
have resolved the past by remapping my governing scenes, the more
I am able to respond to my children in the here and now. It takes
a lot to achieve soulful parental love.

I would describe parental love as the willingness and courage
to make a passionate commitment of time, attention, learning, self-
disclosure, and teaching, for the sake of your own self-transcendence
and the empowerment of your child's uniqueness.

MEETING CHILDREN AT THEIR MAP OF THE WORLD

Second order change allowed me to meet my children at their
map of the world. To meet them at their map of the world meant
establishing rapport with them. When I establish rapport with someone, I stand in their shoes, I experience the world from their point
of view. I attempt to understand the meaning they ascribe to things.

There are many ways of establishing rapport, of meeting our
children at their map of the world. I'd like to describe some of these
ways.

Mirroring

The most basic kind of rapport is called "gross body mirroring." I
learned about gross body mirroring in a workshop led by Leslie
Cameron Bandler, one of the pioneers of NLP, or Neuro Linguistic
Programming. (In Chapter 6, I described an NLP strategy called reframing.) At the workshop we divided into groups of three. One
person in each group was the facilitator and had the job of physically
aligning the other two. I was to mirror the person I was aligned with.
Our facilitator positioned my head at exactly the same angle as the
head of the other person. I was to breathe in exactly the same rhythm
as my partner. As I achieved the exact same spatial placement, posture, and breathing pattern as my partner, the facilitator asked me,

"What must I be sure of?" I answered almost instantly, "Not to show my fear!" I actually felt fear as I said it. Then the facilitator checked this out with my partner, who acknowledged that she was very afraid and was trying to hide it. I was amazed! Just by being physically aligned with her, I was able to feel and know what my partner was feeling and thinking. Try this with someone sometime.

Gross body mirroring such as this is more difficult with children because of the discrepancy in size between adults and children. I recommend sitting, squatting, or kneeling when talking to children, in order to be on the same eye level. This is not possible all the time, but it is a valuable way of communicating when encouraging, problem solving, setting limits, and dealing with other important issues.

A further level of rapport can be achieved by mirroring what children say and the *way* they say it. What the child says is the content of their message; the way they say it is the process. We mirror the content by repeating the words the child has said. We can mirror the process through gross body mirroring and by looking at their face and *watching* for their feelings. Feelings can be detected by observing a child's facial muscles, brow, eyes, lips, and breathing patterns. Sometimes we can't be sure of exactly what the child is feeling. In such cases, we can gain rapport by simply reporting what we observe. For example, I might report that "your jaws are tight," "your teeth are clenched," "your eyes are cast down," or "your lips are pursed."

Learning how to achieve rapport is simple but difficult. It takes practice. You need to be willing to take the time to work on it. I mentioned earlier how foreign *hard work* was to my notion of love. Learning to achieve rapport is a good example of the work of love.

Let me give you a concrete example of the rapport I'm describing. Recently I was waiting to see a doctor. A young mother was in the waiting room with a child of about 4. The child was nervous about going to the doctor. She kept taking the magazines from one table and putting them on another table. The receptionist, a nurse who looked like "Mother Patriarchy," was annoyed. The child was bothering her a lot. Any of us with patriarchal repression have issues around a rambunctious child. The parental voices start in with, "God, that child's a brat! She sure needs some discipline, etc." I've learned to stop doing this, and I was curiously watching this child. The nurse finally couldn't stand it anymore and came over and stopped the child, taking it on herself to publicly correct her. The child was frightened, shamed, and then angry (a common sequence). The mother mirrored the child with her body and said, "It seemed like you were having fun changing the magazines and now you are angry." The child looked down (another flash of shame) and then looked at her mom and said, "I didn't want to come to this stupid doctor anyway." The mom said: "You wanted to stay home and you feel angry because we're here. Is that right?" The child timidly poked her mom and said, "I'm angry at you." The mom said, "I hear that you are angry at me, and I can see it on your face." Then the little girl begin to play with her shoe. Shortly the doctor came to get her.

This mom was superb. She stayed in her own boundaries and served her child in a valuable way. She validated her child's feelings. The child felt *safe* enough to tell her mother that she was angry at her. The mother acknowledged her anger, nothing more, nothing less. She didn't bribe her or try to change her anger. She didn't threaten punishment or scold her. She had to bring her child to the doctor. The child didn't like it, she was afraid and angry. That's it. A real typical *human* situation. One of the unpleasant ones that we have to face in life as responsible parents.

The scene I just described is typical, but the way the mother handled it was *not* typical. She met her child at the child's map of the world.

Contrast it with the scene I saw in a department store yesterday. A boy about 5 years old was diving into a pile of pillows on the floor in the linen section. The pillows the kid was attacking looked great. They were white with red apples on them. This child was antsy and needed to let off some energy. His mother was talking to the salesperson and broke away to exhort him to "stop that immediately." She was across the room and he knew he had some time before the pillow diving would be dangerous. The mother kept looking over and yelling threats. Finally she walked over and bent down and started whispering something to him. He started to cry, and I could see that she was *pinching him* on his neck and shoulder blade. As he cried, she told him to be quiet. She started to leave, and he whimpered again. She stood there threatening him until he was totally quiet. She left him sitting alone on the floor.

Imagine the impact of this transaction. Mom was annoyed and embarrassed by the boy's behavior. I know the feeling. It's a typical mystified response. The boy's behavior touches our *image* of ourselves as parents. Since almost all of us have been raised in patriarchal environments, most of us have issues with children's exuberance. We will often let the child do these very behaviors at home. But in public, we have our inhuman image of being a "good parent." So-called well-behaved children in our culture are often brainwashed, fearful automatons. They are not messy, wiggly, antsy, and impatient like real children. This mother is probably reenacting a similar scene from her childhood. The neck pinching is a particularly painful little unloving transaction. How would you like to have your best friend whisper to you in public as she pinches you, sending striking pain down your shoulder and arm?

This boy was also coerced into repressing his sadness. The crying and tears are the spontaneous responses of his natural psychic immune system. Grieving would allow him to integrate this scene. But in our patriarchal culture there is a taboo on weeping, especially for males. The "no feel" rules in dysfunctional families are especially rigid when it comes to weeping. The child's weeping triggers the adult's repressed reservoir of sadness. To allow the child to continue to weep beyond a certain point would activate the adult's need to weep and render the adult vulnerable. Vulnerability is the special nemesis of patriarchy. Vulnerability risks being shamed.

The boy also needed to express anger and have his anger validated. If his mom modeled respectful anger to him, he *would learn how to express his anger respectfully. This is especially important when we lose face and are humiliated.*

Having Empathy

A second way to meet our children at their map of the world is to have *empathy* for their feelings. For example, I used to like to playfully tease my son. Sometimes he liked it, other times he tolerated it, and yet other times he hated it. It was not until I was demystified that I could really read his signals. I can remember teasing my son, thinking he was having fun, and suddenly realizing that he had started to cry. After passing it back, I was present enough to *hear* when he was telling me he wanted to stop. Adults can often overstimulate children. The child starts off having fun and then gets tired or overwhelmed by the adult.

Children have different levels of intensity. Some are naturally more fearful, sensitive, and prone to shame than others. We must be present to them. When they say "I don't want to play" or "I'm afraid," they *really mean it*. When they cry, they are *really sad*.

I remember counseling a couple through their divorce. They had four children, ages 15, 14, 5, and 4. It was a fairly amicable divorce. The older kids seemed accepting and stable. But the younger kids—two adorable little girls—were very upset over the divorce. A couple of times during therapy, I saw the parents and older children grin and giggle as these young children, with quivering lips, told how sad they were. They were angelic-looking and adorably dressed. The others in the family treated them like cute little dolls, completely discounting their sadness. They were meeting these little girls at their own (teenage/adult) maps of the world, not at the girls'. When we meet children at their map of the world, we will respect their feelings.

Sexuality is an area where it is particularly crucial to respect our children's maps of the world. Liberated parents may see nothing wrong with being naked around their children. But it is possible to be just as rigid about being liberated as our parents were about modesty. What is important is to pay attention to your child's needs. If a child is overwhelmed by parental nudity, the child will blush, feel uncomfortable, and be embarrassed. This signal needs to be respected. Beginning around age 3, children start to be sexually curious. They want to know about sex and learn by exploring. A child is not equal to an adult in knowledge and power. They can easily be overwhelmed by their older sibling's or their parents' sexuality. Good sexual boundaries are the responsibility of a parent, not a child. Parents need to respect their children's need for privacy.

Each child is unique, and no two children understand or respond to the world the same way. If we will use our eyes and ears, our children will tell us how *they* map their world.

Matching Language

A third way to meet children (or anyone else) at their map of the world is to match their language. We all like people who speak our language. Really good communicators learn how to match people's language. This is much more difficult than it seems. Milton Erickson often pointed out that "no one understands the same word the same way." Try a word association test with a group of people. Ask them what comes to mind when they think of a circus. Have each person write down their first response. One person might write "cotton candy," another "elephants," another "clowns," another the "smell of animal dung," another "music." Each person will have associations based on his or her own unique experience. Or try words like "love," "wealth," "happiness," and "wisdom," and watch how different the associations become.

Richard Bandler and John Grinder, the founders of the NLP model of change, gathered detailed and extensive data on three of

the truly effective therapists of our generation: Fritz Perls, Virginia
Satir, and Milton Erickson. They found that all three of them were
masters of mirroring. Each of them intuitively understood that people
tend to represent their experience through one of three primary
representational systems. Some people are primarily visual; they are
see-ers; others are primarily kinesthetic, they are *feel*-ers; and still
others are primarily auditory, they are *hear*-ers. Each representational
system has its own typical predicates. So visual people say things like
"the way I *see* it is," "the future *looks* dark," and "I'm drawing a
blank." Kinesthetic people say things like "I was *moved* by what you
said," "you *touched* me when we spoke," "I can't *grasp* your ideas,"
and "I'm trying to get a *handle* on what you're saying." Auditory
people say things like "that *sounds* good to me," "that *rings* a bell,"
"something *tells* me," and "I just can't seem to *hear* you." There are
also some olfactory/gustatory people, who say things like "I think it
stinks" and "I *relish* being with you."

Bandler and Grinder found that the great therapists mirrored
language by matching the person's primary representational system.
Try this sometime. Listen attentively as your child speaks. See if you
can pick out any pattern in the way he or she represents reality. If
you do pick out a pattern, match it. For example, if you discover that
your child speaks in visual terms, speak to your child in visual terms.

We can also mirror and match a person's content. Talk to your
children about the things they are interested in. Combine this with
the other forms of rapport and you truly begin to enter their map
of the world.

Leading

Meeting your children at their map of the world does *not* mean that
you simply accept their perceptions about everything. Part of growing
up is expanding our map.

Once you're mirroring and matching (sometimes called "pacing") your children, you can start leading them to a wider way of
knowing. Soulful teachers do this intuitively. And soulful parents need
to be good teachers. I've watched mothers talk baby talk to their
children for a while and then ever so surely lead them to more
mature and expansive words. Similarly, soulful parents mirror their
children's specific developmental level and gradually lead them to
more mature and expansive ways of behaving.

In *Uncommon Therapy*, Jay Haley tells a wonderful story about
Milton Erickson. It is a brilliant illustration of a parent establishing

rapport by mirroring and pacing and then leading a child to a larger awareness.

One day Erickson's 3-year-old son Robert fell down the stairs, splitting his lip and knocking an upper tooth back into his jaw. As Dr. and Mrs. Erickson ran to help him, he was bleeding profusely and screaming loudly in pain and fright. No effort was made to pick him up. Erickson told him, "That hurts awful, Robert. That hurts terrible." As Erickson later explained:

> Right then, without any doubt, my son knew that I knew what I was talking about. . . . Therefore, he could listen respectfully to me, because I had demonstrated that I understood the situation fully.
>
> Then I told Robert, "And it will keep right on hurting." In that simple statement, I named his fear, confirmed his own judgment of the situation.
>
> The next step for him and for me was to declare, as he took another breath, "And you really wish it would stop hurting." Again we were in full agreement and he was ratified and even encouraged in his wish. . . . I could then offer a suggestion with some certainty of its acceptance. This suggestion was, "Maybe it will stop hurting in a little while, in just a minute or two." This was a suggestion in full accord with his own needs and wishes and because it was qualified by a "maybe it will," it is not in contradiction to his own understanding of the situation. Thus he could accept the idea and initiate the response to it.

Having mirrored and paced Robert's actual situation, Erickson began to lead him to a broader question about the significance of his injury. Everyone's sense of wholeness is ruptured psychologically by a physical injury. Erickson comments:

> Robert knew that he hurt; he could see his blood upon the pavement, taste it in his mouth, and see it on his hands. And yet, like all other human beings, he too could desire narcissistic distinction in his misfortune.

Erickson engaged Robert's narcissistic attention by saying, "That's an awful lot of blood on the pavement. Is it good, red, strong blood? Look carefully mother and see. I think it is, but I want you to be sure."

Erickson's statement captured Robert's need to know that his misfortune was quite significant in the eyes of others. It was also an important way to reframe Robert's attention. Erickson now began to focus on the question of the goodness and redness of his blood. He directly led Robert by stating that it would be better to examine the blood "by looking at it against the white background of the kitchen sink." Both Dr. and Mrs. Erickson examined the blood and both expressed the opinion that it was good strong blood.

As Robert was absorbed in the important question of the quality of his blood, he was picked up and carried to the bathroom, where water was poured over his face to see if the blood had its proper pink color when mixed with water. Erickson then raised the question of whether Robert's mouth was "swelling" properly. After careful inspection, Erickson reported that the swelling was developing exactly as it should. Robert felt comforted by knowing that his blood was strong and red and that his mouth was swelling properly.

The next question was focused on suturing Robert's lip. Erickson stated respectfully that Robert would have to have stitches in his lip but that it was doubtful whether he would have as many stitches as he could count; it was doubtful whether he would even get ten stitches, which was less than the seventeen stitches given his sister Betty Alice or the twelve his brother Allen had gotten. But he would probably get more stitches than his siblings Bert, Lance, and Carol.

Erickson accomplished several goals with these *leading* statements: He bypassed any negative reaction to the stitches by stating the issue of stitches in a positive way, and the way he discussed the stitches opened up a new and important frame of meaning. Haley comments:

> The entire situation became transformed into one in which
> he could share with his older siblings a common experi-
> ence with a comforting sense of equality and even superior-
> ity. In this way he was enabled to face the question of
> surgery without fear or anxiety, ... imbued with the desire
> to do well the task assigned to him, namely, to be sure to
> count the stitches.

Erickson comments that "At no time was he given a false statement, nor was he reassured in a manner contradictory to his understandings." Once rapport was firmly established, Robert was led to a resolution as an interested participant.

So many parents would try to comfort their hurt child with

reassurances and minimizations, saying that "it wasn't that bad." These statements are dishonest and ultimately invalidate the child's experience.

UNDERSTANDING DEVELOPMENTAL NEEDS

The fourth major way to meet our children at their map of the world is to know as much as we can about the stages of childhood development and the child's needs at each of these stages. You don't have to be an expert in these matters, but you do need to know some basic things. Shame-based parents go either too fast or too slow; they try to hurry their children's development or keep them immature. The child experiences polarized parental demands, which are more than human (stern discipline) or less than human (spoiled indulgence). Either extreme causes problems.

And remember that even accurate developmental information can be misapplied. Children do not mature at the same rate. Age is not a good criterion for maturational readiness. Not all five-year-olds have matured at the same rate and not all five-year-olds have the same innate predispositions and mental capabilities. This is why it is so important to mirror the child's *actual* experience. The actual living, concrete specific flesh and blood child offers the only true data to go by. The actual child must guide our teaching.

Most of the parents I know didn't really know what they were getting into by becoming parents. I think it would be great if high school students could take courses in child development. Students could have "lab periods" in which they spent two afternoons a week helping young couples with their children. It would be a darn sight better than some of the courses taught in high school. We learned many things in school that, while interesting, hardly prepared us for real adult life. Schools originated for the purpose of teaching life skills. Two afternoons a week of helping with children would not fully prepare anyone for the tasks of parenting, but it would go a long way.

The two most important questions that soulful parents must respond to are these: What does the child need at each stage of development in order to become fully *human*? What does the parent need to provide to the child so that the child's soulfulness can emerge?

In responding to these questions, there are, I think, two basic ideas to keep in mind:

A child needs to feel special.

Each child is a human person and, as such, has incomparable value. Children are born with an inherent sense of their own value. Each child is unique. Each will follow life's biological plan in a slightly different way.

Parental love insures that a child's specialness and uniqueness can unfold. The "specialness" each child has is the difference that makes a difference.

A child is inherently strong.

I was an overprotecting and fearful father. My parents were overprotecting and anxiety ridden. My mystified inner child learned to distrust everything, including life. Animals have an innate trust of life. We can learn from them. They care attentively for their young while the young are helpless but then just as surely "let them go." They push them out of the nest somehow knowing that life has provided adequate strength for their development.

The parents' job is to slowly but surely work themselves out of a job.

The human maturation process asks us to move from environmental support to self-support. Self-support starts with separation and individuation. In human development there are special times of ripening, states of readiness to learn certain things. Knowledge of developmental stages helps us to recognize these appointed times, and I will outline the needs of these stages in the following pages. But no two children do it exactly the same.

Basic Security

Infants need to be held a lot. They have a basic need for physical warmth. Most authorities believe that you cannot spoil an infant. Marcel Gerber was sent by a United Nations committee to study the effects of protein deficiency on Ugandan children. She found, to her surprise, that Uganda's *infants* were developmentally the most advanced in the world. It was only after about two years that the children began to be seriously damaged by tribal taboos and food shortages.

Ugandan infants were almost constantly *held* by their mothers and mother surrogates. They went everywhere with their mothers. The physical contact with the mother and the constant movement seemed to be the factors that propelled these infants to maturity beyond Western standards.

Infants need the echoing and soothing voice of a mothering person. This allows them to gradually internalize sounds of nurturing safety to draw upon when their mothers must leave them. These internal voices become the core of our self-soothing internal dialogue.

Infants need a feeling of welcoming security. This comes from the *way* they are touched and spoken to. If the mothering source does not really want them, they will feel the sense of rejection.

Infants need to learn to trust that the source of their security will be there no matter what. No mothering source is perfect, so there will be delays. But the breast or bottle *will* come. There will be reassurance and comfort.

Infancy is a legitimate time to be admired and made a fuss over. This is how a child comes to feel special. When infants know that they will not be abandoned, that they will be taken care of, and that they are special, then their healthy narcissistic needs are taken care of.

At some point around 7 months the stirring of innate curiosity will move children to begin exploring their surroundings. Exploration will focus on sensory experience, as the child is busy touching, smelling, and tasting the world. Space is what is most needed, a safe space where the child can practice sensory enrichment. What I would do if I could do it all over again is *lighten up* (and be more patient). Children need to test their limits, to see how far they can expand. But they also need the protection of limits if they are to embrace their own humanity.

Discipline

The exploration and separation stage continues and intensifies as the child begins toddling toward autonomy and individuality. Somewhere around 18 months each child will begin to test his or her willpower. The toddler will be obstinate and maddeningly stubborn. This expression of willfulness is the child's true self emerging. I think families should celebrate the first time a child says "No" or "Mine," just as much as they do the child's first word or first step. Saying "No" and "Mine" is the beginning of our second, or psychological, birth. The child is separating and becoming his or her own self. This is a benchmark in becoming a human being.

This first unbridled autonomy is a raw energy, primitive and narcissistic. It needs to be tempered with limits. The first experience of selfness is exhilarating and intoxicating. The child is learning about *power,* as they hold on to things and let them go. Dropping things is fabulous! Anything in their path is fair game! Look at what *I can do,* Mommy, as he holds the family heirloom! The budding image of self rejoices in its power to hold on and let go. It is thrilling! The power extends to things that are upsetting to parents. Things like refusing to go to the bathroom when Mom puts you on the commode and going when you're in the middle of the department store. This is a first experience of power.

If Mom and Dad are still children themselves, the clash of wills can be ferocious and the child will lose this battle. Whatever was forbidden to the parent lives on as a self-to-self transaction within the parent. The parents can't let the children have their *willpower* and anger, or sexuality, because the parents are forbidden to have their own. Whatever trances the parents have created will be replayed and reenacted on the child. The parents will be like their own parents and do to their child what was done to them. Or the reverse can happen. Very needy parents may refuse to set limits and may let their children do to them what their parents originally did to them. Without resolution of the past, the offender/victim identity trances will be activated. The scenes of childhood will trigger the trance.

As the child goes through each developmental stage, the parents will have to deal with their own issues at that stage. If the issues are unresolved, the parents will age regress. Many parent-child transactions are really child-to-child transactions. An inner-child-to-child power struggle often ensues at this developmental stage. The terrible twos are a declaration of war. The child's will against the parents' wills. The 2-year-old child *cannot* be allowed to go unrestrained. *To refuse to set limits is abusive* and often causes severe insecurity in the child. It's like being on a tightrope without a net underneath when this is your first attempt at walking the tightrope. Children need practice as a preparation for life. They need time and the protection of a safety net. Firm limits give the child protection. They provide aid and support when the often tyrannical little people get themselves into natural messes of shame and embarrassment.

A child-proof room can be of great value, as can a planned environment with sensory stimulation. (You're a single mom who works, and you have three children and live in a small apartment. You're thinking as you read this, "This guy is nuts! How can I child-proof a room? I barely have enough room to live in!") And the answer is, of course, you can't. You just do the best you can. (If you're lucky there's a playground nearby.) I'm simply letting you know what's going on in the toddler. Your toddler is *not bad or perverse*. Her willfulness is not an innate inclination toward evil. She is a normal, rambunctious, exuberant child following the urges of 15 billion years of the unfolding life force who is struggling to be psychologically born. If you shame and punish everything she does, you will block her new drive toward individuality.

Setting limits means that you must *do some* blocking. What I urge is that you minimize the shaming. To tell a child "I'm angry, I'm trying to read and you keep interrupting me. I want you to play with your toys and be quiet" will certainly not always work. But it lessens the risk of shaming and mystification. To tell a child "You're being a brat; stop being so selfish. One more sound and I'll spank you" might not be disastrous. But it greatly increases the risk of shame binding your child.

In the first example, the parent is setting a clear boundary. Here's what's going on under my skin. I'm angry, and here's what I want from you. In the second example, the parent is indicting the child's very being. This is hardly soulful, although many kids find their soul by developing courage in the face of these threats. Don't take this example and exaggerate it out of proportion. I've bribed my children and threatened them on occasions after my demystification. No one transaction is the end of the *world*. The chronicity of transactions is what creates mystification.

Emotional Empowerment

Children need to have their emotions recognized, named, and affirmed. One of the greatest advances in the last forty years is our understanding of the primacy of emotions. The clinical psychologist Silvan Tomkins has pioneered a whole new classification of neurotic and character disorder behavior based on the primacy of emotion.

For simplicity's sake, let me just say that the first thing one notices about a child is emotion. They may be frightened, smiling, interested, joyous, curious, crying, or angry. The popular theory that all emotions are based on thoughts has a long way to go to explain what depressing thoughts babies are thinking when they are crying or angry. Children do not develop consistent logical thought until around age 7, but they are emotional beings from the very beginning.

A major task in childhood development is to be able to recognize feelings and stay connected to our own feelings. We also need to learn how to differentiate a thought from a feeling. Highly functional people can think about feelings and be in touch with their feelings in relation to their thoughts.

Learning to differentiate thinking and emotions is an important preschool task. Parents need to identify their own emotions—"I'm sad right now," "I'm angry," "I'm very happy"—and they need to name their child's emotions—"I see and hear that you are angry right now." Instead of punishing a child for expressing anger, we should acknowledge the anger. Like saying no, anger is a boundary. When children are angry, they are defending themselves. Anger is the emotion that moves our energy to fight for what we want.

Children cannot always have what they want, but their anger needs to be acknowledged. Anger is the stuff of revolutions and the passion for confronting evil and injustice. Without anger a child becomes a doormat and a conforming people pleaser, often standing up for nothing. This is what every patriarch wants—a person who obeys and who will not make waves.

Anger is often confused with behaviors such as hitting, destroying property, name calling, and cursing. These destructive behaviors are not the same as the feeling of anger, although they often accompany it. We can teach our children (and ourselves) to feel and express anger without acting it out in destructive ways.

Many mystified parents who have had their own anger repressed try to be nice moms and dads till they can't take it any longer and then they explode with rage. Their child gets the accumulations of many little angers in one big dose. Sometimes the child gets the parents' *past* anger also. When a parent rages and yells, the child represses their own anger. The more the parent controls the child this way, the more the child is being set up to rage at their own children later on.

If parents can negotiate their child's anger in a valuing way, the child will be well equipped to handle life's many threatening events. Without anger a child is ill equipped to handle these threats.

At the other extreme, children will also not fare well in social life if allowed to scream and yell and control their parents with their anger. Society will not tolerate what Mom or Dad was willing to allow.

Our standardized rationalistic and patriarchal parenting rules have demanded the repression of emotion. Children are so emotionally shame bound that shame has been called the master emotion. But our emotions are personal powers. They are the energy fuel we use to signal danger, loss, violation, and satiation. Our emotions send us information about our basic needs. They signal us that we are in danger and we must fight or take flight for our safety.

When we are emotionally shame bound, we must numb out. The trance of sensory numbing stops us from feeling and freezes the moment and the pain.

When we numb out, we try to find medicines to help us deal with our feelings. Many addictions, like alcohol and drugs, allow us to feel. Other addictions stop sad, lonely, and fearful feelings. These avoidance addictions include sexual addiction, gambling, work addiction, and the most common, eating disorders. Children are taught to eat feelings—to put something in their mouths when they cry, to eat candy or ice cream when they are angry. They are taught to eat sadness and anger.

The Virtue of Prudence

If I had to do it over again I would work harder to help my children develop prudence. Prudence has lost the powerful meaning it had in bygone days. For moderns it means timidity and avoidance of risk. For the ancients it was the secret life of all the virtues. Prudence was defined by Aristotle as right reasoning in things to be done. He understood prudence to be the *virtue* of all virtues. Justice, courage, and temperance flow from prudence, because each involves right reasoning in areas of action.

Virtues are strengths that come from life-affirming habits. Prudence is a virtue of the practical intellect. This is the part of us that makes judgments and choices about the things we do, working together with our will and emotion. Aristotle was very clear that the crucial issue in developing prudence, the virtue of good actions, was what he called a "right appetite." We develop tastes for things. We can develop psychic tastes as well as physical tastes. *Psychic tastes that lead to virtue are about depth, value, and the sacredness of life.* The child's soul has a natural predisposition toward these things. Children who experience the wonders of creation and have parents who love and value the preciousness and mystery of life will come to desire life. When we taste and experience that something is good, we want more of it. Spiritual masters suggest that if we were confronted with the absolute good and could grasp that it was the good, we could not turn away.

Nowadays most children live in cities, all too often in squalid conditions. They are fed diets of junk food and TV violence. A child may live years without a true experience of natural life. Children need to plant flowers and watch them grow. They need puppies, kittens, and rabbits. They need to experience life, to experience the birth and death of their animals. Children need laughter and joy and celebration. They need the freedom to develop their natural creativity. Someone said that *creativity overcomes violence.* Creativity enriches the imagination, and imagination is the primary activity of the soul.

MODELING

Children learn values from the model the parent provides. If the parent loves life and displays passionately held values, the child will be deeply influenced by this.

Mrs. B. was exuberant. When I talked to her, I felt her presence. She listened attentively, validated, and asked interested questions. Life fascinated her and she would spontaneously move toward it. I remember the first time I met her. We were on a cruise ship. During one of our trips ashore, I was paired with her. As we walked together, she saw a garden full of beautiful flowers. Suddenly she was rushing over to get a closer look. She was touching the flowers. We walked some more and she heard some birds chirping in the trees. She would not move on till she had seen them. Later in the trip, I met her young children ages 5 and 6. They were curious and assertive. Her daughter wanted to feel my beard. Her son talked in an animated voice, detailing things we had seen during the first days of the cruise. I was amazed at the richness of his memory.

I've often envied people who seem so intimately involved with the details of life. For years I felt so sensorially numbed out and dissociated that I seemed to miss a great deal of it.

Parents who love life teach their children reverence and awe. I passed Mrs. B. on the beach. She was playing in the sand with her children. They were listening to the ocean roar in the shells they were finding. She was carefully telling them about the ocean and its importance in our lives. She spoke slowly but with great enthusiasm, almost with the rhythm of the ocean itself. I caught the gist of her words. "The ocean was our great mother," she told her children. She then described how the ocean becomes the rain that waters our plants and how when we eat green beans and lettuce the ocean becomes a part of us and nurtures our lives. The children were fascinated. So was I. She spoke with imagery that was concrete but which made them reach a little for the meaning.

Sometimes she stopped and asked them questions that piqued their imagination. She asked them what it would be like to be a fish and live underwater. The children were pensive for a few minutes. Then her daughter asked her why fish lived underwater and humans lived out of the water on the land. Mrs. B. told her that she did not know, that it was all part of a great mystery.

On one night the passengers were asked to present skits. Mrs.
B and her children performed a skit about three fishes who took a
land cruise and stopped at ports of call that were bodies of water.
Instead of going ashore, they stopped at different oceans and went
into the sea. They ended with a song and dance routine that won
first prize.

I later learned Mrs. B. had lost her husband in Vietnam three
years earlier. She spoke of her grief work and how well her children
were doing. She told me that she was a lawyer by profession but that
she didn't have to work and had chosen not to work while her
children were young. Most single parents do not have this kind of
financial blessing, but I'll bet Mrs. B would have been a soulful model
no matter what.

VALUES FORMATION

In addition to modeling, parents can actively teach children the process for forming values. They can *give their children choices*. The
choices need to be age specific, especially as children may not be
able to grasp all the consequences involved. A 4-year-old who wants
to go to kindergarten in his underpants cannot be allowed to make
such a choice. A child this age cannot grasp the power of social
consequences. He could, however, be allowed to choose which socks
and shirt he wants to wear to school. Well-defined little choices in
the beginning will lead to the habit of making more important
choices later on. Just having a choice and exercising it is the beginning of responsibility and freedom.

Values are based on freedom. Values must be acted on habitu-
ally, as well as cherished and publicly proclaimed. Parents can model
making choices on the basis of values and encourage their children
by recognizing and stroking such choices when the children make
them. Many mystified parents simply reenact their own parents' behaviors. Instead of really making value choices, they fall back unthink-
ing on their parents' vocabulary and model trancelike responses.

We have failed miserably with moral education because of our
literalistic, moralistic patriarchal methods. You cannot command
value. You cannot order people to love life. Such commands are
baked in perfectionism and blame and create people who do what
they do out of fear of punishment or to shut up the violent inner
voices of guilt. This does not foster soulfulness.

I like to recall the biblical story in which Solomon must make a
judgment for two women who claim to own the same child. Solomon

ponders and then suggests that the child be cut in half! One woman is immediately willing to give the child up. Solomon then judges that the child belongs to her. His soulful judgment was based on life. The power of life is the essence of the soul. To live with joyous stimulation of life-affirming parents is the way to develop the "habituation of desire." We develop a right appetite for life by experiencing the pleasures of life. To make valuable choices a child needs right desire. This is the way of prudence.

One thing I take comfort in is the realization that children know in powerful intuitive ways about their parents. No one has ever seen through my phoniness in a more penetrating way than my children. But I also believe they have chosen to actualize elements of my deepest being. In some ways my son is actualizing parts of me I have been afraid to express.

Refueling Sources

Throughout childhood, children also need what developmental psychologist Margaret Mahler calls refueling. Even as they separate from us, they need to come back to the security of the parental bond. Childhood is a prolonged farewell. From the moment children are born, they begin the process of actualizing their own unique identity. Their natural curiosity moves them to explore and expand their experience. Every explorer needs a home base to return to and to get fresh supplies from. "Refueling" is a way to describe the need every child has for an unfailing source of security. In toddlerhood children venture out a little bit at a time—perhaps just across the room—and always keep their parents (the refueling source) close at hand. As children grow older, they venture farther and need to refuel less and less. One day they leave home physically. Usually by middle age we have also left home psychologically. Maturity calls us to be our own refueling source.

Children need different forms of refueling as they grow. School-age children are moving out into a larger social sphere. They need to have friends and to learn to give and take, to play, and to compete. Learning how to win and lose is an important personal issue. Children need continuing support from their parents when they go to school. Although schools are now in transition, many are still traditional patriarchal systems, and children are often at the mercy of administrators and teachers, who themselves are pressured. At school, children learn quickly that our society has rigid standards of judgment. School can be tougher than a dysfunctional family! Schools are often rigid and perfectionistic. They are often undemocratic and authoritarian.

Children also learn quickly that some kids are rich, or athletic, or physically attractive, or are WASPs, while others are poor, or unathletic, or unattractive, or are members of racial or ethnic minorities. Children learn, in short, that there is polarization. And God help a schoolchild who is thought to be gay or lesbian!

What you can do as a parent is give your school-age children time and attention. Make home a *home*—a place to refuel when they feel overburdened by school, homework, and their new-found sense of social inequality. Be especially gentle with children who are not physically attractive or athletically inclined, or who are different in any way. This difference may later become the core of their soulfulness, but school and peers may drive it underground unless you offer consistent support.

WHAT PARENTS NEED

I hope I've been very clear that you don't have to have a perfect family in order to provide soulful support to your children. I cannot imagine a time when all dysfunction will be eliminated. But, while no family will ever be perfectly functional, most can be highly functional in the human sense I've defined it. Functionality means *dealing with* the problems, crises, and suffering that life and fate will present us with. Functional parents are able to respond. They've developed the personal skills and the solid personal discipline that it takes to solve most normal life problems. And they get help when they don't know what to do.

Healthy Shame

Parents need their healthy shame. Someone said that good parents are like reference librarians: They can find things out but do not profess to know all the answers. In contrast, many people act "shameless"; they present their opinions and actions as if they were perfect. I've had many a client say, "My mom/dad would die before admitting making a mistake."

I remember one summer at West Twin Lake in Minnesota. We decided that it was time for our son John to learn to ride a bike. I had long waited for the moment when I would teach my son how to ride a bike. It was one of the things that my dad never did with me. So John and I started out on the bike. Within five minutes he was very upset and I was shouting! But we kept at it until my wife intervened. I tried again the next day to no avail. Then my wife suggested that we hire a university student, someone younger and more patient, whom John might easily relate to. I reluctantly agreed. I felt angry and ashamed. I'll never forget the experience though. The next time I saw John, he was sailing by on his bike waving to me!

Parents need help. We don't have to have all the answers and engage in power trips. We are limited in our perceptions. Buddha's first truth that "to be human is to suffer" is rooted in the fact of our limited awareness. I am appalled at books with titles like *Unlimited Power*. Our finitude causes our ignorance. I like to write the word like this, *ignore-ance*. This makes it clear that as human beings we *ignore* a lot of reality. We can't help it, it's part of the human condition. Just as I'm excitedly focused on one child's accomplishments—"John took a step all by himself!"—I'm ignoring my stepdaughter Brenda who wants my attention.

There needs to be a big place for mistakes in a family. Mistakes are our great teachers. We need to be able to apologize for our big mistakes and laugh at our little ones. Laughter, joy, and fun in a family perhaps are the greatest medicines of all. Humor is one of our especially *human* traits. When family members can laugh with one another and can laugh at themselves, this is a sure sign that the family is rooted in healthy shame.

Realistic Expectations

Perhaps the most subtle aspect of my mystified parenting was my belief that if I found out the best ways to parent and did everything by the book, then my children would be everything I imagined that they would be. I did a lot of parenting by the book and my children did not live up to all my expectations. The fact is my children are unique and incomparable just like yours are. They march to their own drumbeat. Their souls have their own idiosyncratic and fateful journeys to take.

Mystified parenting is not just the result of *how* we parent; it is also rooted in how we *see* our children, in our expectations. When my children, following their own inner destinies, departed from my expectations, I often went into a shame spiral, believing that their behaviors were about my defective parenting or that I was being punished for my past sins. I often envisioned my children loving me

PARENT

IDEALIZED	SOULFUL	DEGRADED
• Has perfect marriage without conflict—"Ozzie and Harriet"	• Deals with marital conflict	• Chaotic marriage Corrupt marriage
• Always knows what is best to do	• Sometimes confused Asks for help	• Never knows what to do
• Personally fulfilled and happy	• Mostly happy Experiences normal human emptiness Sometimes in crisis	• Repressed and miserable
• Always patient and in control	• Sometimes loses temper or acts impatiently	• Violent, rageful Out of control
• Aware of all feelings and models them	• Does best to be aware of and model feelings	• Numbed out and unaware of feelings
• Disciplines with just and natural consequences	• Works at being humanly consistent in disciplining child	• Arbitrarily punishes Uses corporal punishment
• Superb teacher	• Works at learning and growing	• Teaches nothing
• Superresponsible	• Able to respond	• Irresponsible
• Lets child separate without struggle	• Struggles with child's separating	• Won't let child separate

a certain way, and when they didn't, either they were bad or I had defective genes.

No matter what we do or expect of our children, there will always be some aspects of their behavior that is uniquely their own. Recognizing this will help us to have realistic expectations.

CHILD

IDEALIZED	SOULFUL	DEGRADED
• Perfectly obedient	• Often rebels during toddlerhood Gradually obeys more and more until adolescence	• Rebels against everything
• Never gives any trouble	• Occasionally gets into trouble	• Always in trouble
• Speaks when spoken to Never interrupts	• Speaks out of curiosity Interrupts a lot during preschool	• Always interrupts Needs center stage
• Does chores without murmuring	• Sometimes rebels and complains about chores	• Rebels against chores Is destructive
• Rarely needs discipline or punishment	• Needs limits Does not need to be spanked	• Needs frequent discipline and spankings
• Never needs	• Has dependency needs	• Always whining and needy

POLARITY EXERCISE

Polarized thinking is a product of the fantastic imagination and creates our unrealistic expectations. Polarity thinking flows out of the realistic imagination and creates realistic expectations.

The preceeding two charts are exercises in polarity thinking. To get the most out of this exercise, you may want to try charting your own expectations in a similar format. To establish what is humanly realistic, it's also valuable to dialogue with other parents and observe children other than your own.

Parental Boundaries

When Mom and Dad are growing in their marriage, they are getting their own needs met through their loving relationship. The children will not have to constantly please their parents or spend their energy taking care of their parents' needs.

I've often pointed out that functional families must have a *generation gap*. Good solid intimacy between parents is what creates the gap. Children need to see that Mom is the most important person to Dad and vice versa. Mom and Dad need to have some life apart from their kids.

When love between the parents is lacking, or if the marriage ends, one or both of the parents may turn to the children for intimacy. I described the danger of such enmeshments in Part One.

Mom and Dad are also the primary models of intimacy for their children. We first learned what intimate love is by observing our parents. Too often what we learn is a mystified form of love. By providing a functional model of intimacy, parents provide an environment conducive to the creation of soulful love.

This does *not* mean that single parents are doomed to enmeshment with their children. Many single parents maintain a strong, separate adult life that allows their children to be children. And many single parents also model loving relationships with a circle of friends and with an extended family.

CONSISTENCY AND FLEXIBILITY

Although occasionally inconsistency is human, consistency is very important for children. Consistency gives children a sense of security. Children have a lot to cope with. Inconsistent parents create a lack of predictability and add to a child's confusion.

But consistency does not mean rigidity. As mystified parents, we are stuck in rigid responses. By stopping and imagining a new behavior, we can come up with alternatives to the old mystified way of behaving.

Imagination is the faculty of soulful love. Parents need lots of imagination. Patriarchy, with its stress on blind obedience, is highly unimaginative. When we grow up with it, we don't know that we have choices. Freedom is crushed because freedom rests upon *seeing* alternatives. I have to envision a new image before I can change my behavior. New images are the work of my realistic imagination.

Flexibility is an important aid to the development of imagination. There is more than one way. Parents can challenge children to find new ways of behaving. By being flexible parents, we can model imaginative choices.

Flexibility and consistency can coexist. For example, a family rule might be that the children are responsible for doing the dishes. Suppose the children worked at extra jobs and earned enough money to *hire a dishwasher* for the weekend. The rule would be fulfilled. A boy in my neighborhood did this with yard work. He hated yard work. On weekends he worked at a grocery store and hired someone to do the yard work.

It can be valuable for parents to find or create a support group with other parents for discussing more effective methods and interactions with their children. Sharing experiences can lead to new and imaginative alternatives. I know of a group of parents who shared the expense of periodic sessions with a child psychologist. She gave them some solid alternatives to try out. No one approach works with every child every single time. The more choices we have, the more flexible we can be. Flexibility is a component of mental health and soulfulness.

Letting Go

Letting our children separate is the most important task of parenting. If we don't gently push and help them to separate, they cannot form a separate self.

Boys who do not break the bond with their mothers become men who are terrified of commitment. I acted out my mother bonding by going to a seminary to become a celibate priest. This was a way for me to stay connected to my mother. I married Holy Mother Church and was reenacting my mystified family of origin role. My celibacy was a kind of sexual anorexia.

My dad's abandonment set me up to care for my mother's pain and loneliness. Being a priest was a family-authorized, honorable, actually heroic, way to stay faithful to my mom and to not risk engulfment with another woman. My later patterns with women were dysfunctional reenactments of this failure to separate from my mother.

Mother-bonded men, having failed as children to achieve object constancy, tend to act out all-or-nothing patterns. At the beginning of a relationship they'll see a woman as the Goddess Incarnate and then, after going with her for a while and experiencing her normal human faults, they'll see her as the Whore of Babylon. They shower her first with accolades, then rivet her with raging curses. Once her humanness begins to show, once she fails to meet their needs in a fairy-godmother-like way, or has needs of her own, she is no longer the "good mother." Her humanness touches the man's infantile need for a mother who *never* fails. Now she becomes the "bad mother" and receives the primitive rage that the little child could not express to his real mother. I did this in my marriage. My ex-wife used to say, "It doesn't matter what I do, you will be angry." And that was often the truth.

Women who are not allowed to separate from their mothers often become the victims of abusive men. They cling to physically, sexually, or emotionally abusive relationships out of terror of separation and abandonment. Such women often carry deep depression because their mother repeatedly rejected them for attempting their normal developmental separations. They have set up very strong trance defenses against this depression. These defenses may involve oppositional trance identities, one of which is a weak and helpless person and the other of which is assertive but ravished by *guilt* for being so. Men can have this polarity also.

Fathers set their children up for mother bonding by physically or emotionally abandoning their wives.

At the other extreme, some fathers are over-protective. Because of our own unresolved vulnerability, we refuse to allow our children to be vulnerable or to fail. If I could do it over, I'd love my children more by letting them develop the strengths that come from accepting vulnerability.

Fathers often use money and influence to protect their children, thinking they are doing them a favor. More often than not rescuing children from pain sets them up for greater pain. There *is* a place for loving protection. Here we need to walk a fine line. We need to know our children's capacities and limits, so we can let them take risks while guarding them from overstimulation and overwhelm.

Separation and individuation must take place if a child is to be *psychologically born*. When parents are operating out of their undifferentiated mystified child, they either rush their child or cannot allow their child to separate.

Parenting requires more than taking care of our children's immediate needs. Wise and soulful parents allow their children to take risks. They also have a sense of the power of fate. They know that there are factors in every human life beyond anyone's control.

KAIROS MOMENTS

In Chapter 5, I made a distinction between clock time (chronos) and times that are of major significance for our whole life (kairos). I spoke about changing a limiting belief as a kairos moment. Other kairos moments occur when:

• We have insights and new awareness.

• We make a decision to take a risk.

• We meet someone who positively impacts our life.

• We experience our own uniqueness.

• We feel especially loved and valued by someone else.

• We experience deep love and closeness for someone.

There are kairos moments in childhood for both parents and children. I had several such moments as a child when:

• My mother and aunts refused to follow the authorities' advice about schedule feeding. They snuck in my room, held me, and gave me a bottle.

• My mother read the novel *The Robe* to my brother, sister, and me.

• I went to my Dad's company picnic and I threw his baseball so hard that all my father's friends were impressed. He was proud of me.

• My father and mother divorced and I rode my bike to baseball practice weeping all the way.

• I sat at the bus stop on Fairview Street one Good Friday and knew that I was going to do some of the things I'm doing now.

I experienced kairos moments with my children when:

• I watched my son being born.

• I listened to my stepdaughter as a tiny little girl explain what her allowance should be.

• I heard my son scream "It's a miracle! It's a miracle!" as he found his new red drum one Christmas morning.

• My stepdaughter confronted my rage and in a trembling voice told me she would not be afraid of me any longer.

• My son was the lead in his high school play, and I heard him sing for the first time.

GRACE

My son stood at the top of the stairs at 4 years of age and asked me
to bring him his breakfast on a tray! My first reaction was patriarchal.
"Who do you think you are?" I heard my inner voice say. Then a
powerful thought occurred to me. This is a great opportunity to let
him experience grace. Grace is a gift without any strings attached.
There is nothing you can do to earn it. Grace says you are lovable
just because you are you. The sacred scriptures of all religions teach
about this kind of grace. How can children who have been battered
with standardized, rigid rules of self-sacrifice and duty ever grasp that
there is grace in the world? Parents have many opportunities to give
their children such an experience. *Try it sometime.* Give your children something that is wonderful! Surprise them with an unexpected
gift that they do not have to earn or be in debt to you for. You'll
enjoy the experience. You'll be giving a gift to yourself as well.

As tough as parenting is, let me tell you that your children will
be gone in the twinkling of an eye, so fast you may not really believe
it. Fill the unforgiving minute with them. What your children want
more than anything is to matter to Mom and Dad. "Special time"—
Julie's two hours with Dad on Saturday—can go a long way to make
up for the absences that work and the pressures of life lay on us.
Children want your time. Their souls know that what you give time
to is what you love. If I had it to do over, I'd give them more time.

CHAPTER 9

The Love of God

Who am I? Where have I come from? Where am I going?—are not questions with an answer but questions that open us up to new questions which lead us deeper into the unspeakable mystery of existence.

HENRI NOUWEN

Though I speak with the tongues of men and of angels, and have not love, I am become as sounding brass, or a tinkling cymbal.

And though I have the gift of prophecy, and understand all mysteries, and all knowledge; and though I have all faith, so that I could remove mountains, and have not love, I am nothing.

1 CORINTHIANS 13:1–4

When I was 22, I thought I had it made with God. It was the end of my first year in seminary, and my mother, my aunt and uncle, and their two children had come to Rochester, New York, to celebrate my taking first vows in preparation for the Catholic priesthood. I took vows of poverty, chastity, and obedience, the traditional vows for most Catholic religious orders. With the vow of poverty, I promised to live without attachment to material things. This included renouncing all private ownership of property. Chastity asked for renunciation of all sexuality, even sexual thoughts. And obedience asked me to give over my will to the will of my appointed religious superior and to obey the rules of my religious community.

The vows asked a lot but they offered the spiritual compensation of restoring my soul to its absolute purity, untainted by any former sins. I was told that these vows made me pure as the driven snow and ready for an immediate ascent into heaven.

MYSTIFIED LOVE OF GOD

I had a very raunchy adolescence, whoring and drinking and risking hellfire, warts, and blindness through chronic masturbation. But on the morning I took my first vows, I had not had a conscious sexual thought in three hundred and seventy-five days. I had sometimes guiltily hoped for "nocturnal emissions" (these were excused as long as you didn't go to sleep praying for them or give yourself predream suggestions during the day). But only two had occurred in this long, long year.

I was ready for heaven. This world was just a valley of tears and a mountain of heartache. All my childhood suffering stood me in good stead, since the more you suffered, the more rewards you gained in heaven, if you "offered it up." I had not only offered it up, I had received Holy Communion on the nine First Fridays. This, according to the promises given to Saint Margaret Mary in a vision, meant I would not die without a chance at final repentance. This was quite comforting. Years earlier Sister Mary Grace had terrified me with the assertion that you could live a near perfect life up until the last minute and then commit one mortal sin just before you died and go *straight to Hell*!

After I took my vows we were going to drive to Toronto, Canada, where I was to finish my university education.

When I met my family, they failed to see the depth of my holiness. They kept talking to me and treating me just as they had before I left for the seminary. Oh well! My rewards were not to come in this life.

As we drove to Toronto, I prayed we would have a car wreck and I would die. "This is the best shot I will ever have of going straight to heaven," I muttered to myself. I had not worked out what would happen to my mom, my aunt and uncle, and their two children. But I knew God would take care of them. At one point my uncle offered to let me drive. I had no driver's license and had never really learned to drive. As I took the wheel, I thought, "It's happening. God is going to take me. I'm going to heaven."

I feel disbelief as I write these words. But I assure you every word is true. This moment of supreme faith and purity was a culmination of twenty-two years of severe religious mystification. That's how I see it now.

I approach the whole issue of God and Higher Power with trepidation. My references to God should always be understood as modified by the phrase "as you understand God."

The majority of people believe that there is some higher power at the core of life. Most call their higher power God.

The fact that a majority hold these beliefs evidences an ongoing human concern with the question of an ultimate meaning for our lives. Paul Tillich, the great Lutheran theologian, believed that you can find out about a person's love of God by observing their ultimate concern in life.

Many people who profess to believe in God do not manifest that belief. Their lives are not a living witness to the God they profess. Anyone—Christian, Jew, Muslim, Hindu—whose life is a moving picture of lust and avarice is hardly a believer in the God of their religion. "By their fruits you shall know them" makes a lot of sense to me.

Faith is a love commitment that cannot be made on the basis of intellect alone. Faith without doubt is not faith but knowledge. For faith to be faith, it *cannot* have self-evident certainty at its root. Otherwise, what would be the value in believing? Where would one find the need for risk or courage? It is the commitment in the face of doubt that makes believing a morally courageous act.

How a Mystified Family Leads to Mystified Religion

Those who are mystified move easily into religious mystification. I moved from a patriarchal upbringing to an almost pure patriarchal religious system. My mother's family were devout Catholics. I went to Catholic schools and was indoctrinated by Catholic nuns and priests. I was told as early as the fifth grade that I had a religious vocation. This meant that I had a special calling from God to enter the priesthood and do God's work.

Earlier I described my lack of fathering and my enmeshment with my mother. Being a celibate priest was a perfect way for me to "act out" my surrogate spouse marriage to my mother. The religious trance deepened the parental trance. Children deify their parents, and when they remain internally bonded to them, they *parentalize* the deity. The seminary was the sacred and holy fulfillment of all the

patriarchal elements I grew up with: blind obedience, the relin-
quishment of my feelings and needs, and the complete repression of
my will. The cultic elements of my family were embodied in the
religious order that I entered.

Mine was a fervent and passionate mystified love of God. The
intensity and sacrifice of my love were great. The same is true for
many people with a mystified love of God. I don't want to denigrate
the subjective commitment I and others have made. I was a noble
young man ready to give up my life and sexuality for God. I did it
for quite a while. My soul was there, burning with the same fire I
now feel in my reformed love of God, which aims at reclaiming my
own and others' wounded inner children. Taking my first vows and
doing what I'm doing now have the same intensity. But the ends are
quite different.

DESTRUCTIVE POWER OF A MYSTIFIED LOVE OF GOD

I now believe that however well-meaning and committed, a mystified
love of God is ultimately destructive to what is human and what is
divine. I could write pages on holy wars and religious indoctrination.
They have caused untold suffering and pain throughout history. And
all of it in the name of God.

The particular menace of a mystified love of God stems from
the fact that it deals with "the ultimate source" and the "supreme
good" of all reality. It is much more difficult to grasp the destructive
aspects of a delusional trancelike love when one believes that the
object of that love is the Supreme Being or the Highest Good.

There have been a number of clinical studies that underscore
the destructive power of a mystified love of God. Let me briefly
discuss three of them.

Intrinsic and Extrinsic Religion

One of the great empirical studies on the difference between soulful
and mystified love of God was done by Gordon Allport, a Harvard
psychologist. Allport studied the nature of religious behavior and its
relationship to bigotry and prejudice. He found that a majority of
churchgoers—of whatever religion—were what he came to describe
as *extrinsically* religious. The extrinsically religious person *uses* religion.
Going to church is useful to boost one's status, to bolster self-confidence,

and to win friends, gain power, and have influence. Allport found that some people used their religious belief as a defense against reality. Most often, people used it as a super-sanctioning of their own formula for living. This kind of religious love assures people that God sees things their way, that their righteousness is God's righteousness. According to Allport, the extrinsically religious person *turns to God but does not turn away from self.* Thus religion is primarily a shield for self-centeredness, serving the person's deep need for security, status, and esteem.

Allport's empirical tests showed that the extrinsically religious tended to be prejudiced and bigoted, and that this was true regardless of what religion they belonged to.

Allport also found people who were *intrinsically* religious. These people were a much smaller group in the sample he studied. According to Allport, they had a deeply interiorized religious faith and were totally committed to it. Their love of God was integral and all-encompassing. It was an open faith, with room for scientific and emotional facts. Intrinsic religious love was a hunger for and commitment to oneness with God and all others. The intrinsically religious had little prejudice or bigotry. They practiced what they preached and evidenced a striking humility.

Allport's intrinsic religious life has many of the elements of what I'm calling a soulful love of God.

Soulful and mystified ways of loving God cut across religions and denominations. Muslims, Buddhists, Christians, Hindus, Jews can be either soulful or mystified. The same goes for those who believe in God but do not identify with any religious faith.

Extrinsic Religion and Blind Obedience

One of the major consequences of a patriarchal upbringing is that we lose our ability to direct ourselves through our own willpower. In strict patriarchy children are *not* allowed to express any form of self-will. A strong-willed child is considered especially dangerous. Children are considered good if they learn to obey and conform to the will of authority figures. In many cases authority includes *any* adult figure. This is what I was taught. I was to obey any adult simply because they were adult.

This rule has set many children up for molestation. I remember hearing an interview with a child molester who stated that when he stalked children at a playground, he looked for the child who was

EXTRINSICALLY RELIGIOUS

- **Turn to God but not away from self**
- **Use religion like a big Bayer aspirin**
- **Use religion to: boost status**
                 bolster self-confidence
                 win friends
                 gain power
- **Use religion as a defense**
- **Tend to be prejudiced and bigoted**
- **Use religion to sanction their own life-style**
- **Engage in totalistic thinking**

the most deferential and obedient. He watched the children's faces and eyes for clues. The child who seemed shame based and conforming became his prey.

Blind obedience is sometimes referred to as obedience without content. This means that it is virtuous to obey no matter what one is being asked to do. At the Nuremberg trials some Nazi war criminals pleaded innocence on the grounds that they had obeyed their legitimate commanders. They murdered untold numbers of Jews and others because of their trancelike belief that they were part of a "master race," and because obeying orders made them feel they were good and virtuous.

The issues raised at Nuremberg dramatically underscored the unnatural consequences of patriarchy. Blind obedience destroys one's inner life. It is incompatible with true conscience.

True conscience can only be formed on the inside. It is built on a foundation of inner strengths and good habits. Blind obedience and punishment force us to live by rules that are external to ourselves. The rules become internalized and function like posthypnotic trance voices. To form a conscience, we must test the rules we learned in childhood in the waters of experience. We ourselves must ultimately choose or reject the rules we internalize in childhood. When we choose them, they become our own.

INTRINSICALLY RELIGIOUS

- **Turn to God and away from self**
- **Have deeply interiorized faith**
- **Walk the walk that they talk**
- **Are accepting of other beliefs**
- **Are open to scientific and emotional facts**
- **Show striking humility**
- **Have little prejudice or bigotry**
- **Engage in polarity thinking**

Obedience and Responsibility

The second classic study that illustrates mystified religious behavior was conducted by Yale psychologist Stanley Milgram. Milgram designed an experiment to test how far an ordinary person might bend their personal moral values when called on to obey an accepted authority.

He asked for volunteers from the community to help him with a scientific experiment. When the volunteers arrived, they were told to sit on one side of a table across from a partner. The volunteer was told that an instructor would be asking their partner a series of questions. Whenever the partner answered the question wrong, the volunteer was to press a buzzer that electrically shocked the partner. The voltage increased with each wrong answer. The maximum voltage was excruciatingly painful.

The catch to the whole experiment was that the partner was an *actor,* who was to pretend to grimace with pain when "shocked." The volunteers did not know this. *They thought they were actually shocking their partners.* The volunteers turned out to be a pretty good cross-section of ordinary American citizens. Most were people who professed a high degree of morality.

The surprising result of Milgram's study was that the majority of the volunteers continued to shock people even as the voltage kept increasing. With their partner doubling up and screaming in pain, they continued to hit the buzzer. They could clearly see and hear the pain they were delivering to their partner.

Later, when asked if they had been aware of how much pain they were inflicting, most avoided taking any responsibility for it.

Some said the person who organized the experiment was responsible. They argued that they were carrying out orders as they had contracted to do by volunteering for the project. They were just following instructions.

Some said that they thought the experiment was awful but that they did not try to figure it out. It was for the purpose of science and they knew very little about science. Even though they saw and heard the anguish they were inflicting, they figured there was some higher purpose. The *fact* that they perceived themselves as hurting another human being did not supersede their sense of duty and obligation. Once they agreed to be subjects of a scientific experiment, *they refused to think about the data their senses were giving them.* They relinquished all responsibility for their behavior. Here the power of authority rested in science as a kind of God.

Blind obedience and punishment set us up to relinquish our own will and to let someone else think for us. They set us up for extrinsic religion and a mystified love of God.

Cultic Religion

In my description of cultic families in Chapter 2, I drew on a study called *Thought Reform & the Psychology of Totalism* by Robert J. Lifton. I've listed the elements of a cult again here. Cults are the most extreme form of mystified love of God.

Lifton's study discusses how brainwashing was used on American prisoners during the Korean War. This brainwashing was carefully undertaken. Over a period of time, the prisoners were given highly selective information. Negative thoughts about themselves, their loved ones, and their country were continually reinforced. In addition, the prisoners were at times starved and randomly tortured. The starvation caused mood alteration and the random torture, with its lack of predictability, reinforced a sense of helplessness and confusion. Rewards and pleasures were given for ratting on fellow prisoners and for confessing one's own personal defectiveness. In time some prisoners "snapped" and entered a state of trancelike mystification. Their torturers used simplistic words and phrases over and over again for reinforcement. Once the "snapping" occurred, these words and phrases functioned like posthypnotic suggestions and automatically triggered the trance state.

As Lifton writes, "Totalistic language is repetitiously centered on

ELEMENTS OF A CULT

- **Sacred doctrine**
- **Absolute obedience**
- **Obsessive confession**
- **Closed system –
  control of environment**
- **Totalistic thinking**
- **Language of nonthought**

all-encompassing jargon, prematurely abstract, highly categorical, relentlessly judging, and to anyone but its most devoted advocates, 'deadly dull.' " Every far-reaching and complex human problem is reduced to a thought-terminating cliché—a brief phrase easily memorized and easily expressed.

The Holy Writ of any religion requires years of study and high levels of scholarship. Reducing the mystery of God to simplistic formulas is grandiose and downright idolatrous. Such a reduction destroys the soul itself.

Totalistic forms of God talk are directly antithetical to soulful religion. Totalistic thinking is mystified thinking. All you have to do is blah! blah! blah! and life will be all joy and no sorrow. All or nothing is the oppositional split fostered by toxic shame. One pole must be right and the other wrong. Such thinking leads to simplistic righteousness and to an attempt to deny the complexity and suffering that come with seeking truth. When we deny this legitimate suffering, we destroy the human. What happens to the "fear and trembling" and "seeing through a glass darkly" that the Scriptures refer to?

Nazism was certainly a cult, and it is a good example of how a secular political system can become a "salvation system." Creating the "master race" was a supreme goal of Nazism. Some people were saved and some were not. Those who were unfit by blood had to be destroyed.

Rigid patriarchal family systems and the cultic families described in Chapter 2 set their children up as prey for both secular and religious cult systems. And while we seldom see secular cults as horrifying as Nazism or religious cults as horrifying as that of Jim Jones and his followers, there are elements of cult in all mystified forms of the love of God.

TYPES OF MYSTIFIED LOVE OF GOD

I like to divide the mystified love of God into two general types: Apollonian and Dionysian. These terms were originally used by nineteenth-century writers to describe two key elements of any creative product.

Apollonian refers to the formal structure of a work. Apollo was the Greek god of form, the one who gave definition to and put limits on things.

Dionysian refers to the undifferentiated energy at the creative center of the work. Dionysus was the Greek god of ecstasy, wine, and intoxication.

If you look at the chart below, you can see some of the ways in which these two types can be used to describe mystified faith. Each type represents a polarized end of the spectrum. What they have in common is that they are *both* extrinsic. Both are rooted in toxic shame. And in both types of faith, people feel they are "special," the elect of God.

MYSTIFIED FAITH

APOLLONIAN	DIONYSIAN
• **Authoritarian**	• **Enthusiastic**
• **Repressive**	• **Expressive**
• **Mind Closing**	• **Mood Altering**
• **Cultic**	• **Addictive**
• **Legalistic**	• **Exclusive**
• **Judgmental**	• **Judgmental**

Apollonian Mystified Love of God

Apollonian forms of religion are authoritarian. They are characterized by blind obedience to a sacred doctrine or scripture, which is spelled out in concrete and simplistic detail. They use totalistic jargon and effect cognitive closure with endlessly repeated thought-terminating clichés.

For example, as a child I heard over and over again that my church was the "one true church." Later, in the seminary I remember arguing with a Dominican priest who tried to prove that all Protestants were going to hell.

I have also seen TV evangelists who take the most complicated human problems and reduce them to a Scripture text or to the oft-repeated phrase "Jesus is the answer." These simple phrases can become brainwashing and trance inducing. They can polarize our thinking into *us* and *them*.

Members of Apollonian groups are expected to continually strive for perfection and to watch over the moral righteousness of fellow members. They confess their imperfections and report those of others. Emotional repression is the norm. Spontaneity and exuberance are dangerous because they lead to lack of control. A somber environment promotes sensory numbing. The status quo is glorified, while original ideas are unwanted and rigid boundaries keep new ideas out. Those in the group consider themselves saved and all others unsaved.

Apollonian belief systems are inhuman and antilife; they crush the very souls they profess to save. Being in control is the highest priority, and Apollonian religious groups are prone to be sadistic and masochistic. Love is confused with abuse and cruelty. The religious father beating his children for the love of God and for their own good is a familiar image in Apollonian type systems.

The continued subjugation of one's will to the will of authority creates a kind of personal closure. People simply cannot know they have choices if they have no will of their own. To this loss of will, add practices like fasting, self-denial, and mortification of the flesh, and the person begins to experience a kind of mood-altering, and highly addictive, adrenaline rush. I used to kneel for hours at a time. I developed large calluses on my knees. The physical pain of kneeling began to have a kind of sweetness to it. The same kind of mood alteration occurred when I fasted. Years later, working with anorectic patients, I came to believe that anorexia, like my fasting experiences, had an addictive quality.

Feeling self-righteous is also addictive. In my first years of priestly training, I often prayed for the world and for unbelievers. There were aspects of this that were soulful, but it too often ended in waves of feelings about myself as special and uniquely good. At the time, this sense of uniqueness and specialness was mostly unconscious. But it moved me to greater duty-bound self-sacrifice.

There are many subtypes of Apollonian mystified love. These range from severe self-punishing puritanism to more benign authoritarian religion. All in all, the Apollonian experience creates a trance-like and frozen state of being. It is not open to new experience or to imagination.

Dionysian Mystified Love of God

Dionysian forms of mystification are more difficult to grasp because they are outwardly less rigid. They look quite different from the Apollonian. They are more emotional and expressive. Dionysian groups look freer because of the ecstatic expression they allow. Followers may experience speaking in tongues, being slain in the spirit, and being born again. They may take pride in the fact that their church is spirit-filled and beyond denominationalism.

Yet Dionysian forms of religion are often more rigid and authoritarian than their dreary and somber Apollonian counterparts. They demand obedience to a sacred scripture and a rigid interpretation of Scripture. They are often fundamentalist, holding that every word of their Holy Book is the revealed truth of God. Authority is often vested in one charismatic person, who has the final say in everything. There is no room for any real individuality or difference.

Holiness is standardized and the members are considered the elect. This appeals to the mystified person, who often has deep feelings of worthlessness.

Ecstatic religious ritual can effect sudden conversion. In *one act* of belief a person can be freed from the dungeons of sin. Just take the risk, get out of your seat, let Brother So-and-So touch your forehead, and a lifetime of shame will be healed!

What a trip to lay on God! A new self is born—usually just as false and mystified as the old self. We might even call religious mystification the highest level of mystification. Certainly no addiction is more difficult to deal with than religious addiction. No addiction has a greater *denial* system. The entranced self is doubly entranced by the snapping of the religious conversion. This double level of mystification can also come from growing up in mystification and having your mystification reinforced by your family's religious system. The mystification of the righteous, the saved, the elect, the one true church is double digit mystification. Neither cocaine nor heroin nor any other drug can touch the *adrenaline rush of righteousness*.

In this state one *knows* God, is often spoken to by God, is given special gifts from God, is possessed by God, knows who is saved and who isn't, knows the will of God and follows it rigidly.

I know the feeling. I was there. I had it the day I took my first vows of poverty, chastity, and obedience.

Prayer itself becomes magical in this kind of faith. Certain kinds and numbers of prayers can get people out of purgatory (a holding zone before you're allowed into heaven). One deals in the miraculous, one looks for it, one believes in it. TV is loaded with ministers who lay on hands, heal the most heinous illnesses, and slay people in the spirit.

I personally believe that human beings have been healed by the power of God. I've personally had what I believe are true spiritual experiences. I've seen some studies on glossolalia (speaking in tongues), being slain in the spirit, etc., and they indicated that some deep personal changes occurred in the people who had those experiences. I further believe that charismatic "born again" religious experiences can be very powerful for the person who has them. I don't know whether they come from God or not. I tend to doubt that they do. But I would not argue with the fact that the people having them truly believe they are God-sent.

The problem is that most of these experiences are uniquely subjective. Their meaning is entirely personal. They cannot be made normative for an entire community.

ADDICTION AS A MYSTIFIED RELIGION

I suggested earlier that addicts are living out mystified forms of religious behavior. By this I mean that addicts are often spiritually bankrupt people who seek to fill their emptiness in an ecstatic or self-transcendent way.

An addict is a human being with a toxically shamed self. He or she may also have some genetic predisposition toward the object of addiction. I have suggested that in mystification our soul is marred by violence and by the defensive trances it develops in order to survive. The soul is marred but not lost. Remember the drawings in Chapter 5 of the soul as the star at the center of the circle. The star, our soul, seeks spiritual growth. When this growth is blocked by our false self, our soul comes out in covert ways. One way is in our dreams; another way is in our problematic symptoms. Our symptoms may consist of reenactment of the original being wounds we endured. We may reenact them on ourselves, on others, or we may get others to reenact the abuse on us. *The symptom is a metaphor of soul.* By looking at the metaphor we can understand something of the original violence. The metaphorical behavior is the soul's special revelation. The symptom is the soul's way of reminding us of itself and what happened to it.

The soul uses a kind of perverse spirituality to make itself heard. In seeking ecstasy, addicts follow the urging of their soul, of their spiritual nature. In childhood they were wounded by someone who was acting shameless. The abuser played God—acting righteous and perfect. Victims of this abuse, longing for God, yet having experienced only false gods, are confused. They find a substance (alcohol or drugs), an experience (false self), an activity (sex), a person (lover), or a thing (money) that offers self-transcendence. This becomes their idol, their god.

The addictive cycle begins with devotion to the addict's god. In his book *Out of the Shadows,* Dr. Patrick Carnes described this cycle. I've adapted his description for the figure on the next page.

The addict's Sacred Doctrine is formulated from toxic shame and the mystified self. The addict believes, "I am only lovable when I'm not myself. I'm flawed and defective." The first addiction is to the false self.

The second box represents the addict's distorted thinking. His post hypnotic self-talk becomes a kind of formulated prayer. The addict confuses abuse with love and selects a false god, or idol—the primary addiction. This god may be alcohol, drugs, sex, food, money, work, or some person. The addict may also have lesser gods, or secondary addictions. The addict believes, "I'm not okay unless I have drugs (sex, alcohol, money, etc.)." No religious cultist was ever more faithful to the faith.

The third box represents the acting-out cycle. The first element of this cycle is the addict's obsessional thinking. In a self-to-self trance induction, the addict obsesses on his god. A cocaine addict may spend hours, even days, obsessing on the images and scenarios related to getting or using cocaine. The obsession functions like a meditation, a mantra, or a prayer.

The second element consists of *rituals* related to acting out the addiction. Activity addicts (e.g., those addicted to sex, work, or gam-

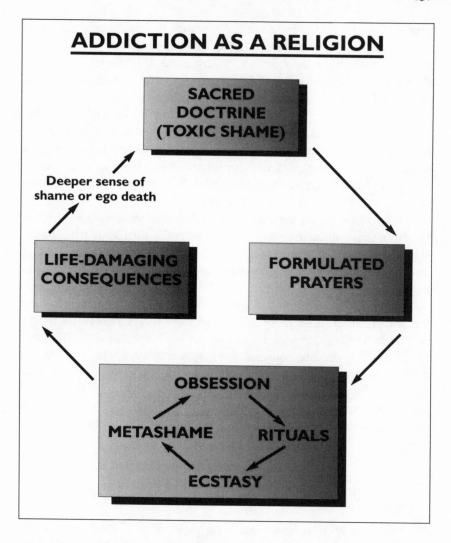

ADDICTION AS A RELIGION

SACRED DOCTRINE (TOXIC SHAME)

Deeper sense of shame or ego death

LIFE-DAMAGING CONSEQUENCES

FORMULATED PRAYERS

OBSESSION

METASHAME

RITUALS

ECSTASY

bling) spend hours in ritual behaviors before and while acting out. Similarly, there are rubric-like procedures for using crack, smoking grass, and so on.

Then comes the moment of ecstasy. This is the high, the big score, the orgasm (sex), the big hit (gambling), the big commission (work). At the moment of ecstasy addicts feel they have arrived. It is an at-one-ment. There is a sense of wholeness. *The addict is possessed by the god.*

In genuine religious experience, this sense of wholeness endures, though perhaps less intensely. But in the aborted religion of addiction, ecstasy is inevitably followed by *metashame*—the fall from grace. Now the addict feels rotten. It wasn't that big a deal. It wasn't satisfying. The longing begins again. The metashame is the shame resulting from the consequences of acting out. It is not the core toxic shame which lies at the root of the addiction. The metashame actually covers up the toxic shame.

The fourth box contains the life-damaging consequences, the worst of which is an increase in the intensity of shame and mystification. This shame leads the addict back to the sacred belief or core sense of being flawed, defective, and unlovable. Now the addict seeks the addictive idol (god) again in order to feel okay. The cycle has gone full circle. It is self-perpetuating.

Addictions are an extrinsic mystified way of seeking God. Addicts turn to an all-embracing savior but never really turn away from themselves. The deep shame core of the mystified self is never healed or transformed. The real idol is one's own self-will, which has turned in on itself.

The soul is still at work in addiction, and there is a point where the addict has *a moment of demystifying choice*. Between the fourth box and the first, the addict hits bottom—however briefly. The false self crashes. There are consequences, suffering, and pain. The pathology opens up the possibility of breaking the trance. This is the moment of grace. I'm thankful for that moment, although it took my soul seventeen years to get my attention. I think of this moment as the major *kairos* moment of my adult life. Let me describe the events that led me there.

THE LANDSLIDE FALL FROM PERFECTIONISM

My desire for an immediate holy death left me as I began my studies in philosophy and psychology at the University of Toronto. Slowly, over the next year, I began to neglect my rigorous religious devotions. I stopped praying and spending extra time in the chapel. "My studies are my prayers," I reasoned. One day I started smoking again after eighteen months of abstinence. This activated my toxic shame. The addictive thought patterns kicked in. Since I was not able to be perfect, I now started slipping in my resolve to live a perfectly celibate life. I started moving to the other polarized extremes. My mystified religion simply could not support my imperfect humanity.

Sexual abstinence can be mood altering. I suspect it has certain similarities with physical fasting. And when it is accompanied by feelings of righteousness, it is intensely mood altering. As my feelings of righteousness were diminished by shame, I began to feel the stirring of sexual desire. I was 23 years old. At that age you can only repress sexual feelings for so long.

One day in my cell (the liberating name given to our rooms in the seminary!), I noticed that the cushion on my desk chair was torn and that the lining was coming out. I decided that it was beyond fixing and that it would be good for me to sit on a hard chair while I studied. I could offer up the discomfort as a little act of mortification. So I pulled the lining out. It was a piece of foam rubber about two inches thick. I put it aside without much reflection and went on with my studies.

Later that night as I lay in bed, I started thinking about a woman I had seen the day before. I had walked behind her for at least three blocks and could not help noticing the lines of her panties beneath her very tight slacks. Now I saw her buttocks again and for the first time in a year and a half I was physically aroused. I felt excited and frightened. I got up and went to the window and prayed. Somehow my sexual feelings subsided.

All during the next day, the image of the woman returned to me. I went to the library and checked out a book I remembered reading during my first year in seminary. It was the life of a saint who had suffered great sexual trials and had triumphed over them. That night when I got into bed I started reading about this saint. As I read, the sexual image of the woman's buttocks kept peering through the pages. I felt that the Prince of Darkness was besieging me. I tried to pray, but this time it didn't work. I *wanted* to obsess on the woman now. I wanted to give in to my arousal. I looked over and saw the piece of foam rubber lying on my nightstand. I grabbed it. It felt spongy and resilient—like the touch of skin. I put it on my genitals. Waves of pleasure swept over me. It was wonderful.

All day the next day I guiltily obsessed on what I had done. For the first time in eighteen months, I missed receiving the sacrament of Holy Communion. I finally went to my spiritual director and asked to confess. He was kind but firm, warning me that I could not be ordained if I masturbated.

I was terrified! But in the following months I was masturbating more and more. The more ashamed I felt, the more I did it. I started drinking again. Whenever I could, I volunteered to put away the altar linens at the end of the morning Masses. The priests leave a bit of wine in the cruets used at each altar. There were twenty altars. I'd drink what was left in each cruet as I put things away. I'd knock back a fair bit of wine each morning. At night I'd sneak into the wine cellar and consume more wine. The drinking progressed to where I was sneaking fifths of Scotch into my room.

Later I added tranquilizers and sleeping pills to my drug diet. I became callous and contemptuous; I was too deeply mystified to leave the religious order and delusionally believed that I really wanted to stay. I raged at the seminary authorities, projecting my self-hate onto them.

There is a tragic quality to all of this as I reflect on it now. I was lonely. So lonely I could die. I knew several Basilian priests who I believe died of loneliness. That will never be admitted by the order or other believers, and I surely can't prove it. One of my mentors, the priest who first taught me philosophy and who was a great inspiration to me, ended his life in dire isolation and loneliness. It's as if he did not want to live alone anymore, and he didn't know how to leave the celibate priesthood. I knew others who seemed to die the same way.

One night my drinking and self-sexing reached an apex. I roared down the seminary halls drunk, cursing the authorities and screaming out my pain.

I was exiled to teach at the University of Saint Thomas. My days were numbered. I was given a teaching load of three hundred sophomore theology students, an English class, and the advanced philosophy group. My selection of material for my courses expressed my inner darkness. Included were Faulkner, Hemingway, Dostoevski, Nietzsche, Kafka, and Kierkegaard. I was trying to find some light for my own darkness. At Christmas, I broke down completely. I asked to see a psychiatrist. After four months of tranquilizers, MAO inhibitors, and sleeping pills, I made the decision to leave. Strangely, this was one of the hardest decisions I ever made. I had spent nine and a half years in the Order of Saint Basil. I had relationships I will never forget. They represent a decade of my life.

After leaving my study for the priesthood I felt completely lost. I felt I had lost my faith. I was 30 years old. I could not drive a car. I didn't have one to drive anyway. Father Caird, my immediate supervisor, had abruptly handed me $400 and told me to leave that day. The $400 was to buy my clothes, find an apartment, and make my way in the world. Not *one single person in my religious family* said good-bye to me. I had lived with them for ten years. I loved many of them as brothers. This was strangely inhuman. Inhumanity is the key element in the mystified love of God.

THE DARK NIGHT OF THE SOUL

Without realizing it, I was entering a period that I now think of as my soul's dark night. Spiritual masters describe the dark night of the soul as ego death. Ego death in my terms is a time of demystification, when the false self collapses and the person reenters the confusion that preceded the formation of the false self.

Patriarchy teaches us to dread confusion and to avoid it. During the "dark night of the soul" we cannot escape confusion. As Francis Thompson says of God in his poem "The Hound of Heaven," "I fled Him, down the labyrinthine ways." But finally there was no place else to run. My drinking led me to be fired from the first two jobs I took. I tried to make it in a 12-step program for alcoholism but could only attain limited periods of sobriety. Each failure brought me greater shame. I quit trying to control my drinking and wound up on a seventeen-day bender, hiding in my apartment. I remember only one part of this. I remember frequently going to the mirror and staring at myself. In the horror of this drunken nightmare, the only way I could be sure I was alive was by staring at myself in the mirror.

The episode ended when an alcoholic friend drove me to Austin State Hospital. He was so terrified of my seventeen-day binge that he had no idea what to do with me. A year earlier I had committed him to the state hospital and it had temporarily helped him stop drinking, so he decided to take me there. I was so out of it that it seemed like an exciting adventure to me. When I woke up in the locked ward of my state's hospital for the hopeless, the joyride was over. Ward 8 was deadly serious. The disorders there ranged from mental illness to criminal insanity. Patients received electroconvulsive therapy and huge dosages of psychoactive drugs.

Dressed in the state's clothes, I was led before the staff of some forty doctors and nurses. I was queried about my condition and asked what I wanted to do. My commitment was voluntary, which meant that I could not be held against my will after ten days. I was terrified but radiantly clear. I had hit bottom. I was no longer mystified. *I knew that I did not know who I was.* I knew that I needed help. I was empty. My false self had collapsed and I wanted to *live.* This was a soul day, a kairos moment. "I want to go to Houston and work my 12-step program for alcoholism," I told the doctor who was questioning me. My sincerity and resolve must have shone through my degradation and confusion. The next day I was on the bus to Houston. I still cannot think about it or write about it without tears coming.

That day when I thought that all was lost, in the midst of the darkness and chaos, I was saved. What an irony! What a contrast with my profession of first vows at Saint Basil's novitiate in Rochester, New York.

In retrospect, the mystified religious practice was not the prayer or the fasting or the devotions to the Blessed Virgin Mary. Rather, it was my more-than-human polarized behavior—the behavior that sprang from my shame-based, all-or-nothing self.

One can love God soulfully in a monastery. But, if you are intensely mystified, beware of entering such places. There are too many payoffs. It is too easy to mood alter the shame with one's exhilarating feelings of righteousness. It's the extremism and the payoffs that often make this form of the love of God so mystified. Rigid, authoritarian, duty-bound, and self-negating forms of religion are usually reenactments of the cultic dysfunction one was raised with. These religious structures are perfect for projecting one's fantasy-bonded inner child onto God.

THE SOULFUL LOVE OF GOD

Soulful religion is a quest that has no answers, and this is often exasperating, frequently painful, and sometimes excruciating. The soulful love of God is a quest for a deepening love and for fuller awareness. God is the deepest mystery of life. The quest for God can only be a journey of deepening, never one of explaining. When we deny that the quest is arduous and even painful, we deny our humanity and kill our souls. When we reduce the paradox that surrounds the love of God into tidy formulas, when we use our holy books as battering rams, when we pontificate as if the Bible were a how-to book with simple solutions for every human problem, we destroy the temple of the sacred.

In the Gospel According to Matthew, Jesus tells several mysterious stories concerning the end of the world and the last judgment. In one of them, the King calls those who are saved and blesses them because they visited him when he was sick and in prison, fed him when he was hungry, clothed him when he was naked, and took him in when he was a stranger. The Blessed are surprised and puzzled. When did we do this? they ask. And the King answers: "In truth I tell you, in so far as you did this to one of the least of these brothers of mine, you did it to me."

The Blessed did not know that in their deep human caring, they were loving God. This is the paradox of soulful love! I think this is one meaning of this passage. Those who love God soulfully are not worried about whether they are saved. The soulful are busy with life. They are living life to the full. They are loving with all their hearts. Their love is expansive and reaches out to others. Because it encompasses the breadth and depth of life, it is unselfconscious.

Once Born and Twice Born

William James, in his famous *Varieties of Religious Experience*, saw ego death and the adult experience of emptiness and confusion as the domain of the "twice born" religious person. The twice born are often reformers and great religious prophets, people like Augustine and Luther, who had complete conversion experiences. They were going in one direction and experienced a sudden rupture of their lives and changed direction completely. The sudden rupture marked the death of a habitual way of being and behaving, the death of a false self. Ego death is demystification. It is a kairos moment.

James also talked about the "once born," by which he meant those people who had not unduly struggled or suffered in their quest for God. The once born have an easier time in seeking and loving God. The twice born, according to James's model, lived out a tumultuous and painful life that ultimately stripped them of all human security and precipitated a dark night of the soul. The once born seemed to have had a more balanced childhood and achieved a fair amount of emotional stability. I think of Billy Graham as once born. He is as constant and unwavering as the North Star.

The lives of the once born seem less dramatic. In my scheme the once born are those who are graced with soulful love from the beginning. They developed along the lines of their true self. They seem to rarely have any doubts about their love.

The twice born are born out of mystification. They never achieved psychological birth as children and had to wait for a kairos moment of grace. I identify with the twice born. My birth came at Austin State Hospital.

The once born and the twice born are not in competition! Both have soulfulness, each in their own way. The twice born evidence the power of soul breaking through the shell of shame and degradation. "Soul," as Thomas Moore points out, "often appears in the places where we feel the most inferior or where one would least expect to find it." That was certainly true for me.

Where Have You Trembled?

It is hard to arrive at a place of needing and wanting, when we have remained attached to the authoritarian religion of our childhood. Too many answers were given to me before I knew the questions. Søren Kierkegaard, the great Danish theologian, once asked, "How do you become a Christian when you are one already?" The basic question could be addressed to a member of any religious group. It implies that it is very difficult to come to emptiness and seeking when you have grown up with some authority figure making you memorize answers to questions that you didn't ask and hadn't even thought of yet. Religious readiness follows the childhood stages for cognitive development. The questions will arise as one develops the cognitive structures to support them.

Cultic, authoritarian religion creates a kind of cognitive closure. The language is so pat, so clear and rigid, that it closes off areas that the mind would naturally be stimulated to investigate.

The natural language of religion is analogy, symbol, and story. Over half of the Judeo-Christian Scriptures consists of myths, parables, psalms, dreams, and prophetic visions. These are ultimately all forms of symbol. Paul Tillich taught that all religious language is symbolic. God cannot be contained in linear thought forms. This is why we need imagination.

I have often found God where I least suspected. The answers have always led to larger questions, and I have never felt completely secure in the expression of my love of God.

Sometimes our misery cries out like Job, "Let the day perish in which I was born." Then the comforters come on the TV screen from the pulpits of the saved and tell us that all is well. "It's simple," they tell us. "Just read the Scriptures, just accept Jesus, just go to church." Like Job, we need to answer these defenders of God who are really defending their own unholy terror and lack of love. Job cries out, "I have heard many such things. Miserable comforters are ye all."

Soulful love of God avoids the trap of becoming God's defender. We need to sit together in the face of the mystery.

SIGNS OF THE SOULFUL LOVE OF GOD

Soulful love of God asks for mutuality, self-sacrifice, long-suffering endurance, and solitude. But being true to its own passionate nature, soulful love also appears as individuality, self-appreciation, spontaneous letting go, and social action. In Chapter 1, I spoke of duty, obligation, long-suffering, self-negation, and codependent mutuality as characteristics of mystified love. Existing alone they are mystified. They stem from the overidentification with one extreme of opposites. Soulful love of God embraces *both* poles of opposites and synthesizes them in a balanced way. This synthesis creates a new level of depth, often revealing something that expands our imagination and opens up new possibilities.

By synthesis, I do not mean *compromise*. Compromise involves placing opposites side by side and giving up a part of each. Compromise is veiled conflict and diminishes the unique power of each polar opposite. Soulful love of God is not a compromise. Let me illustrate by examining some of the fruits of soulful synthesizing. Four of the main fruits are community, power, creativity, and compassion.

Community

Community is a synthesis between mutuality and individuality. The truer the community, the more solid the individuals within it. To put it another way, people best achieve individuality in a true community and they create a true community only when they have achieved individuality.

Mystified religious communities are bonded by toxic shame, loneliness, fear, and insecurity. Their members have failed to achieve selfhood, and, therefore, are enmeshed with one another. Members give up their will and mind for the sake of absolute security—including a guarantee of a safe passage to heaven after death. Mystified religious communities are collectivities and not true communities.

Mystified religious communities engage in *monologue*. The authority figure is the one who speaks. There is no real dialogue, no interest in new ideas or new ways of doing things. Matters are never openly discussed. This crushes individuality and makes personal development and growth impossible.

Soulful religious communities are bonded out of individual choice. Soulful religious communities engage in *dialogue*. They are willing to discuss different points of view. Growth comes through deepening insight and understanding.

True community is not a static entity. It is a living organism, which struggles, makes mistakes, and is willing to change.

We need community because we are social by nature. Our lives began with a mirroring face, a relationship. This primal scene was internalized and, if we managed to achieve healthy separation, became a model for establishing all other interpersonal bridges.

If we were not able to separate, we created a fantasy-bonded self-to-self trance. When we are mystified, we seek a sense of infantile security. Mystified people are not capable of real human community because they have not truly separated and established an identity.

The great benefit of a soulful religious community is that it safeguards our demystification. The community creates a context for feedback. Subjective experience is submitted to the community consciousness. The community demands our *presence* and provides us with real interpersonal contact. As we know and love the others in our group, we experience their unique maps of the world, and each time we experience a new map we become more than we were. To be part of a religious community gives us a sense of solidarity and of strength. We feel like we belong and we overcome the aloneness that came with the achievement of separation and identity.

A religious community is the major source for experiencing the rituals that connect the present to the past. A religious ritual is a way of remembering which allows us to see that the mighty acts of God which took place in the past are present in the here and now. The whole community is committed to uphold religious rituals. Rituals provide a way to feel a sense of continuity with our spiritual forebears. They help us remain focused on the consistency and spiritual depth of our religious tradition. They anchor us. They extend the interpersonal bridge into the past and into the future.

Power

Power synthesizes self-effacement and self-enhancement. Soulful people affirm and embrace their power—their own physical and intellectual gifts, their own individuality, eccentricity, creativity, and passion.

In contrast, mystified religious people often claim to renounce power and worldliness. Yet if we refuse to own our power, we become its victim. We make a fetish out of our body, our intellect, our physical good looks, or athletic ability. Our emotions own us, and we suffer from them rather than using their energy as the fuel to nourish and protect our most basic needs.

Real saints are powerful. They are remembered as much as military heroes. True humility is not victimhood.

Owning our soul's power also means embracing our shadow. "Shadow" is the word Carl Jung used for the repressed and unowned parts of ourselves. For example, when I was a child, I was told anger was one of the seven deadly sins. So I repressed my anger and overidentified with its opposite—excessive niceness. I had a frozen smile and always *justified* people's violations. I was almost always *nice*. When I began drinking, my anger came out in primitive rage. I felt completely out of control when I raged. As Virginia Satir said, "Repressed anger is like a hungry dog in the basement." It has an irrational power. In my good-guy, people-pleasing polarized self, I was *never* angry. I was *innocent* and good. Anger was evil and bad.

The religiously mystified present themselves as good and innocent. Such innocence professes to reject all worldly gain and love of power. Yet the supposed rejection of power is often a power trip. Those who have a polarized view often either totally reject the repressed "I want what I want" part of the self or totally identify with it by regarding themselves as sinners. Such a total identification with or rejection of one's shadow side is a barrier to the realization of genuine power. Rejecting one's dark or shadow side leads to violence. Thomas Moore writes, "Violence has a great deal to do with shadow, in particular the *shadow of power*."

Neutrality is not the domain of the soul, because the life force itself is never neutral. The power of the soul is not like the power we get by strategizing and planning. Rather, the power of the soul is natural. It is like a great ocean that has a mysterious depth not yet fathomed. No one fully understands the depth of being human, and our soul has goals and motives that we only partially understand.

To achieve the power of a soulful love of God, it is useful to embrace confusion and emptiness. In my mystified state I always tried to instantly fill up any feelings of emptiness or confusion.

Religious literature and scriptures are filled with urgings to embrace the void. We are asked to tolerate our weakness. Using strength to *cover up* weakness leads to the shamelessness of perfectionism, control, and pseudopower. Authoritarian religions are experts at cover-up. But their power is always pseudopower.

When power is repressed, it returns in monstrous forms. When the life force is squashed, it reappears as violence. As I mentioned, one of the most surprising responses to my PBS series "Bradshaw On: The Family" was the literally thousands of letters I got from people serving time in penitentiaries. Their letters had an overarching theme. They thanked me for helping them to grasp the roots of their violent behavior. In letter after letter people described childhood experiences of incest, beatings, emotional abandonment, and abuse. Their natural spontaneity and exuberance were squelched in the most vicious way. Their life force was repressed and later reappeared as violent behavior. Repression leads to a compulsion to repeat. In almost every case, the prisoners writing me had reenacted the wounds they received on some innocent person in society.

The repression of our soul's power leads to sadomasochism. With genuine power there are no victims and no offenders. In mystified religion, where power is rejected as if undesirable, there is actually a strong element of sadomasochism. There is a violent offender authority figure who is in control and a victim who submits. Behind its professions of innocence, violence is hidden. The faithful are portrayed in images that imply weakness and submission. But power is there in the attempt to control either by one's authority or by one's submission.

I counseled many people who had a strong sense of moral righteousness and victimization. In many cases they had violated other people's rights. They always tried to *control* what I did with them. They wanted me to find a way to straighten out their spouse, their boss, their children. The more they identified with being the victim, the more they were trying to control everyone around them.

Virtue is never genuine when it becomes the polarization of vice. As Thomas Moore writes, "We only sustain violence in our world if we fail to admit its place in our own hearts."

Creativity

Creativity results from the synthesis of long-suffering discipline and spontaneous intuition.

When we are creating, we are the most like the Creator, and, since almost all religious faiths posit God as the Creator and source of life, creativity is one of the sure signs of the soulful love of God.

The Creator as a model of the soulful love of God is far removed from the mystified model of the blindly obedient churchgoer. Mystified religious authorities would find the model of Creator blasphemous.

According to the Thomist philosopher Jacques Maritain, every great work of art has two elements: *poesis*—creative intuition—and *techne*—the art or skill of its form. This division corresponds with the Apollonian-Dionysian division. The Apollonian is the hard work and skill that it takes to give form to a creative work of art. The Dionysian is the creative energy that is its core. A great work of art is the perfect balance of these two polarities. The same is true of creative love. Soulful love of God requires both hard work and creative energy. Mystified love of God, as we have seen, takes either one of these polarities to the extreme and overidentifies with it.

Compassion

Perhaps the clearest mark of soulful God love is compassion. Compassion synthesizes fervent personal commitment with openness to others' points of view. It involves the action of caring for others while being rooted in the solitude of self-valuing and contemplation of the divine.

Mystified love of God posits that anyone not of the faith is totally wrong. Soulful love of God accepts that nobody has possession of all truth and that no one is perfect. In Allport's study the intrinsically religious were open to other points of view and other ways of life.

Soulful love of God is rooted in healthy shame, which when developed becomes the virtue of humility. Healthy shame gives us the permission to make mistakes and learn from our mistakes. It regards those who disagree with us as possible teachers through whom we can expand our vision and love of God.

With the soulful love of God we reach out to all others, especially those who are less fortunate. Compassion is rooted in humility and care, and caring comes as close to the full expression of our humanity as anything I can think of.

Compassion calls us to service. It asks us to actually help our fellow human beings. With compassion we walk the walk that we talk. True compassion is never overly public, like the Pharisees who opposed Jesus. The Pharisees acted religious in public in order to make an impression. Jesus called this hypocrisy. *Impression management* is the mark of extrinsic, mystified religion. True compassion is an intrinsic virtue; those who possess it are not very interested in press clippings.

The great religious models of compassion are often said to have a special calling from God. As early as the sixth grade, I was told that I had such a calling, and the result was severely mystifying. Today I am much less interested in the notion of a "call."

I have, however, come to believe that my whole life has been a preparation for what I am doing now. I think of my work as a priestly work. I am caring for other people's souls by doing workshops and writing books that aim at restoring people to personal power and wholeness. I owe a great debt to my Catholic formation and the education I received from the Basilian fathers. I have also *reformed* my Catholic roots in the fires of my life experience. I think this *re-*

formation has been necessary for me to love God soulfully. My personal reformation is a second order change.

I am now most interested in the "saints without names." They are ordinary folks who will never make any headlines or be considered for canonization. We have been taught to look for saints and heroes in the "more-than-human" Who's Who Book. The saints without names stumble and fall and live in the mundane messes of human life. If we could stop creating fantastic images of holiness, I believe we would all be able to find a sense of sanctity within ourselves. Most everyone has cared for someone else in a special way. We are all called to the priesthood of caring.

I'll never forget a man, let's call him Sam, who died of AIDS. This was in the early days of the epidemic, and at the time I had never heard of the disease. One of Sam's friends, Maxwell, came to me for counseling when Sam was dying. He told me about Sam's love for life, his humor, and his spontaneity.

Sam died within a week of Maxwell's visit. Maxwell called me and told me that he was having trouble finding anyone to conduct Sam's funeral. He asked me if I would create the rituals for the funeral and preach the eulogy. At first I turned him down, primarily because I am not an ordained priest or minister.

Maxwell called the next day, sobbing as he told me that he had gotten permission to have the funeral in a Catholic church but that the priest had refused to perform the service because Sam was not a Catholic. I agreed to do it.

The next morning, I had Sam's coffin placed in front of the first pew. There were nine men sitting there, and one woman who was a client of Maxwell's. Sam's mom and dad were sitting all alone toward the back of the church. It was so sad! There I was in the pulpit with the body of a 26-year-old man before me with twelve people attending the service. I had a sermon all prepared, but when I looked out on that bleak and empty church, I just started talking. I spoke of how fragile we all are and how fateful and tenuous life really is. I told them I had no idea how AIDS fits into the overarching theme of God's grace. I told them I believed that we can have few certainties about life and none about death.

I compared the twelve of them to the twelve disciples and I compared Sam to Jesus Christ who died alone and forsaken. I believe that we often find Christ where we least expect him. And I'm glad that I could be there for Sam that day.

CHAPTER 10

Self-Love

To the extent you hide your feelings, you are alien-
ated from yourself and others. And your loneliness is
proportional.

Dorothy Briggs

It takes more than a sudden leap to change a life. It
takes a conscious act, a decision to take our life into
our hands.

Mildred Newman and Bernard Berkowitz

"Don't you ever think of anyone but yourself? Stop being so selfish."
I heard this over and over again as a child. And as happens with an
oft-repeated parental message, I internalized it as one of my inner
voices. Until I began my personal reformation, this voice functioned
like a posthypnotic suggestion. I heard it most often when I was
really enjoying something pleasurable or just goofing off and having
fun. It was hard to love and value myself with this voice playing in
the background.

Another message I heard a lot was "Who do you think you are,
mister? Don't you know that pride goeth before a fall?" I was never
absolutely sure what this meant. I knew it was aimed at my not loving
myself too much. In fact I was taught that you shouldn't love yourself
at all. My family specialized in self-negation and self-sacrifice. Any
kind of interest I took in myself was called pride. Pride was one of
the seven deadly sins. Father Walsh, the fiercely respected pastor of
Saint Anne's church and school, said that pride was the deadliest sin
of all. Pride knocked off Lucifer, who was the smartest angel in the
hierarchy of purely spiritual beings. If pride can knock off the highest

angel, think what it can do to us! Any hint of self-love or self-enhancement activated my "Who do you think you are?" voice.

This voice gradually became the core voice in my symphony of
shame. It fanned the flames of my feeling like an imposter whenever
I did anything successful or received any honors. This feeling is one
of the telltale traits of mystification.

THE FALSE SELF

Self-esteem starts in an interpersonal relationship, with our survival
figure's mirroring face. When that face is spitting out indictments like
the ones I've mentioned, the binding wound of toxic shame pene-
trates to the depths of our very being and severs the interpersonal
bridge. We turn our eyes *away* from the mirroring source which is
our lifeline to self-love and self-esteem. We create a self that is acceptable to our source figures. We hide our face and put on ten pounds
of makeup so that no one can really see us anymore. We create the
image we want them to see. Our false self-image may look self-
content, powerful, mean, happy, or joyous, but it is flimsily built on
a foundation of confusion. There is no substance to it; it is fantastic
(ideal or degraded), rather than real. Either more than human or
less than human, our false self-image is *inhuman*. Once we have
created an inhuman self, we guard it with hypervigilance. We become
addicted to it. We try to get our basic needs met with it. We become
attached to it and delusionally believe that this false self is who we
are.

In early adolescence I became attached to a "good guy, people-
pleasing" false self. I also secretly fanned grandiose feelings of self-
misery and special suffering. Look what I had to go through! This
was one payoff that came from my misery. I had grown accustomed
to toxic shame's ugly face and feared anything new. By guarding my
misery I avoided taking any risks.

I had also survived much of my loneliness, sadness, and confusion by getting into my head and analyzing, explaining, and intellectu-
alizing everything. In my active alcoholic days I used to drive people
crazy talking about philosophers no one had ever heard of. (Try
Alcer of Clairvaux, the pseudo-Augustine, or Siger of Brabant!) Head-
tripping is a great defense, and it also takes people off their guard
when you beat them to the punch with a stunning analysis of the
etiology of your *own grandiosity*. Mystified intellectuals are a breed
unto themselves. I was one.

My false self certainly caused me suffering. Constantly being on guard and trying to control everyone is a full-time job and one that is quite exhausting. It is also very lonely. I was in fact too dissociated to feel how lonely I really was. I actually loved to be *physically* alone. Once I could close and lock the door, I could let my guard down, I could relax. When you are pretending all the time, not to have to pretend gives you an adrenaline rush. I could be spontaneous, drop my shorts on the floor, be sloppy, belch, and be completely un-guarded. My opposite trance self, "I want what I want, I'll do whatever I want to do," was free to operate. It felt more real than my false self. The rush I got from physically isolating helped block my awareness of how lonely I really was.

I remember five years ago almost yelling on the phone to one of my friends because I was solidly experiencing the *feeling of loneliness*. There I was, excitedly telling my friend, "I'm lonely! I'm really lonely! I feel it!" My friend was energetically supporting me in having my feelings! God knows what an operator listening in might have thought! As strange as that may sound to you, it was a high-water mark in my journey to self-love and self-acceptance.

SOULFUL SELF-LOVE

I am much less clear today about the full scope of my identity than I was fifteen years ago. False selves are defined and limited; true selves are not. I know that there are unarticulated parts of myself that are still lying dormant. I don't believe we have unlimited powers. That would be inhuman. I do believe we have unlimited *possibilities*. Ten years ago, if someone had told me I'd sell three million books, I would have said they were crazy. If they had told me I was even going to finish writing a book, I would have had serious doubts. I had been messing around with ideas, saying I was going to write a book, since 1972. People had grown tired of hearing me talk about it. By 1980 I had pretty much given up the idea. *But* there was *something* in *me* talking about writing a book. And I was fascinated by *The New York Times* bestseller list. I used to look at it all the time. This kind of energy is usually about one's *soul,* although I sure didn't know it at the time. It never entered my conscious mind, but soul is more often on the fringes of consciousness.

The more I am connected with my soul, the more I wonder what things I still have in store for myself. Many parts of myself that were active in childhood and lay dormant during my battle with booze have surfaced in the last twenty years. I believe that there are surprises still to come.

You can count on the same for yourself. There are parts of your real self that are lying dormant, and they may surprise you in the future.

THE CURATIVE POWER OF SHAME

Learning about shame was a real turning point in my story. I wrote a book about shame, and I recommend it to you. The second half of the book is comprised of every way I could find to help heal the shame that binds you. The exercises can open you up to surprising insights into your own self. Much of our shame is maintained by the blaming, comparing, and self-suppressing posthypnotic voices that echo those we heard in our childhood. We can learn to install new voices and remap our governing scenarios.

I've grown in my understanding of shame. I feel that what I talked about at the end of *Healing the Shame That Binds You* is worth expanding on. In that book I suggested that embracing our shame is a way to *externalize* it and that the only way out of the shame is to enter into it. Shame is the core of mystification, so embracing our shame is the chief pathway toward demystifying ourselves. Our soul leads us into the depth of the dark woods. If we are willing, something happens which is both *revolutionary* and *revelatory*.

Shame As Revolutionary

Shame is revolutionary because by embracing it we come out of hiding and isolation. The very act of embracing our shame starts the process of change.

I embraced my shame the day I went to my first 12-step meeting. My false self feared exposure more than anything. I knew that confusion was lurking just below the surface. I hated to go anywhere where I would not be able to maintain control. I did not know what to expect when I went to my first meeting. I felt vulnerable and exposed. Walking into a 12-step meeting for the first time, feeling raw and unguarded, is what I call embracing my shame. Going for treatment or therapy, being honest with someone about your secret behaviors, telling the truth about yourself—in short, showing your face—is the way to embrace your shame.

We would not be able to embrace our shame unless we had hope. Without hope you wouldn't lift your finger. To be willing to embrace shame means that you want to change and that deep in your soul you hope you can, or you wouldn't even try. Being willing to embrace your shame means that you are also tired of the way life is going. I got sick and tired of being sick and tired. One day the suffering was too great; it just didn't have any payoff. My loneliness was just too lonely. *This is the way soul awakens us. It works through loneliness, boredom, pain, and confusion.*

If you identify with being mystified, I hope that your soul will lead you down the path to powerlessness and confusion. At that point, you have to surrender and reach out. Asking for help, if only from yourself, is a truly human act. You cannot receive unless you ask. When you ask, you have already started receiving help. Shame is about hiding and isolating. To ask for help is to come out of hiding.

Gertrude Mueller Nelson, in her marvelous soul book *Here All Dwell Free,* tells about a woman who broke both arms by tripping over a dog. This woman had lived behind a facade of independence and self-sufficiency. This is a common cover-up for vulnerability and shame. It is a way to control, so that one is never caught off guard. The woman described how humiliated she felt:

> Can you imagine what it feels like to need my husband and my daughter to spoon cereal into me in the morning? Can you imagine needing my husband to put on all my clothes for me, my underwear—tie my shoes ... to wipe my bottom? This is total reduction. And yet I've learned from it ... how controlling I was in my independence. But the most important thing I learned was how to be still. And how to ask vulnerably. . . .

The day I asked for help was the day I began my revolution. In 12-step programs this day is valued and honored. December 11, 1965, is my sobriety date, the day I asked Norris for help. That was the day he took me to the state hospital. I admitted I was powerless and my life changed radically. I learned the paradoxical language of soul making. By admitting I was powerless, I instantly began to regain my power. I have gone through several cycles of growth since my first great awakening at the state hospital. Nothing has been the same since that day.

Soul Days

I think all of us should honor our special kairos times—the day we hit bottom, the day we quit our addiction, the day we found God, the day we quit our stifling job, the day of our divorce, the day of our marriage, the day we finished writing a book, the day we met a certain person.

We honor and celebrate national victories like the Fourth of July, the Day of Independence. I'm for having personal days for honoring *ourselves*. These could be called "Soul Days." They could be any day in the drama of our lives when we truly began to love ourselves, when our soul broke through and made itself known.

Shame As Revelatory

Embracing our toxic shame can bring about self-revelation and self-love. But confronting our demons is a terrifying prospect. We need courage in order to take the risk. Greek myths often represented self-confrontations as a journey into the underworld. They also presented moments of self-revelation in boundary situations—situations where we are at the limits of our sovereignty, where all the protective coverings are stripped off. The hero or heroine must truly face Job's question, "What is man?" Or Lear's question, "Is man no more than this?"

My family and Father Walsh saw any act of self-enhancement as pride. Their view was polarized. Not every act of self-enhancement is pride. Some are acts of self-love and self-valuing. Our acts are prideful when they are too puffed up and grandiose, when they are based on perfectionism, righteousness, criticism, power broking, and blame. This is pride in the sinful sense, because it refuses to accept human limits.

The ancient Greeks called this problem *hubris*. This is also the basic issue in the biblical story of Adam and Eve. Their downfall came because they refused to accept their limits.

Sophocles' tragedy *Oedipus Rex* gives us an indelible image of *hubris,* which Sophocles understood as that quality in human beings that defies the very nature of our humanity. As the play opens, Oedipus is the king of Thebes, powerful and revered by all. But his city is being ravaged by a plague, and the seers suggest that Oedipus himself is the cause. Oedipus is furious with denial at first. But then, with mounting terror, he confronts the secret of his identity. He cries:

Let all come out! However vile, however base it be, I must
unlock the secret of my birth. . . . I shall not be shamed. . . .
I ask to be no other man than that I am and will know who
I am.

Like all of us, Oedipus must go back to his origins to find out about
his mystification. What he discovers was later made famous by Freud's
Oedipus complex: that *in his ignorance,* he had killed his own father
and married his mother, Jocasta, the queen.

And yet the evidence was there all along. Oedipus means
swollen-foot. He was named this because of his wound—a wound
given to him by his mother and father. Laius and Jocasta, the king
and queen of Thebes, were warned in a prophecy that their newborn
son would someday kill his father and marry his mother. In order
to circumvent this prophecy, Laius pierced the baby's feet with an
iron pin to prevent him from crawling and secretly gave him to a
shepherd with orders to abandon him in the mountains where he
would die of exposure. Oedipus was rescued and raised by a herds-
man and his wife, but he could not escape his fate.

Oedipus had to accept the limits of his humanity symbolized by
the wounds to his feet. This lesson is for all of us to learn. When we
try to be perfect or too powerful, we play God and forget that we
are finite, earth-bound *footed* creatures.

Another Greek myth makes it clear that we must be willing to
embrace some painful paradoxes in order to love ourselves. The
Jungian psychologist Robert Johnson tells the story of Eros and Psyche
in his book *She*. It is the story of how Psyche is initiated into full
womanhood by learning to accept *her limits*.

Psyche means soul, and in this myth the woman who bears this
name is the embodiment of the inner life. She was so beautiful that
she threatened Aphrodite, the goddess of love and beauty, who became so jealous that she condemned her to marry Death, the ugliest
and most horrible creature possible.

In order to be sure of Psyche's death, Aphrodite engaged the
assistance of her son, Eros, the god of love. As Eros goes to do his
mother's bidding, he accidentally pricks his finger on one of his own
arrows and in consequence falls in love with Psyche. He takes her
for his bride with the restriction that when he comes to her each
night, she must not look at him or inquire about any of his ways!
Psyche agrees to this, and everything is wonderful until her two envious sisters try to sabotage the marriage by advising her that her

husband is really a loathsome serpent who will devour her. They tell
her to get a lamp and look at him while he sleeps. She does this,
and to her amazement he is the most beautiful creature she has ever
seen. She is so moved she lets go of the lamp and a drop of oil falls
on Eros and wakes him. Outraged, he carries her out of their paradise
garden, drops her on the Mountain of Death, and flies away.

Psyche goes to her mother-in-law, Aphrodite, and begs for
mercy. After a tyrannical speech, Aphrodite gives her four tasks which,
if achieved, will save her life. With each task, she risks death, but if
she successfully accomplishes them, she will attain full womanhood
and expanded awareness.

Psyche is a classic Caretaker. She must learn, as I did, that caretaking can be full of pride and a cover-up for toxic shame.

The tasks are like four stages of a journey to individuality and
wholeness. The fourth task is the hardest and the most dangerous.
In this final task, Psyche must journey to the depths of the underworld and obtain from Persephone, the goddess of the underworld,
a little cask of her own beauty ointment. Psyche is to take two coins
and two pieces of bread.

On her journey, she must first *refuse* a lame donkey driver who
asks her to pick up some sticks he has dropped. She is to pay the
ferryman at the River Styx with one coin, and as she crosses the river
she is to *refuse* the groping hand of a dying man as he reaches out
of the water. She must *refuse* to assist the three women who are
weaving the threads of fate. She then must toss one piece of bread
to Cerberus, the three-headed dog who guards the entrance to hell,
so that while the three heads are quarreling, she can slip past his
guard. She must *refuse* to eat anything that Persephone offers her.
Ultimately the ointment will awaken her to her own sense of beauty,
to her own I AMness, her own self-love.

Psyche's four refusals can be seen as different aspects of saying
no. The *creative no offers form-giving limitation* to our life. Refusing
the lame man and the dying man goes against our instinct for caretaking as a way of self-love and self-valuing. The three women, the
weavers of the threads of fate, are trying to control the fate of their
children by weaving. They refuse to accept their powerlessness in
relation to their children. They refuse to let their children go.

The nurturing soul mother in all of us must learn that we will
love and serve our children and our lovers better by attending to
our own fate, by healing our own unfinished past, our own time of
enchantment and mystification. Only by confronting this past can we
make it real and transform it.

We fear the darkness of our soul's inner regions because we are so polarized. Just as we polarize the world outside us, we polarize the world within. We feel that we must be all light with no darkness, that we must be perfectly clear with no confusion. Instead, what we really need is reconciliation. This reconciliation can only come if we embrace the shame that we fear so much. Until we enter our shame and mystification, we do not have a chance.

Paradoxically we fear our own underground not only because we are afraid of finding flaws and defectiveness but also because we are afraid of finding our authenticity and uniqueness. In his fine book *Owning Your Shadow,* Robert Johnson writes:

> To draw the skeletons out of the closet is relatively easy, but to own the gold in the shadow is terrifying. It is more disrupting to find that you have a profound nobility of character than to find you are a bum.

I see my journey from toxic shame to self-love and self-esteem as having three stages: Recovery, Uncovery, and Discovery. You may not travel these stages in the linear sequence that I will outline here. And your experience may be quite different from mine. The soul can never be defined or contained in such stages. But the stages help me to sort out my own experience. Each connected me with myself, and each enhanced my self-love and soulfulness.

STAGE ONE: RECOVERY OF WILL

I call this first stage recovery because it begins with the recovery of our *willpower*. In Part One, I mentioned that our false self is a hypnotic identity and that hypnotic trance is characterized by a narrowing or fixation of consciousness, a feeling of being out of control, and deep trance phenomena. I was an active alcoholic for seventeen years. My addiction reinforced each of these elements. I obsessed on alcohol; it was my most important need. My thoughts about drinking were pervasive. My horizons were narrowed.

I have already discussed the ecstatic quality of the addictive trance. Addicts also speak of the compulsion to drink and I certainly experienced that. But what most interests me now is how I *stopped my addictive urges*—and, by extension, how anyone can stop an addiction. I smoked for twenty-six years. One day I decided to stop and I did. How is it possible to stop compulsive behavior?

If you recall the earlier discussion of hypnosis and trance induction, you will remember I stressed the fact that an induction cannot take place *without our willingness* to be hypnotized. I also discussed Stephen Wolinsky's thesis that *we choose the particular deep trance phenomena that best insure our survival*. We created the deep trance phenomena. Because they worked so well, they became automatic and were extended to the environment in general. These early choices combined to form our symptoms or problems.

In my case, the emotional part of my alcoholism, the urge and compulsion to drink, was always triggered by some threat in the present that activated an earlier scenario, together with the original defensive trance. For example, when I left the seminary at age 30, I had great fear and anxiety about finding a job. I had been out of the work force for ten years, and my previous job experiences were those of office boy and grocery checker. I did my most serious drinking during the year and a half transition between leaving the seminary and getting settled in a job. I felt raw and exposed. This triggered my sense of shame and powerlessness. It activated childhood memories involving fear and confusion. The positive memory of how alcohol eased my fear, coupled with dissociation from all the past disasters that resulted from drinking, created the urge to drink.

Reowning Choice

The key in the recovery stage is the realization that I have a *choice*. I create my own trance induction. If I learn how I do, I can stop doing it. For me, this realization came from my face-to-face contact with a group of recovering alcoholics who were working the 12-steps. Telling my shameful story and seeing myself accepted in the mirroring faces of others restored the interpersonal bridge. This is the only way back from the psychological death of toxic shame. You can read self-help books geared toward self-esteem till hell freezes over, and nothing will change until you restore the interpersonal bridge. I had tried to do it *alone*. Most people in a self-to-self trance try to get well alone. The original rupture of the interpersonal bridge creates deep mistrust. You first come to believe that you cannot depend on anyone except yourself. Later you depend on your mood-altering drug of choice. You depend on it till it starts delivering severe pain. Your soul speaks through pain. It gets your attention.

Listening to group members speak about their own addictive patterns helped me to see mine more objectively. Listening to other people's stories and receiving lots of encouragement and support from them was a way out of the trance. It was a pattern interruption. The way the program worked was to only commit to one day without a drink. It was also taught that the first thought about drinking is what gets you drunk and that you had to stop the first thought. That was the trance stopper. You do this by immediately replacing a thought about drinking with another thought. Or you say one of the slogans that cover the walls of the meeting room—slogans like "This too will pass," "Let go and let God," and "One day at a time." These became my new posthypnotic suggestions.

These affirmations can be used to break the patterns of any problem resulting from a mystified state of being. The same is true of the 12 steps. They work well with any form of mystification.

To break the *seemingly* automatic pattern of the addiction is a powerful breakthrough. One gradually begins to communicate with what Wolinsky calls "the self behind the trance." As he points out, it is the self that can change the trance and, hence, the complex of symptoms that produce the alcoholism or other addiction. I believe that the self behind the trance is what I am calling the soul. The soul creates the protective trances in childhood, and the soul leads us to the crisis that calls us back to itself.

Coming out of the trance is simple, but difficult. Recovery is the stage of trance breakthrough—or what I earlier called demystification. Usually it is precipitated by the person bottoming out in some way because of some crisis or trauma. But not always. In Chapter 6, I described several other ways that demystification takes place. Awareness can do it. This awareness could come from talking to a friend, reading a book, being confronted by a loved one or a therapist, or going to a workshop. It could also come from an intervention or a religious conversion.

Recovery begins with the decision to stop doing whatever it is that is causing self-destruction. It is the decision to accept powerlessness.

The decision to accept powerlessness is a decision to take our life into our own hands. Paradoxically, by accepting powerlessness, we reown our own power. This is the restoration of freedom and an activation of the will.

Accepting powerlessness leads to asking for help. In my case it meant joining a 12-step group. For you it may mean turning to a friend, seeking out a support group, talking to your pastor, minister, or rabbi, going to a therapist, or seeking out a treatment center or program. It may mean joining a 12-step group for you, too.

Groups have enormous power to break trance states precisely because they restore the interpersonal bridge. Seeing a loving acceptance of ourselves in the *eyes of others* restores the mirroring process. Sharing our shameful feelings and experiencing love and acceptance in spite of our failures restores us to self-acceptance. The friend, therapist, group, or community can give us the support we failed to get as children. The developmentalist Margaret Mahler calls such support "refueling." I spoke about this in Chapter 8. Children need lots of refueling as their newborn psychological self begins to emerge. But if we didn't get it as children, we can still get it as adults. It's never too late to develop the strengths we did not learn as children.

Giving up the mystification leaves us with our original pain. The new mirroring relationship in the group allows the self to begin to emerge. But it is fragile and needs lots of support. The group is a *refueling source*.

The group can also serve as a reality check. It is very easy to fall back into the trance defenses. Anything that is threatening can cause us to fall back. And, since the protective covering has been removed, we are even more vulnerable.

Over time the experiences of being loved and accepted makes possible a loving acceptance of self. If the group sees me in all my secret shame and they still accept me, I can accept myself. Self-esteem originally began and ended with our source relationship. Mystification is a state of psychic death. To be born psychologically, we need someone—a mirroring face in which to see ourselves.

We need to have some form of social support throughout our further development. We may replace the group or the individual people in it, but we continue to live in a social context. In the next chapter I will talk about the importance of friends for developing a sense of identity. The important issue in recovery is to move from the intrapersonal self-nourishing trance to a truly nourishing social life. Love of others cannot really begin until one has achieved self-love. For the person seeking demystification, self-love begins with the *acceptance of another's acceptance*. This gradually leads one to self-acceptance, self-esteem, and self-love.

As I became a recognized member of the group, I felt a sense of belonging and security. I began to trust the people in the group. They told their stories and shared their shame secrets. I knew that they knew about shameful drinking behavior. The value of joining a group of people with the same problem is that we are able to identify. This identification creates a foundation for trust. As I made the decision to trust, I made a *decision* to share my own shame secrets. By sharing them, I exposed my most vulnerable self to them. This was the dark region that I hadn't wanted anyone to see.

Sometimes my closest and most trusted fellow members confronted me. I learned a lot about myself from these confrontations. We can't know what we don't know. What we don't know are the trance defenses that have become automatic and unconscious.

This is the power of trances. They really work. Others can experience our lack of presence, our spontaneous age regressions, our positive and negative hallucinations, and our time distortions. If they confront these behaviors, we can become conscious of them. We can become aware of our own experience. We can begin to connect with the self behind the trance and grow in soulfulness.

Dangers in Stage One

Each stage can lure us into a kind of complacency. As a mystified person, I am vulnerable to mood alteration and addiction. The recovery stage had great appeal. I've never had a more exciting year than my first year of recovery. It is exhilarating to come out of hiding, to enter into a community where you feel welcome, and to give up the phoney act and the pretense. In the beginning I often went to more than one meeting a day. Sometimes it was necessary; sometimes I just enjoyed the camaraderie and the sense of security and belonging. There are people who get stuck at this stage or even addicted to it. Going to 12-step meetings, therapy groups, church, and workshops becomes their way of life. Every other relationship and personal interest becomes absorbed in personal recovery. Rather than find balance in their program, they polarize their program and make it an end in itself. Their way of recovery becomes a salvation system. I know many people who have been indoctrinated by their 12-step sponsor, minister, therapist, or workshop guru. Suddenly there is only one way to be in recovery. The 12 steps or a particular therapy become rigid and authoritarian.

In contrast, the founders of the original 12-step program—Bill W. and Dr. Bob, who were geniuses in understanding how to deal with toxic shame and polarization—taught people to find the way that worked best for them and to follow it. They refused to standardize any official way.

At our treatment center in Rosemead, California, we teach the therapists to take the same flexible approach. They are trained in many kinds of therapeutic techniques. We have learned that when we get too attached to a theory or technique of therapy, we have standardized it, and if it doesn't work for a patient, the patient might experience shame. Sensitive clients know when their therapist is disappointed in them. They are shamed by not measuring up. In essence the therapist has made the client meet their map of the world, rather than tailoring their approach to the client's map of the world.

STAGE TWO: UNCOVERY

Stage Two involves understanding how we became stagnated in our mystification. We must come to understand what really happened to us, the *truth* of our childhood. We must grasp the violence of patriarchal parenting and the specific impact it had on our lives.

Above all, we must connect the symptoms of the violence with the violence itself. The symptoms of the violence are things like hypervigilance, excessive control, somatic disorders, amnesia, hypermnesia, age regression, time distortion, catastrophizing, sleep disorders, accident-proneness, reenactment, compulsive/addictive behavior, and codependency. As we develop a false self trance, we lose the connection between these symptoms (the clusters of deep trance phenomena) and the original violation. The moment we connect the symptoms with the violence (i.e., understand that the symptoms are a direct result of the violence), we start *uncovering* our mystification. We see that the symptoms are not idiosyncratic character traits, but natural consequences of the violence.

The effect of this awareness for me was an immediate reduction of the shame I had been carrying. In effect I became aware that I was not a flawed and defective person. Most of us are victims of a fated multigenerational violence. As survivors of a kind of psychic violence, we can love ourselves for the pain and suffering we have endured.

Legitimate Suffering

Having uncovered our violations, we must grieve our wounds. The grief work is about finishing pieces of unfinished business. Until the pain we once completely avoided is connected with and grieved, we cannot make contact with the deeper regions of the soul. Grieving is suffering, and as Jung said, "it is a legitimate suffering." Our trance symptoms are a defense against the legitimate suffering we need to accomplish in order to integrate our earliest trauma.

This grief work is also self-revelatory. In Chapter 7, I described one way to do grief work. But there are many roads that can take us over this mountain. Life itself is the vale of soul making, as Keats observed.

Grief can be triggered by a death that takes us back into our pain. A parent's death is often the occasion for this. My father's death took me to new depths of demystification and of soulfulness. I quit smoking two weeks after he died, one of his greatest gifts to me! Once I had put aside my false mask, I felt like a little boy again. I had to deal with this boy whose soul longed for a father. My father's death led me to the legitimate suffering I had avoided all my life.

Although therapies can also help us grieve, there is no right method. *There is certainly no John Bradshaw method.* Many have begun asking for that. But methods get standardized. Sometimes a standard method can be useful for stabilizing someone in crisis. It's good to have a name for something to help focus our problem and get the process started. And I do firmly believe that the original pain must be uncovered and dealt with. But no one way is the only way.

Inner Child Work

One way that has worked for me and for many others is what I call finding your inner child.

For me one of the most significant consequences of imaginatively embracing my inner child was that it gave me a way to be compassionate with myself. When I look in the mirror, even now, the old voices of blame, comparison, and self-contempt start playing. Even after years of hearing new voices in my friendships and community fellowship, I can hear those old posthypnotic tapes. For years I read books that offered techniques to help one love oneself. I stared in the mirror and said, "I love you, John" over and over. It helped for a few minutes and then the voices just got worse.

Techniques are basically useless until one has restored social contact and self-acceptance. We need social support and we need to *emotionally* embrace our rejected and split-off parts. The image of ourselves as a child is the fastest and soundest way I have ever found to embrace these parts.

The idea of a child living in me came from Eric Berne, the founder of Transactional Analysis. Reading Berne's work made me realize that I had been experiencing spontaneous age regressions— like the pouting and raging at my wife and children I described earlier. One day I closed my eyes and saw a little boy. His picture is now inside the back cover of the paperback version of *Homecoming*. I felt immediate love for him. He was standing on the front porch of a house on Fannin Street in Houston, Texas. This was the house where I was born. He was resting his chin on cupped hands and gazing out in wonder at the world. I felt so much love I began to cry softly. I couldn't believe the depth of emotion. My soul was at it again! As I embraced this image of myself as a boy, I *embraced* myself. It was powerful and transformative. I loved myself in this image of a boy. Through him I could accept myself unconditionally.

The Question of Narcissism

Inner child work is sometimes interpreted as egocentric and narcissistic. In most cases, this is a fancier psychological way of saying what my internalized parental voices told me: "Stop being so selfish."

Narcissism is named for another figure in Greek mythology, Narcissus, who fell in love with his own image in a pool of water and died trying to unite with it. This is in fact a perfect image of the mystified self-to-self trance that inner child work is designed to end.

As infants we had healthy narcissistic needs. We needed to be admired, to be taken care of, and have every part of us unconditionally loved. If we did not get these needs met, we went on to try and get them met in other ways. When we try to meet these needs ourselves, they become distorted and toxic.

Toxic narcissism is the more-than-human form of mystified self-love. It is based on defensive power. To interact with another is too dangerous for the fragile toxically shamed self. The outwardly pompous self-love of narcissism is a clue that the person displaying it is lacking in true self-love and self-acceptance.

Fritz Perls, the founder of Gestalt therapy, once described narcissism as sitting in a room surrounded by nothing but windows, looking out, and seeing nothing but *oneself*.

Mystified self-loving narcissists believe that they can manufacture and control their own self-love and self-acceptance. They try to force it. I read manuals on self-love for years trying to do this. But soulful self-love cannot be manufactured or controlled. In the beginning we must discover it slowly by seeing love in the eyes of others.

Inner child work leads to second order change. It is truly unfortunate that it is confused with narcissism. Loving and accepting oneself is the deepest call of soul. Self-love and self-preservation are the ground of our humanity. If we lack an inner relationship of self-love, our outer love becomes an obsessive search for self-validation. Spiritual masters from the beginning of time have taught us this. It is a foundation of Jesus's teaching.

Inner child work helped me discover a deeper, less contaminated version of myself. The image of my inner child brought me both unexpected emotion and new self-value. The image we see of ourselves as a child is far more numinous than our frozen false self. Looking at my image in the mirror, I see the hardness and limitations of the mystified false self. This image was manufactured to fit my need for survival. It is defensive and frozen.

The image of the inner child is open to change and growth. In my meditation dialogues I touch myself in my early state of being where possibility was my destiny. It is a healing embrace. In my dialogue with my inner child, I feel the confusion, the feelings, and the needs that I put aside long ago. It is a fruitful meeting in which I touch a depth of myself I had only known unconsciously.

Championing

Championing the child is a metaphor I used in *Homecoming* for making a commitment to myself. It is a commitment to expand and grow. Once I have uncovered and reclaimed my rejected parts, I need to nurture the child I have found. We tend to parent our inner child the way we were parented. So championing involves the hard work of learning to be better parents to ourselves. Just as a good parent helps a child grow to adulthood, I need to help myself complete the developmental tasks I missed as a child.

Homecoming suggests many experiences that can help one learn developmental tasks one could not learn as a child. Championing is a form of corrective experience. By championing my inner child I learn the skills that give me better tools for loving.

Championing has many facets. One of the most important is values clarification. Challenging old family rules is the beginning of this task. The family system rule of denial can be turned into self-awareness and rigorous honesty. The "don't feel" rule can be changed by learning to discover what feelings really are and how to define our own emotional boundaries. Triangulated communication can be transformed into open and honest communication. All this means hard work. Like any other skill building, it takes time and practice. Discovering your own values is the gift of this work.

As I found new ways of being and caring, my self-value intensified. I became more of the person I wanted to be, more of the kind of person I could really love. I discovered that what I believed about love was not love at all. My relationships were based on mystified notions of love.

It was very freeing to discover this. It freed me from beating up on myself so much. Instead of using all my energy to shame bind myself, I used it to learn things like assertiveness, saying no, asking for what I really wanted, and expressing my feelings and needs. A lot of times I felt like I was just learning to walk. I was awkward at first in the way I expressed myself. It was like learning a language. I had to practice a lot. But I discovered something about myself in the process. I discovered that I was willing to change and grow. I was willing to bear the discomfort and embarrassment of my awkwardness. I discovered that I loved myself enough to embrace my shame. I was willing to invest in myself and grow.

The process of *imagining* new ways of behavior and trying them out can create incredible new ventures. One false self role I challenged at this stage was my Mr. Nice Guy. This was a part of me that I was really addicted to. But being nice, as a phoney act, is very shallow. John Friel, a pioneer in the deep uncovery work I've been describing, recently sent me his new book, *The Grown-Up Man*. In it he quotes Garrison Keillor, of "Lake Woebegone Days" fame:

> You taught me to be nice, so that now I am so full of niceness, I have no sense of right or wrong, no outrage, no passion.

Boy, does that speak to me! Perhaps nothing is as soulless as pretending to be nice. I gradually came to terms with my niceness. I came to see that I *am* nice and that it's okay. But niceness does not mean that we agree with everyone to such a degree that there is no confrontation, no difference of opinion.

In the beginning I had to practice being assertive. I would write out what I wanted to say to someone and practice saying it with someone I trusted. The first times I actually said no or expressed anger, I was pretty shaky. It gets easier with practice.

Recently I have had occasion to confront personnel at two airlines about services I had paid for and not received. I made it clear that I knew the flight attendants were not personally responsible, but that I wanted someone to get the message. Ten years ago I would have said nothing, making excuses for the airlines in my internal dialogue. Now I've found that I can be firmly assertive and still value the person I'm talking to. My polarized "all nice" or "all enraged" behavior is being replaced by the polarity of being able to be nice and yet being able to be appropriately angry and to stand up for myself.

Dangers in Stage Two

The feeling work is very powerful. It is wise to be cautious about it. When you have been in the trance of sensory numbing for years and years, it can be ecstatic to start feeling your feelings. The flow of feelings is like a dam breaking.

Any feeling can become the object of obsession. Mystified people are to some degree addicted to feelings of fear and shame. Stage Two allows us to experience our anger and sadness. You can get stuck in either of these feelings. Some people have come to my skill-building workshops and gone away disappointed. "It was not as *intense* as your other workshops," they will tell me or write in a note. You can get addicted to feeling workshops and feeling therapy.

Inner child work can also be addictive. We can sentimentalize and become maudlin about our inner child. We can discover the new image of ourselves and get stuck in our own innocence and purity, forgetting that we have to grow up, that that's the purpose of doing the work in the first place. I've seen people become blaming of their parents and self-indulgently bask in martyrdom and victimization. You can cling to your misery and fail to embrace your pain. Embracing the pain is grief work, and the end of grieving is to be alive again and move on.

Grief work is about finishing our unfinished business. It is about forgiveness. By forgiving we extract ourselves from the enmeshments and fantasy bonds we created in the past. We may choose to put strong boundaries between ourselves and our source figures or whomever we're forgiving. We may have to choose to leave an offender parent to his or her fate. The important thing is to move on toward self-love and fulfillment. The gift of forgiveness is also the gift of forgiving ourselves.

Many people get *stuck* in one of the stages of grieving. They may stay in minimization and denial, refusing to do the painful work that grieving entails. I've seen a lot of 12-step people get bogged down there. Some people get stuck in sadness and hurt, others in anger and remorse. All of these stuck places stop us from further self-revelation and deeper soulful love of ourselves.

There is a clear choice at this stage. I can achieve a certain level of comfort here. I can find predictability and security. But I can go deeper. I can love myself more fully if I want to. If I choose to move on, I enter Stage Three.

STAGE THREE: DISCOVERY

Once we have uncovered our mystification and made peace with our internal and external family, we are ready to go deeper into self-discovery and self-love. It isn't that this happens on some exact time schedule. Soul is like a vast reservoir of meaning. We can have meaningful glimpses at any time or in any place. And soulfulness cannot be controlled. So what I'm depicting could happen anytime, although for the sake of clarity I call it Stage Three. It is a stage of spiritual awakening, which brings us deepening insight and wisdom about ourselves.

There are spiritual disciplines, secular and religious, that offer us ways of deepening our relationship with ourselves. The secular disciplines include internal remapping, dream work, active imagination, meditation, and imagery work. The religious disciplines include meditation and contemplation, prayer, and compassionate action.

My 12-step program brought me back to several spiritual disciplines I had experienced earlier in my life. In my seminary days, we had a practice called monitions. It was a method of self-confrontation through daily inventories. We also prayed daily and began each morning with meditation. Monitions always felt judgmental, and after leaving the seminary I dropped the practice very quickly. I tried to continue with meditation, but I had never really learned how to meditate. My prayer life was very important to me, and I never really lost contact with it. My 12-step program included self-monitoring, meditation, and prayer.

The program also emphasized the discipline of compassionate caring for others who suffered with alcoholism. I did a lot of carrying the message in the first decade of my recovery. I later came to see that I needed to extend my scope of compassionate action.

Self-Monitoring

Step 10 of my program urged me to *continue to take personal inventory and, when I was wrong, promptly admit it*. This was my old seminary monitions work in a new form. It is crucial for self-deepening.

The program's discipline consisted of rigorous honesty, delaying gratification, being responsible and prudent, and living in the now.

Rigorous honesty requires overcoming the compulsive need to cover up mistakes and to always be right. Always being right is one of the major issues in the more-than-human cover-ups for mystification. So is the opposite polarity, always being wrong. Someone said that enlightenment is lightening-up. The habit of self-monitoring helps us to accept our responsibility, but it also helps us to loosen up.

Delaying gratification requires overcoming feelings of scarcity and thinking positive thoughts. Much of our need for immediate gratification comes from feelings of scarcity. A voice saying there isn't going to be enough plays like an almost audible broken record. This voice tells us to get it now while we can. It may never come again.

Self-discipline is a habit. It consists of installing new self-talk. Telling myself "There will be enough" is helpful. Asking questions like "How many times have I starved or gone without my basic needs in the last few years?" helps me even more. I may even laugh when I ask such a question. When I answer it, I realize how fear distorts my thinking. Self-monitoring asks one to develop good habits, to be virtuous.

Virtues are strengths that become like a second nature to us. Once they are formed, once a certain threshold is reached, they function automatically and unconsciously.

This step helped me to accept my human frailties. I stopped fantasizing about perfection and I stopped expecting it. If my self-monitoring shows me real areas of fault, I can take action and do something to change myself. It is human to make mistakes and okay to admit it. Once I humanize my expectations, I enjoy myself more.

Prayer

Step 11 of my program asks that we seek *through prayer and meditation to improve our conscious contact with God as we understand God*. This was another part of my Stage Three work in pursuing spiritual growth.

In prayer I acknowledge that there is something or someone greater than myself, a Higher Power. Prayer in some form is held by all religious traditions to be a way to express gratitude and adoration to a Higher Power. Prayer has also long been held by most religious traditions to contain potent healing power.

For me, prayer is a way of staying grounded in my healthy shame. Prayer is a highly personal matter. I would not pray unless I believed that the infinite mind was personal. I have always been convinced by Paul Tillich's statement that if there is a God, God cannot be less than human. Interpersonal life is our crowning human achievement. It would be strange if the *ultimate source* of interpersonal life was not personal. I find it easier to interact with the concrete *humanity* of Jesus as the revealer of God. My philosophy courses taught me many abstract representations of God, but I could never relate to them. On the other hand, Scripture tells us that Jesus was like us in all things save sin. I can be intimate with one who is like me. I don't even believe that Jesus never sinned. I think that is *inhuman* mystification.

As a friend and brother, I can be intimate with Jesus and I take great consolation in praying to Him and with Him. The kind of love that He says is expressive of His Father (God) is a love that is forgiving, nonjudging, unconditional, and compassionate. This is the only God that speaks to my soul.

For me prayer has a stern criterion: does it engender love? What that means to me is, does my prayer lead me to care for myself and others?

Prayer leads to doing. I remember reading a story about the great theologian Rabbi Heschel who was marching for civil rights in Selma. Someone challenged him: wasn't his real place at home praying? "My feet are praying right now," he replied. My sense of prayer leads me to take action. When I first entered my 12-step group I found a little green card that suggested some daily actions that flowed from prayer. The card said that just for today I will do two things I don't want to do. And that just for today I will help someone without anyone knowing about it. This card became my guideline for several years. I did simple things that I needed to do but often pushed aside till the last minute. When I am self-responsible, I love myself more. I also needed to learn how to be unobtrusive about helping. My grandiose false self loved to boast and let people know all that I was doing to help them or others. I can't honestly say that I never do this anymore. But I have changed dramatically. I dislike myself when I brag and compulsively need to have my self-value authenticated on the outside. I love myself when I do unobtrusive acts of kindness and love.

It is impossible to love myself when I am distorting my limits. In prayer I acknowledge my limits and express my gratitude to my Higher Power, the source of my being. The more I know my limits, the more I accept myself as I really am. I cannot love myself unless I know who I really am.

Before suffering and ego deflation, I prayed a kind of self-righteous prayer. I know now that a lot of my prayer was, like everything else I did then, a form of mood alteration. As I began to understand my human limitations and *felt* my emptiness, I could really begin to pray. Tiny moments of tasting the fullness of something beyond myself are enough to make me want more.

Meditation

My seminary training did not teach me any methods of meditation. I meditated for nine and a half years and never really knew what I was doing. I did not think about formal meditation for the first dozen years of my reformation process. But as I got deeper into my own work, I began to discover that there were many ways to meditate. Daniel Goleman, a psychologist at Harvard, researched the most commonly used methods of meditation around the world. He found that simply becoming mindful of breathing is both the simplest and most universal technique for meditation. I bought an audio tape of his and felt that it led me to a very nice inner place. Later on I used Steven Halpern's tape called *Spectrum Suite*. It helped me deepen my meditation. Some time later, Steven and I created a tape together to help others get started in meditation.

I also experimented with using words and tried focusing on a mantra. I've never had the dramatic results my fantastic imagination envisioned, but I still continue the practice each day. When I began meditating, I expected to have visions, maybe even hear God's voice! I had to learn.

The most important part of meditation for me has been working on a deeper and more loving relationship with myself. The technique one uses to meditate is not meditation itself. What I mean by meditation is an altered state of consciousness somewhere between full consciousness and full sleep. As an altered state, meditation is a conscious trance that I choose as a means of knowing and loving myself in greater depth. I have to be frank and tell you that nothing interests me quite as much as my own identity. That has not always been the case. For all my earlier grandiosity, I was never really interested in my self. I was too busy covering it up.

The mystified false self manifests what the philosopher Heidegger calls *Gerede*, which roughly means "prattle." Prattle is the endless noise of empty speech between two or more mystified people. The Buddhists tell us that prattle is also the endless self-talk that goes on in our heads. With prattle we surround ourselves with noise and loneliness. Prattle is the language of self-rupture. In order to know our soul we need to be grounded in *silence*.

Silence is a natural haunt of the soul. Silence is not useful; it is unproductive, and it is generally regarded as valueless in our modern world of "human doings." But there is great healing in silence. Every good counselor knows this kind of silence.

Getting one to the opening of silence is the aim of every technique or method of meditation. But it is not the technique that gets one there. The silence is already there, as it was in the original beginning of all things.

Going into this silence demands discipline, but it is more like learning to get out of the way than learning to *do* something. I must not try to control or guide the final process in any way. I prepare myself through discipline and ask and wait to receive.

Spiritual masters suggest that when we are in silence, we have a faculty available to us that we do not ordinarily experience. That faculty is a kind of intuition or knowledge that has a quality of immediate certainty. This knowledge comes from the inside. There is no other way to get it. It cannot be gotten from the outside.

During meditation, I have had experiences of self-acceptance and self-continuity that I do not know how to express adequately in words. I have had the experience of somehow *always having known* things that are happening to me now. In *Homecoming,* I wrote about rediscovering childhood memories that still had energy connected with them. Those memories were somehow connected with later periods of intense creativity. The experience said to me that somehow I sensed long ago what was going to happen. Some theories about the soul hold that as children we had larger visions of ourselves than we do in adulthood. Carl Jung stated that "childhood sketches a more complete picture of the self, or the whole man in his pure individuality, than adulthood."

I've also experienced a sense of assurance that what I need will be given to me. I accidentally run across passages in books right when I need them, I hear a lecture on exactly the ideas I need to move on in my work, and I experience countless other seeming coincidences. This inner sense of assurance has deepened over time.

Most important, the inner work of meditation has given me a strong sense of what Erik Erikson called ego integrity. What this amounts to is an unconditional acceptance of my life as something that had to be. The experience sends the clear message that everything I've done in my life had a larger purpose than I knew at the time. I accept all of my life with its wounds, its defenses, its failures, its fateful elements and circumstances, and all the choices I've made. When I look back on my life in the light of what I know now, every part of it (except the part of being celibate for nine and a half years!)

has value and significance. From my soul's point of view, it was all perfect. This acceptance holds true for me most of the time. I have some moments of regret, but they do not last too long.

Another fruit of meditation is a clear awareness of the uniqueness of my own life. My ancestors are surely important to me. I'm indebted to my grandfather, Joseph Eliott, for the things he taught me—commitment, endurance, honesty. I also believe that I am living out my mother and father's most cherished dreams. I'm glad of that, and I'm grateful to them for having dreams. Still, the most creative parts of my life are the product of my own unique soulfulness.

POLARITY CONSCIOUSNESS

Meditation also helps me to gain broader consciousness of polarity. It helps me see things as both/and rather than either/or. Stilling the inner hypnotic voices quiets our ego. Ego in this sense is our narrowed consciousness, the domain of our false self. Ego is always on guard, defending against the many threats the wounded child constantly sees. As we heal the wounds from the past and the ego is gradually demystified, it can rest easier. The unfinished business has been more or less finished, and the compulsion to repeat has subsided. At this point, meditation can help us let go of control a little more.

As we relinquish control, our vision expands to creating a future rather than defending against the fears of the past. We open up and begin to extend ourselves.

We also become more capable of entering other maps of the world. We deepen our love for others and identify with them emotionally. As we do this, we expand our own being. We begin to see our unity and interconnection with everything. With this awareness we deepen our own self-love. All of our being is acceptable. We can see how we have either idealized or degraded ourselves out of our polarized mystification. To embrace our polarity leads us to a balanced acceptance of ourselves.

On the next page is an exercise I've done several times in working on my self-love and self-acceptance. The responses here are recent ones for several important areas of my life. The "real," or polarity column is what I think of as an expression of soulful self-love.

Love in Action—Moving Outward Again

The twelfth step in my journey to soulful self-love urged me to take loving actions. It says: *Having had a spiritual awakening as a result*

SELF-ACCEPTANCE EXERCISE

IDEALIZED	SOULFUL	DEGRADED
	HONESTY	
• I am righteous. I see the speck in my brother's eye, but not the log in my own.	• I need feedback, because my viewpoint is limited.	• I am a liar
	FAILURE	
• Blame others: it was their fault.	• I can learn from my mistakes. I accept that some things are beyond my control.	• Self-blame: I'm a failure.
	SUCCESS	
• I did it all. I am superior.	• I used my talents and I found the right context.	• I just got lucky. I'm really an imposter.
	SELF-IMAGE	
• I spend most of my time packaging myself. I'm obsessed with appearance.	• I accept my body as it is and care for it with good nutrition, sleep, and exercise.	• I'm ugly. I'm a slob. What's the use of trying to look good?
	WILLPOWER	
• I overcontrol myself and try to control others. I'm rigid and self-denying.	• I can hold on and let go in the appropriate contexts. I live with passion and desire.	• I'm out of control. I'm impulsive and self-indulging.
	NEEDS	
• I need nothing from anyone.	• I recognize and express my needs.	I'm needy; insatiable.
	BOUNDARIES	
• I put up walls. I let no one in.	• Semipermeable. I can let you in or keep you out.	I'm totally enmeshed. Anyone can get in.

of these steps, we tried to carry this message to other alcoholics and to practice these principles in all our affairs. Anyone reaching Step 12 is already moving into action. A sense of self-love and goodness has its own internal push to expand. One cannot truly love oneself without wanting to pass it on and share it with others. The 12 steps enlarge the spiritual awakening brought about by the ego death of hitting bottom. Part of the spiritual awakening was healing the mystified past and its frozenness. Living in present time, we can take action about the actual things that are happening.

In the early days of my recovery I worked with alcoholics and other drug addicts. In my uncovery period I worked with teenage drug users and their parents. I also began work with clients in private counseling. I learned a lot about mystification by helping others. I gradually came to understand the adult child as the wounded inner child. I discovered my own toxic shame and saw it as the roots of mystification and addiction.

Later on I saw clearly that addiction includes much more than substance addictions. This insight led to my understanding of the violations of dysfunctional families as the *training ground for all addiction.* I saw how severely all children are oppressed by patriarchal parenting rules. I saw that these rules were themselves the result of childhood oppression. They were the product of shame-based adult children who were covering their fear with power and control.

I then began to realize that the power and control issues in patriarchy are part of even larger and more complex problems concerning our political and economic systems. All of these problems are rooted in the assumptions implicit in our Western cosmology, our view of the world.

Power and control dominate our economic thinking in relationship to the earth. Just as we do not think of children as sacred beings with inherent dignity, we do not view the earth as a sacred living organism with inherent dignity. We use it as an object, just as we objectify children. Power and control systems are most dangerous at the level of governments. Political systems hold the control buttons for spaceship earth. They will have to implement the *new vision* of the planet which has come from the awareness that the earth's internal guidance system is no longer on automatic. Our scientists have uncovered the very process of life itself. They have split the atom and decoded DNA. Those great revelations have placed the control of the planet on *manual,* that is, in our hands.

This brings me squarely back to the question of childhood abuse and mystification. The task ahead of us is one that clearly involves issues of creating love. It would be a monumental challenge, even if we had an earth filled with fully functioning people. *We do not have that.*

I decided to make my commitment to awakening people to the truth of childhood and to helping them become demystified and start loving themselves. It is impossible to love and connect with others if one lives hidden in an isolated self-to-self trance.

I have picked up the banner of Maria Montessori and Alice Miller, pioneers in the effort to awaken people from their mystified trance and from their compulsion to protect their parents.

Erik Erikson remarked that Freud's great legacy was to raise our consciousness about our new ethical responsibility to children—to the child within us, our own children, and other people's children. That is my clear ethical responsibility as I see it. I believe with Maria Montessori that "no social problem is as universal as the oppression of the child." She wrote this in the early 1920s, and the oppression of children is still our crucial problem as we prepare to face larger planetary issues. The violation of children's rights by our *normal* patriarchal parenting rules is outrageous, especially in a country that has fought and died for democracy. The problems of the homeless, of teenage gangs, drug addiction, alcoholism, criminality, and sex addiction are all partly rooted in childhood violation. We must change our methods of socialization, the relationships between parent and child, if we want to change our world culture. There are many urgent social problems, but none more urgent than this.

The adult-child movement, with its discovery of childhood mystification, has been one of the great sources of new awareness in our time. I am committed to this movement with all my might. My self-love demands that I continue to join the many new voices and continue taking action to awaken people to the tragedy of mystification.

CHAPTER 11

The Love of Friendship

To the ancients, friendship seemed the happiest and most fully human of loves; the crown of life and the school of virtue. The modern world, in comparison, ignores it.

C. S. LEWIS

We are here because there is no escape finally, from ourselves. Until a person confronts himself in the eyes and hearts of others, he is running.... Where else but in our common ground can we find such a mirror ... *together* we can take root and grow ... not as the giant of our dreams or the dwarf of our fears, but as a man/woman ... part of a whole with a share in its purpose.

DAYTOP VILLAGE, INC. (a drug rehabilitation agency)

Recently my mother gave me some old photographs from my childhood. One of them particularly grabbed my fancy. It was a picture of four young boys standing together, each with right arm dropped over the next one's shoulder, intertwined like the four musketeers. I was second from the end, looking very head-shaven and young. The other guys were Joe Danna, Dick Stephens, and Bobby Hallett. I know where Joe and Dick are, although I've lost track of Bobby. I'm not friends with them anymore, and when I look at the picture, I feel sad about it. There was a wonderful sense of safety in being the four musketeers. And those were days of some real joy in my childhood. It was a time when we lived in our house and didn't have to live with relatives. I was about 11 years old. Freud calls this the latency period, meaning that the sex drive is latent. Boys did not really want to hang around with girls except to tease them. My buddies and I (the four musketeers) were considered very stupid and immature by the girls who lived around us, especially our sisters. But we didn't care, we were boys and they were girls. What could you expect from dainty do-goods?

The girls thought we were slobs and had their own friendships going. They banded together, whispered and giggled, and had what I called stupid slumber parties.

Friendships are an important part of childhood. In my friends' eyes everything about me was okay. This allowed me to experience my beingness, my unique sense of self. My childhood friendships provided fertile soil for the emergence of my soul.

Many developmental psychologists believe that good peer group friendships are as essential for a child's growth as good parenting. Some maintain that the quality of a child's peer group friendships is more important than anything else in determining their psychological health.

MYSTIFIED CHILDHOOD FRIENDSHIPS

Certainly when we are children it's mainly in our relationships with parents and peers that we can experience our beingness. By the same token, parents and peer groups can be the major *blocks* to our having the experience of soulful childhood friendships.

Parental Bonds

Bonds with parents can be a major source of disruption in peer friendships. A common dyadic enmeshment role is "Dad's Best Buddy." A child who is set up in that role can be retarded in developing his own friends.

I had a college drinking buddy, I'll call him Xavier, whose father used to tell him, "It's you and me against the world; you can't trust anyone." Xavier claimed he had no friends in childhood. His father had an arsenal of weapons, which he taught his son to use. Each week they would play mock war games, pretending that they were under attack. The father was an alcoholic, and often when he got drunk he'd wake Xavier in the middle of the night, terrifying him by telling him that he'd just been shot or that the house was surrounded by thugs who were going to kill them.

Xavier was already alcoholic when I knew him. He was unable to sustain any kind of adult relationship. He died in a drug-related suicide. He left a long, rambling, paranoid note suggesting that this was his only way out.

Xavier's friendship with his father was more costly than most parent/child friendships. But the bottom line is, children need to have their own peer group friendships.

The same problems are possible when mothers create exclusive friendships with their daughters. I call this the "Sorority Sister" syndrome. I know a woman who was her mother's best friend and sexual confidante. Her mother hated her husband, the girl's father. She gave her daughter graphic details about his rotten lovemaking. She demeaned men and told her daughter that sex was awful. The woman I know has no female friends and continually reenacts her mother's hatred of men by having affairs with married men, whom she ultimately rejects in anger and contempt. She can only achieve orgasm when she imagines that she is her mother!

Opposite sex parent/child friendships also take place. They often have a romantic or sexual component to them.

Parents need their own same-age friends. When they have a need to make their child their best friend, something's out of balance in their life. Their soul is trying to tell them something.

After children grow up, friendships between parents and children are possible. They require the same hard work as any other love relationship.

Peer Group Shaming

Those friendship bands of dainty do-goods were often hotbeds of fairly abusive peer group pressure and shaming. For many women the wounds of childhood peer group games of *inclusion* and *exclusion* are deep and painful. Young girls can be cruel in their games of loyalty and betrayal. Power friendships are brokered daily by preteen and early teenage girls.

Teenage male peer groups are just as vicious. I can hardly believe the cruelty of my tenth-grade high school group toward a boy named Bob. I was his companion during the ninth grade. When we began our sophomore year at Saint Thomas High School, something changed. The tough-guy peer group didn't like Bob. He had his own

Cushman motorbike, and there was a lot of jealousy over that. He also had a good-looking Saint Agnes girlfriend. Somehow he became the group scapegoat. I just couldn't take the risk of continuing to hang out with Bob. The peer group was life and death, the difference between daily humiliation and belonging. I abandoned Bob.

I'll never forget what Bob went through that year. He finally moved away to Saint Louis. I really pray that he got a new lease on life. He was water-bombed daily on his Cushman. On numerous occasions after school he was surrounded and his pants were taken off. He often tried to defend himself physically but was overpowered by the biggest guy in the group. I've often pondered the "why" of this level of cruelty. I think it's about the vulnerability of early adolescence to being shamed. Puberty is a time of extreme vulnerability. Whatever shame has been internalized is exposed again as one repeats one's earlier life stages. Shame fears exposure. If someone can be found to scapegoat, then no attention will be drawn to me. Thus, a dozen acne-faced frightened adolescents make someone in the group their scapegoat. Bob got the projected shadow of all of us.

Right now I prefer to look at the picture of the "four musketeers." It is more joyous. I've never *ever* recaptured the camaraderie and the spirit of friendship that I experienced then.

ADULT FRIENDSHIP ISSUES

"People are so busy that they usually put their profession in front of their friendships." This statement was made by Jim Spillane, one of the people we interviewed for my PBS series, "Creating Love." Jim went on to suggest that friendship comes after business and romantic relationships are taken care of. Most of the other people interviewed agreed with Jim's assessment. One man suggested that the idea of friendship was "unrealistic and a waste of time." I was a bit shocked by his outright rejection of the notion of friendship until I remembered that a major change in my life started with the realization that I really had no deep friendships. I had a lot of acquaintances but no real friends.

This recognition, which did not come until my early forties, was part of my uncovery process. I realized that my mystified inner child expected friendships to just magically happen without my doing anything.

At that time my situation looked like this: I had some compan-

ions and God knows my Episcopal priest friend, Mike Falls, had
worked to have a friendship with me. But I was too busy for friendships. I had a wife, stepchildren, my natural child, and the ladder of
success to climb. I was still in my Caretaker, Star role and was working compulsively, overachieving, and trying to prove that I wasn't an
"imposter." I had forgotten about Joe Danna, Dick Stephens, and
Bobby Hallett. Anyway, that was okay for young boys but of minimal
importance in the dog-eat-dog adult world.

My Father's Death

My awareness of my need for and the importance of real friendship
was triggered by my father's death. Something soulful and demystifying usually happens when a parent dies. At least a whole lot of people
have reported their experience of one or both of their parents' deaths
as kairotic. No matter what your actual relationship was, the finality
of a parent's death changes you forever.

The issue for me was about growing up. It was about my fears
of being *the father* now that he was gone. I had made an overt
reconciliation with my dad. I had taken him to his first 12-step meeting. He was twenty-six days behind me in sobriety. We had some
time together sobering up and going to meetings. There was no deep
intimacy in our relationship, because neither of us knew how to
express our feelings. But there was soul. It squeaked through the
cracks of our silences and our self-conscious breaking of eye contact.
Before he died I told him I loved him. I talked to him about dying.
I asked him if he was afraid. I was. He said he wasn't. I felt like I
had finished my business with him. But I really hadn't. I probably
never will.

The emptiness I felt after he died led me to work on my internalized images of him. I was still carrying some old degraded images.
They popped up at the funeral. They reappeared some months later.
I had to do the internal work on the father I had created in childhood. I had to give up my little boy's fantasies about having a powerful father who would protect me from all harm. I had to grow up. I
needed to become the father of my own household, the begetter of
my own life. As I worked through these issues, I came to a place of
deep fear and anxiety about loneliness and death. Dealing with loneliness and fear of death, I realized that I had no real friends. I decided
to investigate that.

My lack of male identity created a deep sense of fear and insecurity about myself as a man. It is very difficult to have any real friend-

ships without a sense of identity. This is the thing my father's death forced me to honestly confront.

Mystified men without any real identity who crave to be loved with infantile intensity *do not make good friends*. It is not just their relationships with women that are one-sided, superficial, and irresponsible. The same pattern characterizes their relationships with men. They are excellent companions and do well in men's organizations like golf, tennis, and gun clubs. Camaraderie in these clubs is superficial and nonintimate. This was exactly the predicament I found myself in.

Homophobia

In my generation, once you hit puberty, there was great suspicion of any close adult male friendship. The suspicion stemmed from a deep-seated homophobia, a fear of homosexuality that has been passed down for generations by patriarchal attitudes. Grown men with arms entwined like the four musketeers of my picture would have been quite suspicious in my adolescence. This homophobia has diminished somewhat as a result of our expanding awareness about patriarchy and as consciousness has been raised about genetic factors in sexual orientation.

A friend of mine whose brother was dying of AIDS told me a tragic story recently. He was at his brother's deathbed. Their father, who is a mystified homophobic religious bigot (I say this in all charity), was there for his duty visit to his dying son. A group of the dying man's friends came to see him. As they left, the father shook his head and clucked his tongue. "God, I'll never understand what this is all about," he said. "Try love and friendship," my friend answered in disgust.

TYPES OF MYSTIFIED FRIENDSHIPS

Because mystification is a defensive self-isolating trance, it is impossible to truly maintain a friendship until some demystification begins to occur. A mystified person will create pseudofriendships, which are either reenactments of source relationships or attempts to fill up their own emptiness by fusing with another person or a group. I distinguish several types of mystified friendships.

Elitist Groups

Mystified persons tend to join groups that give them a sense of special-ness. These groups—economic, social, religious, esoteric—have a cul-tic quality. Members of elitist groups consider anyone not of their kind to be beneath them and often will have nothing to do with so-called ordinary people. Such groups have little to do with friendship, although their members may profess great friendship toward one another. The purpose of the elitist group is not the pursuit of the common good or of common interests. The purpose is self-aggrandizement.

Another form of elitism is the pursuit of "power friends." We all know the "name-dropping" person who has made a career out of acquiring certain kinds of friends. By being associated with celebri-ties, with those who are wealthy, influential, and/or powerful people, these folks gain a sense of potency and identity.

Mystified Friendships in Patriarchal Systems

In general, patriarchy is opposed to real friendships. The system has greater value than the individual, the kingdom takes precedence over its subjects. Friendship is feared because of the power that comes from friendship. Two people or a group of people are more powerful than one person: The king wants a nice uniform country with nobody making any waves.

The religious community I was in had a passage in its rule against "particular friendships." This prohibition was based on the spiritual doctrine that asked us to live a "common life" with equal love for everyone. It was believed that friendship had a special exclu-sive quality. If one person is my friend, than someone else is not. That was the official reason given.

However, patriarchy does encourage some types of mystified friendships. Patriarchal schools with authoritarian rules capitalize on their students' human needs for friendship and community. The school may set itself apart as an elite school. The students are indoc-trinated into a certain "school spirit" and "school loyalty." The school song becomes a sacred hymn of loyalty rather than a soulful remem-brance of an important experience and stage of life. One is expected to become a team member, giving up any true individuality. Differing with school traditions or long standing school policies is considered to be a grievous violation. School uniforms or codes of dress further destroy individuality.

Religious schools often use these tactics to indoctrinate children into a particular religious system. Codes of behavior are clearly delineated, and when students are behaving the "right way," they are told that this is the way good Muslims, Christians, Jews, etc., behave.

For many folks, military service has been a source of powerful friendships. This shows that real friendships are possible under certain conditions of patriarchy. The cooperation and courage needed to survive can lead to extraordinary bonds of love. But, because of its patriarchal structure, the military has the potential for severe mystification. Military atrocities, such as the incident at My Lai during the Vietnam War, are commonplace events in human history. The tragic homelessness of great numbers of Vietnam veterans testifies against the military per se as a place for building soulful and lasting friendships. I recently heard that suicides among Vietnam veterans are almost twice the number of Americans killed in the war itself.

Friendships As Schools of Vice

Mystified friendships play a major role in groups based on vice, criminality, sex, cultism, devil worship, etc. The history of the Mafia offers many strange and paradoxical examples of such distorted friendships. In such groups there is an illusion of true bonding and loyalty.

Some gangs have an element of deep soulfulness in them, but it is distorted by a polarized us-against-them stance. Becoming a gang member is equivalent to an anti-identity family bond for many violated and abandoned children. Some gangs also profess a revolutionary creed and claim to fight against social oppression. But such gangs often demand extremely violent proofs of loyalty and total subordination of the individual to the group—to the point of death.

Drinking or Drug Buddies

Another kind of mystified friendship is friendship with drinking or drug cronies. I had many groups of drinking buddies over the years. The guy I mentioned as my high school best friend was not really a friend at all. As an adult, I realized that our bond was based on father abandonment and early alcoholism. I had to own that I didn't even *like* him.

When I left the seminary, I developed ties with several groups of drinkers. One group consisted of unmarried drinking buddies, another of couples who built all their socializing around drinking and partying.

When I sobered up, I found that it was painful to be around these groups. I tried on several occasions to go to the couples' weekend bashes and abstain from drinking. I remember one party that started at six on Saturday evening and was still going when I left at eleven the next morning. To abstain completely in such a setting was painful. A few hours into the evening no one was coherent. The fascinating intellectual discussions I used to look forward to at these parties turned out to be solipsistic monologues of varying degrees of coherence. As I stopped pursuing these people I had called my "best friends," they stopped any contact with me. My drinking cronies and I were bonded by booze, not friendship.

Codependent Friendships

Mystified people feel empty and unfulfilled. They look for someone who can fill up their emptiness. Relationships that are based on emotional emptiness and hunger are called codependent friendships. Each friend uses the other to fill up their own emptiness.

Codependents often agree never to disagree. This is a pure mystification based on the unrealistic expectations of our fantastic imagination. I think of such friendships as magical child-to-child friendships. Each friend is *expected* to fulfill the other's infantile wishes for unconditional love and absolute support. Those that have poor boundaries enter into this kind of mystified friendship. They have trouble saying no. In many cases they were abandoned as children for expressing anger, and they abhor anger. Sometimes one person controls the friendship with anger.

The inability to set boundaries by saying no or expressing anger creates a relationship without limits. There is no way to negotiate conflict or sort out differences. This inability to have respectful ways to fight over differences rules out any real contact and intimacy. This results in lots of false-self pretense and pseudointimacy. I've been in several such relationships. They are laborious because a kind of duplex communication is often going on all the time. You are saying one thing (what your friend wants to hear) and thinking another (what you really feel). Josephus is telling me about the rotten conditions he has to work under. He talks about what an asshole his boss is. Just about every time I spend any time with him, he goes into boring detail about what his boss says and does. Same song, ninety-ninth verse! I smile a lot and nod sympathetically while he is talking. I let out brief exclamations like "Wow!" or "That's awful!" or "What an asshole!" What I really want to say is "Why don't you quit and find another job? I'm sick of listening to you whine!" Why don't I say this? Because I'm afraid of offending him. I'm afraid of his anger and my own. I'm in my "nice guy" act. I fear that if either one of us blows up, we will end our relationship (abandonment fear). I'm a nice guy, and nice guys don't have anger.

One day it will happen. One of us will blow up, and it is usually not a pretty picture. All the repressed anger connected with the tedious hours of listening will come roaring out. Enraged and energized, I will tell my pseudofriend to get lost and I will never see him or speak to him again. I've done this a few times. It feels rotten.

In my current friendships with Michael and my brother Richard, we have a signal when the other is starting to retell an oft-told story. We look right at our partner and start nodding our head up and down vertically. It infuriates me when one of them does this, but it is a very good agreement. We also have a commitment to each other to tell the truth.

Codependent friendships are not about sharing common interests or cocreating common projects. Their goal is to fill up emotional hunger and emptiness.

Professional Codependent Friendships

Work settings can lead to true friendships, but more often they lead to a kind of dog-eat-dog codependent pseudofriendship.

Men frequently band together at work in "victim" subgroups. This is especially true in companies that are large and bureaucratic and/or rigid and patriarchal. Along with the in-group of victims, there is an *out* group (the bosses) and there are scapegoats (often the people on the fringe of the in-group). There seems to be camaraderie among those in the in-group, but it is really an illusion. Underlying the camaraderie are constant criticism and sarcasm. Such so-called friends are bonded by anger, shame, and a sense of injustice. They are also highly competitive with *one another*.

One of the persons interviewed on my PBS series "Creating Love" spoke about this. He said, "You'd break off into little cliques, and it would break up the camaraderie and loyalty ... certain groups would be talking about you, and other groups are forming sides. I think it defeats the whole purpose of loyalty." Work is very often not a friendly place. If you are promoted out of your codependent peer group, *you* may well become the scapegoat.

Many women form victim friendship groups in a slightly different way. They do not show overt competitiveness and are often in denial about how competitive they really are. They have a lot of passive aggressive discussions about other women in the office.

The wives of professional men sometimes form victim friendships groups of their own. They may spend hours on the phone every day discussing their husband troubles, their financial situation, or their life in general. But confrontation on personal issues is taboo. Any woman who decides to change and moves toward improvement is slowly banned from the group.

Friendships between *mystified* women are characterized by sharing of pain and secrets as a substitute for taking action. Many married women share a lot about their husbands with women friends but do not confront their husbands.

Mystified male friends, on the other hand, do a lot together (golf, tennis, fishing, etc.) but rarely share anything personal. When they interact on a personal level, the interaction is often shaming and sarcastic. Men in mystified male friendships spend hours playing the one-up game. They are obsessively competitive and envious.

SOULFUL FRIENDSHIP

Friendship is the *most fully human* of all loves because it is based not on hormones or blood ties, but on free choice, and free choice is what makes us most human. We need friendship because we are social by nature. The human group, the tribe, has been essential in human evolution. Bonding together in tribes had great survival value. We would have very likely been eaten by woolly mammoths had we not been able to band together.

But we don't just bond together for survival; we long for real human community. Our basic need for social interaction is an expression of our basic need for love. Friendship calls us to our humanness and to our soulfulness. Those who say that friendship is not important and that the love of friendship is not soulful and substantive have never had a friend.

A friend can help our soul to find and express itself. My friends have inspired me and motivated me to stretch myself. They have helped me to grow.

Developing a soulful friendship requires hard work. We must be willing to extend ourselves for our friend, giving them some of our time and attention. Soulful friendship also requires elements like attraction, common interests, special time together, negotiability, and openness to growth.

Dynamics of Friendship

Intimate friendships take time to develop. We can like someone instantly and look forward to being with them. We can be instantly attracted to someone and desire them sexually. We can "fall in love" overnight. But friendships take time.

More often than not a friendship begins when people who are together for some reason start liking each other. They may work together, belong to the same fishing club, or go to the same school or church. The potential friend is at first a casual *acquaintance*. With an acquaintance one exchanges formalities, but that's about as far as it goes. Often by chance some need arises for two or more people in a group to cooperate. Cooperation is the matrix of friendship. C. S. Lewis suggests that friendship was much more cherished in the past because life was bound by the need to cooperate. Survival depended on cooperation.

When people who are casual acquaintances are put into a situation that requires cooperation, they often become *companions*. Terry Gorski describes companionship as a relationship in which activities are shared and in which the activities are the reason for being together. In other words in companionship the activities take precedence over the person. One may have several companions in the fishing club. When one wants to go fishing, any companion who likes to fish will do.

Over time, real interest in one or another person may develop. You may discover that your companion likes to cook gourmet meals or that they, too, are actively involved in conservation. You come to realize that you and your companion have some very special things in common. Now you begin to pursue that person more and more. You spend more time together. You learn more about each other. At some point a real affection begins to emerge. Slowly, that affection leads to the love of friendship.

Now the *person* is more important than the activity. The person is your *friend,* and you choose to be with them. You really want their company more than you just want to engage in the activity. Being with them enhances your experience of the activity.

I'm an interested golfer, and I will play with another companion if I am really desperate to play. But that almost never happens. I love to play golf with four friends, especially my brother, Richard, my Episcopal priest friend, Michael, and my friends George and Johnny. We have wonderful golf games, because we let our hair down, laugh a lot, and play matches with the emphasis on play. We also agree to follow some of our own rules. I like the basic activity of playing golf, but it is my friends that make it really desirable.

Friendships Born in Conflict

My friendships have not always developed in the way I just outlined. Our soul has something to say about our friendships. Soulful love is mysterious, and the initiation into the love of friendship can be quite unpredictable. For example, one of my best friendships began in conflict. Mike Falls and I got into serious theological debate when he first came to Palmer Episcopal Church. He was raw, right out of the seminary, and ready to let the world know that a powerful young theologian was on the scene. Mike was used to being in the limelight. He had been an All-American football player at the University of Minnesota. Later he played for the Green Bay Packers under Vince Lombardi. At the apex of his football career, he was a starting guard for the Dallas Cowboys under Tom Landry.

I was the adult theology lecturer at Palmer when Mike arrived, and I was getting tons of accolades for my theological presentations. I was quite mystified, puffed up, and grandiose. For Mike, the new guy, to challenge me, the authority, caused sparks to fly. I wouldn't have given you a plugged nickel for a long-lasting friendship, cer-tainly not one of twenty years.

I hardly had anything to do with Mike during his first two years at Palmer. I felt outright animosity toward him for a while—you know, the kind where you walk the other way so that you won't run into a person and have to talk to them.

In hindsight, I think Mike represented a *shadow* part of me. He was very honest. If an overly zealous and moralistic person in the church made a comment that Mike disagreed with, he would confront it. I remember an incident that raised a furor in the church. One of the great benefactors of the church was playing "ain't it awful" about sex outside of marriage. Mike told her he thought we should also look at sexual immorality inside marriage. Well, no one, and I do mean no one, had ever done anything but echo Old Mrs. Moneybags. In the hoorah that followed, I pretended to be upset by Mike's lack of politics. But I knew inwardly that Mike was being rigorously hon-est, and that was a part of my shadow I needed to own. My overidenti-fication with my good guy, people-pleasing polarized self left rigorous honesty in the dust. Mike disagreed with me on several occasions. Sometimes he was in a power play, but most often it was a genuine disagreement.

I remember having very critical discussions about Mike with several people on the staff. My soul nudged me during those discussions as if to say, "Come on, John, quit being so phoney." Our soul always nudges us when we are being phoney.

Mike projected some shadow stuff onto me, too. I am very energetic and an indefatigable worker; Mike is too fun-loving to work as hard as I do. That may be a part of his shadow that he doesn't want to own.

Mike's political skills have been sharpened over the years, as he has become older and wiser. I have been willing to tell the truth more often, even if it meant being unpopular, or God help me, being disliked. Mike and I have learned from our conflicts with each other. We have both grown, because we are willing to work out our conflicts, which still come up sometimes.

Some of our initial conflict had to do with the fact that Mike and I are very similar. We have the same kinds of wounds and the same kind of soulfulness. At the time we met, neither of us had done any original pain work. Since we committed to a friendship, our love has grown. No one could support my success with any greater energy than Mike, and I am the same with him. He has been my greatest fan, and I have pushed him to stretch himself. I've helped motivate him to become a full-time workshop leader. I'm urging him to write a book.

Negotiating Conflict

If our friendships are *growing,* they will move us toward higher levels of intimacy. Greater intensity and intimacy is a choice friends have. If friends make this choice they must be willing to deal with conflict. I find conflict the most difficult area of any relationship. In my prerecovery days my so-called friendships were basically agreements never to disagree. In several instances when I started feeling conflicts, I simply began to withdraw, making up excuses as to why I was unavailable. Gradually, the withdrawal led to real separation and emotional and physical cutoff. Mystified friendships are based on avoidance of conflicts.

I'm grateful for the fact that my brother and sister are both in their own programs of personal growth. After years of on-again, off-again closeness and withdrawal, my sister and I are building a friendship with each other. In our family the pattern was to build up anger until we couldn't handle it anymore and then explode, ventilate, and withdraw. As we grew older, the withdrawals meant not speaking to each other, sometimes for months. What we are now learning is that we can be angry at each other without leaving the relationship. I am learning to negotiate conflict with my brother and my sister.

No matter how much two friends have in common, each is unique and sees the world from their own perspective. So both must commit to deal with their differences. We can grow by experiencing another person's point of view. A friendship can be a great arena for this kind of growth. It is by *experiencing aspects of my friends that are different from me that I expand my humanity*. For example, I needed my friend Marc in order to grow out of the stereotypes about Jews that I grew up with. True friendship breaks down the polarizations resulting from mystification. It is a spiritual experience to be able to meet Marc at his map of the world.

Commitment

Friendships require commitment if they are to grow. This is what I was never willing to give in the past. I now choose to work on my friendships.

Work means putting energy into the relationship. This takes many different forms. Mike and I get our calendars out and block out time for golf games, and whenever possible we plan part of our summer vacation together.

I mentioned the head-nodding signal that we use for too often repeated stories. We also listen to each other. I'm committed to listening in all my friendships. Sometimes I don't feel like listening; sometimes I'm slightly bored with what friends are saying, especially when they are talking about their children, in-laws, or family of origin. However, I know that there are times I need to listen, just as there are times when I need someone to *hear* me. There is an art to listening, and we know when someone is not really listening to us. The skills for listening to children that I wrote about in Chapter 8 also apply here. All of us just want to blow off steam sometimes, and for that we need a nonjudging, nonshaming, *noninterrupting* friend. Sometimes we need to be listened to in a way that allows us to see and hear ourselves more objectively. A problem that seems heavy and overwhelming in our self-to-self trance can become much more manageable when we can freely express it to someone else. Sometimes the problem can even become downright silly! Sometimes we need to be confronted!

Listening well cannot happen unless we have a strong commitment to work on our friendship. After all, most of us have mastered "fast getaway" techniques to use when we don't want to listen to someone.

We also need to take the time to disclose our feelings for our friends. This is especially hard when it comes to either end of the feeling spectrum—angry feelings or tender, loving feelings.

Growing Affection

As time passes and friends see each other in all kinds of situations, certain idiosyncrasies and character traits that would not have been attractive in the beginning become very familiar and very dear. Friends might joke about one another's idiosyncrasies and traits, but the jokes are expressions of affection.

C. S. Lewis writes: "Affection almost slinks or seeps through our lives. It lives with ... private things, soft slippers, old clothes, old jokes...." You grow to love your friend's walk, the neat or sloppy way he dresses, his funny hats, his nervous twitches. These are the basis for deepening affection.

My buddy George has a sweetness about him that I didn't see in the beginning. George is a very skilled and powerful trial lawyer. He can be devastating in a courtroom. But he is very kind. I've watched him patiently play chess with my son or take a young child for a walk. He's been very nurturing to me in legal matters. I get really frightened by anything that could lead to lawsuits. George has fathered me in these matters.

My friend Johnny is very antsy and nervous. He can't sit still a minute. I've grown to love his nervousness and impatience. He and I have a lot of wounds in common. At times Johnny appears gruff, yet, when he expresses his feelings in our share group, he is the most vulnerable man I've ever known.

My friend Kip and I share intellectual and therapeutic interests. We've spent hours discussing the nature of shame. We were both philosophy majors in college and we love to talk about the theories of Kant or Whitehead in relation to our clinical work at my center in Rosemead, California. We both did a lot of crazy philosophizing during the days when we were actively addicted to alcohol. By "crazy," I mean that I once got into a barroom brawl over the philosophical proofs for the existence of God. Yes, I did! Kip used to enthrall whole barrooms with his interpretations of Whitehead's theory of reality as a process. Kip recently gave me his timeworn copy of one of Whitehead's classic works. I will treasure it. Kip and I know that most of the time those who did not major in philosophy don't know what we are talking about and could care less. We do it for ourselves, not for anyone else.

Kip and I also share on the deepest feeling level. We've been very vulnerable with each other. I've watched the miracle of his second order change over the last ten years.

THE DARK SIDE OF FRIENDSHIP

We cannot avoid the dark side of friendship. Jealousy, envy, and betrayal are part of its polarity.

When a friendship is deep and soulful, it has less jealousy than almost any other love. But precisely because we cherish someone, jealousy is always lurking in the wings. I have been jealous of a friend's love and affection for someone else. Jealousy is my fear that another person will take what I have; it is the Scarcity Rule applied to my friend. This kind of jealousy has lessened since I've been in the process of demystification. I believe that the healthier one's friendship is, the less likely that there will be jealousy. And the healthier the friendship, the more likely that it will be strengthened, not weakened, by the addition of new friends. I'll have more to say about jealousy in Chapter 12.

Envy is more likely to plague our friendships than jealousy. Envy is the desire for what another person has, and it is much more likely to arise in friendships and affectionate family relationships than in erotic love. It is human to experience envy, even for a friend. We see that our friend has qualities that we really desire to have. But when envy becomes chronic and obsessive, it is a serious contaminant to our lives. Chronic envy is rooted in mystification.

Envy can be an occasion for soulful growth; it is a symptom. Thomas Moore writes, "The pain in envy is like pain in the body: it makes us stop and take notice of something that has gone wrong and needs attention." To transform envy into soulfulness, we need to use imagination. The task for the imagination is to ask our envy what it wants.

A person can easily get attached to envy. I can remember the self-pity my envy engendered. When I came out of the seminary, I was 31 years old. I looked around and saw that my high school friends had families, owned homes, had good jobs. I had been an office boy and a grocery checker. At 31 years of age, that was my entire work experience!

I can remember how passionate I was in my envy. Like a religious missionary who wanted converts, I tried to get people to support my envy.

One day one of my 12-step companions got fed up with my endless whining and comparisons. He told me that my story was getting old. He pointed out that I had been out of the seminary for three months and still didn't have a job. I had spent a lot of my energy wishing I had what my old friends had. I also fantasized about someone coming to me and offering me a job. I had a grandiose sense of entitlement. The fantasies of envy are potent and consuming.

My companion, Mike S., suggested that all the energy I was putting into my envy was a way of avoiding the grief and emptiness I felt about leaving the seminary. He further suggested that my envy was a way for me to avoid dealing with my anger over spending almost ten years in the seminary without fruition. He asked me to confront my own sense of failure and my fears of starting a new life.

This hit me where it hurt. Mike was right on. I was terribly afraid. I had not really grieved all those years I gave to my study for the priesthood. Mike S. taught me something about good friendship. He and I became good friends. He died a few years ago. I'll always love and remember him.

After Mike's confrontation, I started looking at my envy in an honest way. I stopped trying to elicit sympathy and started taking real action. When we are envious, our soul is asking us to look for *deeper levels within ourself*. When envy comes up in our friendships, we can learn to view it as an invitation.

Betrayal is always possible in the love of friendship. I betrayed my friend Bob during our sophomore year of high school. I was betrayed by a friend who stole a girlfriend from me. It is the very depth of the relationship that makes betrayal possible. If I don't care about you and you leave me, I will not feel betrayed. I can only be betrayed when I love deeply.

FRIENDSHIPS AS DEMYSTIFYING

In his book *The Fantasy Bond*, Robert Firestone writes:

> Close friendships stand in opposition to bonds. They provide companionship that is non-intrusive and non-obligatory, qualities that lead to self-awareness and encourage a person to emerge from an inward and isolated posture.

Friendships are demystifying because they lead us away from our fantasy bonds. They have therapeutic value. The daily interaction of friendship keeps us in a nourishing interpersonal (self-to-other) relationship. This is an important factor in confronting our destructive posthypnotic voices. My friends frequently call me to my power and self-worth.

Recovery Groups

My most lasting friendships started in 12-step groups. I believe that the recovery movement has made great contributions precisely because it promotes friendships. The promise of support based on common problems (alcoholism in AA, eating disorders in OA, sexual disorders in SAA, etc.) has enabled an enormous number of people to come out of hiding. Their mystified trances had kept them in self-to-self transactions, creating severe and pathological loneliness. Before joining 12-step groups, these people were often social misfits. The recovery process, with its group support and resocialization, has helped literally millions of once isolated individuals to become contributing members of society.

I mentioned Mike S., the man who confronted my envy when I left the seminary. He took me to some of my first 12-step meetings and spent a lot of time with me. He was a bit younger than me, which I resented at first. But he always made a lot of sense, and I listened to every word he said. As I mentioned earlier, my sponsor was a man named Fran, who was older and a university professor. In my mystification, I would not have trusted anyone of lesser status! Fran was a great teacher. He gave me a solid foundation upon which to stay sober. I love him like I love my good teachers and coaches. They are soul mentors, and I'll say more about them at the end of this chapter. Yet, although these relationships are deep, they are not really intimate. Mike S. was a true friend. He kept me honest. As I achieved more and more sobriety, I spent more time with Mike. We had long talks and shared deeply. He helped me come out of my mystified trance.

Support Groups

I met George twenty-eight years ago. He was attending his first meeting. He and I had a kind of instant rapport. This was before the state hospital. I had some more drinking to do before I would accept my powerlessness over alcohol. When I finally decided to recover my will and to change my life, George was there for me.

For about fifteen years George and I called each other best friends, but we were both pretty out of touch with our feelings. We never moved beyond a certain level of intimacy. After my dad's death, George and I connected more deeply. George had started doing some deep feeling work. I met him to play tennis one day and I knew he had changed. As he told me what he was doing, he was animated and emotional. I had never experienced him so open and unguarded.

In 1982, when I began doing my own feeling work, George and I decided to start a support group. We chose to keep our meetings closed—to invite into the group only people whom everyone in the group had agreed upon.

We started the group with six members. This is when my friend Johnny came powerfully into my life. We agreed to avoid all therapizing and head-tripping and to stay focused on our feelings and on giving sensory-based feedback about feelings. We made a verbal contract to abide by these simple rules.

Sensory-based feedback means staying with the data you can see and hear. For example, instead of saying "You seem to be insecure," we would say "You were moving your hands a lot as you talked, your voice was high-pitched, you were breathing rapidly, your facial muscles were taut, you looked frightened." Sensory-based feedback helps us avoid *interpretation*. This is especially important when you are coming out of mystification. It helps you to safeguard yourself against negative or positive visual and auditory hallucinations. For mystified persons interpretations are continually contaminated by deep trance material from the past. As children in patriarchal families we were not allowed to really be present. ("Children are to be seen and not heard.") Our perceptions were often severely shame bound. Most of us were also bombarded with our mystified parents' crazy-making hallucinations. My being called selfish all the time was really about my source figures' own frustration over the fact that what I was doing did not fit their comfortable level of *control*. All of us do this occasionally. It's called "laying your trip" on others.

In my support group, we work at staying focused on our experience and validating one another's feelings.

My support group has not been all sweetness and light. Early on I felt angry at George. We had somehow miscommunicated about new members in our group. I thought we had agreed that no one was to bring in a new member without getting everyone else's consent. But George brought in some new people without consulting the rest of us. I stopped going to the group, and I was able to tell George how angry I was. That was a high-water mark in our friendship. We changed the meeting site and started another group.

We have let several people in our group who did not fit in well. We have disbanded twice and started over. George, Johnny, and I now have eighty-two cumulative years of 12-step work together, but we have had our difficulties too. A core threesome is always in danger of triangulating, and we have on a few occasions.

A few years ago I got angry at George and punished him with my mystified age-regressive pout. I refused to call or tell him what I was angry at. This was old behavior, and, although it took nine months and almost destroyed our group, we finally worked it out. I had snapped back into my mystified childhood strategy of defense. George wrote me a very touching and vulnerable letter, which broke my entranced state.

Expressing Tenderness

As I learn to deal with anger and conflict, I'm also learning that I have a hard time expressing feelings of love and affection. All love needs to be replenished with genuine positive stroking. A stroke is any kind of physical or emotional stimulation. Children can die because of a lack of positive physical strokes, and we are all wounded in childhood when positive emotional strokes are lacking.

We can give positive emotional strokes by saying things like "Thank you for being concerned about me," "I like it that you always remember my birthday or sobriety date," "I love you," "Thank you for listening to me," or "I like the way you are assertive, like when you kindly asked the waiter to take the fish back and cook it the way you wanted it." This list could go on and on.

In our patriarchal society, men can only hug following sports victories, when loving a woman, and when playing with their children. This is changing. I hug my friends now every time I see them, and sometimes we even kiss on the cheek. The taboos against kissing are cultural. We've all seen Mafia movies where the toughest and most cold-hearted criminals hug and kiss each other. It will take a long time for our cultural eyes to get used to men kissing, but there will come a day.

By making tender disclosures of love, friends become closer to each other emotionally. Get in the habit of expressing tenderness with your friends. Here's an exercise you might want to try:

Periodically sit down with a friend. Each of you tells the other at least *three* things you like about them. Take turns—no more than five minutes apiece—telling these things, and be very concrete and specific. Then take a few minutes to tell each other something you *wish* had been mentioned. The purpose of this is to root out something that your friend may not realize you want to be stroked for. For example, I am most often the unofficial chairman of social planning among my friends. I like doing it, and I realize others might do it more often if I was less energetic about it. All the same, I'd like to get more strokes for my well-planned creations!

Another exercise that can help you keep your friendship up-to-date is for you and a friend to express three things you *dislike* about your friendship. Once again, be very concrete and specific. Be sure you are not upset when you do this exercise, and use self-responsible "I" messages. Those of you who have trouble with conflict might try this exercise regularly for a while.

Spiritual Growth

There are many benefits to being in a long-term support group. For men and women who were never soulfully loved by the parent of the same sex, same-sex support groups can meet our deep need to be loved by others of our sex. This is one of the biggest payoffs for me. I've gained a much deeper sense of masculinity by being vulnerable with other men whom I love and trust. I find that I've stopped flirting with women just to get the charge that comes when they show interest in me. I've changed my whole attitude towards sex. I'm much more spontaneous and far less needy. Sex does not *have* to happen when I'm spending time with my sweetheart. I don't have to prove my masculinity.

Another benefit comes from just knowing that several other human beings *know me* as fully, and sometimes more fully, than I know myself. I know that I can count on them to give me truthful feedback. I have some companions who tell me what I want to hear. My support group tells me what I *need* to hear.

It is also extremely valuable to know *other* human beings as fully and completely as possible. Psychologist Carl Rogers once said, "Whatever is most personal is most general." What this means to me is that when I listen to my support group friends and come to know them intimately, I realize how alike we humans are, that a lot of what

I thought was my own weird stuff is really very common. At the same time I also come to see how each one of us is uniquely shaped by our own fated history and our own unique beingness.

The guys in my support group are "soul brothers." They are as close to me as my blood brother, Richard, with whom I share a half century of experiences.

All my friendships have caused me to grow. If love has a measure, spiritual growth comes the closest to being that measure. George brings out strengths in me that have not blossomed with anyone else—he is my brother, but I have also asked him for a lot of fathering. Johnny has taught me what it means for a man to be vulnerable. I have been able to be more vulnerable because of him. Michael has given me permission to let my child play and enjoy life to the full. With Richard, Kip, and Marc, I have also grown in my ability to be fathering. Each of them is my brother, but each has also allowed me to be part of his empowerment.

CRISIS AND KAIROS TIMES

When my friends are in crisis times or kairos times, I make it a point to pay especially close attention. Johnny's mother died a few years ago. All of us need more help when we are grieving than at any other time of our life. When we are grieving, we can't think. We age regress to the earliest childhood stages. We are, as Tennyson put it, "an infant crying in the night with no language but a cry."

Johnny needed to talk a lot about his mother's death. He began to deal with the issues of his own mortality in a new and frightening way. That required that I listen a lot. Listening is an act of love and requires patience and skill. I'm glad I could listen and be there for him.

My friends were wonderful during my divorce which, though carefully decided on and very amicable, was still painful.

Recently George's son won the highest national honors in equestrianship. I know the whole story of his son. This success was a monument to the paradoxical nature of soulfulness. This was the one child in a sports-centered family who was not interested in athletics when he was growing up. I celebrated with my friend George and his wife, Claudine. These are the soulful moments when we want and need our friends.

REALISTIC EXPECTATIONS

It is crucial to have realistic expectations of our friends. The fantastic imagination can really botch things up here; it is the basis for the "absolute agreement" rule. It is unrealistic to think that close friends never disagree. It is also unrealistic to think that our friends will never let us down. That's an inhuman expectation. You can hope for it, but be prepared for your friends to be human.

Try out this exercise for developing realistic expectations in friendship:

Exercise: Images of Friendship

1. (a) Imagine yourself in the best friendship you could ever have! This is your dream friend.
   What does she/he look like?
   What does she/he say and do?
   What is special about this friend? Give two examples.
   (b) Imagine yourself in the worst possible friendship. Repeat as above.
2. (a) Have you ever seen, been around, or experienced friendships like either of these?
   (b) Where did you get the ideas and images for this best and worst friendship? From the movies? From TV? From books?
3. Outline the best two experiences you have *actually* ever had with a friend. Outline the qualities of the best friend you have ever had.
4. Have you ever been someone's best friend, good friend, friend? If so, what did they say about you as a friend? Did your friend act like your dream friend? How was he/she the same as your dream friend? How was he/she different?
5. Interview five people about their friendships. Make a composite list of all the qualities they talked about. Notice what they actually experienced as the best and worst in friendship.
6. (a) Now redo (1), changing any *inhuman* and *fantastic expectations* and images that you created.
   What is your realistic pictures of your friend?
   (b) What behaviors do you need to change in order to have that friendship?
   What steps can you take to create the love of friendship *now*?

SOUL MENTORS

I've suggested that true friendship is intimate and is based on equality. But there is another kind of relationship that is not based on intimacy or equality, yet is still deep and soulful. We don't really have a word for this. It is the love we have received from someone who has helped us grow in some unique way. They may have been our high school teacher or coach, a college professor, a boss, a therapist, a sponsor in a 12-step program. These people helped form us, helped us discover the power of our souls. The relationship was mostly one-way, and limited. It may have been short term. But it was also profound. Our time with them was *kairos* time.

At the end of January I went to Dallas to do a four-day event. I encountered two people who helped me focus on this kind of friendship.

"An Old Friend"

When I got to my hotel room on the first evening, there was a note on hotel stationery requesting me to call Karl Vogel. It gave a phone number and ended with the phrase "an old friend." I literally felt a surge of energy when I read it, although I hadn't seen or talked to Karl in twenty-five years. When I go to a city to do workshops, I often receive calls and notes from people who claim to be friends or distant relatives. I almost never want to call them. I was surprised at the energy I felt for Karl's note. I hadn't thought about him in fifteen years.

I wanted to call immediately, but I had a radio interview to do and didn't have a lot of time. I also felt something else which is hard to express. I felt it would not be appropriate for me to call back impulsively. I felt it would be in some way irreverent.

Instead, I talked about Karl to Winston Lazslo, my friend, manager, and longtime associate. I surprised myself by the enthusiasm and liveliness with which I recalled details about my relationship with Karl. Until now I had forgotten so much.

On the way back from the interview, I looked forward to calling Karl. So I called him. I was excited. We talked about some mutual colleagues from the past. I talked to his wife, whom I had never really gotten to know. I liked her instantly. Karl kept saying how *proud* he was of me. He told me he had been following my career. I could hear the pride in his voice.

I found out about his life and a terrible tragedy he had endured fifteen years earlier, when two of his children died within the space of a few weeks. One of the children was the age that my son is now. I told him I could not imagine that kind of suffering. He told me that later he and his wife had adopted a child, and he gave me enthusiastic details about this son, who was now 13 years old. I talked to Karl for a long time.

When I hung up the phone, a wave of sadness came over me. I started weeping. I was surprised by my response. I don't know how to express the feeling. Here was a kind and wonderful man from my past. Twenty-seven years ago he had hired me when I was at a low point in my life. I had gotten fired from the first job I took after leaving the seminary, because of my alcoholism. Karl was the district sales manager of what was then Lakeside Laboratories, a pharmaceutical company. He hired me for my second job.

I was in the early days of my 12-step recovery and was still in a lot of denial. But for a while I did well in the job. After working hard and staying sober for eight months, I decided in a moment of insane mystification to drink again. I was at a sales training meeting in Dallas, and I went out with another salesman who had fixed me up with a date. Women terrified me! I started drinking to ease my anxieties. I made it through the first night, got up the next morning, and made it through the first day of training. All day long I thought about drinking. By that evening I was obsessing on it. Then it all gets blurry. I'm out drinking again. I'm at a girl's house at 3:00 A.M. I'm hearing voices in my hotel room, but I won't get up. There is noise all around me. I won't get out of my bed.

The training went on without me. A phone call woke me. It was Karl telling me he was coming to get me, telling me that he had to fire me and we needed to go to Houston to get the company car that had been assigned to me. We flew to Houston together. I was feeling very sorry for myself, talking about my pain and loneliness.

Karl confronted me. He was gentle but firm. He told me loneliness was when you couldn't be with your loved ones. Karl clearly loved his family. One son had severe learning disabilities, and Karl spent hours playing games with him when he was home. His frequent business travel was painful to him.

Karl was an inspiration to me when we worked together. He was what I would call a truly good man, not pious or patronizing, but solid through and through. He was a mentor. I was working on what was really my first job other than teaching. Karl patiently showed me the business, modeling attention to detail, hard work, and rigorous honesty. If ever anyone was truly moral, it was Karl. Aristotle once said, "If you want to know what a good man is, go find one." Karl was the man. I'm not talking here about the hellfire and brimstone brand of morality. I'm talking about a gentle, honest sense of commitment to love, responsibility, and principles.

I realized why I was crying. Karl had been *my friend* and had made an impact on my life. Friends do that. We liked each other, Karl and I. We had worked together like partners, rejoicing in our triumphs when we made sales and supporting each other when we had to lick our wounds. No one was more proud of my progress on the job than Karl. He was my brother, not my boss. At one point I was sixth in the nation in sales. Karl truly rejoiced for me. I knew his care was for me, not himself.

When he had to fire me, he was in deep pain and I knew it. That knowledge exacerbated my pain and my shame.

Why hadn't I ever called him? I heard myself telling him on the phone, "I've thought about you five hundred times, but I lost your phone number dah! dah! dah! dah!" The words droned themselves out as I spoke them. *That wasn't the reason.* The reason was I was too ashamed to call. Being fired is shameful and I deserved to be fired. Then, as the years went by, I became so absorbed in my own survival and my own growth that I forgot about Karl. We humans do that to one another all too often. We get so engrossed in our mystified living, in our defensive trances, that we forget to love our friends!

Tears are the soul's expression of something that cannot be expressed in words. Mine spoke to me of the time lost with Karl. They pierce me now, as I think of my friend's great tragedy and how I wish I could have stood by him.

I was crying for joy, too! I had talked to old Karl. I was seeing a split screen. On one side was a shamefaced guy scurrying to get the samples and supplies loaded into the company car in order to give it back to Karl that painful summer night. On the other side was my picture in the *Dallas Morning News* with a long article about my success.

Then I glanced over at the book that was lying by my bedside table, *Wind, Sand, and Stars* by Antoine de Saint-Exupéry. I hadn't been quite sure why I had brought it with me to Dallas. Suddenly I got it! I remembered Saint-Exupéry's description of his friend, Mermoz.

The book is about the early days of flying and the pilots who flew the mail for a South American airline. Mermoz was one of the pioneering pilots. He had to fly a plane, which in those days had an absolute ceiling of 16,000 feet, over the Andes, a mountain range that rose more than 20,000 feet. His job was to search for gaps in the cordilleras. In the course of his career Mermoz had crash-landed on several occasions: in the desert, in the sea, and in the mountains. Then, one night, he radioed briefly that he was cutting off his rear engine. Silence followed. Saint-Exupéry writes:

> We waited. We hoped.... Slowly the truth was borne in upon us that our comrades would never return.... Life may scatter us and keep us apart, it may prevent us from thinking very often of one another, but we know that our comrades are somewhere "out there." ... Nothing can match the trea-sure of common memories, of trials endured together, of quarrels and reconciliations and generous emotions.

I feel the same way about Karl Vogel and I want to honor him.

The Waiter at the Palm

I met the second person on the third night of the Dallas workshop. I was with two associates at quite a formal restaurant. When the waiter came to our table, he took one look at me and exclaimed abruptly, "I've been waiting twenty-five years to tell you how angry I am with you."

I was startled and thought it was some kind of joke, but he continued, "You taught me freshman English at Strake Jesuit College Preparatory. Our whole class was excited about going to school every day. I had never looked forward to school in my life! And then you left, you went away and left us high and dry." He softened after he told me this. I murmured some stuff about my earlier problems with alcoholism. (Strake Jesuit was one of the jobs I was fired from be-cause of my drinking.) He said that they all knew about my drinking and that what I had done to them was not mitigated by my being an alcoholic. He then went on about his business of serving our meal!

I pondered his words for several days. I thought there was some-thing soulful about running smack-dab into these two people from twenty-five years ago. One a mentor that I had deep and soulful feelings for, and another a student that I had failed as a mentor. My former student's anger was a soulful matter. I had awakened his soul and then left it to wither. That was a deep wound. I remembered a mysterious quote from Paul Claudel. He said, "We are the condition of salvation one for the other." He believed that we alone can offer a *kairos moment* to our brothers and sisters, without which something powerful that could have emerged in them is passed over. That is what I thought my ex-student was telling me. I was there at a precisely right moment in his life. I touched something profound in him. His soul was opening up to new dimensions, and right at that moment, I left him. Something in him was passed over in an *irreparable* way. To call it a loss of trust is too shallow. Some slumbering part of his soul was left asleep.

I had never understood this consequence of my alcoholism. Because of my ex-student's confrontation, I understood better than ever that soul-mentoring is an evolutionary vocation and each of us is called to it. We are all connected to one another in a mysterious way, and, if we fail to be responsible at a certain time and in a certain place, everyone is wounded because those particular moments are irrecoverable.

Hearing from Karl and being confronted by my ex-student taught me something about the soulful and mysterious depths involved in the love of friendship.

CHAPTER 12

Spousal Love

Marriage is "yes" and "no" and "maybe"—a relationship of trust that is shaped in the primal ambivalence
of love and hate.

SAM KEEN

We would have broken up except for the children.
Who were the children? Well, she and I were.

MORT SAHL

My early beliefs about love being natural and easy were quickly dis-
pelled by marriage. In hindsight it is clear to me that my very decision to get married was the product of mystification. Being in love
made me vulnerable to my Caretaker false-self role and the need to
please that went with it. The longer I was involved in courtship, the
more I felt the pressure to get married. That you could love someone
erotically in a long-term commitment and choose not to marry was
not part of my belief system.

When I married, I thought I knew a lot about love and intimacy.
I was teaching courses in couple communication and methods of
enhancing intimacy. Early on I had taken refuge in my head as a way
to avoid my unresolved grief. Knowing all about love and intimacy
gave me the deluded belief that I could *be* intimate.

But I knew nothing of my mystified inner child's need to work
out his original source relationships. And I had no idea that I saw in
my spouse a nurturing mother who would take care of my infantile
needs without engulfing me.

Toward the end of my first year of marriage, I began to feel a
kind of sexual neutrality. I went from the passionate sexual desire of
courtship to a kind of asexual sensuality, feeling comfortable with

hugging and kissing, but feeling frightened if I moved beyond that. This was confusing to me and my spouse. I focused on our friendship, our parenting partnership, and our work relationship as more significant signs of spousal intimacy. As the years went on, I slowly swept all sexual desires under the rug. I lived in a state of delusion, which is sincere denial.

Later, I found out that there was a name for what I was experiencing and that some clinicians believe it is the most common sexual problem in marriage. It is called "disorder of desire," and it is the product of family dysfunction.

Disorder of desire is not a dysfunction of sexual performance. Nor is it about the sexual attractiveness of your partner or your love for them. It is a kind of erotic apathy that sets in when we come from families where sexual expression has been severely inhibited, or where we have been bonded to a source figure with unresolved sexual issues.

When people marry, they re-create the feelings and behaviors they saw modeled by their source figures. If sexuality was never expressed in either person's family, it will feel *unfamilyiar* (to coin a phrase) to express it once you have married and started a family of your own. This is a common factor in disorder of desire.

For me, being my mother's surrogate husband set up a more unconscious dynamic. As a child, taking on the adult role of my mother's companion was overstimulating and fearful, so I repressed my own sexuality. When I married, my *sexual repression and dissociation trance* was induced. The reentrancement coincided with my wife's pregnancy and intensified after our son was born. His birth made my spouse a mother and made us a family, and just as I had done earlier in my family of origin, I shut off my sexuality.

The tragedy is that most of this is unconscious. A blood test is certainly an inadequate preparation for understanding these recycled scenes of enchantment.

Our cultural models of spousal love have been highly polarized on the side of idealization. From Ozzie and Harriet to the stylized groupings of political families, we have been deluged with fantastic images of spousal love.

I suspect that a lot of this idealization is a mystified cover-up for the many disappointments spawned by unrealistic expectations and, in those who experience it, for the disorder of sexual desire.

The daily news reports of domestic violence show how quickly the idealized polarization of mystified love can shift to its degraded opposite. It is a warning sign of the tremendous power that lies in spousal love, a power that can be used either to create soulful love or to push us into the depths of mystification.

SPOUSAL COMMITMENT

Marriage is the most common form of spousal love, and I will focus a lot of my discussion on marriage. Keep in mind that what I have to say has equal application for long-term or live-in gay, lesbian, or heterosexual relationships.

It is important that we see spousal love as a long-term commitment that involves a willingness to learn and to acknowledge our vulnerability, hard work, courage, an acceptance of the mystery and uniqueness of our partner, and a preparedness for what fate may bring. A spousal commitment includes some or all of the following decisions:

- To be committed to continuous personal growth and to support your partner's personal growth

- To affirm your partner's strengths and be willing to be patient, forgive, and negotiate conflict and differences

- To make and abide by agreements about relationship rules and roles

- To stand by your partner in sickness and health, in bad times as well as good

- To be willing to negotiate ending the relationship if one or both of you are no longer spiritually growing and you've made *real* efforts to resolve your differences, including professional therapy

- To bear or adopt offspring

- To invest whatever time and effort it takes to work out conflict during the time of your offspring's developmental dependency needs and to divorce only when it is clear that your offspring's well-being is jeopardized by your staying together

No one makes this commitment in a single act of choice. It starts out with small decisions. As a relationship continues so do the choices. The couple passes through some clearly predictable stages, each of which involves a kind of crisis. These crises are times of increased vulnerability and potential growth. And each calls for new decisions and renewed commitment.

The process of creating spousal love also involves synthesizing a number of polarities:

ECSTASY	*DURATION*
• Moments of supreme oneness. Kairotic sexual experiences. Wonderful times together.	• Enough time to truly trust and to grow in our knowledge of each other. Experiencing a history together.

EMOTIVE WARMTH	*CONFLICT CAPABILITY*
• Good feelings about the beloved. Pleasure from sensuality, sexuality. Emotional strokes.	• The trust and honesty necessary to express anger and resentments.

SELF-DISCLOSURE	*PRIVACY*
• Allowing the other to know us as we are really are. Expressing our feelings, need, and wants.	• Allowing the other his/her solitude and privacy. Not having to share everything.

ACCOUNTABILITY	*NEGOTIABILITY*
• Asking for what we want. Having a sense of duty to the other person; being accountable to him/her for our time and activities. Spending time together. Listening to each other.	• Being able to say no. Being able to negotiate our own private interests and growth needs. Pursuing separate interests. Spending time by oneself. Enjoying solitude.

These polarities take time to synthesize fully, usually fifteen to twenty years. When they are not balanced, *polarization* takes place. When the spousal commitment is polarized, it is either idealized or degraded.

Each stage of the relationship demands that we give up some illusion of safety and stretch our sense of self-identity to allow for greater awareness, freedom, and commitment. We are, in a sense, always becoming aware of ourselves. Our sense of self continues to expand and deepen throughout our lives. Spousal intimacy allows us to discover parts of ourselves that we buried long ago or didn't know we had. This is one of the great gifts of intimacy—discovering our unique selfness.

Soulful spousal love asks us to grow up. Our unresolved devel-

opmental dependency needs are manifested in every spousal commitment. The mystified wounded child in both partners has a new
opportunity to resolve his or her issues of enmeshment, abandonment, neglect, and abuse. As Harville Hendrix points out in his book,
Getting the Love You Want, spousal commitment "can be an arena for
personal growth that matches or exceeds ... psychotherapy, religious
discipline, and social revolutions." I have grown far more from my
spousal commitments than from all my therapy combined. Spousal
love offers us a great opportunity for soul making.

EXERCISE: UNCONSCIOUS PATTERNS

In the sections that follow I'll look at the stages in the journey to
soulful spousal love. But first please try this introductory exercise.
Following the format of the chart on the next page, write down the
names of the people with whom you have had your most significant
erotic love relationships. Then, for each name, write down what you
liked most about that person and what you liked least. (Try for at
least three items in each category.)

Also note any patterns that emerged in the relationship. For example, did you originally think your lover was very strong, only to
find out later that he or she was very needy and weak? Or did it start
out like a fairytale and end like a nightmare? Or was your lover
emotionally available during courtship but then withdrawn after you
married or moved in together?

When you have finished writing, look to see whether there are
any similarities. Do certain patterns repeat? Do you tend to fall in
love with unavailable people—someone who lives far away or already
has another partner? Are you always the one to end the relationship?
Or was one relationship or person a mirror image or polar opposite
of another?

Now close your eyes and take a trip down memory lane.
Find the earliest house you can remember living in and
think about your most significant source figures. These figures are often Mom and Dad, but there are lots of exceptions. My grandfather was a much more significant figure
than my father in my early life. What you are looking for
are the source figures that taught you about relationships.
Notice what you really like about each of these people. Notice what you dislike about them. Try to find at
least three likes and dislikes. Add these to your list. Now

YOUR MOST SIGNIFICANT EROTIC LOVE RELATIONSHIPS

NAME	LIKED MOST	DISLIKED MOST	PATTERNS
	1. 2. 3.		
	1. 2. 3.		
	1. 2. 3.		
(more)			
Source Figures			

ask yourself whether there were any patterns in your relationships with your source figures. You may have always taken care of your mother's sadness and pain. You may have always been disappointed by your father. You may have wanted source figures to tell you that they loved you or that they were proud of you.

Now look to see how what you have written about your source figures relates to what you wrote about erotic love relationships. There may be direct similarities, or your erotic relationships may be just the opposite of your relationships with source figures. These opposites, too, are a kind of connection. Generally, there will be some startling connections—and, the more mystified you are, the more connections you will find.

When you see these connections for the first time, it can be quite shocking! After the shock, it may become clear to you that you've never fully left home.

This does not mean that you have to reject all positive and negative traits of your source figures. I love some of the positive things about my mom and grandfather. And I know that to want the positive trait means that I have to be willing to take the shadow side of it too. The difference is that if I am demystified, I can make this choice consciously.

One way to distinguish soulful from mystified spousal love is to ask *how much a person has really changed their family of origin rules and roles*. Soulful spousal love creates something new—a second order change. Mystified spousal love reenacts the family of origin rules and roles. I believe that until you finish your source relationships, you are never really in another relationship.

THE STAGES OF INTIMACY

Whether we are reenacting mystification or creating a soulful love, all spousal relationships seem to follow predictable stages that closely mirror our childhood developmental stages. If you have read *Homecoming,* you may recall my discussion of the four major stages of childhood: codependence, counterdependence, independence, and interdependence. Drawing on the work of Barry and Janae Weinhold and Pamela Levin, I described how these stages are in fact recycled throughout our entire life.

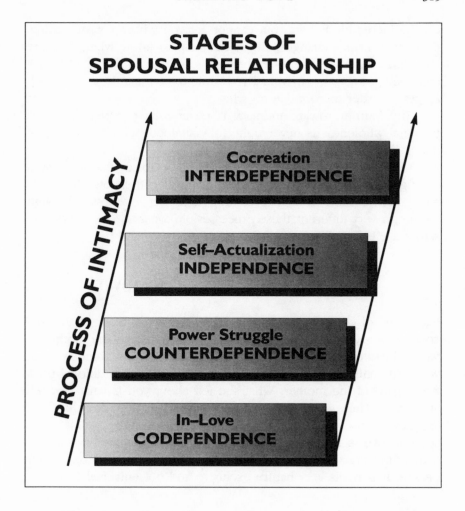

STAGES OF
SPOUSAL RELATIONSHIP

PROCESS OF INTIMACY

Cocreation
INTERDEPENDENCE

Self–Actualization
INDEPENDENCE

Power Struggle
COUNTERDEPENDENCE

In–Love
CODEPENDENCE

Later, I discovered Susan Campbell's book *The Couple's Journey,* which reports on in-depth interviews with fifty couples who had been together from three to thirty years. Two-thirds of the couples were married, and one-third were unmarried but living together. They had been referred to her because they were engaged in developing greater awareness about intimacy. Campbell's work focuses on the *process* of intimacy.

In what follows, I will synthesize Campbell's research with the four stages of childhood to describe the journey to intimacy. I will show you how each of the first three of these four stages can be either mystified or soulful. Stage Four is only soulful. It is the fruit of soulful loving in the first three stages.

Knowing the stages of the process is like having a map. A map can be incredibly helpful, but cannot get you where you are going. Each stage brings changes, and it can help to know when they are most likely to take place. As each stage is completed and its obstacles overcome, new tasks emerge. The couple must meet these new challenges in order to continue growing.

The journey toward intimacy is never fully completed, just as personal wholeness is never quite fully attained. We need to accept this at the start.

One way to describe the entire journey is to say that it involves a struggle in which two people learn to develop their own identities while at the same time overcoming their separateness. Although seemingly very different, these processes of *individuation* and *togetherness* are essentially *inseparable*.

STAGE ONE: CODEPENDENCE (IN-LOVE)

Stage One of childhood is infancy. The essence of infancy is healthy codependency. In that stage there is only one other—the mother. It would be literally true for an infant to say "I am nothing without you." The child's self-foundation depends on the unconditional positive regard of the mother. What she felt about you is what *you* felt about you. There are no boundaries between mother and child.

Lovers also say "I am nothing without you." In its first stage, spousal love is rooted in erotic love. Erich Fromm writes, "Erotic love is the craving for complete fusion, for union with one other person. It is by its very nature exclusive and not universal."

Soulful In-Love

Over twenty-two years, I counseled more than eight hundred couples. During the course of my work, I discovered a curious fact. I used to begin my couple counseling with the question "Of all the people in the world you could have married, why did you choose her (him) to be your spouse?" The answers were always vague. They usually ended with "I guess I just loved her (him)." Inevitably, as I learned about the couple's romantic history, I found that each had married someone with the positive and negative traits of their source figures. This was not always a deficit. The people with little mystification prized and cherished their parental love relationships. They wanted the parental qualities in their partner. They could also see their partners as really different from their parents. And marriage gave them a chance to work on their own internalized parental traits and their own idealized images. Being "in love" was a very positive and wonderful experience.

The experience of being in love is oceanic. It has a sense of boundaryless infinity. It causes us to expand ourselves while being possessed by the image of the beloved. The beloved is godlike and holy. Every aspect of the beloved's being is cherished.

When I fell in love two and a half years ago, I viewed my lady as entirely wonderful. I used to call her on my car phone just to hear her voice. I remember making my friends listen. I'd say, "Just listen to her answer the phone." After they had listened, I'd say, "Isn't that adorable?" They *never* responded the way I thought they should.

Once I took the messages off of her telephone recorder. One message was from me. I was appalled at my 56-year-old baby talk!

Cupid is presented as an infant because when we are in love, we go back to the primal scene. We gaze at our beloved's face just as we gazed at our mother's face. We do talk baby talk!

WHY WE FALL IN LOVE

Many biologists contend that there is a biological basis for romantic love. Some suggest that we instinctually select mates who will enhance our species. In this view men are attracted to young robust women because such women are at the peak of health and, therefore, will be excellent childbearers. Women select men who are strong and aggressive and, therefore, will insure the survival of the family.

Such a view cannot explain the attraction between many men and women, much less between men and men or women and women. Nor can it fully explain the power and intensity of the attraction many couples feel.

A more expansive view of the power of love suggests that we are attracted to those who seem to be more or less our equals. This theory, posited by some social psychologists, is called the exchange theory. It suggests that we go beyond physical beauty and social status. We look for someone who is similar to us in background and values.

I have certainly seen evidence to support this theory. But it cannot explain the huge number of people who seem so mismatched. I once counseled a couple who were deeply in love but very, very different. She was a rigid Roman Catholic who wanted at least six children. He was an agnostic Jew who wanted no children. She was emotionally fragile and quite hysterical. He was emotionally repressed and very logical. He loved classical music. She thought Bach was a beer.

"Why do you want to get married?" I asked. They told me they never imagined having sexual experiences such as they were having and that they equally loved to dance, especially the four-corner shuffle! I did what I have never done as a therapeutic intervention: I *prayed* during one session. They married in spite of my protests. The marriage lasted three months.

LOVE AS DIVINE LONGING

My own way of understanding love goes back to Plato. Plato called love divine madness. He saw the paradoxical quality of love. Love involves pain and struggle along with its pleasure and joy. In his famous dialogue on love in the *Symposium,* he had his characters look at love from many points of view, some of them strangely modern. Aristophanes tells a story that describes allegorically a deeper source of the powerful attraction two people can feel for each other.

In the beginning, says Aristophanes, there were three sexes: men, women, and androgynous beings, who were bisexual. Each being had one head with two faces, four hands and four feet, and two sets of genitals. All beings were round in shape and could walk upright as we do now, or backward and forward. Each could also roll over using their four hands and feet like tumblers.

These original beings had immense might and strength. They also had great ambition, desiring to scale heaven and attack the gods. Zeus pondered their threat. He didn't want to annihilate them totally as that would put an end to the worship and sacrifices they offered to the gods. Zeus discovered another way. He cut them in two, one after another. Apollo was called upon to heal their wounds and compose their forms. The two halves, now walking upright, were then sent in opposite directions to spend the rest of their lives searching frantically for the other half-creature. Reunion with the other half would restore their wholeness.

According to Aristophanes, this explained the intensity and power of erotic love and sexual desire. Men would desire men, women would desire women, and men and women who were originally androgynous would desire each other. Whenever one half of the pair met their other half, they would be "lost in an amazement of love, friendship, and intimacy." The desire for the other was not only sexual desire; there was also something else which the soul of either evidently desires and cannot tell, and of which she has only a dark and doubtful presentiment.

This allegory attempts to explain all forms of sexual preference. It also attempts to explain the power of love and its mysterious quality.

Using Plato as a guide, we might update the allegory as follows:

We do go through life with a mystified wounded child looking for the unique symbiotic bond of infancy in order to restore ourselves to wholeness. No matter how much we have demystified, something dark and doubtful remains when it comes to love. The darkness is love's mysterious depth. We want to fill up our emptiness. And there is no one who will ever be able to do this for us. No matter what we do or whom we love, we will have some emptiness. It is our soul's yearning for the "Good" and for Being itself. The "dark and doubtful presentiment" we touch in our spousal partner may be a reflection of the divine.

For Plato love is always more than it appears. When we experience a fully dynamic and intense earthly love for another, we are being led down a path that will take us into greater depths of soulfulness. In the *Symposium,* Plato called love the *child of fullness and emptiness.* Love promises to heal our deepest wounds. No matter how painful the past experiences of love have been, a new love is optimistically energetic and spontaneous. Love moves us into realms beyond practicality. It is "not made for this world," says the poet Novalis. Thomas Moore asks, "Is love truly blind?" And he answers:

> It may be the other way around. Love allows a person to see the true angelic nature of another person, the halo, the aureole of divinity.

Looked at from a logical perspective, love is illusion. Lovers are out of their minds. But their "madness" may be Plato's divine madness, the unearthly cravings and needs of our soul.

Mystified In-Love

One form of mystified erotic love is love addiction. Love addicts believe time and again that they have fallen intensely in love with someone, but in fact they never really experience falling in love.

In love addiction the sense of emptiness flows from mystification. The love addict's frantic desires and fatal attractions stem from
the wounded child.

When we fall in love, we reawaken the desire for fusion and
wholeness we felt in infancy. But when we are love addicted, we use
our partner to mood alter our emotional hunger and emptiness, to
take away our emotional heartache. Love addicts are in emotional
pain. People who fall in love are not.

The mystified in-love stage can be either idealized or degraded.
It is always a form of addiction. The table on page 322 outlines the
two polarizations, as well as soulful in-love.

IDEALIZED STAGE ONE

In the idealized polarization, the love partner frequently represents
the source figure one liked the most and is most enmeshed with. It
is a reenactment of that relationship. A client of mine, let's call him
Jacques, went with four different women in one year. Each one was
sick two-thirds of the time she was in the relationship with Jacques.
None had been sick when Jacques met them. Jacques' mother was
severely hypochondriacal. She was bedridden two-thirds of his childhood. Is this just a coincidence? Hardly, with four relationships in a
row! Jacques was seeking out women like his mother and reenacting
the same enmeshed fantasy bond he had with her.

In another form of idealized mystified in-love the partners *magically* believe that all their problems will go away. Love will conquer
all. Many people in our culture have been hypnotized into believing
that marriage is magical. Our destiny is to get married, and when we
do, our love will effortlessly grow and our problems will be solved.

In an idealized mystified in-love situation, the partners stop
growing. They bond with each other out of their false selves. There
is considerable dishonesty in this kind of love. It intensifies each
person's loneliness, as each hides their shadow self from their
partner.

DEGRADED STAGE ONE

Being in love is always rooted in the erotic, but the degraded form
is intensely erotic from the start, often from the first date. Both partners want chronic excitement and continuous mood alteration. Relationships of this type are often characterized by obsessive disclosure
of faults and mistakes. There is continuous confession, which aims at

insuring acceptance, as if the person were saying, "Let me confess everything to you so that you will never reject me." Intense discussions of every aspect of the relationship quickly lead to fighting, which is ritually interrupted by mind-blowing sex.

The focus of the relationship is how it makes one *feel*. Each partner tries to test the other and wants repeated proofs of love. Each is more focused on *being loved* than on loving. There is a possessive quality to degraded in-love mystification. Rejection can lead to intense jealousy. In the most severe cases it can even lead to stalking and murder.

THE POSSIBILITY OF GROWTH

The big difference between soulful and mystified Stage One is the degree of self-consciousness. In soulful falling in love, the partners are on their way to self-actualization. They have a strong connection with their own feelings, needs, and wants. They have some sense of their authentic self. Mystified in-love is characterized by self-image actualization and *emotional hunger*. The partners have a false self or no sense of self due to the con*fusion* of intense source figure enmeshment. Neither partner has any real sense of their authentic self.

The good news is that if we can wake up enough, we can use our relationships to break out of the prison of mystification and grow into our true identity.

The Dark Side of Love in Stage One

Each stage of love has its dark side, or painful possibilities. The dark side belongs to the *soulful* stage as well as to the mystified, polarized forms of love. It is the shadow of the good each stage brings us. In risking love, we *always* risk its dark side. Jealousy and rejection mark the dark side of love in Stage One.

The great myths tell us that even the gods are jealous. From a soulful perspective, jealousy may have a deeper meaning than can be accounted for by the wounded inner child and dysfunctional family systems. Thomas Moore suggests:

A first step toward finding the soul in jealousy is to think mythologically, to consider what great context there may be for the intense emotions and profound restructuring we feel in these times.

Stage One
In-Love Codependence

IDEALIZED	SOULFUL	DEGRADED
• Restores fantasy bond with source figure	• A new experience: oceanic, erotic, sense of belonging	• Intensely erotic; based on genital sex; constant excitement
• Partner as magical figure—being possessed	• Experience of beloved's uniqueness	• Distrust; partner needs to prove love—possessive
• Denial of all problems—"love will solve everything"	• Vitalized exuberance; new sense of strength and optimism	• Game-playing; intense probing; chronic discussion of relationship; fighting
• Stops growing; false self intensifies; dishonesty	• Willingness to self-disclose; effects real change—loses weight, exercises, etc.	• Obsessive disclosure of faults and failures, punctuated by mind-blowing sex
• Feels whole and complete; needs no one else; isolation	• Love moves outward, expands to all; wants to show partner to others	• Attachment and insane jealousy; partner as "stash"; rejection may trigger violence
• Self-image actualization; having the "right" partner for social, religious, business purposes	• Self-actualization	• Self-aggrandizement or self-effacement

DARK SIDE
Jealousy
Rejection

What is this larger context? I'm suggesting that when you experience jealousy, there may be a message from your soul in it. If you look for the message, it may keep you from acting out your jealousy in a harmful way.

I remember an ex-girlfriend of mine. I decided to break up with her and I started another relationship. She was *insanely* jealous and morally outraged. She became a detective. Although she fancied herself as nonviolent, she smeared ketchup all over my new girlfriend's car and cut her tires. She called my new girlfriend and hung up every three minutes for about three days. She seemed crazy, and I feared her violence.

Jealousy is a symptom, an invitation to demystify. It is a deep cry from our soul that there is something within ourselves that we are not looking at. We must befriend it. Ask your jealousy, "What are you trying to tell me about myself?"

My ex-girlfriend evidently never let her jealousy reveal its full message. She never went through it to her past history, to her family, to the deeper themes at work. Instead, within three months of our breakup, she married a man twenty-five years her elder. I saw her two years later. She had become obese. Something very deep within her had transformed her beauty into its grotesque shadow.

Her life haunts me. I know a lot about her family issues. When I was with her, she was childlike and innocent. In fact, this is what I could no longer stand. I felt I was with a goody-goody little girl. She was people pleasing and nice to a fault. What no one would have expected of her was the violence of her jealousy, the intensity of her rage. She was so overidentified with purity and innocence, so engrossed in her false self, that she was out of touch with her violence. As Arthur Miller says, "The perfection of innocence is madness."

I think that her obesity is her intolerance and rage turned inward, the price she has paid for not dealing with the message from her jealousy. She felt so good and pure, so righteously justified in her vindictive behavior. I think her jealousy was revealing a need in her soul to be more energetically assertive in her life, to be more spontaneous and free, to balance her shyness and good girl image with her anger and her need to be more of a bad girl. It seems that her soul was thwarted and her defense against the soulful voices calling from deep inside her was to eat, to try to nourish the fury that all her righteousness could not hide.

Another danger of falling in love is that it brings the risk of rejection and abandonment. Rejection is not possible unless you are bonded to someone in a valuing and significant way. To love someone is to risk being rejected by them. This is why love requires courage.

Love is often painful. One should prepare for the possibility of this pain. Some people consciously choose *not* to love again because of this awareness. But if you do decide to love someone, one great fantasy that must be reimagined during the in-love period is that of living happily ever after. Our dreams of perfect happiness, our feelings that we can't live without each other and that we can live without differences or conflict, must be tempered in the fires of reality. The romantic dream inevitably comes to an end. Conflict begins in Stage Two when our in-love fusion is jarred by our individual differences, our self-concerns, and our family of origin rules.

STAGE TWO: COUNTERDEPENDENCE (POWER STRUGGLE)

Three months married, I sat in the kitchen stirring up some anger. The sugar bowl was empty!!! I had noticed it four days ago, but I had let it slide. Imagine, four days with an empty sugar bowl!

You need to know that I had lived alone for fourteen years of my adult life, including four years after leaving the seminary. As a bachelor, I had cleaned my apartment regularly *four* times a year. And now here I was stewing over a sugar bowl and walking around the house like a secret agent looking for dust!

Marriage had kicked in my patriarchal householder rules. Women were supposed to take care of cleaning the house and buying the groceries, and keeping the sugar bowls filled. Never mind that I had done all this for myself for fourteen years. My fantasy image of a good wife had her doing these things. This is what I had seen my mother and my friends' mothers doing. Although there was nothing about this in our legal contract, I expected my wife to live up to my image of how a wife should be.

All my counterdependency issues were emerging now. In childhood, counterdependency begins at about seven months. At this age, children are beginning the journey to personal identity, to self-consciousness and to willfulness. The willfulness is about separation from the mothering source. Counterdependency is later expressed in temper tantrums, saying no, and setting boundaries (saying "it's mine").

In a soulful family, the foundation for boundary building and separation will be solidly in place by about age 3. Object constancy will also be achieved. Well-adapted 3-year-olds will be able to express anger, say no, and have a sense of the polarity in both their source figures and themselves. Their healthy shame tells them that everyone makes mistakes and lets you down on occasion. A 3-year-old is still very immature and impatient, but the groundwork has been laid.

Stage Two of spousal love usually begins with the legal bond of marriage. The marriage contract, as we now have it, is romanticized and idealized. Phrases like "for better or for worse, in sickness and in health, till death do us part" are all very well, but who will fix the commode when it's overflowing, how will we manage the money, and who will wash the clothes and cook the meals?

Disillusionment inevitably sets in. "You're not the same as when we married," says the distraught husband. "You're not the way I thought you were," says the disappointed wife. Disillusionment is a natural part of marriage. It will occur in any relationship that lasts long enough for differences to emerge. Romance knows no boundaries or differences. In romance two people are codependent. This is why being in-love is a *prelude* to love. It is not really love.

Every new couple that enters into the flames of counterdependency has soulful opportunities for a deeper, more profound connectedness. But growth will come only from disillusionment. Buddha called enlightenment *progressive disillusionment*.

The Hatfields Versus the McCoys

The first issues that must be struggled with are those involving the two family systems. Each partner brings into the marriage their family rules, both overt and covert.

These rules cover all the areas of living. There are financial, household, celebrational, political, religious, somatic (illness), sexual, and with the first child, parenting rules. There are also overt and covert rules about sex roles and power in the relationship.

These rules must now be negotiated. We would never critically examine these rules as our spousal partner will do. Questioning these rules and updating them is another way to leave home, another way to grow up. On our own, there would be little occasion to question them.

When people come from similar socioeconomic, political, and religious backgrounds, it saves wear and tear on their colons! People who are from similar backgrounds tend to have similar rules. My wife and I had some different rules in the areas of household, celebration, and money. I had grown up poor; her family was quite well-off. My mother had labored over household chores, washing our clothes by hand. Her mother had had a maid.

Our first Christmas brought some rude awakenings. In my family, we opened our presents on Christmas Eve, we opened them fast, and *we didn't save the ribbons and paper*! My wife's family opened the presents on Christmas morning. You had to wait and watch while each person opened their presents, and *they saved the paper*. These were our overt celebrational rules and they were clashing!

When it came to money, my overt rule—learned from my grandfather—was that if a man could make $500 a month, he was successful. My spouse had come from a family where her father made much more than that during the Great Depression! She had very different feelings and expectations about money. She had some relatives who were ostentatious about money, and any public display of wealth was embarrassing to her.

When I started making some money, my mystified inner child was joyous and very proud of himself. I can remember doing a big workshop for a company that paid me $1,000 for the *day*. This was incredible! I shared this with my spouse, expecting her to leap with joy and be as excited as I was. She was very quiet and polite, and I could see that she felt slightly uncomfortable discussing it. I went away and pouted for two days. Pouting was an *age regression*. I was using the same behavior that got my mother's attention and disguised my anger. My spouse had no idea what was wrong. She asked if I was upset, and I answered, "No, everything's fine," in a sarcastic and haughty voice.

The conflicts over rules are often fiery and stubborn. These conflicts are necessary if we are to find a common ground and melt down the rigidity of the old *familyiar* rules. In these clashes we are armed with whatever *interpersonal skills we learned as toddlers in our original counterdependency stage of development*.

EXERCISE: NEGOTIATING CONFLICT

As a counselor, I sometimes used an exercise I learned from Susan Campbell to help couples become aware of how they dealt with conflict. You might want to try it with your spouse.

The couple sits facing each other with an 8½" × 11" piece of white paper between them. They are told that the paper represents something very valuable. They are further told that there is only one piece of paper and that they each want it very badly. And they are told that only one of them can keep the paper. Each person must hold two corners of the paper, using their thumbs and forefingers.

At the word "start," each has five minutes to try and get the paper from the other person. The players can use any method they know of to get the paper. But if the paper is torn or damaged in any way, both players lose. Try this when you have time.

This exercise can show you a lot about your style of negotiating conflict. It can be an amazing breakthrough to realize that you try the exact ways you used as a child to get what you wanted. Some people just give up, turn their backs, and pout; others try to trick their partner by distracting their attention. Men often try to overpower their partner; women sometimes use seduction to get the paper. It's good to talk things over and share feelings after you do this exercise.

Mystified Power Struggle

Stage Two also flushes out the unconscious images we all carry. Depending on your family of origin, you may have idealized or degraded expectations of your spousal partner.

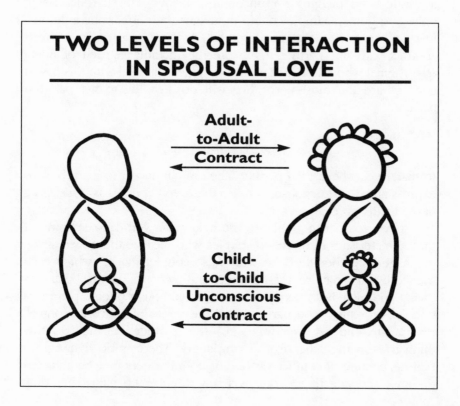

TWO LEVELS OF INTERACTION IN SPOUSAL LOVE

Adult-
to-Adult
Contract

Child-
to-Child
Unconscious
Contract

The most stubborn and high voltage conflicts stem from each of the mystified wounded inner kids trying to fulfill their expectations and get their needs met. When two adult children meet, they interact on two different levels and make two different contracts: an adult-to-adult contract and a child-to-child contract. The child-to-child contract embodies the unconscious and nonlogical decisions that the mystified children made a long time ago. As you can see in my drawing, each spouse's conscious, adult-to-adult contract may be contradicted by the needy child within them.

Unfortunately, our wounded child contract almost always remains unconscious until we are married or in another kind of committed relationship. The marriage itself activates it.

This child-to-child contract must be resolved if the couple is to grow up and create a mature soulful love. Couples often do the very best they can consciously do. But their conflicts are literally infantile. Children are absolutizers. They love to use words like "all," "always," "never," and "ever." Whenever I hear these words used in an argument, I know that the two wounded children are having it out. Sometimes there is yelling, sometimes screaming. What we are hearing is a frantic child begging for unconditional love. Our parents, being finite and human, simply could not give us the perfect unconditional love and mirroring that we deserved. Now we have made a covert contract with our partner to restore the infantile Garden of Eden, our original wholeness. The power struggles that deal with this covert contract are the most fierce. We will do anything to get paradise back.

IDEALIZED STAGE TWO

In marriages where each partner failed in childhood to learn how to express anger and negotiate conflict, the covert contract is "let's agree never to disagree."

If you look at the table on the next page, you can see some of the characteristics of mystified couples who idealize the power struggle stage. Together they create a "false couple image," which each tries to live up to by repressing anger and by pretending to be always loving and nice. Both partners fear anger, although often a pattern is established where one partner uses the threat of anger to control, manipulate, and get their way. The other partner will then do anything to stop the other from being angry. There is no fighting, no real negotiating of conflict. Or one or both partners may be addicted to "joy," always acting joyous as a way to cover up pain. The "duty

Stage Two
Counterdependence

IDEALIZED	SOULFUL	DEGRADED
• Confluence—agree never to disagree; anger phobic	• Contact— negotiating conflict	• Conflict—shaming, "Who's Afraid of Virginia Woolf?" atmosphere
• False couple image; pretending to be nice, happy, loving	• Finding authentic selves by working through family of origin rules	• Reenactment of childhood victim/offender cycle
• Joy addicts; no problems; unrealistic, rigid expectations	• Having tough times, but hanging in; changing expectations to fit reality	• Triangulating children; affairs; nonresolution of problems; expecting the worst
• Pseudo-intimacy based on false-self roles	• Growing intimacy; willingness to compromise; accepting real differences	• Intimacy dysfunction; controlling, battering, punishing
• Self-sacrificing; duty-bound	• Give and take; learning to fight respectfully	• Selfish; "I want what I want"
• No boundaries	• Semi-permeable boundaries	• Rigid boundaries

DARK SIDE		
	Disillusionment	
	Betrayal	
	Anger	
	Grief	

bound" and "self-negating" types of mystified love described in Chapter 1 are commonplace in idealized Stage Two.

Both partners in this type of relationship are highly codependent. They failed to get their childhood counterdependency needs met and thus failed to develop an authentic self. Idealized Stage Two couples often form the same enmeshed fantasy bond they had with their source figure(s). Neither has any real boundaries, and each one is being *used* by the other to fill up their emotional hunger. I like to use the word *confluence* to describe this enmeshed, conflict-avoiding state.

DEGRADED STAGE TWO

In degraded Stage Two, partners may try to really hurt each other in retaliation for the wounds their parents inflicted on them. With each disappointment and disillusionment one tries to spite the other, often shaming them and ridiculing them just as they themselves had been shamed and ridiculed in childhood. Those who were physically abused may become physical and violent. There is a deep reservoir of anger when our childhood wounds are unresolved. Our spouses get this anger.

Each partner feels a sense of betrayal in Stage Two. Each has broken the implicit contract they made during Stage One, when each believed what he or she needed to believe and projected their unrealistic expectations on the partner. The biggest expectation is that our partner will make up for what we missed as children.

But we can never return home. In order to wipe out unworkable levels of expectation, each partner must go into his or her own inner emptiness and its connection with childhood. Attempts to modify unrealistic expectations without going into the original pain will result either in *temporary* acts of will or in emotional disconnectedness and distance. These attempts are often made by well-meaning therapists who teach couples all kinds of techniques for resolving conflict.

Some of these techniques are like the ones I described in Chapter 8. Teaching couples to use "I" messages and active listening can help them to respect each other's boundaries. Assertiveness training can teach couples how to express anger cleanly and ask for what they want. There are also other guidelines for expressing anger and fighting fair. These techniques are *useful for the demystified*. But for the mystified, they become new rigid commands to be obeyed. In my practice couples would do well with them for a few months, but then they would *continue the old fights, this time using their new therapeutic terms*.

This is very frustrating for a counselor. Just when everything seems to be going well, a new, more sophisticated kind of fight emerges. Control and power are at it again, now clothed in therapeutic jargon.

I taught techniques of this kind for the first ten years of my counseling practice. I didn't know what else to do. I stopped teaching them once I became involved in my own family of origin work.

Unrealistic Expectations

The wounded child's unrealistic expectations are also at the root of one partner's desire to change the other. We can become obsessed with our fantastic imagination of the partner we want—and are convinced we *need*.

In order to bring your expectations into line with real human possibilities, it is crucial to embrace your own healthy shame. Seeing the log in our own eye is essential for growing in intimacy. This stage presents us with a great opportunity to embrace polarity. Partners who work out their mystification usually come to see that what they dislike about their partner goes hand in hand with what they do like.

I remember counseling a man who was complaining about his girlfriend putting on weight. He said that he didn't know if he could stay with her and that he felt betrayed. As he spoke, *his stomach hung over his pants,* and the material at the top of his fly was pulled apart because he was so overweight. There were food stains on his tie and coffee stains on his shirt! When I asked him about his own slovenly condition, he got angry and stormed out of my office. He returned later only because I had charged him the full amount for a sixty-minute counseling session. He wanted the thirty minutes that he didn't get when he walked out.

It was clear to me that a slim and trim woman was his fantasy, a projection stemming from his refusal to accept his own overweight condition. In his eyes, an attractive woman made him look good.

On his second visit, he heard me. We had several more sessions. I then made a contract with him. Anytime he had critical thoughts about his girlfriend's weight, he was to think of his own weight problem and do *one* thing to change his own condition. As he focused his energy on himself where it belonged, he stopped his unrealistic fantasy projections. He joined Overeaters Anonymous. As he changed his own image of himself, he stopped pressuring his girlfriend to change. Paradoxically, she began to lose weight. His own slovenliness, coupled with the demands he was making on her, had triggered a great deal of anger in her. She had expressed it passive-aggressively by putting on weight.

I want to make clear that having expectations of our partner is okay, so long as they are contracted for, realistic, and human. It's the unrealistic expectations that are devastating.

Unrealistic expectations and fantastic imagining must be confronted before many of the Stage Two issues can be dealt with. Otherwise the couple is condemned to go back and forth endlessly over particular issues and old arguments. And the areas where we find it *most difficult to change our expectations* are precisely those in which we have our greatest *emotional investment*. Usually the difficulty is based on some disowned part of ourself that we are projecting onto our partner.

Each partner is responsible for their own wound. Each must take the means necessary to do their personal grief work, to finish their own unfinished business. Sometimes this does require professional help.

Soulful Stage Two

When we do our grief work, when we embrace our original pain and legitimate suffering, we come to accept our hurts and disappointments. We know that no adult can give us absolute or unconditional love. Problems and emptiness are part of life. We see that life is one large reasonable gamble and that we must take risks. Things will not always work out the way we want them to. Hurt is part of the incompleteness of being human. We must expect to be hurt, seeing this as the emotional price necessary to attain precious moments and connectedness.

At best two married people can give only *so* much to each other. So also with families. Once we accept the limitations of being human our expectations will be consistent with reality. Acceptance is not dishonest. It recognizes that self and other are not perfect, and that it is all right not to be right. This fosters closeness.

By the end of Stage Two, soulful couples learn to be more flexible. This requires imagination. I would like to share an example of a stuck and mystified relationship becoming more soulful through the use of imagination.

THE IMAGINATION PROCESS IN ACTION

A couple comes for counseling. The wife begins a long diatribe about how insensitive her husband is. She has had just enough recovery to be dangerous. She begins an analysis of *his* dysfunctional family, focusing on their coldness and lack of expressiveness. I ask her to summarize her problem in one sentence. She thinks for a minute and then says, "He just never talks. I don't know what he's feeling. I want him to talk over problems with me." At this point the wife has talked for thirty of our fifty minutes. I have partially allowed this as I like to get a total kinesthetic sense of people when I first meet them for counseling. I say "partially" because I found myself feeling frustrated and angry a couple of times. In truth, I felt it would be hard to get a word in edgewise. After the thirty minutes, I finally jump in and ask the wife to be silent while I talk to her husband. I ask him, "So, is it true you don't talk to your wife?" "I guess I'm just too tired from work," he replies. At which point his wife breaks her promise and starts rapidly talking about weekends, how her husband sits on the couch and watches sports events. I interrupt her (no small task) and again ask her to be quiet. "What about weekends?" I ask the husband. He is silent for what seems like five minutes, then he responds, "I'm sick of her talking. If I answer, she starts talking more. She constantly talks and constantly criticizes me."

It is clear from a family systems point of view that *this couple creates each other's behavior*. As it turned out, each married the parent of the opposite sex. Her dad was quiet and unexpressive. His mom was a critical and compulsive talker. In the marriage, each is acting out his or her wounded child's neediness. This is the hidden agenda, the mystified wounded kids' contract.

I found out that he had been much more assertive and expressive during courtship. He wrote her poetry and was very romantic. She was much more coy and reserved.

This couple are in what has been referred to as "the game without end." She bitches and nags because he won't talk, and he won't talk because she bitches and nags. They are truly stuck. Each has made a real attempt to work their problems out. Both are confused and are beginning to feel hopeless. Neither one *can imagine* a new behavior that would lead to a different outcome.

It is not my job to try and fix their marriage by telling each one that their behavior is wrong, or by taking sides and defending him or her. One possibility I have is to teach them some rules for fighting and get them to practice these rules while they are in my office. Another possibility I have is to separate them and help each one work on reclaiming their inner child and grieving their original pain. This would require a good bit of time and money. The couple had only limited time and money. I decided to let my own imagination work on what to do.

On the next visit, I asked them to sit facing each other. I told them that *verbal talking* was not allowed in this exercise. I realized then that I was using a technique I had learned from my training in Neuro-Linguistic Programming. NLP demonstrates that words often anchor us in habituated patterns of behavior and that people can gain much more flexibility by communicating nonverbally. I hadn't remembered this until faced with the couple that morning.

So I had the couple sit opposite each other. The rule was they could communicate in any way they wanted nonverbally; they could not use any verbal communication. The husband was to tell his wife something that he needed. He began by patting his thighs and pointing to his shirt collar. She looked blank and shook her head no. He then started to unbutton his shirt. She vigorously shook her head from side to side and waved her hand. He then pointed to his shirt collar and pretended he was plugging something into the electrical socket on the wall. He made a fist and started moving his hand horizontally back and forth. I was still in the dark, but suddenly she got a gleam in her eyes and started shaking her head yes. They both began to laugh and hugged each other. It turned out that early in their marriage she used to iron his work pants and shirts. As their troubles worsened, she stopped ironing his clothes. He liked her way of ironing them.

What I reviewed with them was the flexibility he exhibited during the exercise. When one communication didn't work, he tried another. When that didn't work, another. He kept changing his behavior until she understood. This exercise also demanded that they both use their imagination. Ordinarily, they were so stuck in their verbal standoffs that neither could see any other way to behave.

I had them do several more exercises and gave them a similar homework assignment. By their next visit, I could see a visible change in both partners. He looked more animated and alive. She was less talkative and more playful. They came a few more times. I felt they were finished with what I had to offer in terms of their time and finances. I felt that they had truly broken their impasse. They had learned that they had some *real choices*. They learned that there were many ways to work on their problems. I think that I did what good counseling should do—offer people new choices.

It's important to say that this couple might have been helped by any of a variety of interventions and any of a variety of counselors and/or therapists. Imagination is the key. There is no one right way to do anything. There are myriads of possible human responses to any situation. There are many possible meanings we can give to any behavior. We are only limited by imagination.

If Stage Two is resolved, partners will find themselves closer. If the legitimate pain and the nature of the adult human condition is refused, the power struggle can go on until the end, with one partner on their deathbed trying to kick the other one last time.

The Dark Side of Love in Stage Two

The soulful achievement of Stage Two is the deep realization that we cannot get the unconditional love our child wants from our partner by means of power and control. We cannot get unconditional love from them by pretending, threatening, forcing, manipulating, dominating, or playing subtle games. Susan Campbell writes:

> This stage comes to an end when we recognize who we are and what we *do* have and give up our attachment to fantasies of harmony without struggle, achievement without effort, pleasure without pain. When we surrender to life as it is.

Often this kind of soulful awareness is not achieved. Many people stay mystified and refuse to give up their fantasies and infantile wishes. Many chose addiction as a way out of their pain. They act out with chemicals or with eating or with sex. Eating, in addition to filling an ever-deepening emptiness, is often a passive-aggressive way to punish the partner.

Sexual acting out is the most potentially damaging. Affairs are breaches of the commitment of love that was made in Stage One. Affairs are often, although not always, attempts to relieve the tension of deadlock in the marriage. Although many couples survive an affair, there are usually serious consequences. Mystified people have been betrayed in childhood, and the marital betrayal opens up the earlier wound. Those who were severely abused sexually often have used time distortion as a trance defense. They use time distortion once again. The affair becomes the whole truth about the marriage instead of a relatively short time of it. (I am not pointing this out to justify affairs, but only to put them into perspective. And I'm speaking here about one affair, not about the multiple affairs of sexual addiction.) Even where the earlier wounds were less deep, betrayal causes great pain and damages the fabric of trust. It will take nurturing care and time to rebuild the damage.

STAGE THREE: INDEPENDENCE (SELF-ACTUALIZATION)

From approximately 3 to 7 years old children more or less settle down and begin forming their *first identity*. The clashes of the toddler stage are over. This is a period of equilibrium during which children experiment and try things out. They ask a lot of questions and begin to form their core beliefs about self-identity, sexuality, and relation- ships. They find a role—a set of behaviors that give them a sense of significance in the family. And, as I have pointed out, the more dysfunctional the family is, the more the child will create a false self.

Questioning everything is part of the process of finding mean- ings for the confusing relationships and the vast array of sensory data that surround one. Learning that it is okay to clarify confusing communications is an important part of this developmental stage. It will stop the person from doing a lot of "mind reading" in later relationships.

The parental marriage is the first model of a spousal relationship. When that relationship is solid and growing, a child experiences what spousal love looks like and sounds like. By looking at their same-sex parent, children start to concretely imagine what it will be like to be an adult in a spousal relationship.

Owning Our Projections

In courtship we thought our partner's impulsiveness and spontaneity were wonderful because our posthypnotic critical voices would not allow us to be impulsive and spontaneous. In Stage Two we projected our own prohibition against impulsiveness onto our partner and their impulsiveness became an area of conflict.

In Stage Three we need to embrace our own impulsiveness and spontaneity—or whatever parts of ourselves we have rejected and projected. As we own our rejected parts, we become whole and self- connected. We restore our original I AMness. This is a crucial part of the individuation process. We must accept every part of ourselves with unconditional positive regard if we want to feel complete.

Once we've accepted all the parts of ourselves, we stop pro- jecting these parts onto our spouse and others.

The experience of polarity also tells us clearly that *our spouse cannot fulfill all our needs* or *be our only object of interest*. So, we begin to look outside our spousal relationship to develop other inter- ests. In relationships that are demystified and individuating, outside interests do not take away from the marriage. Instead, they enhance it, because as the partners fulfill their desires, they become more whole.

The couple develops a workable and flexible set of rules. They are now creating their own spousal relationship. It may have real powerful cultural influences, but it won't be a cop-out. For example, one may *choose* to live with the more traditional marriage roles—he goes to work, she manages the household. The important word here is "choice." A couple decides on the traditional roles because they want and like them.

Soulful Stage Three

Stage Three is what Susan Campbell calls the stability stage. Partners cool down their conflicts. They are more forgiving and desirous of peace. If they have worked through their grief over the past, they are more present to the here and now. Just going through years of power struggles can teach us toleration. The acceptance of the limitations of our partner and of life itself marks the achievement of object constancy. Partners are no longer hell-bent on "making their relationship work." In fact they are usually confused about themselves and do not have the same certainty about things. As each partner accepts their own limitations, the old confusion comes back. Confusion can be a soulful state. It replaces the false certainty of the false self. We feel we don't know anything for sure anymore.

This stage usually corresponds to mid-life. For most of the couples in Susan Campbell's study, the power struggle stage took ten years. This doesn't mean a couple *has* to engage in a power struggle for ten years. It just means that it often takes that much time to melt down the rigidities from the past. The certainty and rigidity of the past were cover-ups for emptiness caused by toxic shame. The false self gave us definition. So when it collapses, we have feelings of uncertainty, confusion, and emptiness. But our confusion is also the beginning of healthy shame and paradoxical awareness. Because each partner can accept themselves as wounded and limited, they can accept each other in their woundedness. Each partner can be respectful of their partner's wound without trying to fix it or take responsibility for it.

I can see this at work in my own life. As a child, I was enmeshed with my mother and engulfed by her loneliness, pain, and unresolved anger. Love for me meant taking responsibility for a woman's pain and being victimized by her anger. I can still get very frightened when I start to feel too close to my lady friend. My wounded child thinks that love means I must give up myself and take care of my partner's pain, hurt, and anger. I have most often been attracted to women who have my mother's fine qualities but also her negative traits. Before I did my original pain work, I set myself up to take care of wounded women. The pain of those reenacted relationships increased my distrust of women and intensified my anger. Once I grieved my childhood wound and separated from my internalized mother, I modified my projections.

Now when my lady feels the fear of abandonment, I can be accountable to let her know where I am. But I don't have to take care of my lady's abandonment fears. I can be sensitive to them. I can support her in taking care of them. But I need to take care of my own engulfment wound. No woman can do that for me.

Childhood is over, and while we can reclaim our wounded inner child, *it is too late to have a happy childhood*. When each partner is willing to reclaim their wounded inner child, they stop making unrealistic demands on each other. We must take care of ourselves before we can truly care for our spouse. Being responsible for our own wounds and honoring our partner's being wounds is part of the alliance that results from the work in Stage Three.

When each of us takes care of our own wounds, we give each other a great deal more respect and reverence. We listen to each other more. We learn about each other's history. We learn about the caring behaviors our partner values and loves, and paradoxically the love and care that we give each other seems to help us heal our own wounds. What we give starts coming back to us.

Erik Erikson talks about generativity as the adult developmental task that emerges during this time of life. Generativity means creativity and productivity. We don't just rest in our safe marriage and safe job. We start caring for the quality of our life and for the lives of others. The mystified opposite of generativity is stagnation.

Mystified Stage Three

Stage Three mystification is the culmination of the failure to resolve the conflict and polarities the couple experienced over the years. Each partner carries a residue of anger and hurt, and each either feels despair over achieving any real intimacy or believes that what they have achieved is about all they can really expect. They have lowered their expectations to the status quo. Their disappointment usually triggers old shame binds. They may feel that deep love is not possible for them because they are flawed and defective. They may rationalize that "no one is *really* happy."

IDEALIZED STAGE THREE

Some take refuge from personal growth in their job and marriage. The job becomes more and more routine as they achieve seniority. They work four-and-a-half days and head for the lake, cabin, or beach house. Social life with the spouse and a few other married couples becomes a slightly boring ritual. Although the couple may "look good" from the outside, the relationship can easily rigidify and stop deepening. The couple forgets that growth involves risk, uncertainty, and pain.

This is also the point where some couples create a kind of parallel relationship. While keeping up the image of a peaceful marriage, they may "marry" their work or their volunteer activities. She may pursue her career or go back to school. Either of them may have an affair. They agree not to "rock the boat" and give up any effort at working on expanding their relationship. But what looks like acceptance is really a form of hopelessness. The result is a peaceful coexistence geared to distract the couple from their deep terror of going it alone.

Their sex life diminishes to the point of becoming a kind of duty. Or it ceases altogether. Such circumstances are especially conducive to a partner resuming or starting an affair, often with a married person whose marriage is in the same shame boat. Most often partners mood alter their loneliness and lack of connectedness with hobbies, TV, travel, shopping, the children or grandchildren, or with anything else that gives them a respectable way to continue their conspiracy of silence.

DEGRADED STAGE THREE

When we withdraw our fairy-tale projections from one another, we end our grandiose illusion of omnipotence. We are going to die, and we must die alone. All relationships must end. Without our projections, we see each other as we really are, as our all-too-human selves. We may find this terribly disconcerting. We may be terribly disappointed. We can get stuck here in our loss, especially because, since our illusions were unconscious, the loss is totally unexpected.

We can get caught up in remorse about the past or cover our grief by living for the moment. All our accomplishments and our relationships are seen as nothing. Deep depression and low-grade anger set in. We silently rage against the ending of life, but we never come to peace with it. A new kind of selfishness emerges, characterized by nit-picking pettiness. She must have the last word in the argument; he must have his favorite armchair and watch his TV programs. They both become self-absorbed, rigid, and stagnant. Sometimes partners become envious of and competitive with each other.

Depression leads to resentment and cynicism. Partners silently blame each other for the emptiness in their life. Fighting becomes passive-aggressive, subtle, and often cruel.

Mystification gets worse in the evening of life. As the lack of fulfillment intensifies, so does the loneliness. As the whole span of life comes into view, people have an acute sense of how they missed the mark—or how they never even recognized what the mark was. "If only I had known," we hear people saying. "If youth knew, if age could," says an old proverb.

Mystification cannot progress beyond Stage Three because mystified Stage Three ends in *pseudointimacy*. A couple is bonded out of the terror of aloneness, disappointment, and hopelessness.

At this point the couple has created a "false couple image." It is rigid and inflexible. They think they know what their relationship identity is. *They do not know that they do not know what a relationship identity really is.*

The Dark Side of Love in Stage Three

Couples in Stage Three must often contend with sickness, disability, and death. If there is soulful love based on choice, commitment, and the acceptance of fate, almost any of these can be dealt with and worked through.

A spouse's death must be deeply grieved in order to be resolved. Mystified persons often either avoid the grieving process or get stuck in one of its stages. Their earlier disillusionment is intensified. Why go on living? Sometimes a surviving partner will commit suicide or become agoraphobic. Often a low-grade chronic depression takes over. The surviving partner does not want to live the way he or she is living but is afraid to die.

The more mystified the person is, the more they stay frozen and rigid, addicted to their grief. Such people are prime candidates for heart attacks and cancer. And I've been at the bedside of several widowed persons who just quit living.

GROWING APART

Another possibility in Stage Three is that a couple may simply grow apart. When I woke up from my mystification, I saw how completely I had re-created my family of origin trance in my marriage. Over the years I had denied the many differences between my wife and me. Our whole rhythm was out of step. We had grown in different directions. And even though we loved each other, we decided that we were not growing with each other. Our children were grown and gone, so we decided to divorce. I think we made a soulful, generative decision. We remain respectful friends, and each of us is growing spiritually. I have grieved the fateful fact that in spite of loving someone, sometimes it just doesn't work in a spousal way. I believe that Stage Three divorce often requires courage and the commitment to grow.

STAGE FOUR: INTERDEPENDENCE (COCREATION)

The fourth stage of childhood is school age, which spans the years from 7 to puberty. School-age children are learning and practicing interdependence and cooperation. They are acquiring the ability to see from the other person's point of view, to share with others, to play games, to lose gracefully, to agree on rules and guidelines, and to have empathy. All of these abilities are essential for friendship and love.

In Stage Four of spousal relationships, interdependence can occur because each partner has a sense of self-connection. Maturity has awakened them to the realization that security does not reside in anyone else. They have found their own Higher Power and created some security within themselves. Stage Four couples no longer love out of neediness.

Carl Jung wrote:

> We are alone, for our 'inner freedom' means that a love relation can no longer fetter us. The other sex has lost its magic power over us, for we have come to know its essential traits in the depths of our own psyche. We shall not easily 'fall in love' for we can no longer lose ourselves in someone else, but we shall be capable of a deeper love, a conscious devotion to the other.

Stage Three
Independence

IDEALIZED	SOULFUL	DEGRADED
• Bonded out of emptiness; too much to lose	• Coming to a sense of individual identity; bonded out of desire for each other	• Bonded out of terror of being alone
• Take each other for granted; stop growing and working on the marriage	• Taking responsibility for own wounds, own projected parts	• Passive-agressive anger; subtle sabotage; nit-picking pettiness
• "Triangles" involving work, travel, children/grandchildren, etc.	• Supporting the other partner in self-actualizing	• Enabling each other's addiction
• Psychosomatic illness	• Contributing to the needs of the relationship and getting own needs met	• Envy and competitiveness; selfishness and egocentrism
• Pretense becomes congealed as "false couple image"	• New sense of authenticity—formation of a new alliance out of family system rules	• Marriage held together with chronic affairs; "you don't bother me, I won't bother you"
• Pseudointimacy; ritualized and routine sex life or none at all	• Experimenting, finding new enjoyment in sex	• Using sex; marital rape, withholding sex as punishment

DARK SIDE

Growing apart
Sickness, disability, death

The couple in Stage Four is clearly together because they want to be. They are not two half people clinging together to make a whole. They are not needy mystified children looking for their parents. Each is confident about his or her own separateness, and each has faced the hardest truth that comes with soulful aging: *There is no human security. There is no one who will always take care of us.* To know this is to be demystified, to finally leave home and grow up.

In Stage Three the partners separated in order to come into their own as individuals. In Stage Four they come back together and explore unexpected aspects of their intimacy. The range of intimate sharing is as large as the possibilities of relating. Some of the more common forms of intimacy are:

1. *Sexual* (erotic or orgasmic closeness)
2. *Emotional* (empathy or empathic listening)
3. *Intellectual* (sharing the world of ideas)
4. *Aesthetic* (sharing the experience of beauty)
5. *Creative* (sharing acts of creating together)
6. *Recreational* (having fun and playing together)
7. *Work* (sharing common tasks)
8. *Crisis* (coping with problems and pain)
9. *Conflict* (facing and struggling with differences)
10. *Commitment* (mutuality derived from community service)
11. *Spiritual* (sharing ultimate concerns)
12. *Communication* (the source of all types of intimacy)

Partners may see clearly that they have achieved a high degree of sexual, emotional, recreational, and work intimacy but that they can develop more intellectual, aesthetic, and spiritual intimacy. The couple can find a sense of renewal and adventure they never dreamed was possible.

Stage Four partners have reached a kind of expanded awareness which is the fruit of their *interdependence*. True intimacy transcends each person's individual awareness. It is a synthesis of two unique persons' ways of being. It is the fruition of the *process* of intimacy. A unique new reality is created by their interdependent love. It is a true polarity—a synthesis of two persons. Once achieved, this shared being has great power for cocreation.

Couples at this stage often know each other quite intuitively. They can read each other's mind and anticipate each other's desires. The *two people have become one*. Yet they remain uniquely themselves. Each partner experiences the mystery and uniqueness of their mate. Their intimacy is less ecstatic than Stage One but more constant and workable, deeper and more soulful.

My friend Johnny is more in touch with his vulnerability than anyone else in my support group. Recently he was sharing about his wife of thirty years. This was what he said:

> Yesterday I was standing in my bedroom looking at my wife.
> I noticed her wrinkles and that she was aging. I felt a surge
> of love I've never felt before. She was so beautiful, more
> beautiful than she has ever been before!

He wept as he said this. All of the rest of us were crying, too. In his statement I knew something of Stage Four love.

Stage Four is fully *soulful*. It exists in the face of human finitude, of our knowledge that death could take our partner at any time. The risks are much greater at this level of commitment, as the loss of our beloved touches our very being.

Let me sum up with a beautiful saying from a nineteenth-century rabbi:

> If I am I because I am I
> And you are you because you are you
> Then I am and you are.
> But if I am I because you are you
> And you are you because I am I
> Then I am not and you are not.
>
> Rabbi Menachem Mendell of Kotsk

CHAPTER 13

Love and Work

The man who sinks his pickaxe into the ground wants the stroke to mean something. The convict's stroke is not the same as the prospector's for the obvious reason that the prospector's stroke has meaning and the convict's stroke has none. . . . It is using a pickaxe to no purpose that makes a prison: the horror resides in the failure to enlist all those who swing the pick in the community of mankind.

ANTOINE DE SAINT-EXUPÉRY

Work is love made visible.

KAHLIL GIBRAN

Sigmund Freud was once asked what he thought were the marks of maturity. In perhaps the shortest sentence he ever uttered, he answered, *"Lieben und arbeiten"*—to be able to love and work. We cannot reach our potential for soulful love if our work lives are a daily study in mystification.

The Genesis creation story points to suffering in work as one of the major consequences of humankind's fall from grace. But it also suggests that work was intended to be part and parcel of human life. Adam and Eve were to *work even in the Garden of Eden,* "to till it and to keep it." Even in paradise, work is necessary for human fulfillment.

Every spiritual tradition sees work as a crucial part of our soul-building enterprise. When I was in the seminary, physical work was as much a part of our daily rule as prayer, meditation, and liturgy. One of my jobs was to grow corn. I spent some time each day working in my corn patch. Watching the miracle of planting and growing—just being close to the soil—affected me deeply. The activity was soul-expanding in itself. Near harvest-time, I discovered that a lot of my corn had bugs! I was terribly upset. The bugs were like a disease a good friend had developed. I fretted and worried and did all I could to rescue my corn. Some of it survived. We ate it at our common meal supper for several days. I felt very proud.

Soulful work has a healthy narcissistic quality. We see ourselves reflected in our work, and we grow in self-love as we see our work accepted by others.

RIGHT LIVELIHOOD

A hopeful model for the creation of a soulful workplace is presented by E. F. Schumacher in his book *Small is Beautiful,* which has the subtitle *Economics as if People Mattered.* In a chapter entitled "Buddhist Economics," Schumacher offers a picture of what a soulful work and economic order might look like.

One of Buddha's Noble Eightfold Paths is "right livelihood." For Buddha, "spiritual health and material well-being . . . are natural allies." He saw a threefold function of work:

• To give us a chance to utilize and develop our faculties

• To enable us to overcome our ego-centeredness by joining with other people in a common task

• And to bring forth the goods and services needed for a becoming existence

For Buddha, right livelihood is a process involving self-actualization, self-valuing, and self-transcendence. All three of these functions are necessary for work to be soulful. Each contributes to the formation of character, and from a Buddhist point of view, the soul value of work depends on whether or not it contributes to the purification of human character.

WORK AS ENHANCING MYSTIFICATION

Work deepens our mystification when it fails to provide a context for our self-actualization, self-valuing, and self-transcendence. There are three primary ways this happens:

First, the workplace itself fosters mystification through its patriarchal power structure. It does this by:

- Making productivity more important than the life-enhancing quality of its products (and generating, for example, environmental pollution)

- Making the company's productivity more important than the people who work there

- Being rigid, dogmatic, shaming, and narrow-minded

Second, the workplace fosters mystification by the roles it induces us to assume.

- We can continue our false self roles from our families of origin on the job.

- We can re-create the exact same *relationship* we had with our most shaming parent by working at a company that treats us as that parent did.

- We can act out our family's *beliefs* about work.

Finally, the workplace mystifies in that we can become addicted to the activity of work itself, focusing on the mood-altering *process* of work rather than enjoying its products. Or we can become attached to the products of work in the form of money, making money an end in itself.

In what follows I will look at each of these in more detail and describe some ways to create a soulful workplace.

PATRIARCHAL POWER IN THE WORKPLACE

Many of our offices, shops and factories are based on the same patriarchal rules that caused our primary mystification. If you were not mystified in your family of origin or in school, you can still become mystified in the workplace.

I worked as a management consultant for ten years. When I went into a company, I tried to get people to talk about the specific problems they were facing, so that I could assist them in working through some of their actual on-the-job issues. When I could get them to break the company "no talk" rules, the most common pattern that emerged was that the employees thought the company's major problem was the CEO or one of the top managers. The CEOs had frequently risen to their level of success because of their expertise in some special area, like engineering, finance, or marketing. But they were grossly ill-equipped to handle interpersonal situations, to communicate effectively, or to motivate their personnel. They either avoided any hands-on leadership or ruled with an iron fist. More than anything or anyone else, *they were the problem*. They expected their subordinate managers to know how to do the things that *they didn't know how to do themselves*.

Like the parental dyad in a family system, the management team is the chief component of the work system. If the team is dysfunctional and mystified, the whole company will be affected. The problem I found with most of the top managers was the same one we've seen in dysfunctional families: They were patriarchal and secretive, they triangulated communication, and they were out of touch with feelings—their own and everyone else's. They used power, control, shame, and distance as their chief management style. I also found an immense amount of overt and covert prejudice and sexism.

Productivity Versus People

Patriarchal companies are generally committed to unlimited productivity. Their obsession with more and greater profits creates an atmosphere in which greater importance is placed on producing goods and services than on people's growth and self-actualization. Like dysfunctional family systems, the company is more important than the individual, and many individuals sacrifice a great deal of their lives to these inhuman systems.

General systems theory posits that as a system gets more and more obsessive, it becomes increasingly rigid and dysfunctional. Rigidity is manifested in legalistic company policies and in the refusal to change. Comments like "This is the way we do it in this company—don't try any fancy new ideas" and "We've never done it that way before, and we don't intend to start now" are commonplace in patriarchal companies.

Products Versus People

Our places of work cannot be soulful if the *products* of work are not soulful. I can imagine a factory that produces cigarettes sharing its profits and treating its workers with respect and dignity. Such a factory may seem soulful, but it is ultimately not, because the *product* of the work causes massive destruction to human life.

The product of our work must lead to a "becoming existence," one that promotes our own life-style and nurtures all life-forms. How can we love ourselves in our work if the products of our work are life-destroying?

Patriarchal Worldview

The business world's obsession with productivity is rooted in an inadequate view of the relationship between humanity, God, and the world. We have been collectively mystified by a cosmological belief system that most of us have never even considered.

A cosmology is the "beginning" story that every civilization puts together in order to explain the origin of the world and its composition. Once a set of assumptions is formulated to make this explanation, people create a meaning system from those assumptions. Their assumptions form the context for their developing beliefs about law, religion, education, economics, and politics.

It's important to see the contrast between our Western cosmological assumptions and those of tribal or Eastern cosmologies. In tribal and Eastern cultures, God is *in the world*. Matter is never stuff without a soul. There is soul in everything.

The earth is our mother and matter is sacred. In such cosmologies, it is impossible to imagine economic principles like *owning* the earth and unlimited productivity.

Our Western cosmology embodies a different set of assumptions. In the West the sense of the Divine has always been *outside of the world*. The gods or God are transcendent. Human beings have a relationship to God, but the relationship is always one that transcends the universe. The patterns of sacred relationship are human-to-human and human-to-God. *The earth itself is not sacred* in this worldview.

The world is *material,* the primal stuff, which is to be transformed through the human *spirit*.

From the beginning Western cultures have seemed almost driven to perfect the world, to make it better. Our relationship to nature has been oriented toward rearranging it. Nature has had a fearful aspect. There is something foreboding about the wilderness. Nature is "red in tooth and claw," wild, a warlike enemy that needs to be conquered.

As Westerners set out to harness and conquer the earth, they used the earth without constraint and productivity slowly became an obsession.

Mystified Love of the Earth

Patriarchal power with its fallacious cosmological assumptions has led to our current environmental crisis.

At the recent Earth Summit in Rio de Janeiro, Maurice Strong, the secretary general, said: "We have been the most successful species ever. We are now a species out of control."

We are in a crisis, and crisis is a time when soulful and kairotic events take place. We need to create solid images of hope, and it's important that we stay grounded in our realistic imagination.

A mystified love of the earth has resulted in polarization. There are two views of our relationship with the earth, one idealized, the other degraded.

The ideal view of the earth is pantheistic, romantic, and overly spiritual. It sees nature as our divine mother, pure and absolutely innocent. It is sentimental, naive and simplistic. This idealistic view holds nature to be the reservoir of morality and wholly indestructible.

The degraded view is purely materialistic. This view suggests that life and consciousness are accidental by-products of matter and that evolution is motivated by chance and the instinct for survival. Matter is soulless, an inert blob that is subject to humankind's willful fancy. Nature is raw, fierce, dangerous, and totally indifferent, and it must be conquered and ordered by human control. Nature is lovable only when humans transform it.

Soulful Love of the Earth

A more realistic approach sees nature as created, finite, and lovable in itself. Nature has an inner radiant energy that bears the imprint of creative and intentional design. We can metaphorically refer to earth as our mother, but nature is not always nurturing. We are sometimes assaulted by fateful natural interactions, like storms at sea, tornados, earthquakes, volcanic eruptions, and freezing cold.

The realistic view sees the earth as both immensely strong and immensely vulnerable. We humans are inseparable from the earth; we are its consciousness, the earth thinking. We are responsible to the earth as we are responsible for ourselves.

Every cell in our bodies is bathed in the ocean. I recently listened to an audiotape entitled *The Fate of the Earth* by Sister Miriam MacGillis. She is a follower of Teilhard de Chardin, a visionary of human evolution. She says,

Life has a perfect rhythm. The oceans become the clouds, the clouds become rain, the rain becomes our food and water, we take it into our bodies and we become the ocean. The tears we weep are the ocean.

When we assault the oceans, we assault the ebb and flow of life. The communities of life, from the protozoa to the dolphins to the whales, enable the ocean to be alive. When we exterminate a species, we place holes in that garment. The oceans can die. If the oceans become toxic, so will the clouds, so will the rain, so will the food, so will the water, so will the wombs, so will the bodies of our children, and so will our tears.

Power Versus Wisdom

The process of consciousness is very new to the universe. Our planet is very young, and what it knows is the sum total of what the five and a half billion of us conscious beings know. We are the universe thinking. We have the choice. We can either indulge our short-sighted mystification with its scarcity, fear, and greed, or we can create love.

The question is, are we up to the task? Are we wise enough to take over the controls? Can we fly the spaceship ourselves? Sister Miriam MacGillis asks "whether or not we *day-old species,* we *half-hour-grown smart folks,* are working with a full deck of cards when we go into our laboratories." We seem very smart, but are we very wise or loving? The ultimate mystification is the destruction of our living home.

UNETHICAL WORK ETHICS

Another way to compare soulful and mystified work is suggested by Peter Senge, an expert in organizational behavior at MIT's Sloan School. Senge describes systems as "open" or "closed," and in his book *The Fifth Discipline,* he calls for "nothing short of a change in corporate structure." According to Senge, modern business practice is "learning disabled." Only an open system—one that calls on the creativity and contributions of all employees—can provide the basis for new learnings.

Senge believes that the greatest problem in modern business

organizations is that the addiction to profit and productivity creates
a closed system that:

- Makes the system (the company) more important than the individual

- Misses the learning potential of new experience

- Lives by developing skilled incompetence through trying to protect
  the managerial patriarchs

- Thrives on shaming and scapegoating

- Makes inhuman demands on employees' time and loyalty

Senge makes it clear that modern business organizations cannot
survive unless they develop the capacity to learn and create.

I believe that survival also depends on empowering employees.
The powerlessness that many people have felt in the recent economic
recession should give us pause. When tough times come, companies
rigidify and cut jobs almost automatically. No imagination is given to
other possible solutions. The prevailing mood in our country right
now is fear. No matter how hard they work, people have no sense
of job security. When humans are reduced to an item on the ledger
sheet under the heading "labor," there is reason to fear.

For some people, an economic downturn may have a profoundly
demystifying effect. It may lead them to question their work addiction
and their loyalties in a useful way. They may build up their identity
apart from their work. The danger, however, is bitterness and disillusionment about work itself.

For those still employed and working in fear, the demands
placed on their time and loyalty are often dehumanizing and unrealistic. While the physical abuse of labor has been curtailed by unions
and human outrage, the mental and spiritual abuse of the worker has
become part of the professional code of the modern work ethic.

In many companies people who want to advance are expected
to work inhumanly long hours. Those who refuse to do this lose out
in the highly competitive race for higher-paying jobs and positions
of greater power. The demand for greater and greater productivity
creates levels of chronic stress that are driving people into addictions
and even killing them. Unrealistic expectations are the fruit of the
fantastic imagination rooted in greed and a mystified belief in scarcity.
The modern work ethic shows an arrogant disregard for human life
and value. It has lost its spiritual center.

Open Versus Closed Work Systems

IDEALIZED	SOULFUL	DEGRADED
• Everyone's ideas are taken into consideration.	• Flexible. Uses a wide range of viewpoints. Dialogue.	• Rigid. My way or the highway. Monologue.
• Management is always right.	• Accountability. Management is responsible. No scapegoating.	• Skilled incompetence. Energy spent protecting management. Scapegoating.
• No need to experiment, everything is perfect.	• Planned experimentation. Open to learning.	• Defensive. Learning disabled.
• Goals of company and workers are exactly the same.	• Goals of company and individual need to be negotiated.	• Workers' goals don't count.
• Collectivity.	• Community.	• Snake pit.
• Shameless. Righteous, patronizing. No mistakes.	• Healthy shame. Mistakes can be occasions for learning.	• Shameful. Overt shaming, blaming, and terrorizing.
• Product is justified if it makes money.	• Product of work enhances life.	• Product is life-damaging.
• Inhuman. Rigid. Unrealistic expectations.	• Human. Some fun and laughter. Team spirit.	• Dehumanized. Underpaid. Prejudice and sexual harassment.

CONTINUING OUR FAMILY SYSTEM FALSE SELF ROLES ON THE JOB

My experience as a management consultant showed me over and over again how often people reenact their mystified family system false self roles in their jobs.

One notable example of this was my involvement with a group of professionals in Austin, Texas. Five dentists from Austin got interested in my family systems work and asked me to come to Austin to work jointly with their office staffs.

During my first visit I helped each person focus on their family of origin. We spent time looking at the roles they had chosen as a way to matter in their families. We then looked at their current office roles. It was amazing how many of them were playing out the same role in the office that they had played in their family of origin. In fact, at least half of them had re-created their whole family system in their office. All five of the dentists identified their role in their families as Superachiever; two were Stars, and three were Caretakers.

The more rigid the office staff roles, the more problems the office seemed to be having.

Specific conflicts on the job were also very similar to the conflicts each person had experienced in their family. I remember walking past one group and hearing a woman loudly exclaiming to a fellow worker, "Now, I know why I don't like you. You're exactly like my sister." We found that people were often setting others up to act like family members.

For example, one dentist was amazed to discover that in his ongoing conflict with his most qualified lab technician, he was clearly using the trance of negative auditory hallucinations. The technician, who was highly efficient and had a bossy way about her, was frustrated that the dentist did not remember important things she told him. When confronted, he would swear by all that was just that she had never told him about the item in question. But when he heard my lecture on trance defense, he remembered his ongoing conflict with his very controlling mother. It seems she was constantly reminding him of things he needed to do. He defended himself against her boundary violations by using negative auditory hallucinations— that is, he stopped hearing her. He felt that this was what he must be doing with his superefficient lab technician.

I helped them work out some special communication signals for this situation. I suggested that the technician get a box of red poker chips and then write "Not Mom" on one side of each chip with a black permanent marker. Whenever she needed to tell the dentist something important, she was to hand him a red chip. The chip was a symbol of demystification. He could look at it and say to himself, "She's not my mother." Since these miscommunications had been very costly, I suggested he add, "And I want to do quality work and make a profit." After three weeks of this, the trance was broken, and this particular conflict settled in the dust.

In general the work we did created a context for demystification.

It opened up communication and helped build a greater sense of community. Over a two-year period, we were able to effect some dramatic changes in office dynamics.

RE-CREATING OUR MOST SHAMING PARENT ON THE JOB

In over twenty-three years of counseling, I saw many people whose major unhappiness was due to their work situation. More often than not their family of origin mystification set them up for the job they gravitated to. One man whom I'll call Jeremiah literally re-created his tyrannical father in the form of his self-imposed job pressures.

When Jeremiah asked that I spend several sessions counseling with him, it was somewhat puzzling to me. I had originally been seeing his oldest son. The 12-year-old boy was extremely bright but was failing in school and rebelling at home. He was in a stubborn power struggle with his father, especially with regard to doing *homework* and *household chores*. The son was refusing to work—failing in school and rebelling against his father. His mother had brought him to see me.

I had gotten nowhere with the son. He would come to counseling reluctantly and stare at me and refuse to talk. I experienced him as angry, tenacious, and strong. In the few moments of dialogue I was able to have with him, he seemed to really care for his father and to be genuinely confused about his rebelliousness and failure in school. I soon had to admit to his parents that I was confused about what was going on and that I didn't know how to work with the boy. It was at this point that Jeremiah asked for counseling.

Jeremiah worked as much as 120 hours a week. He hadn't taken more than three or four days' vacation in over fifteen years. His presenting problem was the pain and overwhelm he felt about his work. He was weeks behind and just couldn't get caught up. Even though he arrived at work at four o'clock some mornings, his workload was getting worse. I noticed that he had a need to be important to his business partners and was willing to handle all the boring detail work, while they were involved in the more glamorous parts of their company's business. They entertained clients on super fishing and hunting trips. They wined and dined sales prospects at the country club. Jeremiah ground away at his desk.

Paradoxically, Jeremiah's partners were very unappreciative of the work he did. They tolerated him, but complained that he was failing to bring in his fair share of the business, even though he worked twice as much as anyone else. Jeremiah confessed that he felt guilty about not engendering any new business and that his excessive work hours eased his conscience.

Jeremiah was difficult to deal with. He talked compulsively and was what has been called in therapy a "yes/but" player. A yes/but player attempts to defeat every suggestion that the counselor makes. It is a psychological game that is rooted in early conflict with authority. But it is a passive-aggressive form of anger rather than a direct expression of rebellion or conflict.

No matter what I suggested that Jeremiah do to change his work situation, he would tell me yes, and then give me a long diatribe explaining why he couldn't do what I had suggested. Or he would agree to do something one week, and when I questioned him about it the next week, he would give me all the reasons why he did not do what he had agreed to do.

Jeremiah's own father was still alive. Jeremiah described him as a cruel, rageful, and physically abusive man. He told me about his father's viciousness, describing his physical assaults on neighbors, salesmen, friends, and others. But whenever I even intimated that I thought his father was disturbed, he compulsively defended him.

It was clear to me that Jeremiah had deep shame and rage about his father, but that he was also terrified of him.

His father had been especially abusive to Jeremiah whenever he made a mistake. He made Jeremiah recite his homework assignments to him, and whenever he got something wrong, his father hit him on the hands with a ruler. Sometimes he would hit him till he bled.

Jeremiah's work addiction was a way of controlling his deep fear of failure. He stayed so absorbed in work that he had no time to feel his feelings. Even though he worked all the time, he was really quite unproductive. Like many work addicts, the more he worked, the more he worked. He feared his partners' criticism and felt that if he worked twice as much as they did, they would not criticize him.

Jeremiah also felt a great deal of toxic shame and unresolved rage. He punished himself by working all the time. He was *enraged*—that is, his anger was turned inward, depriving him of sleep, relaxation, and anything resembling fun or enjoyment.

He covered up his deep insecurity by mentally obsessing about the details of his work. He was in delusion about how overwhelming his job was, as he was not willing to make any changes. He stayed in control by refusing to delegate even the most menial tasks.

One day it dawned on me that his son was doing all the things that Jeremiah unconsciously wanted to do. His son was underachieving, rebelling, and failing. His son was refusing to *work*.

Jeremiah's work addiction was a way his mystified inner child guarded against the terrors of his father. His wounded inner child sought to keep his father's love through his whole affair with work. By overworking and avoiding failure he could get the only love he had ever known.

CONTINUING FAMILY BELIEFS ABOUT WORK

The chart on the next page is called a family genogram, a map of a family system over several generations. This kind of map can be useful for discovering where you got your deepest beliefs about work. It can be a useful tool for demystifying yourself in relation to your job.

The one I am presenting here belonged to a 75-year-old woman I once worked with. She asked me to use it wherever I saw fit in the hope that it might help someone who was in the same job predicament which she had lived in for thirty-two years.

Lady H had originally come to me because she had reconnected with her inner child in one of my workshops. She began a daily dialogue, using the image of her inner child to get in touch with her feelings, needs, and wants. In the course of her dialoguing, she became deeply depressed over the fact that she had worked at the same job in a large company for thirty-two years and had retired making less than three dollars an hour. Her retirement and Social Security gave her a mere pittance to live on, and she wanted to try and understand why she had compromised her life. Her inner child was enraged over the drudgery and boredom she had put herself through for all those years. Lady H and I spent three sessions together. Her three-generational genogram made several things abundantly clear:

- She had inherited a deep terror (almost paranoia) about life.

- She had been taught that it was not fitting for women to work.

- Her grandfather and father had both worked at one job all their lives and believed that whatever job you had, the important thing was the virtue of doing your duty and working hard.

Lady H had gotten pregnant in her middle teens. Her family had demanded that she get married. Her husband was immature,

Track Down the Beliefs in Your Family System About Work

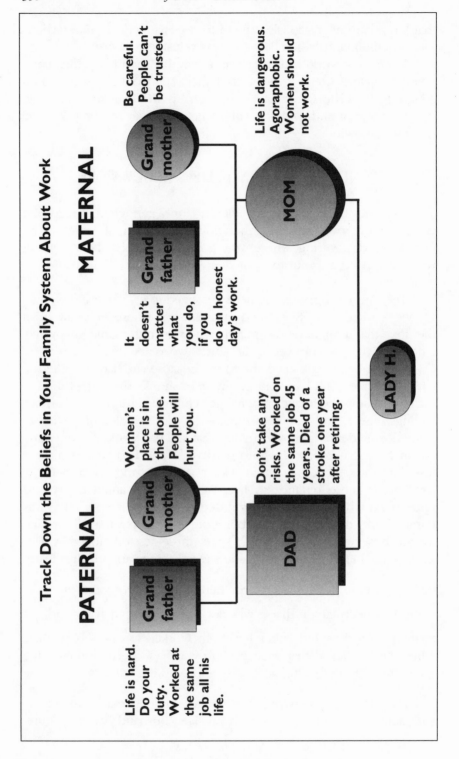

PATERNAL

MATERNAL

Be careful. People can't be trusted.

Grand mother

Life is dangerous. Agoraphobic. Women should not work.

MOM

Grand father

It doesn't matter what you do, if you do an honest day's work.

Women's place is in the home. People will hurt you.

Grand mother

Don't take any risks. Worked on the same job 45 years. Died of a stroke one year after retiring.

DAD

Life is hard. Do your duty. Worked at the same job all his life.

Grand father

LADY H.

CREATING LOVE   359

irresponsible, and later deserted her. At 24 she was forced to go to work. By the time she was 30, she was raising her two children alone. She hated work and felt that she was being punished for her teenage sexual sin.

During the thirty-two years that she worked for the same large company, her work life was a continuous misery. She lived in a state of rage and rebellion. She never did one thing to advance herself. She suffered from constant and painful arthritis, which forced her to take several leaves of absence over the years.

Apart from the dehumanization that this company condoned and passively supported, Lady H herself was responsible for her sad state of affairs.

Lady H was frozen with fear and repressed anger. She found a place to work that was an extension of her patriarchal family. She was an obedient worker, and during her first year she was so sure she would mess up or be fired that she was afraid to leave her desk to go to the bathroom. She worked in a cubicle sorting bills and customer refunds. While her terror diminished over the years, her anger intensified and her work experience was a "living hell"—a prison of mystification. Not surprisingly, her arthritis diminished greatly after retirement.

WORK ADDICTION

For my PBS series, *Bradshaw On: Creating Love,* we interviewed a number of people on the subject of work. One man's comment stands out in my mind: "I think I have always struggled with identifying myself with my job," he said, "and when I don't have work that I'm excited about, I feel at a loss as to who I am."

When work becomes our total identity and is an end in itself, it may become an addiction. But I want to be careful about the issue of work addiction. Many people find great solace in their work. I've heard people (not many) say that their job keeps them sane. We have to make a clear distinction between *passion* and *addiction*. An addiction has life-damaging consequences. It diminishes a person. A passion is a deep desire for something that enhances and enriches one's humanity. Many people have a passion for their work. I am one of them. I can lose myself in my work, and most of the time I love what I do. But there are times when an element of addiction takes over. I am learning to recognize the difference.

Our collective beliefs about work and money set many of us up for work addiction. "Workaholism," writes Diane Fassel, "is the only addiction in society that we boast about, that we're proud of, that we actually support."

Try the following test:

WORK ADDICTION TEST

Answer the following questions by marking an X after the word "yes," "no," or "maybe." Try not to overanalyze the question. Let yourself answer as spontaneously as possible.

1. I think of a total commitment to work as a positive addiction.
   Yes ( ) No ( ) Maybe ( )
2. I like to be busy, doing several things at once.
   Yes ( ) No ( ) Maybe ( )
3. I work overtime a lot, but I never seem to get ahead.
   Yes ( ) No ( ) Maybe ( )
4. I have often called myself a work addict.
   Yes ( ) No ( ) Maybe ( )
5. I frequently commit to doing things involving work without thinking what it will demand of my time and energy.
   Yes ( ) No ( ) Maybe ( )
6. I feel overwhelmed a lot, as if there just isn't enough time to do all that I need to do.
   Yes ( ) No ( ) Maybe ( )
7. I become quite anxious when I'm not in control.
   Yes ( ) No ( ) Maybe ( )
8. It is exciting to have many projects going at the same time.
   Yes ( ) No ( ) Maybe ( )
9. I feel extremely bored when I have nothing constructive to do.
   Yes ( ) No ( ) Maybe ( )
10. I am at the top of my profession and feel depressed a lot of the time.
    Yes ( ) No ( ) Maybe ( )
11. I'm making more money than I ever dreamed possible, but I drive myself to earn more.
    Yes ( ) No ( ) Maybe ( )
12. The people closest to me are concerned about how much I work.
    Yes ( ) No ( ) Maybe ( )

13. My work achievements do not seem to make my parents proud of me, as I had imagined they would.
    Yes ( ) No ( ) Maybe ( )
14. I agree to vacations at the last minute and usually take some work with me or call the office several times.
    Yes ( ) No ( ) Maybe ( )
15. I get angry when my family or friends suggest that I work too hard and too much.
    Yes ( ) No ( ) Maybe ( )
16. I find myself failing to keep promises about cutting down on my work or I secretly stash my work so that no one will notice me working.
    Yes ( ) No ( ) Maybe ( )
17. I feel alive and excited when I have a full menu of work commitments.
    Yes ( ) No ( ) Maybe ( )
18. I procrastinate about work and let the pressure build until I'm in a deadline crisis. Then I work energetically till the work is finished, usually just in the nick of time.
    Yes ( ) No ( ) Maybe ( )
19. I consider myself a perfectionist. I'm extremely upset when I make a mistake.
    Yes ( ) No ( ) Maybe ( )
20. I put far more time and thought into my work than I do into my interpersonal relationships with my spouse (lover) and children.
    Yes ( ) No ( ) Maybe ( )

Evaluation

Assign the number 3 for every *yes* answer, the number 1 for every *no* answer, and the number 2 for every *maybe* answer. Add up the numbers to get your final score.

This test is my own design, but some questions have been adapted from two very good books on work addiction: *Work Addiction* by Bryan E. Robinson and *Working Ourselves to Death* by Diane Fassel. Bryan Robinson's book presents a longer test that is research based. If you scored above 40 on my test, I think your work issues have gotten very serious.

MONEY OBSESSION

Like work, money can become an object of obsession, and when it does, the soulful enjoyment involved in working can be replaced by the narrow pleasure of making money. When money is separated from its connection with meaningful work, it loses its potential for soulfulness. And when profit becomes God, money becomes an enhancer of our mystification.

Money can become polarized into a fantasy of wealth as a defense against poverty, human insecurity, and loss. How much is enough? Thomas Moore points out, "Wealth is primarily what we imagine it to be." For one person it may mean owning a Cadillac; for another it may mean owning a jet airplane. The meaning of wealth is quite subjective.

Even great quantities of money are often not enough for mystified people, and money has the potential for severe addiction. Money may only stimulate our craving for security, and since there is no real human security, the quest for money becomes like an unending pregnancy, without fruition.

Money has a numinous quality. It is attractive, even fascinating and awesome, as well as something to be feared. We have to find the balance that allows us to experience money's polarity. Con games, cheating, embezzlement, avarice, and greed are signs of money's dark side. We've seen a lot of this lately.

We can also get stuck in the opposite polarization: money is evil, poverty is virtuous. Some people may find simple living a soulful choice. But just ask someone who has been poor involuntarily whether it made them better!

Money is part of our human reality, and we cannot refuse to deal with it. One of the worst scoundrels I've ever met continually insisted, "I'm not interested in money," even as he drove around in his Ferrari. Thomas Moore writes: "When the soul of money is denied, it takes on an added measure of shadow." In the last few years, the Ferrari-driver has so overextended himself that he is near bankruptcy. Money is about to get his attention. Or as we say in therapy, "Repress your dark side and it bites you in the ass."

Early in our lives we are often hypnotized into mystified beliefs about money. Families have both overt and covert rules about money. You can use your family genogram to track down the beliefs about money that come from your hypnotic family messages.

Note that your family's overt rules about money may be the exact opposite of the covert rules. For example, your parents may have said over and over again that desiring money is wrong, that money can never bring happiness. But in actuality your parents spent 85 percent of their life energy pursuing and making money.

Money has often had a profound effect on our family history. My paternal grandmother went through a large amount of money early in her life, and my dad spent whatever money he had. They were held up to me as bad examples. My maternal grandfather, who greatly influenced my life, continually stressed frugality and saving for a rainy day. I'm glad he taught me to save. However, I've had a hard time enjoying my financial blessings. In my early years I saved everything and deprived myself of pleasures I could easily have afforded. As I've grown older, I've started spending more, but after I let go and spend, I feel guilty and have to go through a barrage of inner posthypnotic voices.

Money can also aid us in becoming soulful. We can embrace the power of money. We can let ourselves want it and even enjoy having it accumulate. It can offer us a sense of value and provide us with more freedom and security. What counts is our attitude toward it.

These days, I'm much clearer about money. I like it! It frees me to live and enjoy my life as I choose. It provides me with a security I've never known, and it enables me to help others. Most of all, it allows me to go deeper into my own spiritual quest by taking away the stressful pressures of mere survival. Money contributes to my liberation. Only the attachment to money blocks soulfulness.

Mystified work lends itself to the insatiable burden of work or money addiction. It thus deprives us of the healthy narcissistic pleasure we could have in acquiring wealth and seeing the fruits of our labor incarnated in a product that we feel good about.

CREATING A SOULFUL WORKPLACE

I know it is possible to create a soulful workplace. I was involved with a company where we made great strides in developing the kind of environment in which self-actualization, self-transcendence, and self-valuing are allowed to function.

I was the director of human resources at Texas General, a small oil company in Houston, Texas. I was also on the board of directors of this company. Due to the enlightenment of the chairman of our board, W. E. Bosarge, I was able to create several programs that were aimed at enhancing job skills as well as soulful growth.

We had a variety of on-the-job enrichment-type seminars. We had company-paid three-day workshop weekends. We had on-the-job counseling. I met most of the three hundred and fifty people who worked there. Many of them were helped and grew because of the experiences we offered them. Our programs created a sense of community and the commitment to a company goal.

But although we had made great strides, we had not worked out the fundamental issues of worker participation in the company itself. Those were dark days in the economy, just like the ones we're experiencing now. I can remember the lines of devastated people waiting to get their severance paychecks. I knew many of them well. They had been told that morning that they were being laid off.

What is frightening to people is the sense of powerlessness they have in a patriarchal system. Beyond the real unemployment figures lies this sense of powerlessness and layers of fearful fantasy about the future. If companies would develop some kind of participatory system, there would be many alternatives to laying people off. Most people can grasp that in hard times, they may have to sacrifice— even to the point of taking a cut in pay. That is certainly better than losing their job. People cooperate and share mightily when they feel that they are valued, and when they know they are part of a team.

Soulful companies know that people are their primary asset, whatever the accountants put on their books. Buildings and machinery can be lost and replaced, but if the best people are lost, their wisdom, skills, and spirit may never be found again.

EXERCISE: IMAGES OF WORK

- Do you grow intellectually, emotionally and spiritually by being in your job?

- What do you want to change about your job?
  (A) What would it look like if you changed it?
  (B) How would you feel different?
  (C) What would it sound like if you changed?

- Have you ever considered changing jobs?

- If yes, what new job do you want?

- How would you know if you had the job you wanted?
  See (A) (B) (C) above.

- What emotional payoffs do you get out of staying in your old job?

- What stops you from being in the kind of work you want?
  - (A) What images do you create when you think about changing jobs?

    Are these images idealized?

    Are they degrading of yourself?

    What would be a realistic fantasy?
  - (B) What do you have to do to change jobs?

    Visualize the new job in concrete sensory details. See yourself in the new job. Hear the conversation which surrounds you on the new job. How does it feel? Imagine the steps you have to take to be in the new job?
  - (C) What must you do today in order to change jobs? One behavior?

Creativity

To foster soulfulness, the workplace will have to put more emphasis on learning and creativity. John Kao, an associate professor at Harvard Business School, writes: "Creativity is being demanded of managers." He believes that creativity "involves skills that can be taught and learned."

Some companies are using therapists like facilitators, who help management groups by using unconventional methods that stretch the participants' minds, teaching them a *process* for being creative.

The humanistic psychologist Carl Rogers organized an important study on creativity at the University of Chicago in the 1950s. As I understand it, a number of psychologists, poets, therapists, and inventors spent considerable time studying the components of creativity and the psychological conditions that foster it.

The Rogers study revealed that people work most creatively when they are motivated from within. The hard-driving pressure-cooker methods of many managers are too threatening to enhance creativity. When individuals feel threatened, their mystification trance is induced. Excessive outside pressure forces us to defend ourselves. We use our energy to find creative ways to survive rather than to develop better ways to work. Rogers' study confirms that the best environment for creativity is one in which we can respond to reality as it is. Creativity is rooted in the various elements I described as belonging to the natural child—traits like wonder, curiosity, playfulness, spontaneity, resilience and experimentation. In order to actual-

---

CONDITIONS FOSTERING CREATIVITY

Psychological Safety:
    Self-Valuing – individual has a sense of unconditional worth

    Suspension of external evaluation or judgment

    Empathetic understanding

Psychological Freedom:
    Openness to symbolic expression, playfulness, spontaneous juggling of concepts

---

ize these traits, we need a safe environment. To create such an environment, companines will need to stop over-pressuring and overstandardizing. Value must be placed on the uniqueness of each individual.

Kip Flock and I confirmed this for ourselves in an 8-week drug counselor training we did for four years. We decided to create a completely non-shaming atmosphere. We videotaped our therapist-trainees during practice sessions, and while they were practicing, one of us sat behind them as a resource. They were allowed to stop at any point and confer with us, and they could stop the entire session without explanation if they felt too stressed or overwhelmed. Later we reviewed the videotape with them and pointed out *only the things they had done well*. The final week, we showed videotapes of their work at the beginning and at the end of the training. Every single person had visibly enhanced their self-confidence and effectiveness. They had moved from following some very cautious traditional ways of counseling to risking innovative and personally unique approaches to their work.

SELF-VALUING WORK

The patriarchal power structure puts a high value on certain jobs and devalues others. Be a doctor, be a lawyer, be a banker, it tells us, and you will be a success. But status is not the same as soul.

Soulful work is that which gives our life a *meaning*. Work is a way to love ourselves more because of the reality we have created. In work we create ourselves. *No matter what our job is,* it can be truly soulful.

I remember Coy Banks, a man who took care of my lakehouse in Minnesota. Among his other skills, Coy was a self-taught electrician. On several occasions when I was riding in his truck, he would point to a house and say with pride, "I wired that house!" He had every right to be proud. Here was a man who could go home every night knowing what he had accomplished. I know other electricians, painters, plumbers, secretaries, homemakers who love what they do and are proud of their work. They look at it and see themselves reflected. They love themselves more because they see something of their own soul there.

One of the people interviewed for the PBS series was a housewife. When I first read her statement, I thought she sounded too good to be true. Then I watched the video bit of her, and she was completely congruent. Here is what she said:

> My universe seems so small. I don't have twenty-five people reporting to me.... I was worried that I was not making a contribution. But I have two people in my life, my husband and my son ... and I realize that the only real commitment that I could make that might make a difference in the future is to live the life that I'm living as fully and enthusiastically as I possibly can. So if I enjoy it and just live it, I'm doing as much for the history books as I would be in any other position I can think of.

This woman also knew the meaning of soulful work.

WORK AND COMMUNITY

As Buddha pointed out, work helps us to overcome our ego-centeredness by joining with other people in a common task. Saint-

Exupéry says that Mermoz taught him something about the dignity of work: that it "creates a fellowship ... it binds men together." It binds men *and* women together too. One of the people who was interviewed for my TV series was a man named Russell Dalby. Russell had worked on an assembly line, and he talked about how monotonous it was to do this. "You're there eight hours a day, every day for years." What got him through it was the people, the community that bonded together. He told our interviewer:

> And people just talk ... and you have pot lucks, you have Christmas, Thanksgiving dinners. And there's times when people are not doing well—newborns, deaths, people in the hospital—so you know everything good and bad, and you get to know them so well. Some people had tragedies, and when they came to work, everybody pulled together for them. I've had personal tragedies ... and was embarrassed to go back to work and ... people were there for me. So I miss a lot of 'em. I still remember their names and birthdays and stuff. We spent a long time, almost ten years together.

Somehow Russell's words moved me to tears. A lot of soulful human life is there on the assembly line. A bond was created by people just being there for each other, making that drab, dehumanizing assembly line something spiritual.

Russell also talked about a fellow worker who was what I call a soul friend—someone who passes our way and touches us in a way we never forget.

> I can remember Hazel ... she meant a lot to me. She will always be remembered. I went through some really tough times emotionally, and she was always there, and that carries me through sometimes when I think about how she encouraged me.

Until we humanize the workplace on a grand scale, we'll need those soulful Hazels who make our work the human meeting place it needs to be.

EPILOGUE

Fifty years ago we entered a new, as yet nameless era. The judges at the Nuremberg trials dealt patriarchy a mortal blow when they ruled that conscience is a higher authority than obedience. Since these trials took place, several significant human rights movements have evidenced the birth of an awakened antipatriarchal consciousness. There have been movements for civil rights, women's rights, gay and lesbian rights, children's rights (the adult child movement), and the democratization of Communism. Each of these movements calls for shared power and reverence for each person's dignity, and each expands our notion of love.

These movements are the foundation for a second-order change in our consciousness concerning the nature of love itself. This new awareness represents the next great stage of human evolution. Like all matters of the soul, love is a dynamic reality that is always expanding and growing. It can never be defined once and for all. As we make breakthroughs in human consciousness, we understand everything differently. We can no longer base love on polarization, inevitability, genetics, power, control, secrecy, shame, repression of emotion, duty, or self-negation. It must be based on polarity, vulnerability, shared power, choice, creativity, self-love, and a sense of mystery and fate. We still have a long way to go in order to get there, but we have begun.

As we awaken from our collective trance, we realize that we cannot flourish without one another. Learning to create love will necessitate our learning to accept differences as the law of life.

The earth has produced its multiplicity of species over aeons. Evolved differentiation is the condition of life. It's a finely tuned balancing act. As the various life-forms have been worked out, *not one blade of grass or one species of fish is irrelevant.*

Evolution has endowed all humans with language and symbolic thought. All humans are genetically coded to reflect on their reality and to find meaning. But the languages of the earth's people and the meanings of the earth's people are differentiated. Jew, Buddhist, Confucian, Shinto, Christian, and Muslim are all different, and they are all *necessary*. All humans are motivated by life to take their history, their art, their particular meaning system, and their stories, and to weave culture out of them. The cultures of the Eskimo, the Russian, the Irish, the Arab, and of all people are different. Just as all that differentiation on the physical level is essential for the planet to survive and unfold, so too is all this accumulated wisdom, history, and insight essential if the consciousness of the earth is to move forward. Sister Miriam MacGillis says it well: "The differences are not problems: the differences hold the solutions."

Since we *are* the earth thinking, *everyone's* conscious choice is an important part of the power to change. We need a unified field of vision and a unified desire to create love. We must change our hearts. This is something each of us is capable of doing.

C. G. Jung, who more than anyone in this century has called us to soulfulness, wrote:

> The great events of world history are, at bottom, profoundly unimportant. The essential thing is the life of the individual.... Here alone do the great transformations first take place, and the whole future, the whole history of the world, ultimately springs as a gigantic summation from these hidden sources in individuals.

I encourage you to do one thing today to nurture the earth, or to help someone who needs your love. Do something that requires putting yourself out. Do something that no one will ever find out about. By doing one act of love, you can soulfully honor your Creator, love your brothers and sisters, insure that your children and grandchildren will have a richer future, and love yourself for acting in a way that creates love.

BIBLIOGRAPHY

The following books were the major resources for this book. I recommend them with great enthusiasm.

Allport, Gordon. *The Nature of Prejudice* (Redding, MA: Addison-Wesley, 1979). Allport's work presents the most extensive empirical studies that have been done in the psychology of religion. He offers us some solid objectivity in an area where raw subjectivity runs rampant.

Anderson, Meribeth, with David Gordon. *Phoenix* (Cupertino, CA: Meta Publications, Inc., 1981). I like this book. It offers the reader a fast way to grasp the genius of Milton Erickson. Meribeth and David were my N.L.P. teachers.

Bandler, Leslie. *They Lived Happily Ever After* (Cupertino, CA: Meta Publications, Inc., 1978). Leslie also deserves credit for the development of N.L.P. She is an innovative and master therapist and trainer.

Bandler, Richard and Grinder, John. *Frogs into Princes* (Moab, UT: Real People Press, 1979). ————. *Reframing* (Moab, UT: Real People Press, 1982). Bandler and Grinder are the pioneers of a model of change called Neuro-Linguistic Programming. Their strategies for change (still evolving) are useful demystifying and trance breaking tools.

Bly, Robert. *Iron John* (Redding, MA: Addison-Wesley, 1990). Robert Bly is a magnificent American poet. I will forever be indebted to his insights about genius and wounding.

Bowen, Murray. *Family Therapy in Clinical Practice* (Northvale, NJ: Jason Aronson, Inc., 1978). Bowen is one of the pioneers of family systems thinking. My understanding of most of the basic concepts of general systems theory as they apply to families has come from this work.

Briggs, Dorothy Corkville. *Celebrate Your Self* (New York: Doubleday, 1977).

Brown, Phil, ed. *Radical Psychology* (New York: Harper & Row, 1973). See the essay by David Cooper.

Campbell, Susan. *The Couple's Journey* (San Luis Obispo, CA: Impact Publishers, 1980). Susan Campbell's work is extraordinary. She has presented an empirically grounded model of the stages of intimacy. Her work has never received the recognition it deserves.

Carnes, Patrick. *Out of the Shadows* (Irvine, CA: CompCare Publications, 1985). I'm grateful to Pat for his model of the addiction cycle.

Covitz, Joel. *Emotional Child Abuse* (Boston: Sigo Press, 1986). In my opinion, this is the best book available on the impact of emotional abuse and the mystification resulting from it. This is a must-read book for parents and for anyone who may be searching for the roots of their problems.

Dreikurs, Rudolf, and Vicki Stolz. *Children, The Challenge* (New York: Dutton, 1987). I recommend all of Dreikurs' work. Although somewhat dogmatic, Dreikurs is practical and offers some very useful ways of handling children.

Dossey, Larry, M.D. *Recovering the Soul* (New York: Bantam, 1989). Dr. Dossey makes the scientific case for the existence of soul.

Erickson, Milton, and Ernest and Sheila Rossi. *Hypnotic Realities* (Manchester, NH: Irvington Publications, 1976). Erickson's writings are voluminous. The Rossis have made a major contribution in organizing and presenting Erickson's work as well as their own.

Fassel, Diane. *Working Ourselves to Death* (San Francisco: Harper SF, 1990).

Firestone, Robert. *The Fantasy Bond* (New York: Human Sciences Press, 1985). This is a brilliant book which describes mystification and the work of the fantastic imagination. Firestone's writing is sometimes difficult to grasp. But the emphasis on friendship as the way to restore the interpersonal bridge is quite clear. I recommend making the effort to read this book.

Fromm, Erich. *The Art of Loving* (New York: HarperCollins, 1989).

Gordon, Thomas. *Parent Effectiveness Training* (New York: McKay, 1970). Although this book has been around for quite a while, it is still an excellent resource for parenting.

Haley, Jay. *Uncommon Therapy* (New York: W.W. Norton & Co., 1986). Haley is one of the most brilliant and innovative therapists alive today. He has been the leader in packaging Milton Erickson's work and making it available to the public.

Hendrix, Harville. *Getting the Love You Want* (New York: Henry Holt, 1988). This book deals with the issues of the mystified wounded child apropos of spousal love. It is an excellent book to help couples through the stages of imtimacy.

Hillman, James. *Re-Visioning Psychology* (New York: HarperCollins, 1977). Hillman has made a pioneering contribution to the restoration of soul to the modern world. His work is sometimes arrogant but always thought provoking.

Hoffman, Bob. *No One Is To Blame* (Palo Alto, CA: Science and Behavior, 1979). Bob has developed a sound method for separating from our internalized parents.

Jackson, Don D., and William J. Lederer. *The Mirages of Marriage* (New York: W.W. Norton & Co., 1968). A classic work on marriage looked at from a family-systems viewpoint.

James, William. *The Varieties of Religious Experience* (New York: Viking Penguin, 1982). This is a classic work in the field of the psychology of religion. James discusses the "once" and "twice" born.

Johnson, Robert. *Owning Your Own Shadow* (San Francisco: Harper SF, 1991).

Jung, Carl. *Collected Works* (Princeton, NJ: Princeton University Press, 1985).

Kaufman, Gershen. *The Psychology of Shame* (New York: Springer Publishing Co., 1989). Kaufman is a pioneer in applying the affect theory of Silvan Tompkins to an analysis of the syndromes of shame. I have learned a great deal from him, especially his work on "governing scenes."

Keen, Sam. *Your Mythic Journey* (Los Angeles: J.P. Tarcher, 1989) and *Fire in the Belly* (New York: Bantam, 1991). Keen has inspired me for a long time. He embodies soulfulness and has enormous depth.

Laing, Ronald D. Laing has written a number of books presenting his notion of mystification. The case I cited is presented in *The Politics of the Family* (New York: Random House, 1972). *See also The Politics of Experience* (New York: Ballantine, 1981), *The Divided Self* (New York: Viking Penguin, 1965), and *Knots* (New York: Random House, 1972).

Lewis, C. S. *The Four Loves* (San Diego, CA: Harcourt Brace Jovanovich, 1971).

Lifton, Robert J. *Thought Reform & the Psychology of Totalism* (Chapel Hill, NC: University of North Carolina Press, 1989). This is a brilliant study of brainwashing techniques. It has been my major resource in understanding the nature of cults and how families become cultic.

Lynch, William. *Images of Hope* (Notre Dame, IN: University of Notre Dame Press, 1987). Lynch's book is difficult to read but worth the effort. He is a pioneer in grasping the dynamics of the realistic and fantastic imagination and how they shed light on emotional illness and the ways to heal it.

Maritain, Jacques. *Existence and the Existent* (Westport, CT: Greenwood Publications, 1975). Maritain was one of my major philosophical teachers.

Masterson, James. *The Narcissistic and Borderline Disorders* (New York: Brunner-Mazel, 1981) and *Treatment of the Borderline Adolescent* (New York: John Wiley & Sons, Inc., 1972). Masterson is my major resource for the theory of "object constancy."

Milgram, Stanley. *Obedience to Authority* (New York: HarperCollins, 1983). This book presents Milgram's now famous study on the tragic consequences of blind obedience.

Miller, Alice. *For Your Own Good* (New York: Farrar, Straus & Giroux, 1983). Alice Miller describes the consequences of patriarchal parenting in this book. She calls it the "poisonous pedagogy."

Miller, Sherod, et al. *Alive and Aware* (Minneapolis, MN: Interpersonal Communication Programs, Inc., 1975). This is far and away the best book on communications that I know of.

Minuchin, Salvador. *Families and Family Therapy* (Cambridge, MA: Harvard University Press, 1974). Minuchin has pioneered a method of therapy which aims at healing families in which cross-generational bonding has occurred. He is one of the genius pioneers of family systems theory and therapy. His method is called structural family therapy.

Moore, Thomas. *Care of the Soul* (New York: HarperCollins, 1992). This book was a major resource in developing my concept of soulfulness. It is a wonderful book which I hope will find a place on your bookshelf, ideally by your bedside.

Mura, David. See his profound article *A Male Grief: Notes on Pornography and Addiction* (Minneapolis, MN: Milkweed Editions, 1987).

Pastor, Marion. *Anger and Forgiveness* (Berkeley, CA: Jennis Press, 1980). This book offers a step-by-step guide for working what is now called the Quadrinity Process. This process offers a practical way to separate from our internalized source figures. It was originally designed by Bob Hoffman as a result of his personal discussions with the psychiatrist Siegfried Fischer.

Peck, M. Scott. *The Road less Traveled* (New York: Touchstone/Simon and Schuster, 1980). An all-time classic.

Robinson, Bryan E. *Work Addiction* (Deerfield Beach, FL: Health Communications, 1989). A very good book on work addiction.

Rogers, Carl R. The work on creativity is in a book of Rogers' essays called *On Becoming a Person* (Boston: Houghton Mifflin, 1972).

Sardello, Robert. *Facing the World with Soul* (New York: Lindisfarne Press, 1992).

Satir, Virginia. *Conjoint Family Therapy* (Palo Alto, CA: Science and Behavior, 1982). This is a classic in the field of family systems theory.

Schumacher, E. F. *Small Is Beautiful* (New York: HarperCollins, 1989). This is a wonderful little book offering an outline for a soulful workplace.

Senge, Peter, M. *The Fifth Discipline* (New York: Doubleday, 1990). Senge offers some innovative ways to heal our learning disabled workplace.

Stevens, John O. *Awareness* (Moab, UT: Real People Press, 1971). The exercise I asked you to try concerning identity based on repeating the question "Who are you?" is taken from here.

Watzlawick, Paul, and John Weakland. *Change* (New York: W.W. Norton & Co., 1974). This is a book describing the issue of first and second order change. It also presents some brilliant insights into achieving second order change.

Weinhold, Barry K. and Janae B. *Breaking Free of the Co-Dependency Trap* (Dallas, TX: Still Point Press, 1989).

Wolinsky, Stephen. *Trances People Live* (Ashley Falls, MA: Bramble Co., 1991). This book was a major resource in developing my notion of mystification. I think the sections in this book on deep trance phenomena are superb, and I see Wolinsky emerging as a leading figure in designing ways to effect therapeutic change. I look forward to his new work on quantum psychology.

Zukav, Gary. *The Seat of the Soul* (New York: Simon and Schuster, 1989).

For information on John Bradshaw's audio and video cassette tapes, write:

Bradshaw Cassettes
P.O. Box 980547
Houston, Texas 77098

or call (713)529-9437.

For information about workshops and lectures, write:

John Bradshaw
2412 South Boulevard
Houston, Texas 77098

Please send a stamped, self-addressed envelope.